BERTOLT BRECHT:
CRITICAL AND PRIMARY SOURCES

VOLUME I

BERTOLT BRECHT: CRITICAL AND PRIMARY SOURCES

LIFE AND WORK

VOLUME I

Edited by David Barnett

BLOOMSBURY ACADEMIC
LONDON • NEW YORK • OXFORD • NEW DELHI • SYDNEY

BLOOMSBURY ACADEMIC
Bloomsbury Publishing Plc
50 Bedford Square, London, WC1B 3DP, UK
1385 Broadway, New York, NY 10018, USA

BLOOMSBURY, BLOOMSBURY ACADEMIC and the Diana logo
are trademarks of Bloomsbury Publishing Plc

First published in Great Britain 2020

Introductions and editorial content copyright © David Barnett, 2020
English language translations copyright © Romy Fursland, 2020 (unless otherwise stated)

David Barnett has asserted his right under the Copyright, Designs and
Patents Act, 1988, to be identified as the Editor of this work.

For legal purposes the Permissions Acknowledgements on pp. 253–4 constitute
an extension of this copyright page.

All rights reserved. No part of this publication may be reproduced or transmitted
in any form or by any means, electronic or mechanical, including photocopying,
recording, or any information storage or retrieval system, without prior permission
in writing from the publishers.

Bloomsbury Publishing Plc does not have any control over, or responsibility for,
any third-party websites referred to or in this book. All internet addresses given
in this book were correct at the time of going to press. The author and publisher
regret any inconvenience caused if addresses have changed or sites have ceased
to exist, but can accept no responsibility for any such changes.

A catalogue record for this book is available from the British Library.

A catalog record for this book is available from the Library of Congress.

ISBN: HB: 978-1-4742-9942-8
HB set: 978-1-4742-9949-7

Series: Critical and Primary Sources

Typeset by Deanta Global Publishing Services, Chennai, India
Printed and bound in Great Britain

To find out more about our authors and books visit www.bloomsbury.com and
sign up for our newsletters.

CONTENTS

VOLUME I
LIFE AND WORK

Note on the Text and Common Abbreviations	xiv
Introduction	1

Part One Life

The Young Brecht

1. Student Magazine: *The Harvest* — Werner Frisch and K. W. Obermeier — 9

2. 'Ja, damals waren wir Dichter': Hanns Otto Münsterer, Bertolt Brecht and the Dynamics of Literary Friendship — Tom Kuhn — 11

Brecht and the Weimar Republic

3. *Sachlichkeit* (Objectivity) — Philip Glahn — 27

Brecht in Exile

4. 'Changing Countries More Often than Shoes' — James K. Lyon — 39

Brecht in the GDR

5. A Life's Work Curtailed? The Ailing Brecht's Struggle with the SED Leadership over GDR Cultural Policy — Stephen Parker — 49

6. Characteristics of the Berliner Ensemble — Bertolt Brecht — 62

Part Two Work

Plays: Early/Weimar Work

7	Brecht's Plays of the Weimar Period R. C. Speirs	69
8	Review of *Drums in the Night* Herbert Ihering	84
9	Review of *The Threepenny Opera* Monty Jacobs	87

The *Lehrstücke*

10	On the Theory of the *Lehrstück* Bertolt Brecht	91
11	The Lehrstück as Performance Andrzej Wirth	93
12	Review of *The Decision* Durus	102

Exile

13	Theses for Proletarian Literature Bertolt Brecht	107
14	Brecht's Epic Theatre as a Theatre of Exile Ehrhard Bahr	108
15	Review of *Mother Courage and Her Children* Hans Ott	119

Return to Germany/Adaptations

16	Adaptations for the Berliner Ensemble David Barnett	125
17	Review of *Mother Courage and Her Children* Gerhard Wahnrau	136
18	Review of *Coriolanus* Franz Schonauer	139

Fragments

19	The Making of a Document: An Approach to Brecht's *Fatzer* Fragment Judith Wilke	143

Poetry: City Poems

20 The Poet in Berlin: Brecht's City Poetry of the 1920s 153
   David Midgely

Exile Poems

21 'Visit to a Banished Poet': Brecht's *Svendborg Poems* and
   the Voices of Exile 167
   Tom Kuhn

Sonnets

22 Brecht's Sonnets 183
   David Constantine

Later Poetry

23 Brecht in Buckow: *The Buckow Elegies* 199
   Karl H. Schoeps

Prose: The Novels

24 The Anti-Aristotelian Novel: Brecht's Contribution to the Novel
   of Classic Modernity 217
   Klaus-Detlef Müller

The Short Stories

25 The Subject Herr Keuner: Towards a Brechtian Ethics 235
   Sonia Arribas

PERMISSIONS ACKNOWLEDGEMENTS 253
INDEX 255

VOLUME II
THEORY

NOTE ON THE TEXT AND COMMON ABBREVIATIONS ix

Introduction 1

PART ONE NEGOTIATING TERMINOLOGY

Epic

1 *Episch*, or, the Third Person 9
   Fredric Jameson

Dialectics

2 Dialectics and the Brechtian Tradition: Some Thoughts
   on Politicized Performance 17
   David Barnett

Verfremdung

3 The *Verfremdung* of Certain Processes through a Mode of Representation
   Usually Reserved for Customs and Traditions 31
   Bertolt Brecht

4 A Critical Response to Heidi M. Silcox's 'What's Wrong with Alienation?' 32
   Anthony Squiers

Gestus

5 Getting to the Gist of Gestus 39
   Meg Mumford

Fabel

6 The *Fabel* 57
   Bertolt Brecht

7 Brecht, the '*Fable*', and the Teaching of Directing 58
   Craig Kinzer

Historicization

8 Art as the Speaker of History 69
   Astrid Oesmann

9 How Do I Learn to Learn? 78
   Bertolt Brecht

Naivety

10 From Distancing Alienation to Intuitive Naiveté: Bertolt Brecht's
   Establishment of a New Aesthetic Category 81
   Karl-Heinz Schoeps

PART TWO MAJOR THEORETICAL WRITINGS

Notes on *The Threepenny Opera* and *Rise and Fall of the City of Mahagonny*

11 Epic Opera and Epic Theater 97
   John J. White

The Messingkauf/Buying Brass

12 The Drama of Ideas 127
    Martin Puchner

Me-ti

13 Introduction to *Me-ti: Book of Interventions in the Flow of Things* 137
    Antony Tatlow

Theatre Work

14 Brecht's *Theatre Work*: A Foundational Work and its Marginalisation 149
    Detlev Schöttker

PART THREE BRECHT AND OTHER MEDIA

Radio

15 Apparatus without Spectators?: On the Deconstruction of the Medium in Brecht's *Ocean Flight* 165
    Patrick Primavesi

Film

16 Utilizing the 'Ideological Antiquity': Rethinking Brecht and Film Theory 179
    Angelos Koutsourakis

Music

17 Brecht and Music: Theory and Practice 205
    Kim H. Kowalke

Brecht in the Information Age

18 Bertolt Brecht and the Internet 221
    Dorothee Ostmeier

PART FOUR THE PLAY OF IDEAS

The Bible

19 Brecht and the Bible: A Study of Religious Nihilism and Human Weakness in Brecht's Drama of Mortality and the City 243
    G. Ronald Murphy

Shakespeare

20 Brecht as Great Shakespearean: A Lifelong Connection 255
    David Barnett

Capitalism

21 Tracing the Crimes of Capitalism: From Mahagonny to Nazi Germany   269
    Astrid Oesmann

The Natural Sciences

22 Brecht and Science – Science and Brecht?: A Dialectical View   281
    Katharina Brinkert

Thought from the Far East

23 Brecht's Materialist Ethics between Confucianism and Mohism   291
    Markus Wessendorf

Comedy/Humour

24 The Poetic Anthropology of Comedy in Brecht's *Buying Brass*   313
    Ralf Simon

25 On Humour   323
    Bertolt Brecht

Tragedy

26 Brecht and Tragedy   327
    Sean Carney

Gendered Performance/Feminism

27 Brechtian Theory/Feminist Theory: Toward a Gestic Feminist Criticism   339
    Elin Diamond

Postcolonial Brecht

28 A Postcolonial Brecht?   355
    Marc Silberman

PERMISSIONS ACKNOWLEDGEMENTS   361

INDEX   363

CONTENTS   xi

VOLUME III
PRACTICE

Note on the Text and Common Abbreviations   ix

Introduction   1

PART ONE BRECHT AS THEATRE DIRECTOR AND DOCUMENTER

Weimar Republic

1   Brecht's Formative Years   9
    Edward Braun

Switzerland/GDR/Berliner Ensemble

2   Rhythm and Structure: Brecht's *Antigone* in Performance   27
    Bruno C. Duarte

3   Original Interpretations of Brecht Plays   45
    Bertolt Brecht

4   Undogmatic Marxism: Brecht Rehearses at the Berliner Ensemble   46
    David Barnett

Brecht and the Actor

5   Instructions to Actors   63
    Bertolt Brecht

6   Brecht and the Contradictory Actor   65
    John Rouse

Brecht and Documentation

Modelbooks

7   *Couragemodell*: Detail and Arrangement of a Model Book   83
    Kristopher Imbrigotta

Photography/the Image

8   'Was besagt eine Fotografie?' Early Brechtian Perspectives on Photography   91
    Tom Kuhn

PART TWO BRECHT'S RELATIONSHIPS WITH PRACTITIONERS

Caspar Neher

9   Stylistic Devices of a Set Designed by Caspar Neher for Brecht's Epic Theatre   109
    Susanne de Ponte

Helene Weigel

10 Helene Weigel 119
    Bertolt Brecht

11 Weigel's Figuration and Defiguration in Brecht's Texts 120
    Patrick Primavesi

Karl Korsch

12 Brecht's Marxist Aesthetic: The Korsch Connection 137
    Douglas Kellner

Walter Benjamin

13 Walter Benjamin and Bertolt Brecht: Account of a Constellation 149
    Erdmut Wizisla

Kurt Weill

14 'Suiting the Action to the Word': Some Observations on *Gestus* and
    Gestische Musik 161
    Michael Morley

Hanns Eisler

15 Eisler/Brecht or Brecht/Eisler? Perspectives, Forms and Limits
    of their Collaboration 179
    Albrecht Dümling

Paul Dessau

16 Composing for BB: Some Comments 193
    Paul Dessau

Brecht's Female Collaborators

17 Victimhood or Camouflage? The Modesty of Elisabeth Hauptmann 201
    Sabine Kebir

18 '... Now I've Gone and Put Ideas in His Head Again': Notes on Margarete
    Steffin, Brecht's 'Personal Editor' 210
    Wolfgang Jeske

19 Berlau Photographs Brecht's Life and Work – a Collaboration (More or Less) 224
    Grischa Meyer

Brecht's Assistants in the Theatre

20 Notice [3]: *To the Members of the Berliner Ensemble* 241
    Bertolt Brecht

21 Interviews with Claus and Wera Küchenmeister and with Egon Monk
    Joachim Lang and Jürgen Hillesheim 242

PART THREE GLOBAL BRECHT

Europe

22 The Politics of the Body: Pina Bausch's *Tanztheater* 267
    David W. Price

23 Theatre for the People: The Impact of Brechtian Theory on the Production
    and Performance of *1789* by Ariane Mnouchkine's Théâtre du Soleil 276
    Agnieszka Karch

Asia

24 Brecht's East Asia: A Conspectus 287
    Antony Tatlow

25 Brecht: A Participant in the Process of Nation-Building 299
    Amal Allana

Africa

26 African Brecht 315
    Brian Crow

North America

27 New Measures for Brecht in America 333
    Peter W. Ferran

South America

28 Brecht and Latin America's 'Theatre of Revolution' 347
    Diana Taylor

29 Activist Theater: From Brecht through Boal 358
    Steven K. Smith

PERMISSIONS ACKNOWLEDGEMENTS 375
INDEX 377

NOTE ON THE TEXT AND COMMON ABBREVIATIONS

Texts first published in English have been reproduced as they were first printed, with any extracts in German, or other languages, retained as per the originals.

AJ	*Arbeitsjournal*
BBA	Bertolt-Brecht-Archive
BC	*Brecht Chronik*
BE	Berliner Ensemble
BFA	See GBA
BH	*Brecht Handbook*, 5 volumes
BS	Brecht Sourcebook
BT	Brecht on Theatre: The Development of an Aesthetic
DDR	See GDR
GBA	Brecht, *Grosse Berliner und Frankfurter Ausgabe*, 30 volumes and an index volume
GDR	German Democratic Republic
GW	Brecht, *Gesammelte Werke*, 20 volumes
KPD	Communist Party of Germany
SED	Socialist Unity Party of Germany

Introduction

It is difficult to understand the work of any person without appreciating the circumstances under which they produced that work: nothing comes from nothing. It is not, then, that looking at the historical, social and political contexts of Bertolt Brecht's life offers something new or original to the study of the playwright, poet, essayist, theorist, diarist and practitioner. Rather, by presenting such material, this volume can construct a series of connections between Brecht's life and work, although these connections may be understood in a way Brecht himself would have articulated them: dialectically.

Dialectics form the intellectual basis of much of Brecht's approach to the world and art's place in it (and features prominently in Volume II). The dialectic is a mechanism – formulated by the philosopher Hegel and reinterpreted by Marx – that accounts for change over time. In abstract terms, a thesis encounters its antithesis, and the relationship between the two is one of contradiction. When the contradiction becomes too great, change occurs (although the nature of that change is subject to lively debate among dialecticians). In more concrete terms, the tension between thesis and antithesis can be evidenced on a number of levels. Marx saw class struggle as a central dialectical contradiction, with working people driving capitalist profits while receiving derisory wages and living in appalling conditions. Yet, on a more personal level, one can also understand biography as a dialectical process where a contradiction exists between individual and society. That is, any person is born into specific social contexts by complete chance and then has to respond to them over the course of their lives. People inevitably negotiate their place in society in dialogue with the politics, societal structures and values of their times. However, and this is a big 'however', there is *nothing* inevitable about how any individual responds to their circumstances. Dialectics are 'non-deterministic', which means that combining an individual with a set of contexts never leads to a predictable outcome. This is because any individual and any set of contexts are so impenetrably complex that it is impossible to guarantee any particular response of the one to the other. This can be seen in the many ironies of history, but also in the remarkable journeys individuals make through the course of their lives.

Brecht's life was particularly rich in historical ructions and upheavals. He was born in Germany in 1898. At the time, 'Germany' was a relatively new nation, having only been unified from a sprawling patchwork of duchies, principalities and states in 1871. By the time Brecht was sixteen, Germany's international ambitions had led to the outbreak of the First World War, and can be understood as the young nation's bid to attain a similar imperial status to those of its older European rivals. The young Brecht was also born into the middle class, and his artistic leanings set him up for a Bohemian life in the city of his birth, Augsburg. There he led a small group of classmates, writing poems and dabbling with other forms of creative endeavour. The end of the war brought about the collapse of the German aristocracy: the Kaiser abdicated in November 1918 and revolutionary forces believed that their time had come, although that revolution was violently suppressed in the following months. Brecht involved himself in the political ferment to a certain degree and his experiences fed into his dramatic output in the form of the play *Drums in the*

Night. Having moved to Berlin, he then found himself playing a major role in the cultural life of the Weimar Republic, the democratic government that replaced the monarchy. Brecht went into exile when the Nazis came to power in 1933, hopping from country to country as their grip on Europe tightened and finally fleeing to the United States in 1941. Yet even there he faced persecution when the House Un-American Activities Committee, a body charged with smoking out what it considered to be left-wing subversion in public life, summoned him to answer questions about his political allegiances and activities in 1947. Brecht left the United States for Europe the day after his hearing. In the wake of the Second World War and at the dawn of the Cold War, Brecht, after much hesitation, decided to settle in the German Democratic Republic (GDR), the socialist German state informally known as East Germany, and set up his own theatre company. He died in East Berlin in 1956 at the age of fifty-eight.

As is clear from this thumbnail sketch, Brecht's life was marked by radical changes of political context. His brief life accompanied the collapse of three German governmental structures and the birth of a new nation that he hoped would herald a new, emancipatory era for humanity. He would not live to see the imprisonment of GDR citizens behind the Berlin Wall in 1961 or the exponential expansion of the Ministry of State Security, more commonly known as the Stasi. Yet he experienced momentous historical crises and events, and these gave him a perspective that looked beyond the solitary interests of the individual. His work would be typified by its attempts to see the bigger picture and its profound effects on the members of the body politic.

As such, world events were always to make their mark on Brecht's work. Brecht's early years of artistic exploration, for instance, responded to the impact of war, yet his first full-length play, *Baal*, would seem to bear little clear imprint of this experience. Baal is an artist and not a soldier, and the play follows his life in a series of disconnected episodes as he offends bourgeois morality and follows his own rampant desires. Yet a more careful analysis reveals that Baal's radical rejection of the values of his time and his anarchic approach to life are actually a remarkably sensitive reception of a world turned upside down by a war that, for the first time, applied industrial means and magnitudes to battle, with deaths and casualties far outnumbering those of any other human conflict in history.

This short example demonstrates how the dialectical tension between the individual and society could lead to the production of work that was at once of its time and of startling originality. This volume aims to offer readers material that carefully accounts for the contexts in which Brecht was working while setting out his remarkable responses as a collaborative artist.[1]

Here it is perhaps worth noting Brecht's remarkable productivity and the many and diverse forms of his output. The standard German edition of his collected works spans thirty volumes, although there are thirty-two physical tomes, as two of the volumes were too big for a single book. There are nine volumes of plays; one double-length volume of unfinished plays; five volumes of poems; five volumes of prose, including novels and short stories; five volumes of theoretical and critical writings (including one that is double-length); two volumes of journals; and three volumes of letters. In addition, Brecht kept notebooks that are currently being published in German, and more letters and minor writings seem to emerge year on year. Add to this list the theatre work Brecht directed, the interviews he gave, and the occasional films he contributed to, and the picture that

---

[1] For more on Brecht as productive collaborator, see Volume III: Practice.

emerges is evermore rich and varied. In short, Brecht was continually grappling with 'the problems of the world' as one of his biographers, Werner Mittenzwei, called them,[2] and sought a myriad of forms and approaches to address them.

The distinctiveness and novelty of these forms are Brecht's artistic legacy. His restless mind latched on to all manner of sources to fuel his experiments. For example, Japanese Noh plays were central to the development of Brecht's most radical dramatic form, the *Lehrstück*, or 'learning play' as he called it in the only essay he co-authored in English.[3] Yet this form of drama appears to have little in common with the Japanese plays; it seeks to dissolve the boundary between the stage and the auditorium in order to facilitate the experience of painful and unenviable political decision-making. It was the repetitious nature of the Noh plays, however, and their playful reconfiguration of dramatic permutations that made them a model for a form of theatre that was not fixated on continually presenting the audience with something new, a legacy of the Romantic period in European art. It is this relationship of context and product that this volume seeks to expose.

The chapters are broadly organized into two sections: life and work. The 'life' section outlines the various political and social contexts that informed Brecht's work and breaks down into four broad periods: the young Brecht in Augsburg (1898–1918); the Weimar Republic (1918–33); the exile years (1933–48); and the GDR (1949–56). While these periods are, of course, discrete, readers will also note confluences between them and the ways in which certain concerns persist and develop over time. Nobody's biography falls into neat phases, where one thing starts and another stops, and there is no simple connection between the different phases of Brecht's life and the work he was doing.

The 'work' section takes up the lion's share of this volume for reasons that should be evident from the description of Brecht's output, outlined above: there is simply a great deal of it. The essays cover the plays, the poetry, the novels and the short stories. Each essay approaches a particular constellation of work Brecht undertook. The material on the plays and poems reflects the diversity of forms Brecht developed over his career, and the connection between artistic production and historical period is designed to help readers relate the one to the other.

The 'primary sources' selected for this volume include writings by Brecht previously untranslated into English. He rarely wrote lengthy essays, preferring to pick on particular issues or topics, often returning to them later on. The brevity and frequency of the majority of his unpublished writings indicates how he would take up ideas, leave them for a while, and perhaps consider them again. The short essay 'Eigenarten des Berliner Ensembles' ('Characteristics of the Berliner Ensemble'), for example, is the second draft of a set of thoughts on what distinguished his theatre company from any other in the GDR and, indeed, any further afield. The essay builds on and refines ideas of the first draft. Yet even this draft cannot be understood as 'final'. It is difficult to conclude that any of Brecht's ideas can truly be characterized by this epithet as his butterfly mind may simply have turned to another set of topics before he was able to offer a further articulation of his analysis. The essay is almost certainly not his last word on the matter,

---

[2] Werner Mittenzwei, *Das Leben des Bertolt Brecht oder der Umgang mit den Welträtseln*, 2 vols. (Berlin: Aufbau, 1997).
[3] Brecht, 'The German Drama: Pre-Hitler', in Brecht, *Brecht on Theatre*, ed. Marc Silberman, Steve Giles and Tom Kuhn, 3rd edn (London: Bloomsbury, 2015), pp. 119–24, here p. 122.

and the other writings included in this volume should be read in a similar way. That said, the writings may be provisional, but they also convey a need to reflect on experiences and express them as clearly as possible as a means of self-understanding on the artist's part at any given time. They offer snapshots of thoughts and are valuable as a way of gauging Brecht's engagement with certain ideas at particular historical moments.

Contemporaneous reviews of productions of his plays have also been included in the 'work' section to offer the reader a view of their reception. While some of the reviews are taken from the first productions of key plays, others focus on other important productions. That is why there are two reviews of *Mother Courage and her Children*, for example: the first reports on the world premiere in neutral Zurich in 1941 while the second gives an account of Brecht's own production in East Berlin in 1949. This production, a resounding triumph that helped convince the ruling Socialist Unity Party that Brecht should get his own theatre company, served as a model for later productions – Brecht documented it in the *Courage Model 1949*.[4] Ironically, the production did not fully satisfy Brecht's criteria for a successful translation of theory into practice. He feared that the audience spent too much time sympathizing with Mother Courage rather than standing at a distance from her to analyse the choices she made under the circumstances she encountered. That concern hardly discounts its significance in the play's production history, and is included for that reason.

Taken in its entirety, this volume sets up a tension between Brecht the creative artist and the many contexts that informed his work. There is no attempt to suggest direct links between the one and the other, but rather readers will find a presentation of complex circumstances and analyses of what Brecht crafted out of them. This dialectical relationship reflects the shifting forces that act on each other and that produce the incredible body of work associated with Bertolt Brecht.

---

[4]See Brecht, *Courage Model 1949*, in Brecht, *Brecht on Performance: Messingkauf and Modelbooks*, ed. Steve Giles, Tom Kuhn and Marc Silberman (London: Bloomsbury, 2014), pp. 183–222.

PART ONE
LIFE

The Young Brecht

CHAPTER ONE

Student Magazine: *The Harvest*

WERNER FRISCH AND K. W. OBERMEIER
TRANSLATED BY ROMY FURSLAND

In 1913, some grammar school pupils founded a student magazine called *The Harvest*. A small team of editors collected together poetry and prose written by the other pupils and presented it to the teachers and the student body. Max Schneider was among them, and had one of his own short poems published in the magazine:

> 'Unfortunately I don't have any copies of the issues of *The Harvest* that we worked on between 1913 and 1914. The editors were Brecht and Julius Bingen, who was one of the cleverest students in our class. He was killed in 1918.
>
> As far as I recall there were six issues of *The Harvest* altogether, and we were working on the seventh but I don't think it was ever finished. The magazine was A5 size. We had a print run of around 40 copies per issue. We printed using gelatin stencils that one of the girls made by hand. The cover pages were made of drawing paper, a different colour for each issue. It was the same drawing paper as we used in our art lessons. Every issue of *The Harvest* had six to ten pages and cost 15 pfennigs.'

The only remaining copies of the student magazine *The Harvest* are in the possession of Dr Georg Geyer, Berlin. Brecht had the following pieces published in the magazine:

The Tale of One Who Was Never Too Late [Satire]. Part 1	Issue 1, August 1913, pp. 5–7. Bertolt Brecht Archive (referred to below as BBA) 1534/04 and 1278/02.
Balkan War [A parabolic commentary]	Issue 1, August 1913, p. 7, BBA 1534/05 and 1278/01.
Wagner [Commentary]	Issue 1, August 1913, pp. 7–8, BBA 1534/05 and 1278/01.
The Poet	[Probably in Issue 2, September 1913.] BBA 1278/05.
The Burning Tree	[Probably in Issue 2, September 1913.] BBA 1278/04.

Werner Frisch and K. W. Obermeier, 'Schülerzeitung *Die Ernte*', in Frisch and Obermeier, *Brecht in Augsburg. Erinnerungen, Dokumente, Texts, Fotos* (Frankfurt/Main: Suhrkamp, 1976), pp. 58–60.

The Tale of One Who Was Never Too Late. Part 2	Issue 3, October 1913, pp. 2–4. BBA 1534/09 and 1278/02.
Gallery of Class 6A. Part 1	Issue 3, October 1913, p. 8. BBA 1534/12.
The Wish [Ballad]	Issue 4, November 1913, p. 1. BBA 1534/14 and 1278/04.
Gallery of Class 6A. Part 2	Issue 4, November 1913, p. 12. BBA 1534/20 and 1278/01.
The Bible [Drama in 3 Scenes]	Issue 6, January 1914, pp. 1–7. BBA 1278/08-16.
Carnival	Issue 7, February 1914, p. 1. BBA 1534/22 and 1278/06.
The Mother and Death. Part 2	Issue 7, February 1914, p. 2. BBA 1534/23. BBA 1278/07 (Typescript Parts 1 and 2).
The Tango	Issue 7, February 1914, p.2. BBA 1534/23 and 1278/05.
The Prussian Federation	Issue 7, February 1914, p.6. BBA 1534/25 and 1278/04.
Fairy Tale	Issue 7, February 1914, p.6. BBA 1534/25 and 1278/04.

The pieces Brecht contributed to the student magazine are signed Eugen Brecht, E. Brecht, E. B., Bertold Brecht or Bertold Eugen.

A schoolfriend of Brecht's at the time, Josef Schipfel, who also had pieces published in *The Harvest*, says: 'One day Eugen told me that the name Berthold also appeared on his baptism certificate, so from now on he was going to call himself Berthold Eugen. Up to that point he'd only ever been known as Eugen Brecht. In his next few years at the school he used those first names as a pseudonym.'

Brecht carried on using the self-chosen pseudonym Berthold Eugen until 1916; from July 1916 onwards he signed himself Bert Brecht.

CHAPTER TWO

'Ja, damals waren wir Dichter': Hanns Otto Münsterer, Bertolt Brecht and the Dynamics of Literary Friendship

TOM KUHN[1]

I

Brecht was, throughout the span of his career as a writer, quite exceptionally dependent upon the cross-fertilizations, inspirations and practical contributions which he could conjure and cajole from a host of literary and artistic collaborators and companions. The purpose of this essay is to create an image of just one of the relationships at the center of the early Augsburg circle of Brecht and his friends, and to illuminate the dynamics of that circle – particularly in terms of the practices of composition which developed in these years, and of their issue in literature.

The impulse to undertake this reconstruction of a friendship is twofold. Firstly, the images of such relationships in a writer's life are often reduced to crude formulae: 'exploited servant', 'homosexual lover'. There is no concrete evidence that Münsterer was either of these. Secondly, and much more interestingly, the nature of collaboration and of authorship have become central to our understandings of Brecht. This essay seeks

---

Tom Kuhn, '"Ja, damals waren wir Dichter": Hanns Otto Münsterer, Bertolt Brecht and the Dynamics of Literary Friendship', *Brecht Yearbook*, 21 (1996), pp. 48–66.

[1] The title is a nostalgic remark from a poem by Münsterer, 'Ah yes, we were poets then'. The impulse for this paper was provided by the collaborative work on an English edition of Münsterer's memoir: Hanns Otto Münsterer, *The Young Brecht*, trans and introd. by Tom Kuhn and K.J. Leeder (London: Libris, 1992). This book contains, in an introduction and extensive appendix, further reference to issues discussed below, as well as a brief bibliography in particular of Münsterer himself. A version of the paper was presented in Augsburg, in March 1995, at a conference of the International Brecht Society, to whom thanks are due. Thanks go also to Christiane Nuhn and Iain Galbraith, for friendly suggestions. A German language version of this paper will appear in *Der junge Brecht. Aspekte seines Denkens und Schaffens*, ed. Helmut Gier and Jürgen Hillesheim (Würzburg: Königshausen & Neumann, 1996).

to negotiate the terrain between biography and textual comment, but it is above all the *literary* friendship – the friendship made through and for literature, and the literature made through and for friendship – which concerns me.

The advantage of investigating such an early friendship is that it precedes the theorizations of Brecht's compositional practices, both by himself and by his later critics. Although it is true that Brecht, from about 1917, took pains to be unconventional and rejected rule-making where he could perceive it, it is scarcely plausible to suggest that at this stage he was developing a coherently anti-bourgeois attitude to intellectual property. Nor was collaboration yet a practicality of work for the theater or for film. Applied to schoolboys and recent school-leavers, it seems strikingly hollow to invoke notions of the end of the unique inspiration of the bourgeois artwork, or of artistic production as the activity of a socialist collective. On the other hand, although I am inclined to be skeptical about such theorizations, I can perhaps anticipate my argument to this extent: it is exactly in these years that Brecht himself begins to manifest an evident and growing self-consciousness of his practices. Münsterer gives the years of their friendship as 1917 to 1922. These are key years in the development of the self-awareness of the author. And so perhaps they are the appropriate moment when he and we begin to reflect about collaboration theory, a collaborative aesthetic even. The habits of collaborative composition, the marks of this early experience of literary friendship, may be traceable even many years later in Brecht's life.

The advantage specifically of Hanns Otto Münsterer, who was not after all the most important of the gang of friends, is that he has left an extraordinarily detailed account of Brecht's literary coming of age. This is the book *Bert Brecht: Erinnerungen aus den Jahren 1917-22* (Zurich: Arche, 1963, and Berlin: Aufbau, 1966) which has long formed an essential source for our knowledge and understanding of the young writer. There is also an extensive and underexploited collection of papers in the Bayerischer Staatsbibliothek in Munich.[2]

Münsterer's *Erinnerungen* are an unusual document, written for the most part only after detailed reference to his own diary from the same period. At several points in the text he refers explicitly to his diary notebooks, presumably lying open on the desk next to him as he undertook his reconstruction. We can observe the process of composition by comparing parallel passages.[3] Even here, however, some caution is necessary. The surviving diary narrative up to 1921 is not a true diary, but itself a reconstruction undertaken in 1921, partly from earlier documents which were then, it seems, destroyed. Besides, Münsterer clearly used the diary as an opportunity for literary self-stylization. With these reservations, the account which emerges from both the diary notebooks and the published memoir is nonetheless substantially accurate, at least in terms of raw facts. The precision of Münsterer's memories of conversations and of versions of Brecht's texts may seem implausible, but we know that he kept a conscientious record of the remarks

---

[2]References to the *Erinnerungen* are to the Zurich edition. The most important parts, for our present purposes, of the Münsterer-*Nachlaß*, which is held in the Handschriftenabteilung of the Bayerische Staatsbibliothek, Munich, are the extensive collection of Münsterer's own literary manuscripts, the collection of 'Brechtiana' (including manuscripts), and Münsterer's own diary and some letters. Extracts from the diary are published in Hanns Otto Münsterer, *Mancher Mann*, Manfred Brauneck ed. (Frankfurt: Fischer, 1987), 166–71. This volume contains, alongside published and some previously unpublished poems by Münsterer, the only significant essay on Münsterer himself. For further discussion of Münsterer's reliability, and for a fuller bibliography, see *The Young Brecht* (note 1).

[3]E.g. *Erinnerungen* 99–103, and diary notebook *1:45-52* (compare the extracts in *Mancher Mann*, 166–71).

and conversations which seemed of importance to him at the time. Moreover, in many cases he owned an early typescript transcription or a newspaper cutting of the poems he quotes.

Surprisingly, much of the material even readily available has been used uncarefully by Brecht scholars. The editors of the *Große Berliner und Frankfurter Ausgabe*, for instance, make reference to both the published memoir and to the archive in their notes, but they use only what suits. They reflect not at all on the creative processes which led to the poems they publish.[4] Other material from the archive has been misrepresented. For example, the now familiar and potentially significant Brecht diary fragment from 1916 was presented in *Sinn und Form* with no mention of Münsterer's note on an accompanying sheet that it was a 'spätere Abschrift, vielleicht fingiert, bestimmt für Therese Ostheimer' (later copy, possibly fabricated, intended for Therese Ostheimer).[5]

In comparison with the wealth of material about Münsterer, 'Orge' (Georg Pfanzelt) and 'Bez' (the later Bavarian Minister Otto Bezold) remained reticent, and some others of the circle entirely silent. Of Brecht's other early friendships, it is above all that with Caspar Neher which would merit much closer attention, and which has also helped to inform the following account.[6] To an extent, however, my reconstruction, even given these and other published and unpublished sources about Brecht's youth, must remain speculative.

II

Münsterer was born in 1900, two years Brecht's junior, in Dieuze in Lorraine (then German). His family settled in Augsburg before the first world war. It is perhaps above all the congruence of the geographical, historical and cultural perspectives of their youths which makes Münsterer's memoir of Brecht so valuable. In the early years they shared many sympathies and ambitions. In later life they drifted far apart. In striking contrast to Brecht, Münsterer only ever moved as far as Munich (except for a short period of study in Vienna) and he remained in Bavaria throughout the 1920s, throughout the years of Nazi rule and the war, and right up until his death in 1974. In 1933 he married an Augsburg girl, Elsbeth Nebelung. In 1937 Münsterer, whose political sympathies speak clearly through the pages of his memoir, was expelled from the National Socialist Chamber of Literature and forbidden to write. In the 1940s, however, he managed to establish a considerable name for himself as a doctor of medicine, specializing in dermatology and virology; in later life he devoted himself increasingly to the study of popular medicine and religious art.

---

[4]Compare notes 8 and 15. All quotations from Brecht's works are, as far as possible, from the edition mentioned here: Bertolt Brecht, *Werke*. Große kommentierte Berliner und Frankfurter Ausgabe, ed. Werner Hecht, Jan Knopf, Werner Mittenzwei and Klaus-Detlef Müller (Berlin and Weimar: Aufbau; Frankfurt: Suhrkamp, 1988-), henceforth GBA.
[5]The 'diary' entry was published in *Sinn und Form*, 38.6 (1986): 1133–4. The sheets in question are in Münsterer's *Nachlaß*. The issue of self-fictionalization in these sources is addressed below.
[6]The documentation of this includes Brecht's side of a very full correspondence, in *Briefe*, ed. Günter Glaeser (Frankfurt: Suhrkamp, 1981), and Neher's own diary, which is in the Augsburg Staats- und Stadtbibliothek, but which has never been conscientiously deciphered, much less edited or published. Some other valuable fragments of material appeared in *Brecht in Augsburg*, a documentation by Werner Frisch and K. W. Obermeier (Frankfurt: Suhrkamp, 1976).

The friendship between Brecht and Münsterer has furnished us not only with a valuable guide to the young Brecht, but also with a tantalizing portrait of their own relationship. It was a brief friendship, lasting really only a couple of years. For Münsterer, however, it was intense. Brecht was the older of the two, a self-possessed young man, a 'real poet' and self-appointed petty bourgeois rebel from the workers' suburbs. Münsterer was still very much a schoolboy, the son of a cavalry major, whose family had fallen on hard times but still lived in some splendor on one of the main streets of Augsburg. For a short while they saw each other nearly every day. Even much later Münsterer writes with scarcely concealed emotion of their times together, swimming in the Lech and lazing in the grass, or walking under the stars through Augsburg. And yet, from Brecht's perspective it perhaps seemed rather different. We can explain the paucity of letters from Brecht to Münsterer (unlike to Caspar Neher or Paula Banholzer for example) by the simple fact that Münsterer was never far enough away to merit a proper correspondence. The formal address, 'Herr Münsterer', which Brecht used in letters and in the 'Lied an Herrn Münsterer' (Song to Herr Münsterer), has been taken by some to indicate that this was a relatively distanced acquaintance.[7] I would suggest that it became almost a nickname, an ironic, and perhaps somewhat patronizing stylization of the elegantly besuited young man who first came to visit Brecht in the autumn of 1917. That said, it must be granted that the youthful friendships with Cas (Neher) and Orge (Pfanzelt) meant more to Brecht.

III

Although the rest of this essay concerns itself centrally with Münsterer, my remarks cannot be confined to him alone. Münsterer was, as we well know, just one of a whole band of gifted friends. Most of them were somehow 'artistically' active, even if it was only in the way that one might expect of intelligent and sensitive schoolboys. Münsterer describes his schoolmates' derivative poetic efforts from the period before he ever met Brecht; and, when they subsequently did meet, his own poems clearly furnished a persuasive visiting card (*Erinnerungen* 13, and diary notebook 1:34). One surviving poem which unambiguously antedates Münsterer's acquaintance with Brecht, and which Brecht apparently praised, is 'Jonathan' (compare *Mancher Mann* 27):

Ach die Zeiten sind vorüber,
da ich rein und keusch geliebt,
meinen Leib zerfrißt das Fieber
und die Seele ist getrübt.

Damals schenkt ich meine Neigung
einem einzgen schönen Kind,
ihre kleinste Gunstbezeigung
war berauschender Absinth.

---

[7]Brecht, *Briefe* 37–8; the poem in GBA 13:127–28. Even in brief notes to himself Brecht referred to his friend as 'H.O. Münsterer', or 'H.O.M.', see notebooks in the Bertolt Brecht Archive, Berlin (hereafter BBA), e.g. BBA 435/70, 435/85 and 452/92. Letters from 1920 are addressed to 'Hanns Otto'. After the war Brecht settled for 'lieber Münsterer', but signed himself, 'Dein b'. Incidentally, others imitated the formal address: Neher talks in his diaries of evenings with 'bert, orge und Münsterer' (e.g. May 1919); and Orge's later wife remembers the friends as Bert Brecht, Otto Bezold and Herr Münsterer, in: *Brecht in Augsburg*, 104.

Ach vorüber sind die Tage
meiner holden Jugendzeit
und mir bleibet nur die Klage
über die Verkommenheit.

Und ich stolpere durch Genüsse,
die ich nicht genießen kann.
Meerwärts taumeln alle Flüsse,
zu dem Grab ich alter Mann.

As for the rest: Otto Bezold, partly spurred on by Brecht it seems, wrote a novella and several poems, including one entitled, according to Münsterer, 'Der Geierbaum' (The Vulture Tree),[8] Georg Pfanzelt was musically gifted and provided tunes for several ballads and songs. Caspar Neher of course drew and painted, but his diary for this period also contains stories, poems and brief dialogue sketches. In October 1918 alone, we find a dialogue between Christ and Hans, a brief story about Lulu and several poems, including one entitled 'Krieg' (War). And that was by no means the end of it.[9]

It was from the outset not a circle of equals. Brecht himself was very much at the center. Indeed, Walter Brecht goes so far as to suggest that the friends looked upon his brother as 'ein von Geist und schöpferischem Temperament sprühender Messias' (a veritable Messiah sparkling with wit and creativity).[10] However, Brecht's skill was not just to find creative friends whose talents he could exploit, but, crucially, to encourage a creative bent in the friends he had. We can perhaps consider him an 'enabler' rather than an 'exploiter'. It was only gradually, in the course of this period, that Brecht's own ambitions and manipulative inclinations began negatively to influence the group. By that time they were anyway drifting apart for other reasons, dispersing to Munich and elsewhere to study, or settling into bourgeois life.

At the most basic level of literary production, this early team exchanged material and ideas, and (perhaps not unlike later collaborators) furnished raw sketches, some of which Brecht himself transformed into familiar early poems, or else rejected and left for them to complete as their own. But there was much more to it than that. The young friends communicated to an extraordinary degree through and about literature and the arts. They talked about poetry continually. They exchanged books and recommendations and opinions. They showed and read to each other drafts of their work and discussed them in detail. All of this is fully documented in Münsterer's *Erinnerungen* and elsewhere. The

---

[8] A note on Brecht's 'Der Geschwisterbaum' (The Tree of the Brothers) reads, 'Otto Bezold schrieb in starker, auch formaler, Abhängigkeit von diesem Werk ein Gedicht "Der Geierbaum"' (Münsterer-*Nachlaß*). This is one detail ignored by the editors of the GBA, who confidently date (and ascribe) Brecht's 'Der Geierbaum' 1917 and 'Der Geschwisterbaum' 1918. 'Der Geschwisterbaum' was dedicated 'meiner lieben Mutter 1918 zum Geburtstag', but that does not mean it was not written earlier (Münsterer has the dates the other way round, *Erinnerungen*, 39 and 75). Perhaps Brecht's 'Geierbaum', which indeed shows marked similarities of form and language with 'Der Geschwisterbaum', was based on an already Brechtian model by Bezold. Compare the story of 'Tarpeja', below. It is easy to be misled by the documents. Münsterer describes, for example, how Brecht made copies of the poems which pleased him (19). Where we have no other evidence, a Brecht type- or manuscript may not prove much. See also *Erinnerungen* 147–49, for Münsterer's comments on the friends' creations.

[9] Nor is this of course a complete list of the friends. It was a large and fluctuating group. Amongst the other names well-known to Brecht biographers are Heiner Hagg, Rudolf Hartmann, Otto Müller (or Müllereisert) and Ludwig Prestel.

[10] Walter Brecht, *Unser Leben in Augsburg, damals* (Frankfurt: Insel, 1984), 236.

friendship between Brecht and Münsterer flourished above all, it seems, when they read, talked about, wrote, or otherwise shared their experiences of literature.

Nevertheless, Münsterer is often apparently unaware of the extent to which the young Brecht and he himself were also fictionalizing elements of their own lived experience, making literature out of life and life out of literature in a tangled symbiosis. There are some nice examples of the contrast between their stylizations and the rather less splendid reality. Paula Banholzer, for instance, tells how Brecht used to feel sick and scared on the swingboats; whereas for Brecht and for Münsterer the swingboats were an ecstatic metaphor and the stuff of poems.[11] To an extent – as above all Banholzer's memoir makes clear – the whole rebellious, devil-may-care image was a fictional construct. If in their literature they were indeed exploiting experience, it was experience as much dreamt of as lived. Just as the whole gang of friends shared a real life, so they shared also a life of the imagination. Brecht himself was determined that his own life should be 'sein wichtigstes Kunstwerk' (his most important work of art – *Erinnerungen*, 83).

Their diaries provide rich evidence of these constructions. Brecht's diaries and letters are full of stylizations and imaginative flights; and the resulting self-images were evidently deployed, with mixed success, to impress the friends and potential girlfriends. It is difficult to know how much of the diaries were 'private', or how far they were rehearsals for public statements, or indeed already shared amongst the narrow public of the circle of friends. We know, for example, that Caspar Neher sent home leaves torn from his front-diary to Brecht (*Briefe*, 44). And Münsterer's own diary is at times extraordinarily self-conscious and 'literary'.

Nor was it only in their writing that elements of public performance and stylisation are so evident; even the friends' daily conversations could take on a heightened, fictionalized quality. They engaged in conversational games and role-playing; for example, they took on the characters of their fictional creations and spun spirited exchanges. In some cases these may be understood as improvisations towards dramatic situations and dialogues, even 'first drafts' of what were to become literary texts. Münsterer remembers that Brecht expected them to be able to conduct a conversation 'in sauberen Hexametern' (in immaculate hexameters – *Erinnerungen*, 137),

Even if, especially in retrospect, it appeared that Brecht was firmly in control, there can be little doubt that this traffic of inspiration and creation was two-way. Max Hohenester and Walter Brecht both paint in their own accounts that same atmosphere of mutual intoxication which Münsterer remembers: '[Es] herrscht eine fieberhafte Betriebsamkeit nach allen Richtungen, ziellos und um jeden Preis' (There's feverish activity shooting off in all directions, aimless and no matter what).[12]

---

[11] Paula Banholzer, *So viel wie eine Liebe: Der unbekannte Brecht*, ed.Axel Polder and Willibald Eser (Munich, 1981), 139; and see also Max Knoblach in *Brecht in Augsburg*, 176. Compare, for example, Brecht: 'Vom Schiff schaukeln' (GBA 11:18), Baal's comment (GBA 1:48), and several remarks in letters and diary entries; Münsterer: 'Philosophische Betrachtung beim Schiffschaukeln', *Mancher Mann*, 83–4, and *Erinnerungen*, 119. In his own diary Münsterer noted, 'Das Leben ist eine Schiffschaukel, aber – man muß schaukeln können' (diary notebook, 3:38, 17.12.1921; see also *Mancher Mann*, 165).
[12] *Erinnerungen* 105; compare *Brecht in Augsburg*, 107, and Walter Brecht, 236.

IV

A comparison of Münsterer's and Brecht's writings reveals the extent to which they shared their reading, their interests, and this whole life of the imagination. There are a great many thematic and formal links, most clearly in the work which was written in the early years. This is not the occasion to demonstrate them in detail. It is perhaps enough if I say that one poem by Münsterer ends with the words:

> Vergessen habe ich alle Erbarmung
> nur den Himmel niemals, der schön ist und weit.
> (I've forgotten all compassion
> but never the sky, which is wonderful and wide.)
>
> ('Leben eines Wüstlings', *Mancher Mann*, 14)

Another, with the title 'Von den Seefahrern und Kapitänen' (Of mariners and capitans), begins:

> Wohl sind unsre Schiffe von Algen und Tang
> und die Segel von Sonne zerschlissen.
> (Well may our boats be algae and weed
> and the sails worn by the sun.)
>
> (*Mancher Mann*, 17)

There are poems – songs and ballads for the most part – about pioneers and adventurers lost in distant jungles and oceans. There is a later poem about the flight of the aviator Nungesser. Another, entitled 'Von den schwächen der großen Männer' (Of the weaknesses of great men), starts off imagining Scipio with a toothache, and continues with a whole catalogue of the famous (including Hitler and Adenauer) in incongruously mundane situations – exactly as Münsterer describes the game he played with Brecht: 'Oder man stellte sich große Männer in sehr menschlicher Lage vor, Napoleon etwa Eis essend, Christus mit Zahnweh, den erhabenen Dante für seine Beatrice Zwiebel schälend; es lies sich da allerhand ausdenken' (Or we imagined great men in mundane and human situations, like Napoleon eating ice-cream, Jesus with toothache, sublime Dante peeling onions for his Beatrice; there was all sorts we could think up like that – *Erinnerungen*, 159).

All of these pieces are reminiscent to some degree of early Brecht works, whether in details or, more often, in their whole attitude and structures. Indeed what strikes one even about Münsterer's later compositions, from as late as the 1950s and 1960s, is his inability to cast off the models and the preoccupations of his youth in Augsburg. The voice becomes more monologic (particularly under the pressure of inner emigration), the mood more pensive, even melancholic, and other influences make themselves felt – some poems are almost Rilkeesque. Yet, even as Münsterer turns to spiritual comforts and to a religiosity quite foreign to Brecht, he falls back on memories of a poetic youth. In his *Erinnerungen* he cites 'Stadtgraben im Frühling' (Town moat in spring, 123–25):

> Als du ein Jüngling warst, toll von der Maiandacht,
> Weihrauch im Haar noch, trieb es vom Domportal
> fort dich zum Graben. Schaukelnd im Dämmerlicht
> zitternder Ampeln schwankten die Gondeln.
>
> (When you were a youth, wild from May Devotions,
> with incense still in your hair, drawn from the cathedral doors

down to the moat. Rocking in the dusking light
of shaking lamps the gondolas swayed.)

The reference to the 'Maiandacht' and to the boat-hire beneath the chestnut-trees opposite the Frühlingsstraße (now Bert-Brecht-Straße) is clear. The somewhat *larmoyant* 'Lang ists her' (It's a long time ago) from which I have borrowed my title, provides another example:

Ja, damals waren wir Dichter.
Trotz Krieg und Blut war die Welt uns recht
und mein Freund war Bert Brecht – – –
Ja, lang, lang ists her.
(Ah yes, we were poets then.
Despite war and bloodshed to us the world was kind
Bert Brecht was my friend – – –
Ah yes, it's a long time ago.)

(*Mancher Mann*, 95 and 94)

So as not to leave Münsterer's own achievement on such a note, however, let me pick out one more interesting piece from after his time with Brecht. Amongst Münsterer's unpublished papers there is a sheet of his own headed notepaper dated 1938 with an ironic anti-Nazi protest song in the form of a popular chorale.

DEUTSCHER LOBCHORAL (GERMAN CHORALE IN PRAISE)
Lobe den Fisch. Er ist Stumm.
Ewig schwimmt er und dumm
tief in den dunkelen Meeren.
Preise das Schaf,
denn es läßt brav
von seinem Henker sich scheeren.
Lobe das Schwein,
bald salzt der Schlächter es ein
aber es wird sich nicht wehren.
Lobe den Mann.
Froh tritt zum Tode er an
bald auf den Feldern der Ehren.
Zeig dies Gedicht
GeStaPo nicht,
sonst wird sie rasch dich belehren
oder bekehren
mit einem Schuß ins Gesicht
aus ihren guten Gewehren.

There are obvious and striking similarities with Brecht's own parodistic 'Hitler-Choräle' (Hitler Chorales). Yet, cut off as they were from one another, Münsterer would hardly have known that Brecht had experimented with the very same form in exile. This is not nostalgic or slavish imitation, but a parallel, independent development from common roots.[13]

---

[13]'Von den schwächen der großen Männer' and 'Deutscher Lobchoral' are cited from the *Nachlaß*. The other quoted poems are available in *Mancher Mann*. Although some poems, e.g. 'Deutscher Lobchoral', can be dated

V

What Münsterer the poet derived from the friendship with Brecht is clear: inspiration, encouragement, practical advice and creative daring, models of forms, ideas and imagery in plenty. His entire poetic output bears witness to this, and the later wistful memories, especially, bear the scars of this literary encounter. But what, if anything, did Brecht's literary expression derive from such friendships? One can perhaps isolate three more-or-less distinct types of marks which this 'teamwork' (and not just with Münsterer) left on Brecht's early poetic voice.

Firstly, and most straightforwardly, there are the details of material and ideas furnished by other members of the gang. The one story of a schoolfellow's contribution, Armin Kroder's rhymed poem 'Tarpeja', which Brecht transformed, must stand in for the surely many examples of this sort of thing which are no longer traceable.[14] This is a relatively trivial matter. Writers have to get their material from somewhere; it is a matter of passing interest to discover where. Presumably the larger part of the material contributed by friends came anyway not in the form of whole poems and sketches, but rather as 'corrections' to the versions of texts which were passed around or read aloud. According to Münsterer, Brecht 'nahm ... für seine Arbeiten Anregungen und Änderungsvorschläge, die wir ihm nahelegten, bereitwillig an' (eagerly accepted ... for his own work the suggestions and corrections that we proposed – *Erinnerungen*, 148). It was perhaps not an insignificant contribution.[15]

Secondly, working not just together, but in this climate of youthful competition, fuelled all these men's imaginations, including Brecht's. The excitement is abundantly clear from all the accounts. They tell of the rush of contributing forms and ideas, of trying to outdo each other, 'in förmlichem Wetteifer' (in the spirit of a contest), as Münsterer remembers (20), whether in breaking taboos or merely in composing scurrilous rhymes. All this sparked off adventures: in themes, images and forms. It is clear, equally, that Brecht valued these processes. The early notebook collection of poems is entitled 'Lieder zur Klampfe von Bert Brecht *und seinen Freunden*' (Songs for the Guitar by Bert Brecht *and His Friends*, my emphasis), although no one ever seems to want to make anything of that formulation.[16] In that collection, 'Baals Lied' (Baal's Song) is expressly described as having been written, 'Zusammen mit Lud [i.e. Ludwig Prestel] am 7.VII. 18 nachts am Lech' (Together with Lud on the night of 7/07/18 by the Lech – BBA 800/01 and /04). According to Münsterer Brecht once went so far as to suggest they publish their poems jointly (*Erinnerungen*, 147). As late as January 1922, Brecht was still writing to Münsterer from Berlin to solicit contributions (*Briefe*, 75), Münsterer has told, and again material in the Brecht Archive supports his version, of his attempts, with Brecht, to write *Volkslied* (folk song) parodies, possibly with a view even to publishing a whole collection, *Des Knaben Plunderhorn oder Schmatzkästlein des schweinischen Hausfreunds* (The Child's

---

unambiguously, in other cases one has to piece together the internal evidence of the poem, the nature of the manuscript or typescript, paper and so on. First publications are, in the case of Münsterer, a particularly uncertain guide: one poem was published only thirty years after its composition (*Erinnerungen*, 51). Brauneck ascribes dates to only a few of the poems in his collection.

[14]Münsterer-*Nachlaß* and *Erinnerungen*, 148. See also GBA 13:437.

[15]See also below, in the discussion of *Baal*.

[16]The GBA gives a rather rough picture of this activity, concluding, for no very convincing reasons, 'daß die Texte weitgehend Brecht selbst zugeschrieben werden können' (that the texts can be largely ascribed to Brecht himself – 11:289). They may be right, but we have no means of knowing.

Horn of Plunder or The Treasure Kisser of the Swinish House Guest). From the different versions of the several of these which have been handed down to us (and which now, rather oddly, find their way into the GBA) one can reconstruct the atmosphere of exchange and banter, of elaboration and ironization, in which such texts must have been composed.[17] It is not possible to determine precisely what poems, or what aspects of what poems, can be accounted for in these terms. All the same, it is instructive to set much of Brecht's early poetry, with its many voices, unstable meanings and fragmentary philosophies, against the clamoring exchanges of this context. This was surely part of the value and attraction of the Augsburg circle. Walter Brecht even asserted that Brecht 'needed' the friends, 'und sie nie vergaß, ja ihnen ein Leben lang auf seine Weise die Treue hielt' (and never forgot them, indeed was, in his own way, loyal to them his whole life – 236).

Thirdly, if we restore Brecht to his place as the leading spirit of all this activity (which is where he firmly belongs), the friends take on the part of an exceptionally sympathetic and receptive audience, his very first audience and readership in fact. But they were also a responsive, critical and participating audience, one that made its own active contribution to the works. Brecht wrote specifically for them. It was not just a literature derived *from* experience with friends, but one conceived *for* them, and for further excited sessions *with* them.

The experience of this audience probably had two consequences for Brecht's writing. In the first place it presumably helped him to develop ideas of an active theater audience and of active readers of poetry, which were to become central to his later poetics. And in the second place it furnished him with that sensitivity to improvised or quasi-improvised forms, fast and careless ripostes and busked dialogues, which are a characteristic of his work right up to the *Lehrstücke* and perhaps beyond. The following little exchange between Bezold and Brecht is documented by Münsterer and again in the Brecht Archive:

BEZOLD: Er sah die Maid
und dachte, die gefällt mir wohl.
Er hob das Kleid
BRECHT: Und damit wird das Lied frivol.[18]

(Bezold: He saw the maid
his thoughts weren't only chivalrous.
He lifted up her dress
Brecht: And now our song is getting frivolous)

The importance of such a trivial piece of banter lies not in its literary accomplishment, but in its symptomatic presentation of the way in which Brecht and his friends could work. There were certainly hundreds of other exchanges which were not recorded.[19]

---

[17]Münsterer's copies of three poems, which the editors have taken up into the GBA (13:221-24), 'Rudelsburg', 'Der Baum im Odenwald', 'Ballade vom Hauptmann von Köpenik' [sic], are introduced: 'Aus einem geplanten Volksliederparodienbuch: Des Knaben Plunderhorn oder Schmatzkästlein des schweinischen Hausfreunds. Ein Volksbuch für die oberen zehntausend. Gemeinschaftsarbeit von Brecht and Münsterer' (Münsterer-*Nachlaß*). The copies in the Brecht Archive bear the note '(m. Münsterer)' (BBA 2212/02; compare 2212/50 and also Brecht's notebook, 435/70). Compare also Münsterer's diary notebook, 2:55, 20.8.1921; and *Erinnerungen* 185-86.

[18]BBA 2212/45; also in *Erinnerungen*, 80, and in the *Münsterer-Nachlaß*.

[19]A few examples of dialogues etc. are recorded in Brecht's diary too, *Tagebücher 1920-1922. Autobiographische Aufzeichnungen 1920-1954*, ed. Herta Ramthun (Frankfurt: Suhrkamp, 1975), e.g. 27 and 64. Some read like

VI

Thus far I have managed hardly to mention the most important product of these years and these friendships, namely *Baal*. It is clear that this text too benefitted from the climate of unfettered productivity, of collaborative artistic friendship, and especially of dramatic improvisation. Münsterer remembers,

> der ganze Frühsommer 1919 ist durchpulst von Baalischem Weltgefühl. Aber auch das Umgekehrte ist richtig, das Drama, besonders in dieser zweiten und besten Fassung, enthält selbst viel von unserem damaligem Leben.
>
> (the whole of the spring of 1919 was imbued with a Baalian feeling for the world. But the obverse is also true, the play [*Baal*], especially in this second and best version, itself contains much of our life in those days)
>
> (*Erinnerungen*, 109)

Again, the friends read drafts to each other, proposed corrections and improvements. The level of participation and of investment in *Baal* is made strikingly clear in Münsterer's and Neher's diaries, which record progress and alterations in considerable detail, and for some periods speak of little else but Baal. Neher calls it 'sein und mein Baal' (his and my Baal).[20] And it is noticeable how Münsterer describes the evolution of the text in impersonal and passive terms, avoiding almost all mention of an author: 'große Partien ... sind gestrichen' (large sections get cut), 'schon die nächsten Tage bringen weitere Änderungen' (the next days witness further changes), 'die ... Episode wird ... gestrichen' (the episode is cut), 'die ... Szene wird ... ersetzt' (the scene is substituted) and so on (107-8). Münsterer seeks no credit for himself, he mentions only 'ein paar Änderungsvorschläge werden von ihm [Brecht] wohlwollend aufgenommen' (a couple of suggestions for changes are benevolently taken up [by Brecht] – 108). But then he seems anyway inclined, like others later, to efface himself in order the better to reveal what he perceives as Brecht's genius. We know at least that it was Münsterer who was partly responsible for the abbreviated title: Brecht himself had proposed *Baal frißt! Baal tanzt!! Baal verklärt sich!!!* (Baal eats! Baal dances!! Baal transfigured!!! – 22-23).

The most interesting instance of Münsterer's involvement in, if not contribution to, the text is that parts of the dialogue with Johannes in the 'Baals Dachkammer' (Baal's attic room) scene (GBA 1:34-37), where the 'Jüngling' (youth) seeks Baal's advice about sexual relations with his Johanna, echo quite closely formulations in (Hanns) Münsterer's own diary, this time as the record of a real conversation between himself and Brecht.[21] Münsterer glosses this in his *Erinnerungen:* 'bei manchen Gesprächen im *Baal* klafft zwischen historischer Realität und dichterischer Überspitzung keine allzu breite Kluft' (in the case of some conversations in *Baal* the gulf between historical reality and poetic

---

reported conversations, others like pure fantasy.

[20]Neher diary, April 1919, also quoted in *Brecht in Augsburg*, 171. A proper discussion of the relationship with Neher will need to take on board that a good part of Neher's creative contribution was not in words but in pictures. He sketched a great many 'Baals', some of which undoubtedly influenced Brecht's own emerging image of Baal. Hence his 'co-authorship' of the figure. Pfanzelt's musical contributions may, by the way, have performed a similar function to Neher's graphics. The dynamics, however, of the relationships between the different art forms, another important aspect of Brecht's creativity, lie outside the scope of the present essay.

[21]Diary notebook, 1:35. Brauneck somewhat exaggerates this correspondence, *Mancher Mann*, 186.

hyperbole is not all that great – 109).²² My point, rather, would be that historical reality has precious little to do with it; the congruence was guaranteed by the atmosphere of mutual self-stylisation and of shared adventures of the imagination. That this in turn proceeded, to some extent, from the real experience of the participants (often buried deep), or from their real reading experience, is a truism. And the extent is anyway undiscoverable.

There are internal textual pointers too, which reveal *Baal* as a product of the circumstances I have described. The improvised conversations of Baal and Eckart, especially in the earlier versions, both imitate and anticipate the improvisations between friends; and the drunken exchanges and ditties of the 'Hölzerne braune Diele' (brown wooden salon) scene (not in the 1918 text, [GBA 1:58-63]) read like an exaggerated parody (or nightmare) of anything Münsterer can describe of evenings spent in Gablers Taverne (again *Erinnerungen*, 109). We sense in these scenes that the performance is not even meant for us outsiders; we have the sensation of eavesdropping on a process of textual exchange which belongs only to the (intoxicated) participants. Moreover, Baal himself, the poet, is a spinner of yarns and a performer for friends, not exactly a great conversationalist, but at least a social performer and not a lonely literary artist in the post-Romantic tradition. He has a garret, it is true, but that is little more than a throwaway quotation of the Romantic trope (besides Brecht had his attic room too, in the house of his parents). We only once see him alone there sitting over his paper, and then he is driven to the desperate exclamation, 'Ich muß etwas gebären!' (I must give birth to something! – GBA 1:34). Where we in fact see him giving birth to 'literature', he is in the company of others. Indeed, he is almost entirely immersed in quasi-literary relationships and contexts. It is possibly an index of his world-view that his solution to Sophie's disaster is to suggest that she go 'zur Bühne. Oder in den Himmel' (to the theatre. Or to heaven – 57). Not even the reality of a pregnant mistress can interrupt for long his flight of fancy, and of literature. He sees the people on the street as 'Zuschauer' (spectators), and he measures time in 'Acts' as well as nights (34-35). Baal and the pastor argue over whether the world is a circus or a prison (65); there is no prospect of it being a real world.

All this is not to say that *Baal* gives a somehow accurate portrait of the Augsburg milieu and friends. On the contrary, my point is that, at least to the extent that they derived their literature from themselves, so these young men derived themselves from their literature. The lumberjacks laconically sum up the relationship of life and narrative, 'Wir erzählen hier oben nur Lügen. Es ist besser so' (Up here we only tell lies. It's better that way – 38).²³

This image of the genesis and early development of *Baal* gives us reason to see the early history of the text, not as a series of versions or 'Fassungen' ('versions' as the GBA would have it), but as a process of continual and, at least to a certain extent, collaborative elaboration, correction, and renewal. *Baal* emerges as an open fragment, which achieves itself in a heady exchange of performance and composition. This is perhaps why the

---

²²Compare Paula Banholzer's generalized remark that, 'Dichtung und Wahrheit lagen für Brecht sehr nah beisammen' (poetry and truth for Brecht lay very close together), *So viel wie eine Liebe*, 120.

²³Is it worth again stressing here that Brecht's *real* life, despite the surface features often commented upon, was very different? The pregnancy of Paula Banholzer and subsequent birth of Frank, for example, mark a very significant change in Brecht's attitudes; this is a reality for which he has to shoulder some responsibility (see e.g. *The Young Brecht*, 151–55). Nor of course did Brecht murder anyone, drive anyone to suicide, or indeed even drink heavily. Paula Banholzer, in particular, paints the picture of a sexually relatively inexperienced young man, often shy and always courteous (*So viel wie eine Liebe* e.g. 35–38). Compare *Erinnerungen*, 109.

theater versions and the later attempts to recast the play and establish a purely textual coherence are, as Brecht himself recognized, essentially unsatisfactory.

VII

I said at the beginning that I was concerned more with the literature than with the life. The biography of the young Brecht in any case draws us inexorably back into the literature, and it often becomes difficult to hold the two apart. Brecht's life centered firmly on literature. His writing and his friendships turn out to have more to do with one another than one might have imagined.

Perhaps it was his very inability or unwillingness at this stage to invest much in real life that, amongst other things, contributed to misunderstandings and, from 1920, to the gradual estrangement of the friends.[24] The years covered by Münsterer's narrative, in Augsburg and Munich, were for Brecht the years in which his literary career gradually became more important than his friendships. It started as a period of quite exceptional and chaotic productivity. Münsterer describes the stream of works issuing from the friends' and Brecht's uneasy blend of spontaneity and reflection. Brecht himself, however, was becoming increasingly aware of the value for his own creative processes of the protean spontaneities he could derive from collaboration. He began to make self-conscious use of the relationships I have described. One can sense the presence of others in Brecht's work and world of the imagination throughout his *Tagebücher*. His 'need' for the contribution of others is formulated most strongly, however, when everything is beginning to go wrong and no one will help him (e.g. September 1920, 69). By June 1922, Münsterer is confiding bitter thoughts to his diary: 'Sobald er bessere Freunde hat, schmeißt er die alten weg' (As soon he has better friends he chucks the old ones away – diary notebook, 3:76). These years mark the beginnings of a literary awareness in which selfless and glad collaboration becomes calculated and blurs off into exploitation. Münsterer's own role, although certainly not passive, becomes increasingly a secondary and supportive one: as the go-between in relationships with women, then interceding with publishers, writing reviews and so on. In the later stage of their friendship, in his unselfish promotion of Brecht's career and interests, Münsterer begins to prefigure those later loyal followers (many of them women, such as Elisabeth Hauptmann) who effaced themselves in order to serve what they considered to be genius.

But I have sought to describe, not the later, emotionally fraught personal relationships, but the earlier literary friendships, out of which literature was perhaps conjured rather than knowingly extracted. It is a very particular literature which, I believe, owes some of its most striking features to the circumstances of its genesis. One of the characteristics, for example, of the texts of the young Brecht over which traditional accounts of 'life and works' often stumble, is their shifting and inconsistent perspectives and opinions. This is made the worse since the texts, by assertively naming real people, places and circumstances, tempt us to seek a single biographical authority. But as early as the 'Lieder zur Klampfe', the 'author' and his collaborators and 'friends' are already placed as fictional figures inside the text. And the poems themselves are presented as the chatter of their multiple fictionalized voices. The multiple subjects within the texts of the young

---

[24]This is documented clearly in Brecht's diaries and elsewhere, especially Münsterer's diary notebook, 2:21 and 37 (i.e. April-May 1921).

Brecht are striking (and have become very familiar), but we know, of course, that they are not simply the author and his friends. The whole poetics of these works seems to entail the creation of personalities and voices, which can then perform themselves. The filling and debunking of subject positions – of which Baal is perhaps simply the most grandiose – becomes an exuberant game of the literary imagination. In fact one of the best places to trace Brecht's slipping in and out of fictions and careless inventing of personae is not in a strictly literary work at all, but in the letters to perhaps the closest friend of these years, Caspar Neher. Here, rather than in Brecht's own somewhat more monologic diaries, we can see him trying on selves, and letting them speak.[25] The very contrast between these letters *and* the diary gives us some clue to the main profit which Brecht derived from the literary friendships I have described. Brecht and others often talked of how he 'needed' other people in order to write. It was less their specific material contribution that he sought, and more that essential sense of a sympathetic interlocutor with whom one could play the games on which his early work depends.

An investigation of early friendships and their texts invites reference back to those conventional descriptions of Brecht's 'collective' work which I mentioned at the outset. It is remarkable, surely, how many of the inclinations and working methods of the young author appear to anticipate developments and preoccupations in the aesthetics and literary practices of the later and Marxist Brecht. But perhaps we can now establish how little Brecht's famed 'collective productivity', in origin at least, has to do with his Marxism. For it is back in the years 1918 to 1920, thus early in Brecht's career, that literature already begins to establish itself as a process of provocation and riposte, a dialogue, and a site of competing discourses. It is here that literature becomes so embroiled in adaptation and revision, and in performance. And it is here that we first experience literature as productive within a community, and indeed productive of a community. Perhaps the fruitfulness of these ideas for readings of Brecht indeed justifies talk of an 'aesthetics of collaboration'. There are signs enough in Brecht's later work. To cite just one example: a key feature of the 'Lehrstück' (admittedly in the context of a quite different ideological program) is the involvement of the audience in the completion of the work, a work for the community of the participants. One can perhaps see the roots of this sort of project in the Augsburg circle. And the notion of a productive society of 'friends', governed by 'Freundlichkeit' (friendliness) was of course to become a central topos of the later work. The creative atmosphere and exchanges of friendship may even be understood as something of a paradigm of productivity – analogous to the ideas Brecht was later to sketch about love.[26]

That such connections are worth pursuing is hinted at by Brecht's very last note to Münsterer in the 1950s: alongside a transcript of the poem 'In finsteren Zeiten' (In dark times), the author thanks the companion of his youth 'für viele Freundlichkeiten' (for many acts of friendship). [27]

---

[25]The early correspondence in *Briefe passim*, e.g. 41, where Brecht imagines nicknames for himself.
[26]E.g. GBA 18:40. For a stimulating discussion of notions of productivity, compare Darko Suvin, 'Brecht: Bearing, Pedagogy, Productivity', in *Gestos* 5.10 (1990): 22–23 especially.
[27]Münsterer mentions the note, which is preserved in the *Nachlaß*, in his *Erinnerungen*, 190.

Brecht and the Weimar Republic

CHAPTER THREE

Sachlichkeit (Objectivity)

PHILIP GLAHN

In his 2007 book *The Century*, the French philosopher Alain Badiou presents Brecht as 'an emblematic figure of the twentieth century', an era whose subjectivity is 'prey to the passion of the real and placed under the paradigm of definite war'.[1] What draws Badiou to Brecht is the playwright's articulation of the antagonism that defines 'Germany's identity crisis': the tension between a romanticism of Wagnerian dimensions – 'This has less to do with Wagner's genius', Badiou remarks, 'than with its appropriation by petit bourgeois *ressentiment:* the bankrupt shopkeeper in rags mistaking himself for Siegfried in a Kaiser helmet' – and a cynical, paralysing nihilism.[2] Brecht's work 'thinks the enigmatic link between destruction and commencement', finding social, political and dramatic innovation not in the unreserved replacement of the outdated with the new but in the old's 'nourishing decomposition'.[3] Brecht's interest in the *Sachlichkeit* or facticity, the facticity of the city and the masses, of technology and sports, of prostitution and crime writing, lies not in their abolition of romantic or bourgeois notions of individuality or existence per se, but in their chronicling of the demise of the old to make room for alienation and discontent to emerge as a critique that is increasingly harder to suppress. What drew Brecht and his peers to sports was not just the audience's engagement but the contest itself as a technical model of reality where, in the end, the outcome was based on unadulterated, unmediated force. This was the upside of Kracauer's lament regarding the depoliticization of sport: ideology could represent physical competition in *völkisch* terms but, as the National Socialists found out for themselves when Jesse Owens repeatedly shattered the myth of Aryan supremacy during the 1936 Olympics in Berlin, the facticity of the contest defied any racist *Überbau*. Boxing in particular offered a violent deconstruction of the stage without its abandonment. The actor on this stage was accountable for his actions, while their presentation challenged the formal and narrative artifice so integral to the concept of entertainment.

Brecht was one of many Weimar artists and intellectuals who were enthralled by boxing. The avant-garde mingled with the heroes of the ring, like Max Schmeling, Paul Samson-Körner, Hans Breitensträter and Erich Brandl, at soirées organized by the art dealer Alfred Flechtheim and on the pages of his journal *Querschnitt: Magazin für Kunst, Literatur und Boxsport*. A number of artists even took up boxing themselves, among them John Heartfield and George Grosz, the actor Fritz Kortner and the opera singer Michael Bohnen. The rejection of

---

Philip Glahn, '*Sachlichkeit*', in Glahn, *Bertolt Brecht* (London: Reaktion, 2014), pp. 74–92.

[1] Alain Badiou, *The Century* (Cambridge, MA, 2007), p. 39.
[2] Ibid., pp. 39–40.
[3] Ibid., p. 45.

theatricality was the shared, decisive appeal, and any tampering with the material 'realness' of boxing was vehemently denounced. Greater specialization and abstraction, as through the increasing attempt by 'experts' to apply 'a whole nomenclature of technical terms' and 'point systems', and the technical TKO rather than a true knock-out, belied, according to Brecht, a tendency toward 'l'art pour l'art'.[4] The *Querschnitt* even presented reports on matches by fighters themselves, in a language as direct and straightforward as their performance in the ring. Brecht's own boxing stories took a similarly factual approach, using reportage and interviews to effect as direct a perspective as possible.

Brecht cultivated a friendship with Samson-Körner; several photographs show the two spending time together. A staged image of 1927 captures Elisabeth Hauptmann at the typewriter, among a few friends and colleagues, with Samson-Körner sitting at a piano at the other end of the room and Brecht standing in the centre, as if connecting the worlds of the fighter and the Weimar intellectuals. Another photograph, published the following year, shows Brecht and the boxer as complementary characters: raising his fist as if to throw an uppercut, Samson-Körner towers over the diminutive writer, who has his hands in his pockets, gaze turned downwards, a sly smile on his face. But the heavyweight champion has placed his other hand gently on the back of the poet's head in a nearly tender embrace. There is something almost homoerotic in this picture, a curious charge of masculinization that suggests the Weimar cult of the strong, male body as the physical and psychological catharsis of a nation's men maimed and humiliated by war and reparations. Brecht's short story 'The Uppercut' (1925) and *The Vita of the Boxer Samson-Körner*, an incomplete serial novel published in *Scherls Magazin* in 1926–7, emphasize the ambiguity of the boxer image: on the one hand the fighter is gruff and uneducated, brutal, the least likely role model for bourgeois sons or those with *bürgerliche* aspirations. On the other hand, he embodies ideals of masculinity, wholeness and individuality. The form of the interview and first-person narrative also affirm the subjective voice of a coherent self, but in the banality of their language and structure, the lack of psychological development found in the more traditional *Bildungsroman* (a type of novel concerned with the spiritual, moral and social education and maturation of a young protagonist), Brecht's texts defy easy consumption. As in the photographs of Brecht and the boxer, the elements do not quite add up, so they come under scrutiny themselves.

In a sense, these texts resemble the works of the Berlin Dadaists, such as Hannah Höch's collages and John Hearfield's montages, in their 'nourishing decomposition'. The emphasis on construction and constructedness not only makes room for an awareness of the production of language but foregrounds the alienation that stems from experiencing the rift between disparate images and ideas, between the possible and the actual, the picture and the thing. In an article published in the *Arbeiter Illustrierten Zeitung* (Workers' illustrated paper) on the occasion of its tenth anniversary, Brecht addresses the type of reportage offered by someone like Heartfield, who was one of the publication's staff artists:

> In the hands of the bourgeoisie, photography has become a terrible weapon *against* the truth. ... The photographic apparatus can lie just as much as the typesetting machine. The task of the A-I-Z to serve the truth and reconstruct the real facts is of undeniable importance and, I believe, is being solved brilliantly.[5]

---

[4] *GBA*, XXI, pp. 224–5.
[5] 'On the Occasion of the A-I-Z's Tenth Anniversary', *Arbeiter Illustrierten Zeitung*, 41 (October 1931); *GBA*, XXI, p. 515.

Brecht's contribution to this project of truth-telling was the demystification of art and language. Using a historically specific and determined type of speech, he aimed to denaturalize views, positions and attitudes that had been presented as given, transhistorical, inalterable. To Brecht, the images provided by bourgeois art as well as by the Neue Sachlichkeit (New Objectivity) were what Barthes called 'depoliticized speech', which turned history into nature, robbing events of how they came to be, how they function, how they change. 'Things lose the memory that they were once made.'[6] Instead, Brecht looked to historicize the natural in the affirmation of the production of the present. In Barthes' words:

> This is a political language: it presents nature for me only inasmuch as I am going to transform it. ... There is therefore one language that is not mythical, it is the language of man as a producer: wherever man speaks in order to transform reality and no longer to preserve it as an image.[7]

It was in this pursuit that Brecht picked a very public fight with Thomas Mann, while ridiculing the Neue Sachlichkeit's *Technikkult* and accusing Erwin Piscator for his merely formal mechanization of the theatrical apparatus.

In 1926, celebrating its one-year anniversary, the journal *Literarische Welt* announced a number of competitions with the goal of helping young artists gain visibility. In the literary category, Brecht was chosen as the juror for poetry, Ihering for drama and Alfred Döblin for fiction. Rejecting all of the several hundred poems submitted, Brecht instead chose a poem he found in a bicycling magazine and declared its author, Hannes Küpper, the winner. In the article accompanying Küpper's 'He, he! The Iron Man!', a poem documenting a victory of Australian cyclist Reggie MacNamara, Brecht explained his decision, arguing that the young poets had failed to write something that was not old, that they rivalled their precursors in 'sentimentality, insincerity and unreality'. Like that of Rilke, Stefan George and Franz Werfel, the works of these young poets had no 'use-value'. Brecht ends with a provocation: 'I recommend to Küpper to produce more songs of this kind, and I recommend the public to encourage him through rejection.'[8] A considerable outrage ensued, with responses in the *Literarische Welt* and many other publications. Some writers objected to the belittlement of German literary accomplishment; others, including Klaus Mann, Thomas Mann's son, defended the rejected poets against the banality of bicycle lyricism. One of the young poets protested publicly against Brecht's decision, whereupon the playwright advised the outraged contestant to 'subscribe to a cycling magazine', where he would learn that 'in uneducated circles far removed from the *Literarische Welt*, it is considered unfair to reject a judge *after* the race'.[9]

After the war, Thomas Mann, the personification of bourgeois literature, had cast himself as a figure of modernist writing, offering aesthetic autonomy and categorical continuity in times of moral chaos and social upheaval. *Geist*, good taste, *Formwillen* and artistic discipline presented, according to Mann, a necessary antidote to the type of naive revolutionary and largely incoherent literature and theatre of the younger generation, including Brecht. Thomas's son Klaus then took it upon himself to explore the topic of the generational divide,

---

[6] Roland Barthes, *Mythologies* (New York, 1997), p. 142.
[7] Ibid., pp. 146–7.
[8] *GBA*, XXI, pp. 192–3.
[9] 'Bert Brecht's Reply', *Die Neue Zeit*, 5/6 (May–June 1927); *GBA*, XXI, p. 200.

addressing the question of how to bridge old and new while avoiding what he saw as the reactionary *Vatermord*, or patricide, that would leave the vulnerable culture rudderless. In 1926, the literary journal *Uhu* published articles by and a conversation between the Manns. Klaus Mann wrote, 'The father's work stands before us, and we educate ourselves, learn from it.' Thomas Mann contends, 'Maybe it is less the parents who changed than the children, meaning that they have grown older and more reasonable, seeing their parents in the right light.' The younger generation, according to the elder Mann, had lived for some time off the myth of patriarchal tyranny but now, faced with the challenge of warding off the 'wave of analytic revolution' that had swept Europe from Russia, the 'tendency towards the immoral, toward a smug disorder' would no longer suffice. 'The Bolsheviks, they hate the soul', he wrote, and because American modernism was itself soulless, it was left to the tradition of nineteenth-century European – German and French – culture to 'guard the soul'.[10]

This provocation Brecht could not resist. That same month, in the Berlin weekly *Das Tage-Buch*, Brecht took aim at both father and son, displaying obvious dissatisfaction with the fact that the younger Mann had been chosen to represent the new as much as with the declaration that the time of revolutionary youth was over. Brecht presented the 'harmony in the literary forest' as yet another act of active depoliticization aimed at concealing the fact that 'boys' like Klaus Mann were tired from merely watching their fathers and had given in. He further elaborated that the notion of the patriarchal tyranny was far from the reason for the *Vatermord* (patricide): 'Truly, we didn't kill those fathers because they were hard and violent! Instead they did not feel it because they were soft and mushy.' Brecht adds, 'To our controversial fame as *Vatermörder* we will have to add the very indisputable as *Kindermörder* [child murderers].'[11]

Brecht had taken aim at Thomas Mann before, accusing him of inventing things in order to then ironically judge them and characterizing the traditional German novel as a counterproductive distraction from reality. Instead, the playwright advocated a return to the crime story and its *Gaunerjargon*, or gangster jargon, a language existing through agreement (*contrat littéraire*) between writer and reader to describe 'all the occurrences of human life, feelings, gestures, viewpoints, entanglements, situations'.[12] The idea was to put forth a truly new attitude to the present, including 'the creation of *Formschlüssel* [formal keys] that can access the new subjects'.[13] This entailed an approach not unlike that of modern science, rejecting harmony and idealism and creating 'chaos' by restoring the complexity of events and ideas through historical specificity. For Brecht, the acknowledgement of the social and political reality at a given moment would enable that reality's transformation. The chaos to be experienced and known was the schism between the real and the ideal and the acknowledgement of their incompatibility – dialectics not as synthesis but as a constant state of becoming. Useful is the type of art that articulates the reality of the relationship between the material and the idea, the given and the possible; useful are the forms and mediums that remain factual in their presentation. The power to report rather than embellish or divert became the new directive for the arts in general and the theatre in particular:

> Practically speaking, *what is desirable is the production of documents*. By that I mean monographs of important men, outlines of social structures, exact and immediately

---

[10]Klaus Mann, 'Die neuen Eltern' and Thomas Mann, 'Die neuen Kinder: Ein Gespräch', *Uhu*, XXI (August 1926).
[11]*GBA*, XXI, pp. 159–60.
[12]'Squibs about Crime Novels' (1926), *GBA*, XXI, p. 131.
[13]'Word to Old Age' (1926), ibid., p. 168.

applicable information about human nature and heroic presentation of human life, all from typical standpoints and not, regarding its usefulness, neutralized by form.[14]

Sachlichkeit, to Brecht, was thus a form of communication, a technique of representation made possible and indeed necessitated by urban life, sports and technology. Only by maintaining an active and contingent relation between the audience's experience of everyday life and its mediation would this speech remain political. Döblin, in his own assessment regarding the state of fiction writing in the Weimar Republic, put it this way: 'Short stories, as well as short novels, require not only a special technique but the special willingness to establish a modern, close contact with the reader.'[15]

During the mid-1920s Brecht published dozens of stories and essays in a wide variety of newspapers and magazines, ranging from the yellow press like *BZ am Mittag* and liberal dailies like the *Berliner Börsen-Courier* to more specialized papers such as the literary section of the *Frankfurter Zeitung* and the theatre journal *Die Scene*. Poems like 'The Cities' appeared in the magazine *Der Simplicissimus* in 1926, presenting the big city as empty and meaningless without its inhabitants and thus emphasizing the role of the urban dweller in producing modernity. An untitled poem published in the *Berliner Börsen-Courier* in early 1927, on the other hand, advises the reader to forget everything they have ever heard regarding their place and possibilities in the world and their mothers' and society's encouragement to succeed; it counsels that the world is one's oyster, and to realize instead that to learn the 'ABC' is to learn how oppression works. The readers are told, 'This is not to discourage you!'[16] Brecht asks his audience to accept, to *concur* in order to not be deceived.

The social dimension of Brecht's work at this time was for individuals to see themselves as part of a larger whole. At this point, he did not see the proletariat as a revolutionary force, though he clearly was concerned with a redistribution of the ownership of experience and knowledge. The usefulness of the *Einverständnis*, or social agreement, is manifested in the production of a social consciousness of the given, rather than a class-consciousness of the possible. Brecht belonged to a group called Gruppe 25, which included, along with Döblin, the 'raging reporter' Egon Erwin Kisch, who embodied the art of journalistic writing as a form of social participation. Gruppe 25's interest in reportage, questionnaires, radio broadcasting and filmic ways of direct, collective seeing inspired their use of short texts, self-revelatory narration, multiple perspectives and popular, even banal subject-matter. To Brecht, such forms of communications technology themselves interpellated the individual as a collective subject, exchanging psychology and inwardness for an objective, 'seeing from the outside' cognition. But unlike his Neue Sachlichkeit peers, Brecht never confused the technological apparatus with its applications, and he was wary of an undifferentiated embrace of modern progress. His well-known poem '700 intellectuals Pray to an Oil Tank', written most likely in 1927 and published in *Der Simplicissimus* (among other places) in 1929, demonstrates his critical attitude:

> You ugly one
> You are the most beautiful!
> Do violence onto us

---

[14] 'A Bit of Advice for Producing Documents' (1926), ibid., p. 165.
[15] Alfred Döblin, 'Unbekannte junge Erzähler', *Literarische Welt*, XI (1926), reprinted in *100 Texte zu Brecht*, ed. Manfred Voigts (Munich, 1980), p. 51.
[16] *GBA*, XI, p. 164.

> You factual one.
> Erase our individuality!
>
> Make us collective!
> Because not how we want:
> But how you want!

Brecht directly addresses the schism between the promise of liberation and the renovation of dependent relationships as one god is enthusiastically exchanged for a new one in the name of progress and enlightenment. The text ends with an astute analysis of how technology creates symbolic ownership via commodities rather than actual ownership of *Geist,* or intellect. The last verse directly recalls the tone and rhythm of the Lord's Prayer and offers a neologism of Ford and progress (*Fordschritt*):

> Therefore answer our prayers
> And deliver us from the evil of the *Geist.*
> In the name of electrification
> *Fordschritt* and statistics![17]

To Brecht, technology, mechanization and the accompanying deindividuation were meant to empower, not lead to new forms of exploitation and repression. As the capitalist and fascist versions of collectivity became increasingly apparent, Brecht tried to articulate more clearly how his idea of the individual vis-à-vis the community differed from a mass culture of consumption and spectacle ultimately resulting in what Walter Benjamin denoted the *Volksfest* of fascism.[18] In an unpublished note from 1929 titled 'Individual and Mass', Brecht wrote:

> Our notion of the mass is derived from the individual. The mass is therefore a composition. ... The notion of the 'individual' is here based not on separation but on allocation. The divisibility of the individual is to be emphasized (as the belonging to several collectives).[19]

Brecht aims to overcome the exclusive binary of the subject and the social (as well as the private and the public) by turning the idea of the collective into a strategic and dialectical rather than absorbent form of belonging.

In 1927, Brecht had planned a *Ruhrepos*, an operatic revue about the coal-mining and steel works in the German industries' heartland. The project's audience was supposed to consist of 'all parts of the population' gathered to learn about the realities of production and the production of reality: 'But not only the clearly visible achievements of the human *Geist* are to be presented here, but also the worldview of our time itself. Also the image that our time has of itself is worth recording.'[20] The so-called Ruhrpott or Ruhr Valley was a crucial site of struggle over the nation's independence and politics, as under the Versailles Treaty much of the revenue generated in the region was earmarked for reparation payments, and the Allies kept a close watch on potential arms production. But the mines and factories were also the stage where the drama of capital, labour and

---

[17]Ibid., pp. 175–6.
[18]Benjamin, *Gesammelte Schriften*, v/1, p. 243.
[19]*GBA*, XXIX, p. 351.
[20]'Ruhrepos' (1927), *GBA*, XXI, pp. 205–6.

control over the Weimar Republic's political future unfolded. Brecht's opera project was foiled by local politics and financial difficulties; the few songs that survive put a face on the 'unknown worker', while the machines get a chance to tell their own tales. Both workers and machines reflect on their roles, their past and future and their relative bond to one another, which is limited to the fact that both are products rather than producers. The crane 'Milchsack Nummer 4' remarks to a worker, 'You are not yet alive, I am still dead.'[21] Both workers and machines are only vital parts of progress when the subject and the apparatus no longer generate and absorb alienation but work according to their potential.

Brecht joined Erwin Piscator's directors' collective in 1927, established as part of the Piscatorbühne, the playwright's own new theatre, after he had been dismissed by the Volksbühne (people's theatre) in 1926. Brecht admired Piscator's productions because of their attempt to bring politics onto the stage and raise the theatre's technical standards. Working with the collective gave Brecht the opportunity to study technological innovation in the use of sound, film and projections, and stage design. Writing in the *Berliner Börsen-Courier* Brecht defended Piscator, dismissing those who had driven him from the Volksbühne as 'lazy and stupid', as unwilling to recognize or intimidated by the revolutionary power of the new drama.[22] Elsewhere he praised Piscator's efforts to 'electrify the theatre and raise its technical standards'.[23] In a retrospective outburst of generous egomania, he declared Piscator 'the only other capable dramatist'.[24] But Brecht remained sceptical of what this electrification of the stage could actually accomplish. Prefiguring Walter Benjamin's famous differentiation between the aestheticization of politics and the politicization of aesthetics, Brecht remarked that what truly counted was the 'current tendency to regard the Piscatorian attempt to renew the theatre as revolutionary', perceiving 'not politics attempted appropriation of the theatre but theatre's of politics'.[25] According to Brecht, what had to change was not simply what was being staged, but the very relationship between audience and stage. He explained:

> The politically laudable translation of the revolutionary spirit through dramatic effects, which solely create an active atmosphere, cannot revolutionize the theatre and is a provisional solution, which cannot be expanded, but only replaced by a truly revolutionary theatre. This [current] theatre is at its core anti-revolutionary, because it is passive, reproductive. It depends on the pure reproduction of already existing, hence, dominant, types, meaning bourgeois types, and has to wait for the political revolution in order to find its models. It is the last form of the bourgeois-naturalistic theatre.[26]

Brecht's idea of a *sachlich* theatre was different. And even though he was just beginning to articulate a new aesthetic for the stage, he succeeded in producing a true Weimar play, reflecting his preoccupation with providing an insight into the mechanisms of the republic's social and political self-understanding as well as the difficulties in reappropriating the cultural apparatuses and their relationship to the audience.

---

[21] *GBA*, XIII, p. 376.
[22] 'Tendency of the Volksbühne: Pure Art', *Berliner Börsen-Courier* (31 March 1927); *GBA*, XXI, p. 195.
[23] 'The Primacy of the Apparatus' (1928), *GBA*, XXI, p. 226.
[24] 'The Relationship of the Augsburger to Piscator' (1939), *GBA*, XXII, p. 763.
[25] 'Piscatortheater' (1927), *GBA*, XXI, p. 197.
[26] 'Sociological Perspective' (1928), *GBA*, XXI, p. 234.

The Threepenny Opera was Brecht's greatest success and arguably the biggest theatrical achievement of the 1920s. Popular with its audiences (less so with the critics), it ran for almost a year in Berlin, was translated into several languages, put on all over the world and made into a film and a novel. There were several other printed derivations as well as songbooks, concerts and recordings (including the world-famous 'Ballad of Mack the Knife'). Though *The Threepenny Opera* made Brecht a star, solved his lingering financial problems and expanded his opportunities, he was uneasy about its effects and continued working feverishly to develop what is now known as the Epic Theatre.

Sachlichkeit may not come to mind when thinking of *The Threepenny Opera*. Rather than direct and unaffected, 'factual', the play seemed complex, confusing, chaotic. The stories about its origins and methods invoke a plethora of sources from John Gay to Kipling to Villon, various styles of song and language, characters of multiple classes, eras and places, technical choices such as the half-curtain and projections, captions and sudden changes between singing and speaking. Countering the lore of its instant popular success, Elisabeth Hauptmann recalls that the premiere at the Theater am Schiffbauerdamm on 31 August 1928 had anything but a euphoric reception: 'No, the audience was peeved.'[27] Brecht's idea of having the viewer observe the rearrangement of the set between acts was in particular met with scepticism and irritation. The critic for the *Neuen Preußische Kreuz-Zeitung* wrote, 'The whole thing is best described as literary necrophilia, the only remarkable thing the insignificance of the object it was committed on.'[28] Reporting for the other end of the political spectrum, the *Rote Fahne* similarly observed a lack of coherence and significance:

> When one feels weak, one leans on the stronger; when facing the present more or less uncomprehendingly, one flees into the past. … No trace of modern social or political satire. But all in all a multifarious, entertaining mishmash.[29]

The Threepenny Opera was in many ways a thievish play. It began as an adaptation of John Gay's *The Beggar's Opera* (1728), which had been rediscovered and staged in the UK since 1920 with great success. In the winter of 1927–8, prompted by the press coverage of the play, Elisabeth Hauptmann translated Gay's text. Meanwhile, Brecht had been invited to mount something at Theater am Schiffbauerdamm. He had met the composer Kurt Weill in 1927 and collaborated with him on a couple of projects, and they set to work on a full-length opera using Gay's project as a blueprint. Brecht and Weill composed new songs and wrote new lyrics, constantly adding and scrapping material, Gay's as well as their own. Brecht and Weill even spent a summer in southern France working, as Weill's wife, the actress Lotte Lenya, recalled, 'like *crazy*, writing, changing, tossing, writing anew, taking a break only to walk down to the sea for a few minutes'.[30] The project's collaborative structure was made transparent to readers and audiences in both its first print publication with Verlag Felix Bloch Erben in June 1928 and the premiere's programme, which credited Gay, Villon, Kipling, Hauptmann, Weill, Erich Engel, Neher, Theo Makkeben and the Lewis Ruth Band. Gay's original was already a work of various sources and collective effort (Alexander Pope and Jonathan Swift had allegedly lent a friendly hand), to the extent that Gay (and later Brecht) was accused of plagiarism.

---

[27] Cited in Kebir, *Ich fragte nicht nach meinem Anteil*, p. 107.
[28] GI (author's initials), *Neue Preußische Kreuz-Zeitung* (1 September 1928), reprinted in Wyss, *Brecht in der Kritik*, p. 80.
[29] er (author's initials). *Die Rote Fahne* (4 September 1928), reprinted in Wyss, *Brecht in der Kritik*, pp. 82–3.
[30] Cited in Siegfried Unseld, ed., *Bertolt Brechts Dreigroschenbuch* (Frankfurt, 1960), p. 223.

The *Beggar's Opera* was a 'poor play', its poverty, as in Brecht's *Lesebuch*, a means of justifying the appropriation of operatic forms, and as such a critique of the artificial 'nature' of high culture. It is a story about two men, a robber and a fence, who will do anything for money, turn anything – any person, feeling or desire – into a commodity in order to succeed. But Gay's opera is less a progressive critique of social circumstances, exploitation and alienation than a conservative lament about money as a vulgar tool of social mobility. Brecht's version, on the other hand, does not show the ascent of the rabble but, quite the opposite, shows that capitalism itself is a form of robbery. Werner Hecht describes the *Beggar's Opera* as a 'disguised critique of open grievances' and Brecht's project as 'an open critique of disguised grievances'.[31] In a letter to George Grosz, Brecht writes of the *Threepenny Opera*'s plot, 'The main point: The robbers are *Bürger*.'[32] In allegorical fashion, Brecht displays how the struggle of the market and its Darwinian laws of survival are carefully hidden behind seemingly abstract bank transferrals, boardroom meetings and stock-market numbers, as well as a cultural apparatus concerned with categorical questions of truth and meaning rather than a reflection of history and its making. Accordingly, the *Moritat* balladeer famously sings:

> Oh, the shark has pretty teeth, dear
> And he shows them pearly white
> Just a jack knife has Macheath, dear
> But he keeps it out of sight.[33]

In a London cobbled together from Brecht's reading of detective novels and a temporal setting far from authentically Victorian, Brecht produces an armature of juxtapositions, showing the relations among bourgeois traditions and their contemporary application, among social strata and the ideology that unites them, among old and new notions of progress, freedom and subjectivity. The prostitutes and cripples are shown as victims of interrelated circumstances – industrialization, warfare and modern forms of traffic as well as reparations and Weimar prosperity. Brecht's constructions of robbing and owning, of classes and experiences, drives and desires, truths and images reflect the Weimar Republic's rudderless, 'lawless' culture and ideological laissez-faire. The content and the formal devices of narration and representation emphasize the contradictions of the capitalist order; Weill's music, Neher's stage setting and Brecht's characters all lack harmony and coherence. The music is at times antithetical to the action on stage, veering between pop and jazz; the stage itself is a landscape of superficial construction, as are the protagonists, slipping in and out of roles, attitudes and convictions, accusing each other of being fakes, forgers, even 'artists'. Everything is constructed, lending insight into the mechanisms of how things are made. At the same time as being usable, everything is consumable. In his essay 'Zur Musik der *Dreigroschenoper*' (On the music of *The Threepenny Opera*, 1929), Theodor Adorno articulated this ambiguity:

> Society has many ways to deal with inconvenient works. It can ignore them, it can critically destroy them, it can swallow them, so that nothing is left of them. *The Threepenny Opera* has roused its last appetite. However, it remains to be seen how agreeable a meal it is.[34]

---

[31] Werner Hecht, *Sieben Studien über Brecht* (Frankfurt, 1972), pp. 84, 87.
[32] *GBA*, XXVIII, p. 484.
[33] *GBA*, II, p. 231. My translation is adapted from Marc Blitzstein's 1954 translation.
[34] Theodor Adorno, *Musikalische Schriften v/Gesammelte Werke*, vol. XVIII (Frankfurt, 1984), p. 539.

Brecht in Exile

CHAPTER FOUR

'Changing Countries More Often than Shoes'

JAMES K. LYON

Except for the multitude of enemies and handful of friends he left behind, the only mark Brecht made on America at this time was on *Pins and Needles*, the musical review presented by the Labor Stage and the International Ladies' Garment Workers' Union in 1936. Emanuel Eisenberg, a well-known figure in the New York leftist theater, wrote a satire entitled 'The Little Red School House' based on what had happened in rehearsals and production of Brecht's *Mother*. Like many leftists, he had had no sympathy for Brecht as a person or for his type of theater. Presented as one of the skits that comprised *Pins and Needles*, this satire suggests that had he not been so disliked, Brecht might have been forgotten entirely.

Europe, especially Germany, was still the center of Brecht's universe, and he wanted to be near his German-language stage and the struggle against the Nazis. During eight years of exile in Denmark, Sweden, and Finland, he devoted himself to anti-fascist activities that included writing radio broadcasts, giving lectures, staging his antifascist plays, and turning out pamphlets to be smuggled into Germany. In this period he also wrote some of his most brilliant poetry and many plays, among them several of the dramas that later would bring him international recognition – *Galileo*; *Mother Courage and Her Children*; *The Good Woman of Setzuan*; *Round Heads and Peak Heads*; *Private Life of the Master Race*; *The Resistible Rise of Arturo Ui*; and *Puntila and His Servant Matti*.

During his Scandinavian exile, Brecht traveled to Russia, France, and England. He had not forgotten America, but he had no desire to settle there. In mid-1936, a few months after returning from New York, he wrote Erwin Piscator, the German stage director living in Russian exile, and suggested that they travel to America and try to sell a film story. But not until Hitler marched into Czechoslovakia in October 1938, and free Europe began to shrink, did he seriously entertain the idea of America as a refuge.

After the Stalin purges began, Brecht never considered the Soviet Union a haven. Two trips there in 1932 and 1935 convinced him that by now he would be associated too closely with the 'Formalist' heretics Meyerhold, Eisenstein, and his Soviet friend, Sergei Tretyakov. By 1937, when Tretyakov was arrested and tried on a trumped-up charge (he was executed in 1939), Brecht's survival instinct told him to look elsewhere. One by one

---

James K. Lyon, 'Changing Countries More Often Than Shoes', in Lyon, *Bertolt Brecht in America* (London: Methuen, 1982), pp. 21–9 and pp. 356–7.

his acquaintances in Moscow, both German exiles and Soviets, disappeared.[1] In July 1938 he replied to an inquiry about his friends in the Soviet Union: 'I really don't have any friends there. Nor do the Muscovites – like the dead.'[2]

Late in 1938 the Hollywood screen writer Ferdinand Reyher visited Brecht in Copenhagen. Before he went to Hollywood in 1931, Reyher, a brilliant raconteur, not only enjoyed a reputation as a gifted writer himself; he maintained close ties to Sinclair Lewis, Wallace Stevens, Ford Maddox Ford, John Rodker, and a large number of important literary figures on each side of the Atlantic. When he and Brecht first met in Berlin in 1927, they discovered a kinship which grew into one of the closest friendships Brecht experienced in his lifetime.[3] With America very much on his mind during Reyher's visit between October 28 and November 4, 1938, Brecht now recounted to him his plans for a drama on the life of Galileo. Ruminating on it with Reyher, he cocked an eye toward Hollywood's hills of gold and agreed first to write a film story, which Reyher would try to sell, and then to do a drama. From Reyher or others, he learned that to have a film or play of his produced in America would simplify immigration matters greatly. On December 2, 1938 he wrote Reyher saying that within a period of three weeks he had written a play about Galileo instead of the film story they agreed upon. Could Reyher arrange an American production of it? 'It has a monumental role', he went on, 'and if one could get an important, influential actor for it, it might help get a production. But perhaps productions in America aren't dependent on actors as they are in Europe.' His obsession with succeeding on Broadway, coupled with fear for his own safety, now spelled one word – America.

As Nazi agents moved freely throughout Denmark and as the Danish government's ability to resist Nazi demands for deportation of German exiles weakened, Brecht decided to apply for an American quota immigration visa for his family and himself, which he did in Copenhagen sometime before March 1939.[4] Like many who wanted to come, Brecht had been stripped of his German citizenship by Hitler and no longer qualified as a 'German national'. Not only were he and others like him refused special consideration; they were penalized by being placed on a much longer waiting list for those without nationality. Further, American xenophobic and isolationist popular opinion supported pointlessly harsh immigration policies which allowed many State Department foreign service officers to obstruct the entry of German refugees. For many like Brecht, consular whim became a matter of life and death.[5]

From information he received in 1939, Brecht informed friends in America that he would have to wait two years for a normal quota visa.[6] In the meantime, as Reyher wrote a friend, 'Bert Brecht's little green isle of Denmark is getting hot, and I believe will soon

---

[1] Robert Conquest, *The Great Terror. Stalin's Purge of the Thirties* (New York: MacMillan, 1968) gives a comprehensive picture of these years.
[2] Quoted by Walter Benjamin, *Versuche über Brecht* (Frankfurt/Main: Suhrkamp, 1966), p. 133.
[3] James K. Lyon, *Bertolt Brecht's American Cicerone* (Bonn: Bouvier Verlag Herbert Grundmann, 1978), pp. 4–7.
[4] Letter dated May 17, 1940, Brecht to Piscator.
[5] Geoffrey Perrett, *Days of Sadness, Years of Triumph. The American People 1939–1945* (New York: Coward, McCann & Geoghegan, 1973), pp. 96–97, reports that sometimes refugees were forced to return to Nazi Germany because U.S. officials refused to admit them.
[6] According to a letter dated Mar. 16, 1939 from Ferdinand Reyher (who was corresponding with Brecht) to George Seldes.

be untenable for him. He is trying everything to get out and wants to come to America.'⁷ With his little Danish isle becoming, in his own words, 'increasingly like a mousetrap',⁸ he moved to Sweden in April 1939, where he spent another year before continuing his exile in Finland after April 1940. Like thousands of other refugees from Nazi Germany, Brecht found America's golden door opened to him through the exertions and largesse of kind friends and generous strangers, not to mention a substantial portion of good luck.

In mid-1939, the exiled German film director Fritz Lang began soliciting funds from Hollywood personalities expressly to support the Brecht family for a six-month period.⁹ In the next two years, Fritz Kortner, Dorothy Thompson, Kurt Weill, Oskar Homolka, Bruno Frank, and Lion Feuchtwanger all helped financially at one point or another.¹⁰

In June 1939 Erwin Piscator, the German stage director known as the founder of 'political theater', wrote from New York and asked if Brecht remembered encouraging him to go to New York 'because of the enormous opportunities there'. He urged him to heed his own counsel and asked if Brecht would help with Piscator's fledgling Theatre Workshop at the New School for Social Research.¹¹ Later this became a solid invitation that resulted in a quota immigration visa. And in Mexico in the summer of 1939, Hanns Eisler told a young American writer named H. R. Hays, who had seen and admired *Mother* in 1935, about Brecht's genius and plight. Hays offered to help, sight unseen, and Brecht now had someone who later provided an affidavit of support for his party.¹²

On April 17, 1940, shortly after Nazi troops occupied Denmark and Norway, Brecht sailed for Finland and again 'took up the exile's trade: hoping' (GW IX, 822). On the same day he left Sweden, Dr. Alvin S. Johnson, president of the New School for Social Research and father of the 'University in Exile' at that school, cabled him in Stockholm with an invitation to 'join our faculty ... as Lecturer in Literature, with a salary of $1500, the appointment to run from May 1940 (or the earliest date on which you can arrive) to January 1941'.¹³ Many Europeans owed their lives to Dr. Johnson and his idea for a 'University in Exile', born out of dismay at what he saw in Germany in 1932. Normally he invited distinguished refugee scholars and teachers for one to two years at stipends of $3,000 to $4,000 annually, solely to help them get into the United States.¹⁴ Piscator, one of the few refugees to secure a permanent position at the New School, persuaded Dr. Johnson to invite the distinctly non-academic Brecht on the basis of his poetic and dramatic reputation. While this invitation was not enough to bring Brecht to America immediately, it probably saved his life, for it prompted him to go to the American embassy in Helsinki (May 17, 1940) and re-enter the names of his family and a collaborator, Margarete Steffin, on the consul's waiting list.

Brecht wrote Piscator the same day, thanked him and his friends for intervening in his behalf with Dr. Johnson, and stated his plans to come soon on a visitor's visa. Could the

---

[7] Ibid.
[8] Letter dated June 13, 1939, from Margarete Steffin (who was quoting Brecht) to Reyher.
[9] Letters dated July 24, 1939 from Reyher to Lang, and Oct. 4 and Dec. 4, 1939, from Lang to Reyher.
[10] Fritz Kortner, *Aller Tage Abend* (Munich: Deutscher Taschenbuch Verlag, 1969), pp. 318–319; interview, Marta Feuchtwanger; Baxandall, foot note, p. 85.
[11] Letter of June 15, 1939, Piscator to Brecht.
[12] Interview, H. R. Hays. Letter dated February, 1941, Hays to Brecht.
[13] Letter dated May 2, 1940, Johnson to Brecht, reporting on the telegram and confirming the offer.
[14] Laura Fermi, *Illustrious Immigrants. The Intellectual Migration from Europe, 1930–1941*, revised second edition (Chicago: U. of Chicago Press, 1971), pp. 74–76.

New School do anything to speed up approval of that visa? His name, he said, had been on a list for a quota visa since March 1939, but now the situation had become urgent – his wife's and children's Danish refugee papers would expire in August 1940.

Why did Brecht hesitate this long before pressing for quota visas? The most apparent answer lies in the desperate hope that the fight against Hitler would not be a losing battle. Few optimists have had fewer illusions than Brecht and remained optimists. He refused to quit Europe until the situation was hopeless. Only after the Nazi invasion of Holland that same month and the fall of France the next month did he decide to leave for good.

A letter to Piscator of May 27, 1940 reveals a more compelling reason for hesitation – his collaborator Margarete Steffin. Remarking that 'I believe the United States is one of the few countries where one still has the freedom to do literary work and show plays like my Master Race', he asks if the New School could not request a visa for Steffin from the American consul in Helsingfors, Finland. 'She, in fact, is the only one who has an overview of my thousands of manuscript pages. Without her, preparing lectures would mean an enormous loss of time. ... I cannot simply leave her here. For ten years she has been my closest collaborator and is personally much too close.'

Margarete (Grete) Steffin, the intellectually gifted daughter of a Berlin worker, began collaborating with Brecht in Berlin in the early thirties and followed him into Danish, Swedish, and Finnish exile. In many ways she resembled the scores of women who became entranced by this man whose generally unsavory appearance belied a legendary reputation for being sexually attractive. Like many of his women, she played several roles for him – editor, secretary, collaborator, teacher, librarian, and sexual partner. Nor did Brecht maintain a conventional *ménage à trois*. Often he had more than one female collaborator. At this time at least one other woman belonged to his entourage – Ruth Berlau, an actress trained in the Royal Danish Theater who had left her husband, a professor of medicine in Copenhagen, in the mid-thirties and followed him. She, too, played the same roles Steffin and Brecht's other women did. It was unthinkable to leave without them.

At this time, Steffin was by all odds the favorite. In contrast to his feelings for the women involuntarily drawn into his orbit without special effort on his part, Brecht appears to have felt a profound dependence on and tenderness toward her. Her frail health (she had only one lung) caused him a dilemma, for it eliminated her from consideration for an immigration visa. He, however, was unwilling to leave without her. According to his own account, in December 1940 he, his wife, and his children received immigration visas for Mexico, where a number of his German friends had settled.[15] Steffin's visa was denied on grounds of poor health. Against the urging of friends in America to leave immediately for Mexico, he risked everything on obtaining an American visa for her, even if it was a visitor's visa. Throughout his exile years, this unexpected tenderness would intrude into Brecht's coolly rational behavior often enough to amend his 'tough-guy' image. In his relationship to Steffin one sees his ability to care deeply for something beyond his own work. To her and to a few close friends he committed himself with the same irrational devotion which, in promoting his ideas in the theater, brought him the reputation of refractoriness and intractability.

In June 1940 Piscator wrote him that the New School could do nothing to accelerate the visa process. If and when one were issued depended entirely on the American consul in Helsingfors. Mentioning his great difficulty in securing an appointment for Brecht,

---

[15] Brecht, *AJ*, p. 285.

Piscator urged him to thank Dr. Johnson. Brecht did so later that month: 'You can imagine', he wrote Johnson, 'what it means here in war-ravaged Europe to be given such a prospect of continuing cultural activities.'[16]

In late November 1940 Brecht announced to Piscator that the American consul now had promised the visas, but his appointment at the New School was about to expire. Could it be extended? Dr. Johnson quickly sent a letter to 'Dr. Brecht', tendering him an appointment from February through September 1941.[17]

Brecht's journal says almost nothing about the struggle to secure visas for himself, his wife, his children, Steffin, and Berlau. But his penchant for writing occasional poetry preserved some details. A poem entitled 'Ode to a Lofty Dignitary' catches the frustration of one moment while sitting across from Lawrence von Hellens, vice-consul in charge of immigration matters. He, no doubt, is one of the few U.S. Foreign Service officers to be memorialized in a poem in any language. Brecht begins his unflattering portrait with a caustic greeting:

> Exalted vice-consul, deign
> To accord this trembling louse
> The blessed stamp.

Four times, he continues in a mock dignified tone, I have managed to come into your exalted presence; twice I cut my hair for you. I hid my shabby cap, and I wore a hat. I hope some of my words have reached your ears. Then changing the tone abruptly, he demands:

> Don't be afraid, little man behind the desk.
> Your superiors
> Won't mind your stamp.
> ....
> Slap it on, your superiors
> Won't devour you.

(GW IX, 811-12)

Brecht's indignation at this degrading treatment while trying to obtain visas also comes out in one of his *Refugee Dialogues*, semi-autobiographical conversations between an exiled German physicist, Ziffel, and an exiled metal worker, Kalle, which he wrote in Finland in 1941. Speaking of attempts to get an American immigration visa, Kalle describes being sent from one office to another until a consul finally demands that he crawl around the block on hands and knees four times and then get medical certification that he has no callouses. Then he has to take an oath that he 'never had any opinions', but when asked to prove it, he falters, and the visa is not issued.[18] However exaggerated, this account represents Brecht's reactions to the many questions asked to determine that he was never in prison or an almshouse; that neither he nor his parents had been in a mental institution; that he was not an idiot, imbecile, epileptic, chronic alcoholic, polygamist, procurer, vagrant, criminal, or any one of twenty other categories not allowed to enter the United States; and, above all, that he was not excluded by a 1918 law forbidding

---

[16] Letter dated June 12, 1940, Brecht to Johnson.
[17] Letter dated Dec. 6, 1940, Johnson to Brecht.
[18] GW XIV, 1448–1449.

'anarchists and similar classes' from entering and conducting political activity against the established order.

Affidavits of support for his family, Berlau, and Steffin also complicated matters at a time when his family noticed growing numbers of German 'tourists' appearing in Finland. In March 1941, Brecht wrote H. R. Hays asking for an affidavit to support Berlau's immigration.[19] The previous month Hays had sent him his own English renderings of Brecht's poems, one of which had appeared in *New Masses*, and his translation of the *Lucullus* radio play. In the kind of charming letter he was capable of writing, Brecht replied quickly about the affidavit. He explained that Berlau, a Danish citizen, could secure a visa more easily than he and his family. Would Hays forward it to the American consul in Mexico City, their intermediate destination on the way to America? The next day he wrote and changed instructions: Would Hays please send the affidavit to the American consul in Finland? Hays responded quickly, and on March 29, 1941, Berlau received a quota immigration visa.

Brecht in the meantime had been soliciting help from others in America for affidavits and ship passage. Perhaps never before has there been so much humanitarian misrepresentation to U.S. immigration and consular officials as there was in bringing exiles from Nazi Germany to the United States at this time. Many Hollywood personalities inflated their financial statements in order to provide dozens of affidavits of support for exiles stranded in Europe.[20] William Dieterle, a successful director at Warner Brothers who had come from Germany in 1930, and his wife Charlotte, probably assisted over one hundred Europeans personally this way,[21] and friends testify that they contributed up to a half million dollars of their own funds to this cause.[22] Dieterle gained a reputation for the mass scenes in his films designed specifically to employ non-English speaking German exiles in them.[23] Sometime in April 1941 the exile obtained an affidavit of support signed by Dieterle.

With German motorized divisions visible everywhere in Finland and the invasion of Russia somewhat over two months away, Brecht still lacked a sure escape route. In a poem he describes his plight:

Curiously, I examine the map of the continent.
High up in Lapland,
Toward the Arctic Ocean
I still see a small door.

(GW IX, 819)

On his visa application he wrote that he would depart from Bassia, Persia. But, in fact, nearly every exit seemed blocked. He notified Hays that he heard Japan would not let him through via Russia, and that Turkey was also closed off because of the war.

On May 3, 1941 the 'lofty consul' finally stamped and issued immigrant quota visa number 1936 to Eugen Berthold Friedrich Brecht, who was listed as having 'no

---

[19] Letter dated Mar. 3, 1941, Brecht to Hays.
[20] Salka Viertel, interview of Sept. 22, 1972, claims Henry Manckiewicz signed affidavits of support for fifteen people at one time whom she helped bring to the United States.
[21] Interview, William Dieterle.
[22] Interview, Marta Feuchtwanger.
[23] Interview, Marta Mierendorff.

nationality'.[24] He now possessed what Kalle in the *Refugee Dialogues* had called the noblest part of a human-being – a passport (GW XIV, 1383). Two days later, word came that Steffin, who could not pass the physical for a quota visa, would receive a visitor's visa as Helene Weigel's 'secretary'. Though time as well as his 'means of production' (as he called cigars and English murder mysteries)[25] were running low, Brecht delayed another week, waiting for Steffin's visa. He packed, stored the books and manuscripts he could not transport, and purchased railroad tickets to Moscow for the six persons in his party.

Shortly before leaving, Brecht wrote Gorelik saying: 'Where Columbus succeeded, I'll be successful too, though I won't have it as easy as he did.'[26] He also mentions the new play he is bringing (*Arturo Ui*), 'which really ought to stand a chance over there'.

On May 13, 1941, one day after Steffin's visa finally came, Brecht, his wife, his son, his daughter, Berlau, and Steffin boarded a train for Moscow. They had scarcely arrived when Steffin collapsed with tuberculosis and had to be hospitalized.

After great difficulties, Brecht managed to secure tickets for a Swedish ship that sailed for America from Vladivostok on June 14th. Not knowing this would be the last ship he could take, he noted in his journal that he had tried to exchange his tickets for a later ship in order to wait for Steffin.[27] But he was unable to do so, or his concern for her and assurances of friends that the Stalin-Hitler pact of the previous year guaranteed peace in Russia for a considerable time might have lulled him into a fatal postponement. Leaving many of his manuscripts with her, and with arrangements made for her to come as soon as she could travel, he, his family, and Berlau departed Moscow on May 30, 1941, for the ten-day trip across Russia on the trans-Siberian railroad. Daily telegrams reported Steffin's decline, and on June 5th news reached him that she had died the previous day. Her death cast him into a depression that lasted well into American exile. One of several poems on the topic reads:

> Since you died, my little teacher,
> I wander aimlessly, restlessly
> Benumbed in a gray world,
> Without work, like one discharged.

(GW X, 827-8)

In what became a leitmotif in many of his exile poems, he speaks further of his guilt at having survived her.

After Nazi U-boats made the North Atlantic unsafe for ship passage, the Swedish Johnson line had dispatched its small freighter, the *S.S. Annie Johnson*, to the Pacific. Flying a neutral flag which the Japanese respected, it was allowed to shuttle between Russia and America, carrying fifty-one refugees to freedom on each trip. When it sailed, its manifest listed Brecht, his family, and Ruth Berlau among its passengers. Though the voyage was interrupted by a five-day stop in Manila to load copra, the ship spent more than a month on the high seas before arriving in San Pedro, California, on July 21, 1941.

---

[24] Brecht's *AJ*, in an entry of July 13, 1941 recording the events of the past two months, erroneously gives the date as May 2nd.
[25] *AJ*, April 25, 1941.
[26] Undated letter written from Helsinki in April or May, 1941, Brecht to Gorelik.
[27] *AJ*, July 13, 1941.

In his poem 'The Landscape of Exile' (*GW* x, 830) Brecht claims he took the last ship to cross the Pacific before the bombing of Pearl Harbor on December 7, 1941.[28] Perhaps this was poetic license, though he repeated the claim to friends after his arrival. But another set of circumstances was very real. In June 1941, while his ship was somewhere in the Pacific and while Germany prepared to launch its invasion of Russia later that month, the U.S. Government declared that no one with close relatives in Germany could henceforth enter the United States.[29] Having a father and brother in Germany certainly would have made this the last ship for Brecht. His narrow escape might have been reason enough to rejoice, but by instinct and inclination he seldom permitted himself any feelings that dulled his critical habit of mind, and his approach to America was no exception. Calling himself in the same poem the 'messenger of misfortune', he describes his joy at various sights on their trip – the rolling dolphins, the horse-drawn carts of 'doomed Manila', the pink armbands of the matrons there. But of the oil rigs, gardens, and ravines in his new southern California home, he could bring himself to say only that they 'didn't leave him cold'.[30] Soon, however, they would. His exile in paradise, and one of the most difficult periods of his life, had begun.

---

[28] *GW* x, 830–831.
[29] Perrett, p. 97.
[30] Reinhold Grimm, *Brecht und Nietzsche oder Geständnisse eines Dichters: Fünf Essays und ein Bruchstück* (Frankfurt/Main: Suhrkamp, 1979), 11–54 interprets this and related poems. See especially pp. 26–27.

Brecht in the GDR

CHAPTER FIVE

A Life's Work Curtailed? The Ailing Brecht's Struggle with the SED Leadership over GDR Cultural Policy

STEPHEN PARKER

Securing the presence in East Berlin of such an iconic socialist artist as Bertolt Brecht was both a major coup for the leaders of the Socialist Unity Party of Germany (SED) in 1949 and a major headache. Given the same opportunity just two years later, they would probably have declined. Brecht was the most prominent of the German artists who returned to the GDR from exile to participate in the construction of a first German socialist state. However, during the later years of the Weimar Republic and his subsequent exile from Nazi Germany, Brecht already had major differences in his aesthetic theory and practice with artists and cultural politicians who sought to represent an orthodox position for the Communist Party of Germany (KPD) by means of the doctrine of Socialist Realism. In his capacity as editor of the Moscow journal *Das Wort* during the Great Terror, Brecht – himself in Danish exile – clashed in a sectarian struggle with the 'Moscow faction', most notably his co-editor Georg Lukács and other influential figures such as Alfred Kurella and Fritz Erpenbeck. When Brecht had to flee Scandinavia in 1941, he pointedly chose to take refuge not in Moscow, where friends such as Carola Neher had been imprisoned, but in California, where he remained as a 'western émigré' until his return to Europe in 1947. When Brecht moved from Switzerland to Berlin in 1949, the stage was set for the resumption of the sectarian struggle within the new context of the Cold War. As before, major areas of contention were the treatment of the German cultural heritage and dramatic theory. While Brecht engaged in a critical interrogation of the *deutsche Misere*, the wretched path of German history that had reached its nadir in Hitler's Germany, the SED leadership expected artists to provide exemplary, uplifting narratives from the socialist heritage in support of the new state, contrasting the GDR with an unregenerate West.

Stephen Parker, 'A Life's Work Curtailed? The Ailing Brecht's Struggle with the SED Leadership over GDR Cultural Policy', in Laura Bradley and Karen Leeder (eds), *Brecht and the GDR. Politics, Culture, Posterity* (Rochester, NY: Camden House, 2011), pp. 65–82.

Throughout the Cold War, the restricted access to records in the obsessively secretive and security-minded GDR drastically impaired our understanding of Brecht's struggle with the SED's leadership and cultural politicians. There was frequent speculation in the West that Brecht's last seven years in the GDR must surely have contributed to his early death on 14 August 1956, aged just fifty-eight. The official record of his death published in East Berlin stated that Brecht had died of a heart attack. For the GDR authorities, the matter was then closed. Yet almost immediately rumors circulated that the official record was flawed. Fritz Cremer, for example, told the story of his trip to Brecht's flat on Chausseestraße to make the death mask. When he arrived, he found Brecht's corpse sitting in an upright position, with blood running from the mouth.[1] There was, however, no opportunity to test the official pronouncement.

Following the end of the Cold War, documents were extracted from Berlin archives that demonstrated, in much clearer terms than had previously been possible, Brecht's instrumental involvement in the protracted struggle over cultural policy between the SED and the GDR's artistic elite in the East Berlin Academy of Arts.[2] The struggle was at its most intense during two periods. The first was the SED's Formalism Campaign in early 1951. The second followed the SED's proclamation of the Construction of the Foundations of Socialism in 1952. Over a number of months in the first half of 1953, Brecht was subjected to extreme pressure to recant his dramatic theories in favor of a Stanislavskian form of Socialist Realism. However, quite improbably, Brecht and his supporters in the Academy used the profound shock of 17 June 1953 to turn the tables in cultural politics. The outcome in the short term was an uneasy standoff until Brecht's death.

Given the speculation surrounding the possible link between Brecht's health and SED pressure upon him, it is surprising that the official record of the cause of Brecht's death and of the medical treatment preceding it was until recently the subject of only limited re-appraisal. In the absence of firm medical evidence, discussion of the relationship between Brecht's health and his activities has hence largely remained conjecture. The present essay addresses the issue with such evidence, building upon the publication of a first medical history of Brecht and incorporating further details of Brecht's medical condition during his years in the GDR.[3] Those findings are juxtaposed with the record of Brecht's involvement in cultural-political controversies in order to explore four related questions: Can a substantial linkage be established between the two spheres? What was the nature of the authorities' surveillance of Brecht? Did they use their knowledge of his condition in their dealings with him? Finally, were Brecht's life and productivity thereby impaired or even curtailed?

This essay was written during the tenure of a Major Research Fellowship awarded by the Leverhulme Trust.
[1] Fritz Cremer's story, told to the journalist Rudy Hassing, is included in John Fuegi, *The Life and Lies of Bertolt Brecht* (London: Harper Collins, 1994), 606.
[2] See Peter Davies and Stephen Parker, 'Brecht, SED Cultural Policy and the Issue of Authority in the Arts: The Struggle for Control of the German Academy of Arts', in *Bertolt Brecht: Centenary Essays*, ed. Steve Giles and Rodney Livingstone (Amsterdam and Atlanta: Rodopi, 1998), 181–95; Peter Davies, *Divided Loyalties: East German Writers and the Politics of German Division 1945–1953* (Leeds: Maney, 2000).
[3] Stephen Parker, 'What was the Cause of Brecht's Death? Towards a Medical History', *Brecht Yearbook* 35 (2010): 291–307. Subsequent discussion of Brecht's medical history draws upon this article unless otherwise indicated.

BRECHT'S MEDICAL CONDITION ON HIS RETURN TO GERMANY

Brecht's medical history reveals that when he settled in East Berlin in June 1949 he was more seriously ill than has been suspected hitherto. His markedly failing body was carrying diseases that destined him, come what may, to an early death from chronic heart failure. Those diseases and the complications that might ensue were poorly understood. From childhood onwards, Brecht had known that there were things quite seriously wrong with him medically but had remained frustrated in his attempts to establish what his symptoms actually signified. In particular, Brecht carried with him the abiding effects of his undiagnosed childhood contraction of rheumatic fever, triggered by the streptococcal bacterial infection of pharyngitis or 'strep throat', which had attacked his heart and his basal ganglia, triggering carditis and the motorneural condition Sydenham's chorea. Brecht's doctors had simply labeled him a nervous child with an enlarged heart. Only in the 1930s and 1940s did advances take place in medical research that identified strep throat as the trigger for rheumatic fever. It was only from that time, too, that it was possible to supplement diagnosis with antibiotic treatment. In Brecht's adolescence, carditis deteriorated into the lifelong condition of chronic heart failure, the symptoms of which are arrhythmia, or heart palpitations; dyspnea, or shortage of breath; dizziness; and exhaustion. Brecht recorded such symptoms obsessively in his diary as a fifteen-year-old. Then and later, he suffered from frequent bouts of heart failure. His susceptibility increased as his organism deteriorated during the aging process. Meanwhile, Sydenham's chorea, manifested in childhood as a facial tic that the boy held in check with a grimace, recurred at times of stress during his adult years. Again, this condition manifested itself more markedly during the aging process.

Because Brecht's condition was never adequately diagnosed, his doctors were unaware of complications that could ensue from a further disorder, a urological condition that Brecht carried with him throughout his adult life. The condition manifested itself intermittently as kidney stones and pyelonephritis, inflammation of the renal pelvis. The symptoms are fevers, rigors (violent shivering with temperature rises), headaches, and vomiting. The inflammation can easily spread to the heart, particularly, of course, to an already diseased organ, triggering endocarditis, the inflammation of the inner lining of the heart and usually, too, of the valves. Among Brecht's doctors there was no real understanding of how vulnerable he was to the debilitating interaction of urological infection with his underlying cardiac condition. Even without the spread of the inflammation of the heart, when the weak and sickly Brecht contracted urological infections during his adult years he was susceptible to symptoms of chronic heart failure as well as of the urological condition. Records show that he was typically assailed by fever, arrhythmia, dyspnea, and exhaustion. By the time he returned to Berlin, recurrence of the urological condition had become frequent, as had that of the symptoms of chronic heart failure. The threat of the escalation of his condition into endocarditis was always given, with the distinct possibility that death would ensue.

Unpublished correspondence shows that the urological problem plagued Brecht in the period immediately before he moved to Berlin from Switzerland. Brecht wrote to Hans Albers that he was in hospital with pyelonephritis.[4] In a draft of a letter dated 10

---

[4] Brecht's undated letter to Hans Albers is in BBA 507/81. It is estimated that the letter was written in 1947. Subsequent references to files from the BBA are given in the main body of the text.

August 1948 Berthold Viertel asked Brecht what was wrong with his kidneys.[5] Only days after returning to Berlin, on 22 June 1949 Brecht had an appointment at the Catholic St. Hedwig's Hospital on Große Hamburger Straße in East Berlin with the urologist Ferdinand Hüdepohl. Hüdepohl (1902–1980) was then recognized as Germany's leading specialist in the field. In the Germany of the Third Reich he had been a consultant to the Luftwaffe and, from 1934, a member of the SS.[6] It is an extraordinary thought that, only days after his return to participate in the construction of a socialist Germany, Brecht, later the vigilant voice in such poems as 'Der Einarmige im Gehölz' (The One-Armed Man in the Undergrowth), unwittingly entrusted his sickly body to a former SS man. Thanks to his urological expertise, Hüdepohl became Brecht's trusted physician for the next seven years. Until 1956 Brecht played an active part in attempts to secure Hüdepohl's future in East Berlin.[7]

In the report upon his first examination of Brecht, Hüdepohl identified a serious urological condition above and beyond Brecht's susceptibility to pyelonephritis and kidney stones. Brecht was suffering from a urethral stricture with pronounced prostatitis, inflammation of the prostate gland, following a build-up of urine in the prostate. Hüdepohl recommended that Brecht should only be treated in hospital and explained that he had refrained from a further examination out of fear of infection. Hüdepohl admitted Brecht to St. Hedwig's Hospital for three weeks to address the stricture and related issues. The narrowing of the urethra, which causes the stricture, is normally due to scar tissue. The procedure to deal with it is to widen the urethra either by passing a bougie into it or by performing a urethrotomy, a surgical operation. Yet even with surgery, a stricture tends to recur and treatment has to be repeated periodically. As we shall see, Brecht's urological complaint proved to be persistent, his symptoms relating to inflammation of the prostate and of the renal pelvis. Brecht's condition dictated that he regularly consulted Hüdepohl about his urological problems until shortly before his death. There is no evidence that the specialist urologist Hüdepohl was aware of Brecht's cardiac problem.

THE SED'S COERCIVE HOSTILITY TOWARDS THE AILING BRECHT

Against this medical background, Brecht embarked on his postwar career in East Berlin, in which he enjoyed great material support from the state through the Berliner Ensemble. He was driven by his ambition to realize his theatrical vision in a socialist Germany. In

---

[5]In a further draft Viertel thought better of asking such a personal question and omitted it. The drafts of Viertel's letter to Brecht of 10 August 1948 are in Deutsches Literaturarchiv Marbach in A: Viertel, 69.2031/1–3.
[6]For details of Hüdepohl's career, see Slatomir Joachim Wenske, *Die Herausbildung urologischer Kliniken in Berlin, Ein Beitrag zur Berliner Medizingeschichte* (PhD diss., Charité – Universitätsmedizin Berlin, 2008), 132.
[7]In August 1953 Brecht supported Hüdepohl's nomination for the award of 'Verdienter Arzt des Volkes' (*BFA* 30:190 and 555; Doctor of the People of Merit). In February 1955 Brecht wrote to Otto Grotewohl about Hüdepohl, pleading that Hüdepohl should be awarded an individual contract, for which he would not normally be eligible because he worked in a private hospital (*BFA* 30:308). Brecht explained that at St. Hedwig's Hüdepohl only earned the salary of an actor, as a result of which, despite being greatly overworked, he had to perform operations in the West, where he lived. In fact, Hüdepohl had no intention of leaving West Berlin for the Eastern part of the city, where he had severely restricted his activity, and in 1956 he accepted an appointment in West Berlin (*BFA* 30:638).

1949 Brecht wrote his famous lines linking the inevitability of the aging process with the arduous struggles to come, the suggestion being that the latter could hasten the former:

> Als ich wiederkehrte
> War mein Haar noch nicht grau
> Da war ich froh.
>
> Die Mühen der Gebirge liegen hinter uns
> Vor uns liegen die Mühen der Ebenen.

(BFA 15:205)

> [When I returned
> My hair was not yet grey
> And I was glad.
>
> The travails of the mountains lie behind us.
> Before us lie the travails of the plains.

(Poems 415–16)]

Hugely combative yet very protective of his frail constitution, Brecht knowingly accepted the toils that the socialist state would surely have in store for him at a time when he could have chosen a much less arduous path for himself in the West of the German-speaking world. Yet Brecht found the challenge to participate in the establishment of a socialist Germany irresistible. He strongly supported key SED policies for economic and social transformation: land reform through the expropriation of large landowners, nationalization of key industries, and access to further and higher education for the working class. For Brecht, these changes set the GDR on a course quite different from an unregenerate Federal Republic. Yet he was also of the view that progress toward socialism was deeply compromised by the fact that the policies had been promulgated administratively from on high after the Allies' defeat of Nazism, not secured by the German people through revolutionary struggle. Indeed, Brecht himself rapidly came to experience a particular variant upon administrative diktat: SED cultural politicians' coercive hostility toward him personally in the imposition of their agenda.

Brecht's return was heralded in East Berlin with a special issue of the new journal *Sinn und Form*, which was dedicated to the work he had produced in exile, and with the production at the Deutsches Theater of *Mutter Courage und ihre Kinder* (Mother Courage and Her Children, 1939). Both were hailed as great successes. However, even then, before Brecht had actually settled in the city, Fritz Erpenbeck, the influential editor of the journal *Theater der Zeit*, was attacking *Mutter Courage* in terms that would become all too familiar.[8] Erpenbeck criticized the 'negativity' of Brecht's work, particularly the absence of uplifting examples with which the audience could identify. Essentially the same charge was leveled in 1950 against Brecht's adaptation of Lenz's *Der Hofmeister* (The Tutor, 1774). Brecht used this adaptation to initiate his exploration of the *deutsche Misere* in the German classics and among German 'bourgeois' intellectuals. This approach was quite consistent with Brecht's development but wholly at odds with the SED's self-legitimizing needs. The terms of engagement were set for the coming struggle.

Meanwhile, Brecht remained dogged by symptoms relating to his urological and cardiac conditions. His letters to Ruth Berlau from December 1950 and January 1951, when he

---

[8] The following section draws upon Davies/Parker, 183.

was directing rehearsals for *Die Mutter* (The Mother, 1932), chart the recurrence of a bacterial infection, which left him exhausted. Initially, he quite typically emphasized not his own illness but that of the set designer Caspar Neher, claiming that he himself was just a bit tired (*BFA* 30:47). However, Brecht was soon writing that he had contracted a fever and was staying at home, where he had slept the whole day (*BFA* 30:48). On 12 January 1951, which saw the premiere of *Die Mutter*, he was still feeling weak and admitted defeat the following day (*BFA* 30:52). On 15 January Hüdepohl admitted Brecht to St. Hedwig's.

A note in a *BFA* volume edited by Werner Hecht misleadingly claims that Brecht was treated as an outpatient (*BFA* 27:564). Hecht does nothing to dispel this view when he restricts the entry on the matter in the *Brecht Chronik* to 15 January.[9] Brecht was in fact only allowed home on 27 January with a course of penicillin (*BFA* 27:318; *BFA* 30:54, 500). It has hence continued to escape critical attention that Brecht was hospitalized with a serious complaint at the very time when a concerted public attack was being launched upon him in the Formalism Campaign. That Brecht was in hospital cannot have been lost on his opponents in the same way as it has been lost on one of his editors.

Brecht's principal concern in mid-January 1951 was the production of the opera *Das Verhör des Lukullus* (The Trial of Lucullus, 1940). However, he wrote in his journal that the Ministry of Education had once more requested the score (*BFA* 27:317). Brecht was determined to maintain the planned production schedule in the face of the political pressure. However, on 20–21 January the SED launched the Formalism Campaign. First *Die Mutter* was singled out for criticism on account of its supposed formalism, then *Das Verhör des Lukullus*. On behalf of the Ministry for State Security, a request was made on 12 February that a seat should be reserved for one of its officers at the State Opera where *Das Verhör des Lukullus* was to be performed.[10] The Stasi's interest in Brecht can thus be dated from this point at latest. Since all records of that interest preserved in the Ministry appear to have been destroyed, only very limited conclusions can be drawn about the Stasi interest in Brecht. However, the SED leadership itself had a direct interest in the GDR's most prominent artistic personality. On 12 March the Secretariat of the SED Central Committee banned the public performance of *Das Verhör des Lukullus* and instructed that it should be removed from the repertoire of the State Opera. In the face of further attacks, Brecht and Dessau managed to secure a closed performance for an invited audience, which hailed the work a great success. Brecht thanked Walter Ulbricht and others for permitting the performance to take place. However, the ban was re-affirmed on 19 March.

Brecht viewed the SED's approach to cultural policy as wrong but as an understandable product of the time: 'Es ist vorauszusehen, daß bei Umwälzungen von solchem Ausmaß die Künste selbst da in Schwierigkeiten kommen, wo sie führend mitwirken' (*BFA* 27:318; It is inevitable that during upheavals of these dimensions the arts will run into trouble even where they help to show the way ahead, *Journals* 433). Brecht's strategy was to seek a dialogue with Party figures in private meetings, demonstrating his preparedness to make alterations to his work, in the hope of persuading them to change direction.

---

[9]Werner Hecht, *Brecht Chronik 1898–1956* (Frankfurt a.M.: Suhrkamp, 1997), 945. Subsequent references to this work are cited in the text using the abbreviation *BC* and page number.

[10]*Das Verhör in der Oper: Die Debatte um Brecht/Dessaus 'Lukullus' 1951*, ed. Joachim Lucchesi (Berlin: BasisDruck: 1993), 66–67.

Brecht's strategy corresponded reasonably closely to the SED's own, which was to talk to Brecht in private, with a view to prevailing upon him to make corrections in keeping with the Party's position. The conversation about *Das Verhör des Lukullus* involved no less a person than the state President, Wilhelm Pieck, who invited Brecht to his home.[11] Brecht appeared to derive pleasure from the exchanges with Pieck and made alterations to the text. Brecht contrasted Pieck's intervention with the meddling of narrow-minded bureaucrats and took it as proof positive of the SED leadership's appreciation of the contribution that the arts had to make to GDR society.

Yet it became increasingly apparent that, while the respective parties agreed on the ends, they were fundamentally at odds about the means required to achieve those ends. The attacks on Brecht in the Formalism Campaign continued, while the surveillance increased. On 2 May 1951, the Politbüro of the SED Central Committee directed Wilhelm Girnus 'mit Bert Brecht eine ständige politische Arbeit durchzuführen und ihm Hilfe zu leisten' (to undertake continuous political work with Bert Brecht and to provide him with help).[12] Girnus, the editor of the arts pages of *Neues Deutschland*, was one of the most forceful, feared, and dogmatic SED cultural politicians of the early 1950s. He reported upon his discussions with Brecht to Walter Ulbricht.[13] Brecht could be in no doubt that Girnus's attentions meant that he was under regular surveillance. The understanding of Brecht's interventions in cultural politics from May 1951 until the summer of 1953 certainly needs to take into account Brecht's 'special relationship' with Girnus, particularly when considering Brecht's responses to Girnus's attacks on the Academy's Barlach exhibition and on Hanns Eisler's libretto *Johann Faustus* (Johann Faustus, 1953), which Eisler had produced in consultation with Brecht. Brecht's evident concern to maintain a dialogue with the SED leadership, mediated through his regular dialogue with Girnus, set limits to his criticisms until 17 June 1953. However, as we shall see, Girnus did not always accept Brecht's pieces for publication in *Neues Deutschland*.

Exposed to this continuing cultural-political pressure, Brecht was unable to recuperate. He would never recover. Amid concerns for his well-being, Brecht underwent an examination at the Charité hospital, which included x-rays of his lungs and his heart. The report upon the x-rays, dated 25 May 1951, indicates that Brecht was suffering from chronic heart failure. However, neither Brecht nor the doctors who treated him during the last year of his life showed any awareness of these findings. There is no indication in Brecht's frequent statements about his heart in 1955–56 that they were communicated to him.[14]

Efforts to marginalize Brecht increased. In June 1951, the SED's Cultural Department undertook an analysis of the achievements of the Academy of Arts. Noting that the Brechtian mode of theater was dominant, the Culture Department reported Ilse

---

[11] Lucchesi, 185. Pieck also invited his comrades Grotewohl, Wandel, Ackermann, and Lauter.
[12] Lucchesi, 220–21.
[13] On occasion, Brecht worked together with Girnus, the latter wearing his hat as editor of *Neues Deutschland*. See *BC* 1021.
[14] Given Girnus's role and Mielke's boast (see note 34 below), it is conceivable – though it must be stressed that no evidence has as yet come to light – that the findings about this prominent figure were passed on to the authorities and that they were aware of Brecht's condition. In that case, they would have known more than Brecht and the doctors treating him during the final year of his life, particularly that Brecht's urological and cardiac conditions meant that he would most likely die quite soon. The SED's ongoing campaign against Brecht would, of course, take on a more sinister character still if seen in such a light.

Rodenberg's view that Brecht was good, but that his methods must not be allowed to catch on. The Department added that the Performing Arts Section needed new Marxist blood.[15] Official complaints continued. On 25 July Erich Honecker requested the removal of Ernst Busch's name from Brecht's *Herrnburger Bericht* (Herrnburg Report, 1951; *BC 974*). In declining this request, Brecht addressed Honecker as Erich Honegger. On 3 August, Brecht wrote in his journal: 'Immer noch erschöpft, arbeite ich an der Schreibmaschine doch die frühen Vormittage frisch' (*BFA* 27:324; still exhausted, i [*sic*] nevertheless work at the typewriter freshly in the early morning, *Journals* 439, trans. mod.). Typically, Brecht immediately looked for a way to turn debilitating exhaustion into freshness and strength. However, on 26 August his assistant Käthe Rülicke wrote in her diary that Brecht was really worn out and had not recuperated at all (*BC 978*). He was in a virtually permanent state of exhaustion. On 9 October Rülicke added:

> Brecht klagt über einen allgemeinen Schwächezustand. Er käme sich vor wie ein Nüchterner unter lauter Betrunkenen. Seine Kraft reiche kaum für die Proben aus, er sei mittags völlig erschöpft. – Er habe Depressionen, lebe eingleisig, sehr isoliert – habe andererseits Angst, durch Ablenkungen seinen Rhythmus zu unterbrechen.
>
> (*BFA* 27:568)

[Brecht is complaining about a general state of weakness. He says that he feels like the only one who's sober among a lot of drunks; that he scarcely has the strength for rehearsals, by midday he's completely exhausted; that he's depressed and is living on a single track, very isolated; but that he's afraid of disrupting his rhythm through distractions.]

The socialist Germany of the GDR was proving to be a disorienting and dispiriting environment for an innovative artist for whom formulaic Socialist Realism was an unacceptable constraint. Despite his influence on theatrical life, Brecht was a marginalized figure, aware that his approach to dramatic art was anathema in official circles. Brecht was unable to attend the premiere of *Die Verurteilung des Lukullus* (The Condemnation of Lucullus), as the revised version of the opera was now called, because he had a fever (*BC 984*). According to Rülicke, the problem lingered on, leaving him in an exhausted, depressed state throughout that autumn (*BC 988*). In November Horst Bienek, Brecht's 'Meisterschüler' – or scholar – at the Berliner Ensemble, was arrested by the security services and sentenced a year later to twenty-five years' hard labor in Siberia. The specter of the Moscow trials loomed large in the Eastern Bloc.

By January 1952, Rülicke was noting that after conducting two rehearsals daily Brecht was worn out and needed to take care of himself (*BC 996*). But there was no question of the driven Brecht being able to let up. Official measures included a resolution of the Cultural Department of the SED's Central Committee that all Brecht's plays be removed from the secondary school curriculum (*BC 997*). Shortly after, the Cultural Department commissioned an 'Exposé über die Arbeit des formalistischen Brecht-Kreises' (*BC 1001*; Memorandum about the Work of the Formalist Brecht Circle). Girnus and the art critic Kurt Magritz led vehement attacks on the exhibition of Ernst Barlach's 'formalist' sculptures at the Academy of Arts. Brecht confided to his journal words that surely convey his own reduced state, namely that 'die wenigen verbliebenen Künstler

---

[15]*'Die Regierung ruft die Künstler'*: *Dokumente zur Gründung der 'Deutschen Akademie der Künste' (DDR) 1945–1953*, ed. Petra Uhlmann and Sabine Wolf (Berlin: Henschel, 1993), 171.

in Lethargic geworfen wurden' (BFA 27:329; the few surviving artists were cast into lethargy, *Journals* 441). Brecht responded publicly with a measured defense of Barlach's work, acknowledging its weaknesses as well as praising its strengths.[16] Girnus, however, rejected Brecht's piece for publication in *Neues Deutschland*. It appeared instead in *Sinn und Form*.

Despite his abiding exhaustion, Brecht continued to work and, on occasion, to travel. However, on a visit to Warsaw he had to severely curtail his program (BFA 30:115).[17] In March 1952 Rülicke urged Brecht to think of himself and go to Hüdepohl.[18] Brecht tended to put off the distressing clinical procedure to deal with his stricture even though, as we have seen, the corollary was his near-permanent exhaustion and related symptoms. In addition to treatment by Hüdepohl at St. Hedwig's, in early May Brecht again had to visit the Charité for a procedure that could not be deferred any longer (BFA 30:124). Rülicke wrote that she had never seen Brecht so nervous, bitter, and unfair toward others as he was afterwards, when he remained plagued by pains (BC 1014–15). Brecht excused himself from the GDR Writers' Congress in Berlin and declined an invitation to join the executive, citing his doctor's advice that he should take it easy for a considerable time (BFA 30:124).

Brecht worked with Erwin Strittmatter on the latter's comedy *Katzgraben* (1953) in the attempt to produce a dramatic work that dealt with the early GDR's radical social and economic changes from a strongly supportive position.[19] For the depiction of individualized characters contributing to these historic upheavals, Brecht needed a different approach from the familiar Brechtian caricature adopted in the interrogation of the *deutsche Misere*. Brecht looked to Stanislavsky's writings for stimulus.[20] In the 1930s Brecht had opposed Stanislavsky's dramatic theories. Now, however, his needs were different, both dramatically and also in terms of cultural-political strategy, since Stanislavsky was being actively promoted in official quarters as a model for GDR drama in opposition to Brecht.

At Buckow, Brecht initially mustered fresh energy for *Katzgraben*, rising at 6:00 a.m. and working with Rülicke from 8:00 a.m. to 2:00 p.m., then again in the evening for two to three hours (BC 1021–22). However, four years to the day before Brecht died, Rülicke noted: 'Manchmal erschrecke ich, wie grau und zusammengefallen Brecht morgens aussieht [...]. Mir ist erst hier klargeworden, daß Brecht alt wird – vorzeitig eigentlich.' (BC 1025; Sometimes I am frightened how gray and broken-down Brecht looks in the morning. It has only become clear to me here that Brecht is growing old – prematurely in fact.) It was not only that Brecht's hair had turned gray. The SED's pressure upon him since his hospitalization in January 1951 had undoubtedly accelerated the aging process. Around this time, Brecht began to reflect on impending death: 'Ich, Bertolt Brecht, Sohn bürgerlicher Eltern/Hab diesen Sommer im Gefühl, die Zeit sei knapp/Durchblättert

---

[16]For a balanced appreciation of Brecht's defense of Barlach, see Matthew Philpotts, *The Margins of Dictatorship: Assent and Dissent in the Work of Günter Eich and Bertolt Brecht* (Oxford: Peter Lang, 2003), 299–305.
[17]Marcel Reich-Ranicki, who met Brecht in his hotel room, could see no evidence of any illness. See Marcel Reich-Ranicki, *Ungeheuer oben: Über Bertolt Brecht* (Berlin: Aufbau, 1996), 103.
[18]Rülicke's unpublished letter to Brecht of 21 March 1952 is in BBA 972/113.
[19]Strittmatter's wartime service in the 'Ordnungspolizei', which was assigned to the SS, was recently discovered. See Werner Liersch, 'Erwin Strittmaiters unbekannter Krieg', *Frankfurter Allgemeine Sonntagszeitung*, 8 June 2008.
[20]Philpotts, 278–81.

mein Gewissen' (*BFA* 15:263; I, Bertolt Brecht, the son of bourgeois parents/Have leafed through my conscience this summer/With the feeling that time is short).²¹ Brecht further curtailed his activities, writing to the organizers of the Peoples' Congress for the Protection of Peace in Vienna that he could not attend because his doctor forbade it (*BFA* 30:153). Meanwhile, Hüdepohl admitted Brecht for a clinical procedure from 29 January to 9 February 1953 (*BC* 1044).

17 JUNE 1953: AN IMPROBABLE, SHORT-LIVED VICTORY

A fresh phase of hostilities against Brecht began, which culminated in the momentous events around 17 June 1953. In this extreme situation, despite his straitened circumstances, Brecht for the last time demonstrated his great mental energy and agility. The SED's Construction of the Foundations of Socialism was intended to signal an end to the 'compromises' in the arts.²² Brecht and the Academy of Arts were twin targets that were brought into a single focus in a campaign orchestrated by Alexander Abusch. As a Jewish 'western émigré', Abusch had been stripped of all his Party responsibilities and had then been recruited by the Stasi to combat the influence of 'western émigrés' and Trotskyism, though not directly Brecht and the Academy.²³ However, Abusch, ensured that Brecht was confronted in a concerted fashion on those very issues where the SED's need for self-legitimation clashed with Brecht's artistic theory and practice. In an act that undermined the Academy's authority, the State Commission for Artistic Affairs announced that on 17–19 April the Academy would be the venue for the First German Stanislavsky Conference. It was an open secret that the event was designed as an attack on Brechtian theater through which Brecht would be forced to recant his theoretical position. Some people believed the liquidation of the Berliner Ensemble to be on the agenda.²⁴

It counted for nothing that Brecht himself was looking for common ground with Stanislavsky in rehearsals for *Katzgraben*. Intimidation of Brecht included the Stasi's arrest of another of Brecht's 'Meisterschüler', Martin Pohl, who was subjected to sleep deprivation and forced to sign a dictated confession, which he later retracted.²⁵ Brecht intervened on Pohl's behalf until he was released in 1955. In its resigned, weary tone Brecht's journal entry of 4 March 1953 echoes the entry after the attack on Barlach:

> Unsere Aufführungen in Berlin haben fast kein Echo mehr. In der Presse erscheinen Kritiken Monate nach der Erstaufführung, und es steht nichts drin, außer ein paar kümmerlichen soziologischen Analysen. Das Publikum ist das Kleinbürgerpublikum der Volksbühne, Arbeiter machen da kaum sieben Prozent aus. Die Bemühungen sind

---

[21] This and later statements show the untenability of Werner Mittenzwei's contention that Brecht did not begin to countenance death until shortly before the event. See Werner Mittenzwei, *Das Leben des Bertolt Brecht oder: Der Umgang mit den Welträtseln*, 3rd edn (East Berlin and Weimar: Aufbau, 1988), 2:655–56.
[22] The present section follows Davies/Parker, 185.
[23] *Wer war wer in der DDR*, ed. Bernd-Rainer Barth et al. (Frankfurt a.M.: Fischer, 1995), 13.
[24] Werner Hecht, 'Das Vergnügen an einer ernsten Sache: Ein Leben im Dienste Brecht – Erinnerungen von und an Käthe Rülicke', *Der Tagesspiegel* (Berlin), 3 November 1992, cited by Philpotts, 280.
[25] *Denken heißt verändern: Erinnerungen an Brecht*, ed. Joachim Lang and Jürgen Hillesheim (Augsburg: Maro, 1998), 131. The Pohl case provides a plausible background for Mielke's comments about Brecht's alleged accusations of Stasi malpractice.

nur dann nicht ganz sinnlos, wenn die Spielweise späterhin aufgenommen werden
kann, d.h. wenn ihr Lehrwert einmal realisiert wird. (Das gilt, obwohl wir alles tun,
für jetzt, für die Theaterabende, für das Publikum von jetzt unser Bestes zu liefern.)

(BFA 27:346)

[our performances in berlin have almost no resonance any more. the press notices
appear months after the first night, and there is never anything in them anyway apart
from a few pathetic bits of sociological analysis, the public is the petty bourgeois
public of the volksbühne, workers make up scarcely 7% of it. the effort will only
be worthwhile if the manner of acting can be taken up later, i.e. when its didactic
value has been realized. (this is true, although we, here and now, put all we can into
our theatre evenings and do the best we can for the public we have at the moment.)
(*Journals* 454; lower case in original)]

Brecht, for whom intervention in the pressing matters of the day was a matter of artistic principle, found himself in the German socialist state working once more for posterity.

Helene Weigel protected Brecht, as she often did, by representing the Berliner Ensemble against the weight of official voices at the Stanislavsky Conference. Brecht was subjected to pressure on a second front when Abusch orchestrated a new regular discussion forum in the Academy, the Mittwoch-Gesellschaften. The first item for debate was Eisler's *Johann Faustus*. Girnus joined Abusch and others in the deeply coercive atmosphere for a concerted assault on the 'Brecht faction'. But wholly improbably, Brecht and his supporters turned the tables when the strikes and demonstrations of 16–17 June shattered the SED's fragile authority.

There was no question of Brecht placing himself at the head of a popular movement for reform. Indeed, Brecht re-affirmed his support for the SED leadership's achievements. Brecht was, however, instrumentally involved in the formulation of the Academy's recommendations to reform cultural policy.[26] The principal target was the cultural bureaucracy, the baleful effects of which Brecht and others like Eisler and Arnold Zweig had experienced.[27] When publication of the recommendations was blocked, Brecht threatened to resign from the Academy. Publication followed in *Neues Deutschland*.[28] The *Berliner Zeitung* then published Brecht's scathingly satirical poems 'Nicht feststellbare Fehler der Kunstkommission' (Unidentifiable Errors of the Arts Commission) and 'Das Amt für Literatur' (The Office for Literature). Brecht discussed his piece 'Kulturpolitik und Akademie der Künste' (Cultural Policy and the Academy of Arts) with Girnus at

---

[26]The present section follows Davies/Parker, 191–92. The recommendations were first discussed at an Academy plenary on 26 June 1953. In *BFA* 23:549–50 the meeting is dated 16 June and the discussion placed in the context of the New Course without reference to 17 June. In Werner Hecht, *Brecht Chronik: Ergänzungen* (Frankfurt a.M.: Suhrkamp, 2007), 111, Hecht dates the meeting 26 June 1952. This is not an isolated dating error on Hecht's part in that work concerning the events in the Academy around 17 June. For example, Hecht (121) dates the meeting of the Academy commission concerning the future of *Sinn und Form* as 2 June, a month before the meeting actually took place. See Parker, '*Sinn und Form*, Peter Huchel und der 17. Juni: Bertolt Brechts Rettungsaktion', *Sinn und Form* 46, no. 5 (1994): 738–51, here 747.

[27]Although Abusch was not required to report upon the Academy to the Stasi, he reported upon the positions energetically taken up by Brecht and his supporters against the cultural bureaucracy and against Abusch himself after 17 June. See Matthias Braun, *Kulturinsel und Machtinstrument: Die Akademie der Künste, die Partei und die Staatssicherheit* (Göttingen: Vandenhoeck & Ruprecht, 2007), 76–77.

[28]Hecht, *Brecht Chronik: Ergänzungen*, 123–24.

Buckow. It contained outspoken criticism of the cultural bureaucracy. Girnus, now on the defensive, published it without delay in *Neues Deutschland*.

Girnus's record of the conversation for Ulbricht reveals the depth of Brecht's concerns.[29] Brecht had dismissed the SED's entire cultural policy as wrong. He had insisted that the Shdanovite measures deployed in Stalin's Soviet Union were wholly inappropriate for the GDR and that the Formalism Campaign was a Nazi phenomenon, as was the SED's use of the term 'Volk'. Brecht was plagued by the deep fear that the SED was contributing to a resurgence of Nazism by pandering to an unreconstructed institutional and popular racism. This fear informs Brecht's famous journal entry, 'Der 17. Juni hat die ganze Existenz verfremdet' (*BFA* 27:346; 17th June has alienated the whole of existence, *Journals* 454). Immediately preceding that entry are references to Brecht's most important poetic and dramatic responses to 17 June, the *Buckower Elegien* (Buckow Elegies, 1953) and *Turandot oder Der Kongreß der Weißwäscher* (Turandot or The Whitewashers' Congress, 1953). Brecht enlarged upon his fears in the 'Vorwort zu *Turandot*' (Foreword to Turandot, 1953), which concludes: 'Unter neuen Befehlshabern setzte sich also der Naziapparat wieder in Bewegung [...] Unüberzeugt, aber feige, feindlich, aber sich duckend, begannen verknöcherte Beamte wieder gegen die Bevölkerung zu regieren' (*BFA* 24:410; So, under the new commanders, the Nazi apparatus once more set itself in motion. [...] Unconvinced but cowardly, hostile but cowering, ossified officials began again to govern against the population, *BAP* 336).

Brecht's critique of the continuity of such a pernicious mentality informs Brecht's reworking of the *Turandot* material, his exploration during the Weimar Republic and exile of the false consciousness of intellectuals, whom he labeled 'Tuis'. The Tui Ka Mü remarks: 'Und dies hier ist neue Musik. Die wird verfolgt, weil sie nicht volkstümlich ist' (*BFA* 9:183; And this is new music. It's in trouble because it's not 'true to the spirit of the people', *Plays* 8:184). Brecht's earlier confident, satirical treatment of the theme is superseded in the burlesque of *Turandot* by the sobering experience of Stalinist power politics and of the fledgling German socialist state. Henceforth, Brecht's hopes for world revolution rested not with the Soviet Union and the Eastern Bloc but with China.

After the momentous events of the summer, in November 1953 Brecht's thoughts turned once more to the prospect of impending death. In a document that he placed in an envelope for Helene Weigel to open after the event, he stipulated what was to be done after his death.[30] In 1954, Brecht acknowledged for the first time that his creative powers and intellectual resilience were failing him (*BFA* 27:362). His slight frame had become bloated, as had his face. This can be readily attributed to his deteriorating medical state.[31] *Turandot* and other dramatic projects like *Büsching*, which dealt with the economic and social development of the GDR, remained unfinished. After struggling with *Büsching*, Brecht was forced to concede to his 'Meisterschüler' Claus Küchenmeister and his wife Wera: 'Ich kann nicht mehr, das müßt ihr Jungen weitermachen.' (*BC* 1117; I can't do it anymore. You younger people have got to take things forward.) He noted wistfully:

---

[29]Girnus's letter to Ulbricht of 27 July 1953 is summarized in *BC* 1070–71.

[30]The document bearing the date November 1953 in Brecht's hand is in the collection of papers recently acquired by Augsburg city library from Barbara Brecht-Schall. Hitherto this document has been attributed to the same period of time as Brecht's letter of 15 May 1955 to Rudolf Engel, the administrative director of the East Berlin Academy, in which Brecht sets out arrangements for his funeral. This dating is no longer tenable.

[31]When Bernhard Reich saw Brecht in Moscow in May 1955 for the first time in fourteen years, Brecht had changed a lot in appearance. His face was broad and his body stocky. See *BC* 1166.

'Natürlich war ich auch begabt, vor vierzig Jahren besonders.' (*BFA* 1:573; Of course I was gifted too, particularly forty years ago.) Brecht's extraordinary intellectual energy was nearly spent. The irony is that this occurred just as he achieved the international acclaim that he craved: in 1954, the Berliner Ensemble's performance of *Mutter Courage* was hailed for its transformative impact on world theater, when the company was awarded first prize at the Théâtre des Nations festival in Paris. At a time when the GDR had few friends abroad, the SED leadership could bask in the reflected glory of Brecht's renown. However, Brecht's success in the West, not to mention his award of the Stalin Prize the following year, changed nothing in the GDR. In 1955, as the attacks gained fresh momentum, he saw his life as threatened by the forces ranged against him: 'Daß du untergehst, wenn du dich nicht wehrst/Das wirst du doch einsehen' (*BFA* 15:295; That you'll go down if you don't stand up for yourself/Surely you see that, *Poems* 452).[32] The summer of 1955 saw the onset of Brecht's final, protracted illness. After contracting a bacterial infection that affected his kidneys, then spread to his heart, triggering endocarditis and septicemia, he died of chronic heart failure.[33]

As we have seen, Brecht was destined for an early death, come what may. However, the concerted campaign of public attacks, surveillance, and intrigue that the SED leadership conducted against him undoubtedly accelerated the aging process. As a result, Brecht's life and work were certainly impaired. If further material comes to light, it is likely that it will confirm the strong impression that the actions of the SED leadership served to curtail Brecht's life's work.[34]

---

[32] In similar fashion to Brecht's attack on the cultural bureaucracy after 17 June 1953, members of the Berliner Ensemble took the fight to the enemy with pieces in *Theater der Zeit*. Hans Bunge countered Erpenbeck's negative review of *Der kaukasische Kreidekreis* (The Caucasian Chalk Circle, 1944) and Erpenbeck's critique of epic theater in general. Manfred Wekwerth and Peter Palitzsch similarly countered Günter Kaltofen's critical review of the production of Becher's *Winterschlacht* (Battle in Winter, 1942). See *BC* 1154.

[33] See Parker, 'What was the Cause of Brecht's Death?' for details of Brecht's treatment from the summer of 1955 until his death.

[34] The recent discovery of a sound recording of an in-house address by Deputy Minister for State Security Erich Mielke to senior Stasi officers shortly after Brecht's death can only add to that impression. Mielke departed from his prepared text to boast: 'Ich möchte eins der krassesten Beispiele bringen, Genossen, weil es wichtig ist, dass man als Staatssicherheitsmann, nich' wahr, genau weiß, wie diese Brüder gedacht haben ...: dass also in der Staatssicherheit die Verhafteten geschlagen und misshandelt worden sind, auch hier in der DDR. (Pause) Und dass deshalb also der bekannte Schriftsteller (Pause) und, äh, Dramaturg Brecht Strafantrag stellen wollte gegen also einen leitenden Funktionär der Staatssicherheit. Und dann ist der Brecht erlegen einen [*sic*] Herzschlag.' (I'd like to give you one of the crassest examples, comrades, because it's important, isn't it, that we state security men know what these fellows have been thinking ...: that the state security has been beating and abusing prisoners, here in the GDR too [pause]. And that for this reason the well-known writer [pause] and, erm, dramaturge Brecht wanted to bring criminal charges against a leading functionary of the state security. And then Brecht succumbed to a heart attack.) In the final sentence Mielke, seemingly knowingly, placed the emphasis on 'dann' (then). See Peter von Becker, 'Erich Mielke und des Dichters Herzschlag', *Der Tagesspiegel* (Berlin), 15 August 2006. No documents have emerged hitherto that directly substantiate Mielke's boast.

CHAPTER SIX

Characteristics of the Berliner Ensemble

BERTOLT BRECHT
TRANSLATED BY ROMY FURSLAND

It was to be expected, if not hoped, that the tremendous revolution in the way people live, work and think, brought about by the introduction of Socialism, would also bring about and necessitate significant changes in the arts. The changes will not, as some people seem to think, only concern subject matter or only form or only intention in the arts, but all of them together, since they form a coherent, if contradictory, whole. The theatre in particular will be 'affected' by these changes.

Some of the changes to be expected are:

1) In order to bring about an artistic experience, the way the theatre represents people living together must be more 'accurate' than before: in other words, the representations must be realistic.

2) Important insights must feed into the reality being represented, and this reality must communicate certain intentions.

3) Human nature must be represented as capable of change.

4) The representations must be materialist-dialectical.

5) It is vital, since we are dealing with art, that people should be made aware of the materialist-dialectical viewpoint and that it should be a source of pleasure.

6) All these changes (and others not listed here) must be effected within the realm of art which is not the art of today. The development will happen in such a way that the achievements of earlier revolutions will be overturned, in the dialectical sense.

It is advisable to judge changes in theatre and drama on the basis of these criteria.

The most important thing for the Berliner Ensemble at the moment is to examine Point 6.

If the Ensemble follows this advice – as it intends to do – the audience will be guaranteed to have an artistic experience. Contrary to the claims of certain critics, emotions (for example) are in no way 'inhibited' by the Ensemble's acting style, even if some of those emotions are of a different nature. And the training of the next generation of actors

---

Brecht, '[Eigenarten des Berliner Ensembles 2]', in Brecht, *Schriften*, vol. 3 (Berlin and Frankfurt/Main: Aufbau and Suhrkamp, 1993), pp. 312–13.

is certainly not, as some critics claim, undertaken solely in line with one specific and perhaps undesirable 'school of thought'. The special new requirements the actors must fulfil, as mentioned above, call for a very broad education. Actors need to learn how to act in a realistic and natural way which is based on observation, but which is also stylised. In our view, it is plain for all to see that the actors trained by the Ensemble are by no means merely 'Brecht specialists'.

PART TWO

WORK

Plays: Early/Weimar Work

CHAPTER SEVEN

Brecht's Plays of the Weimar Period

R. C. SPEIRS

Whenever a list is made of the 'representative' writers and artists of the Weimar Republic the name of Bertolt Brecht always figures prominently. Yet, when one asks in what sense he was representative of the period one soon encounters problems. If, for example, public resonance is used as a criterion the evidence is contradictory. On the one hand his *Dreigroschenoper* (The Threepenny Opera) enjoyed a degree of success in 1928 which has become an established part of the legend of the 'golden twenties'. Although not quite such a 'smash hit' as the *Threepenny Opera*, his theatrical debut with *Trommeln in der Nacht* (Drums in the Night) in 1922 was also popular with critics and public alike, both in Munich and Berlin. On the other hand, both of these works were untypical of Brecht's twenties writing in certain important respects, and this 'untypicality' may help to explain why they enjoyed far greater success with the public than any of his other plays. If the term 'representative' is used in the sense of being typical of current literary trends, the difficulties in applying it to Brecht do not become any less. In the first place, the literary life of the Weimar Republic was so varied that one cannot properly speak of a period style. In addition to this, Brecht's own literary production and the attitudes to life he expressed outside of literature were so many-sided, complex, even contradictory, that it is difficult to generalize about them. Consequently, the relations of any given work of his to its social and cultural contexts are particularly resistant to short and simple description. Because the subject of Brecht's place in the literary life of the Weimar Republic is such a tangled one, the path beaten through it here is bound to be fairly rough and ready.

Like the Weimar Republic itself, Brecht's first mature play, *Baal* (first draft, 1918), was a product of the First World War. In the first instance this 'dramatic biography' of an anarchic poet with an astounding appetite for life was a reaction to the years of multiple deprivation which the War inflicted on the populations of the combatant countries. Although Brecht was fortunate enough to be spared active service, he could not escape his share of the general misery of the War years. Hermann Hesse's 'novella', *Klingsors letzter Sommer* (Klingsor's Last Summer), written just one year later than the first draft of *Baal*, and read with pleasure by Brecht, took a similar artist figure for its hero and expressed the same intense hunger for experience. Hesse recalled the mood which underlay his story

---

R. C. Speirs, 'Brecht's Plays of the Weimar Period', in Alan F. Bance (ed.), *Weimar Germany: Writers and Politics* (Edinburgh: Scottish Academic Press, 1982) pp. 138–52.

thus: 'Every one of us had the feeling that he had lost and missed out on something, a piece of life, a piece of the self, a piece of development, adaptation and "savoir vivre."'[1] Brecht's close friend and later collaborator, the artist Caspar Neher, who did see active service, welcomed *Baal* as a much needed source of invigoration: 'Your Baal is as good as ten litres of gin.'[2]

Baal and Klingsor both have a particularly intense hunger for life because they share an unusually keen sense of life's transience. The theme of life's brevity and brutality runs through the whole of Brecht's twenties work as an abiding mark of the existential shock administered by a war in which millions of lives, particularly young ones, were buried in the mud over which the machines of war advanced and retreated. The unifying action of the seemingly loosely constructed *Baal* is that of a 'dance with death', a medieval form to which the experiences of 1914–18 had given renewed relevance. As his name suggests, Baal is a figure with a mythical dimension; he is an embodiment of Eros, the life principle, who is locked in permanent conflict with Thanatos, the force of death. Death presents itself to Baal in myriad forms – in the shape of corpses, of course, but also in the guise of social conventions and contracts, or in such images of transitoriness as fallen trees, wind-driven clouds, drifting rivers or the ever-changing but ever empty skies. Yet Death is not only around Baal but is also within him, both as a process of decay and as the energetic will to consume all that he can of other life before he is consumed in his turn. Baal is an embodiment of the cruel vision of life which Brecht had acquired through the War. Yet this horrifying figure is presented more as an object of admiration than of disgust. Brecht's characteristically aggressive response to what seemed an inherently and ineluctably cruel world was to counter violence with violence, to answer nature's indifference to the individual with unconditional egotism. Thus *Baal* came to be written as a fantasy of mastery over life, achieved through a figure whose vitality and ruthlessness enabled him to turn even the sources of pain (such as transience and the related problem of existential isolation) into sources of pleasure and strength.

Deprivation and existential shock were not the only effects the War had on Brecht. When the War broke out he immediately began, as a schoolboy of sixteen, to write a series of poems, stories and newspaper articles of a patriotic nature, urging his countrymen to accept the sacrifices which would be entailed in fighting for the 'holy cause' of the Fatherland. His 'Augsburger Kriegsbriefe' (War Letters from Augsburg)[3] are documents of an intense youthful idealism which he managed to keep alive for over a year, but which then began to sour into bitter disillusionment. This destruction of a set of ideals, which centred on a religiously coloured conception of service to the community, was the third main injury which Brecht suffered at the hands of the War. *Baal* is a vision of a life lived entirely without the help of any belief in a saving ideal. Baal is an animal who 'dies as all other animals die', a bundle of appetites, drives and sensations, a descendant of the apes (he is repeatedly spoken of as an 'Orang Utang') who is destined to become nothing more than food for worms. Although he sometimes dreams of permanence and tranquility in a 'country where it is better to live', he knows that this is an illusory, unattainable state for a material creature subject to the ravages of decay. As he contemplates the corpse

---

[1] *Klingsors letzter Sommer* (Zurich, no date) p. 276.
[2] *Baal. Der böse Baal der Asoziale: Text Varianten and Materialien* (Frankfurt am Main, 1968), p. 99.
[3] There is a compilation of these early texts in Frisch and Obermeier, *Brecht in Augsburg* (Berlin/Weimar, 1975). p. 225 et seq.

of a fellow lumberjack who has been killed by a falling tree, Baal remarks: 'He has his rest, and we have our restlessness. Both of these things are good. The heavens are black.'[4] For Baal peace exists only in death; until then man is the seat of an unceasing organic process of consumption and decay, and the enjoyment of this process is all the 'meaning' there can be in life. The savagery of this view of life as wholly lacking in any possibility of transcendence needs to be seen both in relation to a war in which the term 'Menschenmaterial' (human material) could be invented, and in relation to the grand illusions which had been nurtured in Brecht before the War began. The harsh cynicism of *Baal* was an act of revenge on the part of a disappointed idealist.

Having once been duped into believing in ideals which were shattered by the reality of the War, Brecht was determined never to be anybody's fool again. The aggressive individualism of Baal, who refuses to be anyone's man but his own, is a magnified version of the recalcitrant attitude which Brecht himself adopted in most areas of life. This youthful 'Widerspruchsgeist' (spirit of contradiction) is reflected not only in the character of Baal, but also in the play's implied relations to its cultural context. The immediate occasion of the composition of *Baal* was Brecht's encounter with the works of the minor Expressionist poet Hanns Johst at a seminar on contemporary drama run by Artur Kutscher, a professor of literature at Munich University and biographer of the dramatist Frank Wedekind (one of Brecht's few youthful idols). Having been ejected from Kutscher's seminar for loudly expressing a dissenting view of the professor's latest protégé, Brecht wrote *Baal* as a counterblast to the 'ridiculous view of genius and amorality' contained in Johst's *Der Einsame* (The Lonely Man), a play which cast the late-Romantic poet, Christian Dietrich Grabbe, in the cliché role of the misunderstood, suffering artist. Johst's theme is the typical late-Expressionist one of the conflict between spirit ('Geist') and life, which makes martyrs of finer souls, such as Grabbe reputedly was. When Johst's Grabbe loses his young wife in childbirth the poet's grief, guilt and resentment make him plunge into a life of apparent debauchery, which is, however, one of secret self-laceration. This 'flagellatory', defeatist response to life's indifference to man's ideals and expectations is the diametrical opposite of Baal's tough acceptance of the world as it is, and his ready indulgence in 'vice' and destructiveness as pleasurable ends in themselves.

Although *Der Einsame* caused *Baal* to crystallize in Brecht's imagination, it was really only the starting point for a much broader attack on the values of the many Expressionist writers whose experiences of the War had led them to proclaim the need for man's spiritual renewal. These Expressionists believed that the sufferings of the War were the birth-pangs of 'the New Man' who would herald in an age of pacifism, universal love, spirituality freed from the shackles of a corrupt and materialist past. Their values represented a secularization of the Christian tradition of rebirth through love, and showed the influence of the Romantic philosophy of Arthur Schopenhauer, who preached the redeeming power of art and of compassion. *Baal*, by contrast, shows the influence of Friedrich Nietzsche, the denigrator of Schopenhauer and prophet of the antichrist. Like Wedekind's Lulu, Baal is an offspring of Nietzsche's Dionysius. Baal and Dronysius both embody the world's eternal sameness ('die ewige Wiederkehr des Gleichen'); both

---

[4]*Baal* (Potsdam, 1922) p. 53 An accurate view of Brecht's early work can only be gained if one uses the first published versions of the texts; the versions contained in the standard editions contain revisions which reflect Brecht's later point of view.

are figures of overbrimming vitality who delight in discharging their energies in violent conflict; for neither is there any possibility of neutralizing the will to power through spiritual transcendence. Baal is an unregenerate Old Adam who mocks the Expressionists' dreams of the New Man. His opposition to the God of the Old Testament is conveyed by his name (the rites of Baal were a constant temptation to the Israelites to deviate from their worship of Jehovah), and his rejection of Christian asceticism is made explicit in his angry reaction to a Corpus Christi procession. In short, *Baal* was a declaration of war not only on the idealistic excesses of contemporary Expressionism but also on the whole Judaeo-Christian tradition which provided the ostensible mainstay of Western society.

Although *Baal* rejected the utopian visions of the majority of the Expressionists, it retained certain distinctly Expressionist features. In conceiving Baal as a larger-than-life, mythical figure Brecht made full use of the Expressionist author's licence to overstep the limits of psychological probability. What unites the play is not a traditional plot, nor the empirical sequence of a biography, but an Expressionist 'vision' of life's 'essence' as a struggle between the forces of vitality and decay. Just like other Expressionist heroes Baal has his moments of ecstasy, although in his case the visions are violent rather than pacific: 'My soul ... is the moaning of the corn-fields as they roll under the wind. And the sparkle in the eyes of two insects who want to eat one another' (*Baal*, p. 47).[5] Admittedly there is much more earthiness, concreteness and humour in *Baal* than one usually finds in the frequently rather thin-blooded dramas of the Expressionists, but these differences do not detract from the larger similarities. It has been suggested that Brecht's early plays should be considered as belonging, alongside those of Arnolt Bronnen and Hans Henny Jahnn, to a sub-category of 'black Expressionism'.[6] There is some merit in this, as long as the term is not used indiscriminately, so as to obscure the important differences between these authors: Bronnen, for example, wrote the crudest and weakest plays of the three, while Jahnn was more pre-occupied with guilt than Brecht. Nor should the term be taken to suggest that Brecht's early work belongs to a late, 'decaying' stage in the development of Expressionism; it was, rather, an attempt to recover the vitality of earlier Expressionism and to emulate that of such 'pre-' or 'proto-' Expressionist authors as Wedekind or Strindberg, both of whom Brecht still considered in 1918 to be amongst 'the great educators of the new Europe' (GW 15, 4)[7]. The real debt to Expressionism that is evident in *Baal* should not be minimized, for the freedom it gave Brecht from the constraints of Naturalism, and the courage to use symbolic techniques as a means of giving the modern theatre the generality of reference he considered characteristic of 'the major form of drama' in all ages, was to remain a cornerstone of his writing throughout the twenties, and even beyond.

With the outbreak of the 'German Revolution' in November 1918, it seemed possible that various hopes for a radical change in German society might be realized. Some of the Expressionist idealists (Landauer, Toller, Mühsam) even found themselves at the centre of revolutionary political activity when a short-lived 'soviet republic' came into being in Bavaria. In the event, however, the German Revolution achieved neither the dictatorship of the proletariat which was the aim of the Communists, nor the spiritual renewal which

---

[5] In the two earliest, manuscript drafts of the play these lines are introduced with the stage direction, 'arising ecstatically, full of sun'. *Baal: Drei Fassungen* (Frankfurt am Main. 1969). p. 55, p. 119.
[6] The phrase is taken from G. Rühle, *Theater für die Republik* (Frankfurt am Main, 1967), p. 25.
[7] References in this form are to Brecht's *Gesammelte Werke*, 20 vols. (Frankfurt am Main, 1967).

was the utopian goal of the Expressionists, but rather the abdication of the Emperor and the creation of a parliamentary democracy. Nevertheless, Expressionist dramas dealing with revolt and revolution enjoyed their theatrical heyday in the first years of the new republic. By 1922, however, both public and critics had grown decidedly tired of plays elaborating the abstract dialectics of revolution. The Expressionists' visionary pathos had come to appear increasingly irrelevant to the day-to-day problems of sheer survival in a country where rampant inflation, unemployment and black marketeering had made the resigned acceptance of man's unchanging fallibility seem more appropriate than any enthusiastic belief in change. The success in 1922 of Brecht's second play, *Trommeln in der Nacht* (Drums in the Night), which ends with the hero taking his cynical farewell of the revolution, reflected this change in the public's mood. Yet there was irony in this success, for when Brecht began to write the play in 1919 his object was to deride the rhetorical, idealistic type of Expressionist play and to insult the bourgeois public who might applaud such plays in the theatre but had no intention of permitting any kind of radical change to occur in reality. By the time the play came to be performed, however; the public's own satiation with theatrical idealism meant that *Drums in the Night* could be received with approval by the very people it had been originally intended to provoke.[8]

Brecht's polemic against Expressionism was conveyed both through the hero's explicit rejection of the claims of an 'Idee' on his loyalty, and through the form of *Drums in the Night*. The clear message of the play was that revolution was no more than a dangerous indulgence in romanticism and therefore quite contrary to the interests of the man in the street. Throughout the course of the action the returning infantryman Kragler is shown to endanger his chances of winning back his girlfriend from the stay-at-home war-profiteer Murk whenever he allows himself to become infected by the mood of hysteria prevailing throughout postwar German society, amongst the panic-stricken bourgeoisie as much as their enemies. In order to be able to perceive and defend his true interests Kragler has to learn to behave in a 'sachlich' (sober, controlled, realistic) manner, accepting that life with Anna (even if she has been made pregnant by Murk) is a better and more humane choice to make than an 'honourable' but fruitless death on the barricades. This anti-Expressionist argument was reinforced by the style and structure of the play. Instead of the abstract settings and symbolic figures of the Expressionist drama, Brecht presented an observed contemporary situation and described the difficulties in adjusting to it of an ordinary soldier, who has endured four years in a POW camp; instead of a loose sequence of scenes illustrating a spiritual development or abstract dialectic, Brecht presented a play with five acts and the conventional plot of one man's struggle with another for possession of a woman. These relatively realistic and conventional features of the play provided a foil for the playwright's travesties of Expressionism. He employed sets painted in the Expressionistic 'diagonal' manner, for example, and an all-too-obviously symbolic red moon, which glowed automatically whenever Kragler appeared on stage, so as to convey visually the 'Expressionist' (i.e. hysterical) atmosphere which Kragler encounters on his return to Berlin. At the end of the play Kragler is made to knock down the artificial moon into an equally artificial river in order to signal his emancipation from the melodramatic, illusory clichés which govern the behaviour of most of the other characters, and which

---

[8]Brecht frequently spoke disparagingly of *Drums in the Night*, claiming that he only wrote it to make money. Yet diary entries from the time when he was revising the manuscript indicate that he put much more into the play than he was prepared to admit to others.

have all but prevented him from achieving happiness. Whereas Kragler eventually learns to follow his genuine feelings instead of the lines of the role assigned to him in the 'Theater' which all around him are playing, his earlier failure to resist that role was signalled verbally by the collapse of his speech into helpless Expressionistic stammering. His incoherence at such points was aggravated by the influence of alcohol. Seen in the context of the concrete struggles of the period, so Brecht implied, the 'drunken' Expressionist manner was merely the voice of impotent hysteria.

To describe Kragler's behaviour at the end of *Drums in the Night* as 'sachlich' is to apply to it one of the key terms in the vocabulary of the 1920s in Germany. Its general sense was 'in control of the emotions', and it was used in all walks of life to indicate that one had in some sense moved 'beyond' the illusions and excitement of the last few years in order to look contemporary reality squarely in the eye. The term 'Neue Sachlichkeit', first coined in 1923 as the title for a proposed retrospective exhibition of paintings produced in the last decade and portraying a concrete, tangible reality, has been seized on by cultural historians searching for a convenient label to apply to the art and literature produced after the demise of Expressionism.[9] Unfortunately, the term is an awkward and confusing one since almost everyone wanted to describe his own attitude as 'sachlich', but different individuals and groups meant quite different things by it. If there was a mainstream of 'neusachlich' writing, it was perhaps formed by those works which presented contemporary themes, situations and types with a mixture of ironic detachment, satirical edge and sentiment. As examples of this combination of attitudes one might cite the poetry of Erich Kästner or the mid-twenties comedies of Hasenclever, Sternheim, Kaiser, Zuckmayer, and the many other, more minor, dramatists who were only too glad to meet the public's demand for lightweight comedies, confirming their desire to believe that although one might need sharp elbows and few illusions about one's neighbour in order to survive in a tough world, one could still be a person with his heart in the right place.[10] This type of literature expressed a greater or lesser degree of accommodation to the status quo, and as such it conflicted with the radical discontent which was Brecht's dominant attitude to society throughout the twenties. His damning verdict on this allegedly new objectivity was that it was insidious old hat: 'the New Objectivity is reactionary' (GW 15, 161). It is therefore ironical that *Drums in the Night* has a fair claim to be considered the first 'neusachlich' comedy. Like its successors it was contemporary in theme and setting; it attacked the 'Schieber' (profiteers) who were the favourite objects of neusachlich' satire; it had a hero who won the day by keeping his head while others all around were losing theirs; it also showed the hero as a man

---

[9]H. Lethen argues that the term 'Neue Sachlichkeit' should be restricted to work produced in the years 1924–32; see H. L., *Neue Sachlichkeit 1924–1932* (Stuttgart, 1970). Lethen's reason for this is his desire to establish a causal connection between this cultural trend and the socio-political effects of the Dawes Plan, which reputedly encouraged the 'Americanization' of German industry. Yet the terms 'Amerikanismus' and 'Asiatismus' did not appear for the first time in this period, but had been circulating since before the War, in German debates on the country's cultural identity. Equally awkward for any attempt to link artistic and social change closely is the fact that the Mannheim exhibition of 'neusachlich' painting in 1926 was already able to draw on more than a decade of work.

[10]For surveys of the comedy in this period see E. Schürer, 'Die nachexpressionistische Komödie' in W. Rothe, *Die deutsche Literatur in der Weimarer Republik* (Stuttgart, 1974), and R. Grimm, 'Neuer Humor? Die Komödienproduktion zwischen 1918 and 1933' in *Die deutsche Komödie im zwanzigsten Jahrhundert*, ed. W. Paulsen (Heidelberg, 1976).

with genuine, good feelings behind the armour-plating of cynicism which circumstances forced him to adopt. That Brecht should almost always have felt it necessary to speak disparagingly about his second play now looks like a reaction of exasperation to the ironic twist of history that transformed what was originally conceived as an angry rejection of the hollow and cliché attitudes struck in the revolutionary period, into a herald of the sentimental-cynical attitude that became the new cliché in the years of Weimar's stabilization.

America was an object of great fascination to the general public and intellectuals alike in the Weimar Republic. It epitomized the new, the modern world of technology, skyscrapers, booming cities, business efficiency, a fresh, uncomplicated and unsentimental attitude to life, jazz, films, cocktails, professional boxing, all of them things which elicited responses ranging from excitement to abhorrence. Initially, Brecht could think of America only with enthusiasm, as an alternative to the dullness, decrepitude and impoverishment of life in post-war Germany (GW 20, 10; GW 68–9). However, by the time he came to write his third play *Im Dickicht* (In the Jungle), later entitled *Im Dickicht der Städte* (In the Jungle of the Cities), which he set in Chicago, he had developed a more complex and ambivalent vision of transatlantic civilisation as exemplifying with particular clarity the historical process of urbanization, what Brecht called 'mankind's migration into the great cities'. Although Brecht had read Upton Sinclair's novels portraying the brutality and squalor of American life, and even drew on this knowledge for the milieu of his play. *Im Dickicht* was much more concerned with the existential effects of city life than with providing an indictment of its social and material inequities. The setting of the action was 'a cold, unreal Chicago',[11] and the point of view from which the characters' behaviour was observed was one of 'Relativität' (relativity or relativism) (GW 15, 70). This was a somewhat pretentious term, similar to Nietzsche's concept of 'perspectivism', and was used by Brecht to describe the effects of human individuation. He saw each individual as isolated from all others by his unique personal disposition. Although a person's psychology might be grasped intellectually by another person as the 'typical' product of various circumstances, actual subjective experiences were incapable of being shared: 'every man is the best one in his skin', i.e. each man's life is his own, private affair. The main interest of the play lies in its particular application of the themes of 'subjective relativism and isolation to the conditions of modern urban life.

The jungle image in the title of the play expresses the young Brecht's conviction that, though they live in cities, men are still driven by the same instincts as their ancestors, the apes. The chief of these instincts is the will to power which, in the animal world, issues in the struggle to master a hostile environment, but also in competition with other animals of the same type. In man this will has operated unusually successfully thanks to his superior intellect; its visible achievements are the forms of civilization through which man exploits the rest of nature, and within which individuals can assert their supremacy over other individuals. However, man's intellect is an ambiguous distinction, since it can undermine the achievements of the will by making men aware of the imperfections in their creations or, worse still, by prompting man to ask what the ultimate object of all his activity is. The resultant boredom with material achievements is what gives rise to the wild 'metaphysical struggle' that forms the main action of *In the Jungle*. The two principal characters are an ageing Malayan called Shlink. the unscrupulous owner of a successful timber-business,

---

[11]*Im Dickicht der Städte. Erstfassung und Materialien* (Frankfurt am Main, 1968), p. 134.

and a young white man[12] named George Garga, who ekes out a living for himself and his family (recently immigrated into Chicago 'from the plains') by working, sporadically, as an assistant in a dingy lending library. Shlink initiates the fight with Garga by offering him money in exchange for a literary opinion, because, having spent a lifetime achieving power and security, Shlink is suffering the effects of his own success: boredom, alienation, a diminished sense of being alive as a result of the habitual insensitivity he has cultivated in the struggle to rise in the world. He therefore devises, as a last challenge for his still restless will, a struggle to gain possession, not of something tangible, but of another man's mind and feelings, hoping that the intensity of sadomasochistic excitement will provide him with one 'last sensation' (D. 137) before his death, Garga in turn accepts Shlink's challenge because, as a poetry-loving idealist who dreams of escape to a Gauguinesque simple life in Tahiti, he is profoundly disaffected from the world of work, duty and material success.[13] Yet, despite their common desire to defeat one another, the fight peters out in stalemate because the isolation and inaccessibility of the private self make it seem pointless to go on. Whereas victory for an ape was a relatively simple matter of leaving his enemy bleeding in the undergrowth (D. 93) Shlink and Garga can find no way to measure their respective spiritual strengths, nor can they even know when a 'blow' has truly struck home, nor sense how much pain each has caused the other. Thus the outcome of the fight reveals the 'treacherous' nature of the process of evolution: the mind, having enabled man to civilize nature, ultimately deprives him of the satisfactions of simple, instinctual behaviour by seeking out new, unattainable goals which leave the will to power frustrated. The alienation of man from man in the last stages of the fight takes the general process of man's alienation from nature yet one stage further. The cold, hard, inimical city, itself an image of the process of 'de-naturation', provides a fitting backdrop for Shlink and Garga's harsh insights.

The escape by Shlink and Garga from a life of deadening routine shows that, as far as Brecht was concerned, the Expressionist mood of revolt had not simply been superseded by the cynical or sentimental compromises of 'neue Sachlichkeit'. Certainly, Brecht's sympathetic presentation of Kragler's 'sachlich' choice of his bed in preference to the barricades, remains in evidence in his approving attitude to the willingness of Galy Gay, the hero of *Mann ist Mann* (A Man's a Man, 1926), to transform himself into a 'human fighting machine' in order to save his own skin. On the other hand, Brecht's continuing attraction to irrational, self-destructive revolt is equally apparent throughout the twenties; it can be seen in his adaptation of Marlowe's *Life of Edward II*, in *The Threepenny Opera* (in Macheath's recklessness) or in Jim Mahoney's rebellion in *The Rise and Fall of the City of Mahagonny*. Yet it is not only this variability of standpoint from play to play that makes it pointless to divide Brecht's early work into Expressionist and post-Expressionist or 'neusachlich' phases: for there are sharp conflicts of perspective and value within each individual play. *In the Jungle*, for example, mixes cold, ironical contemplation of the irrational tendencies in modern man with excited participation in the characters'

---

[12]Brecht's choice of a white American and an Asian as his chief characters suggests that he intended to allude to the generalizing cultural debates still current in Germany at that time. His treatment of these 'types', however, is characteristically ironic, for he has the Westerner become increasingly passive in the course of the action while the Asian becomes increasingly frenetic.

[13]The theme of escape from Europe to the South Seas is found in a number of plays written out of the mood of depression that followed the War; see H. F. Garten, *Modern German Drama* (London, 1964), p. 174.

impulses. This ambivalence is reflected in the style of the play. The struggle between Shlink and Garga is presented through the imagery of the jungle, the boxing ring, the Wild West and the Chicago underworld, imagery taken from such forms of popular culture as the adventure novel, the sports arena (a source of images exploited also by many other writers of the time), and the thriller. Brecht, a lifelong addict of detective stories, was also working on scripts for film-thrillers just before he began writing *In the Jungle*. *In the Jungle* interprets these forms, the 'mythical amusements of the great cities beyond The Pond' (GW 17, 948), as providing outlets for the aggressive energies built up in man by the frustrations of modern urban existence. But as well as having a cognitive, 'estranging' function, the violent imagery also invites vicarious involvement in the idiosyncratic struggle. Although Brecht would have been horrified at the thought, the mixture of cold analysis and rational excitement of *In the Jungle* is strongly reminiscent of the work of Gottfried Benn, an Expressionist poet of right-wing persuasions whom Brecht detested; ambivalence about the role of the intellect in human evolution is a further important area of agreement. Similarly, Brecht's *Edward II* at times betrays a sympathetic understanding of the savage excitements of war that is closer in spirit to the work of Ernst Jünger (another right-wing writer) than to anything one finds amongst the writers of the Left with whom Brecht's name is habitually linked. Brecht's early tendency to take a very long view of human history, and to describe it in terms of conflict between such general categories as 'brain' and 'instinct' or 'appetite' is also comparable with Spengler's approach to history in his *Decline of the West*, one of the most popular books of the twenties. The continuing influence of Nietzsche is probably the main reason for such similarities of preoccupation. Even allowing that there are also important differences between Brecht's writings in the 1920s and those of Jünger, Benn or Spengler, the perhaps surprising areas of overlap should not be ignored – even if they do make Brecht's place in the literary life of Weimar harder to define.

Brecht's next project after *In the Jungle* was an adaptation of Marlowe's *Life of Edward the Second of England* (1924). Although this may seem a rather out-of-the-way undertaking to engage in at that time it can be related to the contemporary context in three main respects; as one of a number of historical plays, as an adaptation of a classic text, and as a play about a son's revolt against his father. The producer Leopold Jessner had given the contemporary German theatre a lead in developing a bold, up-to-date approach to the staging of revered classic plays. Using Expressionist techniques of stage design and acting he made *Richard III*, *Macbeth*, and Schiller's *Fiesco* into vehicles for powerful statements about issues of pressing concern. Brecht, following Jessner's lead, went even further in asserting the right of the present to imprint its own concerns on works handed down from the past. Characteristically provocative, he advocated an attitude of ruthless 'vandalism' towards the classics (GW 15. 176–84). His own adaptation of *Edward II* exemplifies his determination to have regard only to the 'Materialwert' (usefulness as raw material) of the earlier author's work: he removed or simplified long sections of the plot, transferred functions from one figure to another, radically re-interpreted the central characters' motives, so as to fashion out of Marlowe's chronicle with its concern for the supra-personal issues of kingship, a lurid, ballad-like vision of life as a sado-masochistic tussle between 'pathological' individuals. This use or abuse of history to confirm an author's own optimistic or pessimistic, political or apolitical vision of the world was widespread at the time: Fritz von Unruh's *Louis Ferdinand, Prince of Prussia*. Ernst Toller's *The Machine-Wreckers*, Hans Henny Jahnn's *The Coronation of Richard III*, Alfons Paquet's *Banners* and *Tidal Wave* all belong to this type of 'historical' drama.

Brecht's individualistic view was shared to a considerable extent by Jahnn, although the latter's Richard III broods on evil and guilt in a way that is quite foreign to Brecht's wholly amoral, blood-lusting Edward. As well as representing an affront to the Expressionists' tragic accounts of the role of 'Geist' (spirit) in history, *Edward II* was yet another example of Brecht's malicious pleasure in taking a pattern of action used by the Expressionists and adapting it for his own purposes. Here he used the theme of a son's revolt against his father as the starting point for a life of insurrection against all forms of authority and convention. His hero is motivated not by indignation at paternal corruption and a desire for a better world, but by existential resentment at the world's resistance to his will and by his sheer appetite for battle.

The comedy *Mann ist Mann* (A Man's a Man) is a parable about the instability of personal identity. Brecht completed it (in 1926) at a time when Pirandello's plays were being much performed in Germany, but this was more coincidence than consequence, since Brecht had had the theme and the basic shape of the plot in his mind as early as 1919. In his original conception the action had a more obvious, immediate relation to the contemporary situation in Germany, in that the characters who induce the protagonist to abandon his old identity and accept a new one were at that time to be a group of 'Schieber' (black marketeers), whose business flourished during the chaos of the immediate post-war period. By 1926 Brecht had re-situated the plot in a Kiplingesque (but quite fantastic) India, where three British machine-gunners inveigle Galy Gay, a peaceful and ingenuous Irish stevedore (who conveniently happens to live in Kilkoa!) into joining the British Army under the assumed identity of Jeriah Jip – the name of the original fourth member of the crew who went missing as a result of an unofficial raid on a native temple. The effect of this distancing of the action was to accentuate the generality of the play's social and philosophical concerns: again Brecht's tendency was to carry on the symbolic tradition of Expressionism rather than follow the 'neusachlich' trend towards naturalism, reportage or, at least, the drawing of characters/types from contemporary German life. The unstoppable advance of the British Army through India and on to Tibet was chosen to symbolize the rapid spread of modern civilization across the face of the globe. The essence of this civilization is conveyed by the crowded troop train which eventually carries Galy Gay-alias-Jeriah Jip towards the Tibetan border at the inhuman speed of one hundred day's marches per minute.

However, it is not only modern, mass society that is seen as a machine in the play. So also are the individuals who have to serve its purposes. Thus the stevedore Galy Gay is transformed into the soldier Jip just as a car might be re-fitted or re-built ('ummontiert'). Yet the levers by which the transformation is effected are natural ones: the marauding soldiers play on the hero's appetites and instincts (principally that of self-preservation) in order to make him change his social persona. In fact, the machine of society develops from the machine that is nature. Society as a whole, like each individual in it, is governed by the mechanisms of appetite: it is the lust for 'gold' that brings the Army of the Queen to India, and it is no less important for the Army's advance that the appetite of its tanks for petrol be satisfied than that the needs of its soldiers for food and drink be met. As with the relation of the cold, hard city to the jungle in *In the Jungle*, so the machine that is society does not represent man's perversion or falsification of nature in *A Man's a Man*, but rather a final revelation of the inherently mechanical quality of life. Consequently metaphors taken from the animal sphere ('elephant', 'mammoth') and from the mechanical sphere ('passenger train', 'car') are used interchangeably to characterize the behaviour of Galy Gay throughout the play. In one symbolic set-piece the interrelatedness of these apparently distinct spheres is neatly captured in the image of the mechanical elephant, which plays a crucial role in the transformation of the hero. The point of all this symbolism is to deny that man has any possibility of escaping or transcending his material determination. The mechanical transformation of Galy Gay is a fierce parody of the spiritual 'Wandlung' (transformation) described and aimed at by the idealist Expressionists. At the same time, the intensity of the imagery is quite unlike the shallow, optimistic similes in which 'neusachlich' writers would liken modern man's toughness to that of his machines. For an artistic use of such imagery comparable to Brecht's one needs to turn to the visual arts (e.g. Georg Grosz's 'Republican Automatons').

It has been suggested that *A Man's a Man* reflected two particular phenomena of the 1920s: the introduction of 'Taylorism' into German industry (i.e. the use of time-and-motion studies and conveyor-belt production methods to increase efficiency) and the advent of behaviourist psychology. 'Taylorization' may have influenced the writing of the play, but it would be wrong to place too much emphasis on this. In the first place, the First World War had already demonstrated the power of machines in the modern age, and the increasing uniformity and anonymity which their use entailed. Secondly, *A Man's a Man* is much more concerned with the machine age as a metaphor than with the immediate experience of working in modern factories.[14] As for Behaviourism, there is no evidence that Brecht knew Watson's theories before the 1930s. In fact, since *Behaviourism* was not translated into German until 1930, it is doubtful whether Brecht *could* even have been influenced in 1926 by the new psychology. Quite apart from this, although Brecht applies the model of a machine to human behaviour, he does not eschew the vocabulary of the inner life (hopes, fears, instincts) which it was the aim of Behaviourism in its strict, scientific sense to make redundant.

Where the twenties flavour of *A Man's a Man* is very evident is in the form and style of the play, which show the influence of the silent film farce. Brecht once described the play as 'a comedy just made for the screen' (GW 17, 973) and noted that it should have 'light, tipsy, functional decor, flimsy and provisional. Chaplin'.[15] The basic pattern of the action is that of the chase in which a 'little man' is pursued by bullies on whom he eventually turns the tables; this primitive type of plot could be found in one film comedy after another. Brecht even seems to have attempted to simulate the mechanical quality that life acquired when seen through the lens of an early cine-camera, by introducing an element of stiff stylization into the speech, and sometimes even into the movements of his characters. As usual, however, Brecht's use of a 'low', popular form was anything but naïve. In his hands slapstick farce became a symbolic form, expressive of man's condition as a stand-up, knock-down clown, pushed this way and that by the determining forces in nature's circus. On the other hand, the light, popular form also suited his preference for laughter rather than tears as a response to this vision of life.

Every one of Brecht's early plays made use of music and song to leaven the dough of the spoken word. For *A Man's a Man*, for example, he had composed a song of the same title and had also prescribed that Widow Begbick's daughters play jazz to entertain

---

[14]Interpreters of the play are fond of quoting the lines, 'Technology steps in. Standing at a vice or at a conveyor belt the big man and the little man are equal, even in stature' (GW 1, 340). Yet these lines were not part of the 1926 version, but were added subsequently by Brecht to increase the immediacy of the play's socially critical implications.

[15]Note in the Bertolt Brecht Archive, BBA 150/44.

the customers in their mother's canteen – but also, of course, to provide Brecht's own audience with yet another form of 'Spaß'. But the works in which the characteristic jazz idiom of the 1920s figured most prominently were the operas on which he co-operated with Kurt Weill – *The Threepenny Opera* (1928) and *The Rise and Fall of the City of Mahagonny* (1929). These two pieces were very different in character. The first, which proved to be the theatrical smash-hit of the period, was a quickly dashed-off adaptation of John Gay's *The Beggar's Opera*, designed to make some money for Brecht and Weill and to meet E. R. Aufricht's need for something new and popular with which to launch his re-opening of the 'Theater am Schiffbauerdamm'. This 'lightweight minor work'[16] looks at the world from the cheerfully cynical perspective of picaresque characters who would like to have some romance in their lives but recognize that they cannot afford to entertain any illusions.[17] The hero, Mackie Messer (Mac the Knife), runs his gang of hoodlums with all the ruthlessness of a hard-headed businessman, but allows his heart to rule his head when he insists on dallying with his whores in Turnbridge despite the fact that there is a warrant out for his arrest. This small indulgence in bravado and vanity almost costs him his life in a world where treachery can be bought for a small sum. However, having made his cynical point about human baseness clearly and repeatedly, Brecht (like John Gay before him) finally allows sentiment and good-humour to win the day by having the queen grant the dashing young hero[18] a pardon, which brings him down from the gallows and into the waiting arms of his Polly. Although this parodies the conventional happy ending of operetta, it nevertheless has the effect of gratifying the expectation of a happy ending which is nourished in the audience throughout by the comic tone of the piece (effectively neutralizing most of its satirical potential), and by its presentation of the desire for romance as something quite understandable even if it cannot be realized. This mixture of sentiment and cynicism, which was perfectly matched by Weill's half-parodistic use of popular music, made *The Threepenny Opera* Brecht's most straightforwardly 'neusachlich' work – and paid off handsomely in box-office returns. The bitter-sweet flavour of the opera clearly hit the mood of a public determined to keep a cheerful face despite hard experiences; but this general appeal may also have been enhanced by the refreshing change it offered from the diet of sickly Viennese operettas that theatre and film impresarios were still offering to the public in large quantities.

Unlike *The Threepenny Opera*, *The Rise and Fall of the City of Mahagonny* did not enjoy immediate and broad popularity. Not only was it a much more demanding composition in musical terms, but it also presented the public, as *The Threepenny Opera* did not, with a devastating vision of the malaise of contemporary society. The city of Mahagonny, situated in a mythical Wild West somewhere between Alaska and the gold fields, exposed

---

[16] According to Ernst Robert Aufricht, Brecht himself described the piece in these terms to him; see E. R. Aufricht, *Erzähle damit du dein Recht erweist* (Berlin, 1966), p. 64.

[17] According to the first published version of the opera (Vienna, 1929), the following text was to be projected on to a screen during the overture: 'This evening you are to see an opera for beggars. Because the conception of this opera was as grand as only beggars may dream of, and yet the production had to be cheap enough for beggars to afford it, it bears the title *The Threepenny Opera*'. Thus the very staging of the opera was to reflect symbolically the discrepancy between aspiration and reality.

[18] The notion that Macheath should be presented as a portly, staid member of the middle classes resulted from Brecht's afterthoughts about the piece, which he decided should be given greater clarity as an allegory of the bourgeois way of life. His original conception, by contrast, was of Macheath as a young gentleman, idolized by the ladies (GW 17, 989).

the aggressions and discontents underlying the surface of economic and political 'stabilization' in the Weimar Republic. The opera's analysis of the fundamentally anarchic character of all human relations (which is accentuated, but not created, by the conditions of life under capitalism) poured scorn on the notion that *any* modern civilization can escape destruction by pandering to and exploiting the appetites of its members. While the masses of Galy Gays will be willing for a while to accept a life of mechanical routine in exchange for the satisfaction of their modest appetites, sooner or later men with a more intense hunger for unconstrained happiness and with less easily lulled aggressions will rebel against the human ugliness mirrored in man's creations, and will bring down society in chaos. *Mahagonny* resembles nothing so much as a blasphemous *Messiah*, since it draws extensively on biblical stories to tell a story of the Hell man creates for himself on earth (rather than the story of God's providential care for his Creation). The opera is an anarchist's dream of revenge on the civilization of the great cities, a fantastic re-enactment in a modern idiom of the fall of Sodom, Gomorrha and Babylon, with the playwright taking the role of a gleeful prophet of doom. Yet, although the destruction of Mahagonny is accomplished through the martyrdom of its 'Messiah', Jim Mahoney, 'a simple woodcutter from Alaska', the opera does not end on a note of revolutionary hope, but in virtual cacophony, as the citizens march around in confusion chanting the dirge, 'Can't help a dead man. Can't help you or me or no-one.' Even by the time Brecht completed *Mahagonny* (1929) the existential pain which had been the main stimulus for his imaginative work throughout the twenties had still not been replaced as a motive for writing by an optimistic commitment to revolutionary change.

There was a lively strain of political theatre in the Weimar Republic, beginning with Erwin Piscator's short-lived 'Proletarian Theatre' in Berlin (1920–21). Brecht's name is habitually linked with this aspect of Weimar's theatrical life, yet the evidence concerning his involvement with it is slight, and the evidence about his attitude towards political theatre contradictory, but indicative of reserve or even hostility rather than approval. The materialist-anarchic direction Brecht took after his disaffection from the cause of German Imperialism meant that he was more likely to be generally sympathetic to the political Left than to the Right. His personal 'bolshiness' was much in evidence during his short period of military service as a medical orderly (he was regularly to be seen hatless and wearing yellow gloves in barracks!), so that his comrades thought him the right man to elect on to a local 'soldiers council' during the period of the revolution. According to Brecht's own retrospective account, however, he lacked both political convictions and enthusiasm at the time (GW 20, 25). It is true that he wrote theatre criticisms for the *Augsburger Volkswille*, the organ of the Independent Socialists, in 1920, and in this capacity he urged local trades unionists to support a production of Hauptmann's *Rose Bernd*, a play which he represented as having more 'revolutionary' implications than it really possessed. On the other hand, his notebooks from that period express scorn for the 'little revolutionaries, those who abolish the Kaiser and introduce Communism' (GW 20, 7) and strong antipathy towards Bolshevism, not because of 'the disorder actually achieved there [i.e. in Russia], but the order actually aimed for' (*Diaries*, p. 45). *Drums in the Night*, which puts the case for the individual's rejection of revolutionary self-sacrifice devastatingly well, could be read not only as an attack on Expressionist idealism, but also on the partisan enthusiasm of the political theatre which was just emerging out of Expressionism as Brecht revised his manuscript.

In 1926 Brecht wrote to his collaborator Elizabeth Hauptmann that he was 'fathoms deep in *Capital*', yet in that same year he replied to the repeated assertions emanating from the Left that art should become a weapon in the class struggle with the observation that 'proletarian art is as much art as any other kind: more art than proletarian. It may be useless, and it is quite certain that it *is* useless during a struggle, but art does not care about that' (GW 15, 66). The years 1926–29 are perhaps the most puzzling of his whole career. On the one hand he was involved to a greater or lesser extent in a number of Piscator productions (*Rasputin, Die Abenteuer des braven Soldaten Schweyk, Konjunktur*); he was learning to use Marxist terminology through his discussions with the sociologist Fritz Sternberg; and he was working on several plays (*Fatzer, Weizen, Der Brotladen*) which were concerned with the problems in the relation of the individual to the collective or with the mechanisms of the capitalist economy, but all of which remained fragmentary. On the other hand, his theoretical writings in this period were critical of Piscator's 'old-fashioned' (i.e. emotive and naturalistic) deployment of his own technologically advanced staging techniques, while Brecht's completed creative works (none of which were produced by Piscator despite his desperate need for suitable texts) show no evidence of commitment to the proletarian cause before the middle of 1929 (i.e. up to and including the *Lindberghflug*). The lack of any political commitment in Brecht's twenties work is matched by the tenuousness or even hostility of his relations with literary groups or trends throughout this period. It is reported, for example, that he took an active part in the discussions held by the 'geistesradikale' (intellectually radical) 'Gruppe 25' (1925 Group), yet his name does not appear on any list of signatories to the group's public pronouncements on matters of public interest.[19] Independence had become his watchword after his early fateful commitment to the Imperial cause, so that, no matter how much he might be persuaded that the coming age would be a collectivist one, any fresh commitment was extremely difficult for him to make. Hence the relatively long period of his 'courtship' with Marxist ideas; hence also the radicalism and completeness of his commitment when the catastrophic events of 1929 forced a decision on him. It was not only as a good Latinist that he knew the truth of the tag *Hic Rhodus, hic salta*.

When Brecht began to write plays of a revolutionary tendency his work was certainly influenced by his forerunners in the field of political theatre, but it also continued to have a marked individuality. Although he made use of Piscator's technical innovations (the split stage, projections, film, the moving and rotary stages, loudspeakers) he laid more stress on enabling the spectator to gain a complex, dialectical understanding of social processes, than on his political passions. However, such distinctions were not hard and fast in every instance; *Saint Joan of the Stockyards*, for instance, was both analytic and agitational. Similarly, when he began to write short didactic pieces ('Lehrstücke') he did not conform to the 'Agitprop' practice of dramatizing topics of immediate political controversy, but preferred to aim at a deeper and more lasting form of political (and aesthetic) education. His 'Lehrstücke' were written to train their performers in the dialectical mode of thinking rather than to indoctrinate a passive audience with ready-made political slogans.

What I have emphasized in this account of Brecht's dramatic work in the 1920s is his non-conformism – what he himself described as his 'Widerspruchsgeist' (spirit of contradiction). Although certain features of his plays can be thought of as 'neusachlich' and others as 'expressionistic', their peculiar mixture of cynicism and passion, realism and stylization means that the individual plays mostly cannot be taken as exemplifying

---

[19]See K.-P. Hinze, 'Gruppe 1925. Notizen und Dokumente', *Deutsche Vierteljahresschrift*, 1980, Heft 2, pp. 334–46.

either trend. It also means that one cannot speak of a clear development in his work from Expressionism through 'Neue Sachlichkeit' during the twenties. This long period of recalcitrant individualism may be seen as the precondition for the radicalism and innovatory character of his eventual conception of political theatre. Had he aligned himself with the reformist, compromising 'sobriety' of 'Neue Sachlichkeit', it is unlikely that he would have become free to develop in a revolutionary direction at the beginning of the 1930s. Equally, had he been drawn into an early commitment to revolutionary politics, as the erstwhile anarchist Franz Jung had been, he might well have gone through the same process of disillusionment and disaffection from the Communist movement.[20] On the other hand, if fewer Germans had shared Brecht's dislike of compromise, there might have been no need eventually to make radical political choices for the red or the brown. Although it expressed itself in an individualistic manner, the cult of irrationalism in Brecht's early plays, up to and including *Mahagonny*, was part of a wider irrationalist tendency running through large sections of Weimar society. Before 1929 Brecht refused to contribute positively to the development of Germany's first democratic republic; indeed he cannot escape some small share of the blame for stoking the fires which eventually destroyed it.

---

[20]See Horst Denkler, 'Der Fall Franz Jung. Beobachtungen zur Vorgeschichte der "Neuen Sachlichkeit"' in *Die sogenannten Zwanziger Jahre*, ed. Grimm and Hermand (Bad Homburg, 1970).

CHAPTER EIGHT

Review of *Drums in the Night*

HERBERT IHERING
TRANSLATED BY ROMY FURSLAND

The exceptional success of Bert Brecht's comedy *Drums in the Night* was new evidence of the fact that, when you take risks, art that is real and powerful will always win out. The young Augsburger Bert Brecht is now twenty-four years old. When he wrote *Drums in the Night* he was twenty, and in this play, set in Berlin during the Revolution, there is no partisanship, no hint of a declamatory tone. All is expression and craftsmanship. Of the many German plays about the Revolution, this is the only one that remains poetic. One reason for Berlin's theatre directors not to stage this play in particular, then. An even more important reason given that the dramatic effect is obvious at first reading. And the most important reason to praise Otto Falckenberg and the Munich Kammerspiele who, in staging this first performance of Bert Brecht's work, have done more for German drama in recent times than all Berlin's theatres put together. Mr Erwin Faber, in the leading role, was frequently exceptional. And this is not just a flash in the pan. Bert Brecht has also written two other plays, which only serve to strengthen the impact of the first.

Herbert Ihering
Berliner Börsen-Courier, 2 October 1922

Never has the tension between the experience of an era and its expression been as great as in our time. But our age was not accused of the crime of unproductiveness for as long as a certain slackness was seen as an understandable reaction to the nervous strain of the war years. People criticised the younger generation and failed to appreciate that it was having to fight harder than any other in the last hundred years. Not necessarily for its material existence. Not necessarily for its spiritual worth. But for something that no other generation – except the one that came after the Thirty Years' War – had been denied access to: experience itself. The horror of the preceding years was not the collapse of a nation but the inability to experience fundamental things in a fundamental way. People were so drained of energy that they experienced apocalyptic events as if they were everyday inconveniences. The worst thing is not pain: it is the inability to feel pain.

Only when we understand the spiritual fate of recent years in this way will we be able to engage with our present-day drama. Only when we acknowledge the grotesqueness

---

Herbert Ihering, '[Review of *Drums in the Night*]', in Monika Wyss, *Brecht in der Kritik* (Munich: Kindler, 1977), pp. 4–6.

of an era that cannot hear its own noises, cannot see its own grimace, can we properly understand its writers. They were isolated, trying to stretch their language across spaces in time where experience could not penetrate. The paroxysm was necessary and had to be resolved at the same moment as the era itself began to dissolve.

There is no doubt that this resolution has begun. It started in poetry. It continued in the novel. And now the miracle begins. There are no coincidences. But even those who felt instinctively that the era must soon break out of its unproductive torpor, even those who had already recognised the creative urge and explosive temperament in Bronnen's work must surely be overwhelmed by the intellectual transformation which a genius can effect with his very first act. The twenty-four-year-old writer Bert Brecht has changed the face of German literature overnight, and brought to our age a new sound, a new melody, a new vision.

The really significant artistic event is not the fact that Bert Brecht, in his first play *Drums in the Night*, gives form to contemporary events that have only been spoken about up to now. It is the fact that the era itself is present as background, as atmosphere, even in the dramas that go beyond contemporary subject matter. Brecht feels the horror of our age in every sinew; it is in his blood. This horror surrounds people, it fills spaces, as ashen air and half-light. It collects in the pauses between lines, in the breaks between scenes. It releases the characters and then swallows them up again. The figures phosphoresce.

Brecht has a physical sense of chaos and decay. Hence the unparalleled vividness of his language. You feel this language on your tongue, in your gums, in your ears, down your spine. It does without conjunctions, ripping perspectives wide open. It is brutally sensual and melancholically tender. There is baseness in it and unfathomable sorrow. Grim humour and plaintive lyricism.

Brecht sees people. But always through the lens of their impact on other people. Brecht's characters never function in isolation. It is a long time since Germany has had a writer so unconditionally bound by these two tragic imperatives: the intertwining of people's destinies and the effect people have on each other.

The mark of Brecht's genius is that his plays constitute a new artistic totality with its own laws, its own dramaturgy. His plays – including *Drums in the Night*, and especially *Baal* and *In the Jungle* – are new celestial bodies in our literary sky. Revealing the laws that control their orbits, and defining the new sense of space (space looms up behind people and overgrows them) and the new structuring of scenes, are tasks for another time. My aim here is to recognise a dramatist whose work is the most stirring, unsettling experience since Wedekind. Who is ostensibly cynical and who moves you with his cynicism. Who is young, but has already peered into the darkest depths of the abyss. Whom you need to hear singing his own songs and poems while accompanying himself on the guitar, if you truly want to feel the exhilarating rhythms of his sentences. Who strips people bare and lets them speak, but with an eloquence and power the like of which we have not heard for decades. In Brecht's plays, you know from the very first word that a tragedy has begun.

The Munich Kammerspiele will go down in theatrical history for having been the first to stage Brecht. Otto Falckenberg had an ear for the sombre melody of the play, although not all the actors were able to carry it off. Some, like the provincial Mr Gluth, blurred the elemental images of Brecht's language by speaking naturalistically, as if these images had only just occurred to them. Falckenberg had a feeling for the characters' attitudes to one another, but not for the scenery – or for the breadth of staging which would have shown the characters in their proper perspectives (as is crucial with Brecht). But Falckenberg did have the right actor for the leading role. Mr Erwin Faber played the returning prisoner of war, who finds his fiancée in the arms of a brash profiteer, with a bewildered tension that was wonderful to watch. His acting is as effortless as it is intense, and he never says a word that is not physically legitimised. He could not quite carry off the risky ending: the prisoner of war turns his back on the revolution and goes back to his fiancée, a fallen woman. Perhaps this is a result of unfortunate cuts made by Brecht himself, and a somewhat obscure composition. In any case, here is an actor whom Berlin has much greater need of than those dull gentlemen from Frankfurt.

Alongside Faber, Hans Leibelt played the profiteer with precision and a human touch, while Max Schreck of the Staatstheater in Berlin, who appeared once again 'on loan' in Munich, indulged in some rather cheap and artificial grotesquerie.

Herbert Ihering
Berliner Börsen-Courier, 5 October 1922

CHAPTER NINE

Review of *The Threepenny Opera*

MONTY JACOBS
TRANSLATED BY ROMY FURSLAND

If new director *Ernst Aufricht* goes on to fulfil the promise of this auspicious opening night, then we might just have the next Piscator on our hands at the Schiffbauerdamm. Everything about last night's performance sparkled with boldness, spirit and verve, and there was no conspicuous toeing of the party line.

Bert Brecht shares in this great jackpot, and here we must repeat the refrain you hear after every lottery win: he was due a bit of luck. For this problematic young talent, an artist through and through, and one of the few writers of our younger generation to bear the hallmarks of genius, was in dire need of another theatrical success. Brecht found it in his reworking of a foreign source text – in a work, therefore, which was by no means his most ambitious. But it is in this work that the best elements of Bert Brecht come to the fore: the poet, the minstrel, the balladeer. Admirers of his poetry volume *Manual of Piety* will find the same explosive art in *The Threepenny Opera*, and in a purer form than in Brecht's frostier comedy *Man Equals Man*.

This 'play with music' is based on *The Beggar's Opera*, a two-hundred-year-old work by the English pastoral poet John Gay. Brecht and Weill's musical comedy, like its British source, is set among a gang of beggars. Only at the end do playwright and composer take liberties with the old parody, which satirises the heroic opera style of Italian touring companies. Meanwhile, Brecht is in his element: writing ballads. His Mackie is the head of a criminal gang responsible for countless misdeeds. But at the same time he is such an elegant, gallant gentleman that *Harald Paulsen* is perfectly cast in the role. In both the *haut monde* and the *demimonde*, hearts skip a beat when Mackie starts to sing. How could Polly – the daughter of a shady gentleman for whom begging in London is a monopoly business – ever hope to resist Mackie? He marries her in a stable, just as he has married many another girl who took it into her head to insist on matrimony. His friend, the sheriff and chief of police, shares in the profits of the gang's operations, and so covers up all their crimes. Only Mackie's former lovers in the brothels persist in turning him in to the police, who would prefer to turn a deaf ear to their accusations. When Mackie finally does find himself on the gallows with his neck in the noose, his fate lamented by several soon-to-be

---

Monty Jacobs, '[Review of *The Threepenny Opera*]', in Monika Wyss, *Brecht in der Kritik* (Munich: Kindler, 1977), pp. 80–2.

widows, the King's Messenger rides in and saves his life. For the King's coronation is being held in London that day, and his Majesty is all the happier to pardon a poor sinner given what a brilliant parody this motif makes of the romantic opera finale.

In this play, which touches on the heaviest of themes, everything is light, and precisely because everything seems so drenched in bitterness, everything is funny. This world, in which a murderous gangster is the most respectable character, wears a jaundiced grin. Fortunately, though, the dark mood produces some excellent gallows humour. The human misery of begging, the human injustice of crime – everything is a business, a well-organised corporate entity. Because the tragedy neutralises itself, however, the atmosphere of this play is so saturated in tragedy that it eventually turns into humour. It is a humour that makes us sit up and think, an atmosphere that goes straight to the heart when the ballad blasts its moral into the audience: don't be too harsh on wrongdoing! Or when, in the strongest finale of the evening, the hungry try to prick the consciences of the full: food is the first thing, morals follow on!

This time, having learnt from experience, Brecht cites balladeers whom he translates: his old source of inspiration Kipling, and Francois Villon, to whom he dedicates such a heartfelt epitaph in the *Manual of Piety*. But the ballads written in his own style, which are interspersed so casually throughout *The Threepenny Opera*, seal the triumph of the evening.

Their integration into the play is one of the major achievements of *Erich Engel*'s production. He works hand in hand with the set designer *Caspar Neher*; positions the orchestra, half hidden behind a mock organ, on the open stage; and draws a shabby little canvas curtain across the whole thing. No machinery, no pretensions: the perfect frame for Brecht's picture. Only the two film projections, a nod to Piscator, miss the mark. Their texts and images are superfluous and at the same time inaccessible. Take them out!

Erich Engel does not need any film titles, not when he is able to get his actors to translate all his intentions so effectively. He has sourced them from all over Germany: *Erich Ponto* from Dresden plays the begging boss, and looks like a shorter Curt Götz, playing tragedy instead of comedy: he is a confident gallows humourist. From the world of cabaret come the sheriff, *Kurt Gerron*, and his daughter, *Kate Kuhl*, both seasoned performers with plenty of experience in singing a chorus and dramatising a ballad. *Harald Paulsen* is borrowed from the operetta; he looks more like Domela the imposter prince than the leader of a criminal gang, but his amiability makes him master of the situation. And who else could play the queen of the beggars, who seeks solace for her woes at the bottom of a bottle, but *Rosa Valetti*? The role of a gangster's moll without any preconceptions calls for an actress of Roma Bahns' spirit. In the casting of the outlaws and beggars (Hannemann, Fürst, Lehrmann) and the spokeswoman of the whorehouse, Erich Engel proves himself adept at promoting new talent.

A good omen for the rest of the run: new boldness where once there was stagnation.

Monty Jacobs
Vossische Zeitung, Berlin, 3 September 1928

The *Lehrstücke*

CHAPTER TEN

On the Theory of the *Lehrstück*

BERTOLT BRECHT
TRANSLATED BY ROMY FURSLAND

The key thing about the *Lehrstück* is that people learn by acting in it, not by watching it. In principle the *Lehrstück* does not need any spectators, although they can of course be put to good use.

The *Lehrstück* is based on the expectation that the person acting in it can be socially influenced by the experience of performing certain behaviours, adopting certain attitudes, giving certain speeches etc.

Imitating highly skilled role models has a key part to play in this, as does critiquing such role models by deliberately acting in a different way.

The *Lehrstück* certainly need not be limited to reproducing behaviours and attitudes that are seen as socially positive; reproducing antisocial behaviours and attitudes (as magnificently as possible) can also be instructive.

Aesthetic standards for character development which apply to dramatic theatre are not applicable to the *Lehrstück*. Particularly unique or idiosyncratic characters do not feature in the *Lehrstück*, unless uniqueness and idiosyncrasy are themselves the learning problem.

The form of the *Lehrstück* is rigid, but only to make it easier for the performers to incorporate sections of their own invention or of a contemporary nature. (In *The Horatians and the Curiatians*, for example, the generals can engage in an improvised verbal duel before each of the battles; in *The Decision*, entire scenes can be added as desired, etc.)

In terms of acting style, the same instructions apply as for *epic theatre*. A knowledge of the V-effect is indispensable.

It is crucial to have an intellectual command of the entire play. It is not advisable, however, to settle on what is to be learned before actually acting it.

In principle, the learning effect can also be achieved if the performer is partnered with people appearing on film.

The musical accompaniment can be played mechanically. On the other hand, it can be instructive for musicians to provide the music for mechanical images (on film), as

---

Brecht, 'Zur Theorie des Lehrstücks', in Brecht, *Schriften*, vol. 2 (Berlin and Frankfurt/Main: Aufbau and Suhrkamp, 1993), pp. 351–2.

this gives them the opportunity to try out variations of their own invention within the framework of what is needed for the performance.

In terms of the acting, too – subject to certain conditions – the aim is for the actors' performances to be free, natural and individual. The point, of course, is not to train people in a mechanical way or to produce average types, even if the aim is to produce high average quality.

Tremendous variety is possible in the *Lehrstück*. During the production of *The Baden-Baden Lesson on Consent*, the playwright and the composer stood onstage and kept intervening. The playwright publicly told the clowns where to perform their act, and as the crowd – with great reluctance and unease – watched the film showing dead people, the playwright instructed the narrator to call out at the end: 'The depiction of death which was received with reluctance will be viewed for a second time' and the film was played again.

CHAPTER ELEVEN

The Lehrstück as Performance

ANDRZEJ WIRTH
TRANSLATED BY MARTA ULVAEUS

I

Reading Brecht's *Lehrstücke* as thesis pieces has become an established tenet of German studies even though there are disagreements over the status of the theses in Brecht's texts. Should they be understood in terms of content or form: as political appeals or as formal exercises in the art of the dialectic (see Steinweg 1972)? But there is also a third possibility: Perhaps the short pieces are performance drafts with intentionally controversial governing principles that have the power to generate a performance (as acceptance or rebellion). Drama therapy as pedagogy: Lehrstück texts are therapeutic sound poems. This hypothesis deserves to be interrogated.

The critical discourse in German studies has overlooked that the Lehrstücke are libretti and can be interpreted only in relation to the vocal, musical, and choreographic performance: The music and the orientation toward particular target groups make the Lehrstücke applied texts, explainable simply in terms of performance practice. The originally envisioned target groups of the Lehrstücke (for example, the workers' choruses of the Weimar Republic) belong to the past. What is learned from a Lehrstück (as 'thesis' or experience) depends upon the composition of the actual target group.

In the Lehrstück project, two utopian concepts meet: the theatre as metatheatre, and society as changeable. Both are equally radical: theatre should function without an audience, society without classes. The short pieces written from 1926 to 1933 are formally the most innovative in Brecht's oeuvre. In the last seven years of his life, Brecht, a theoretical socialist, was confronted with the political practice of a state which called itself socialist. He was able to live in a small state that understood itself as a Lehrstück and had to learn that such a state needed no Lehrstücke from its poets. But this realization doesn't discredit the significance and importance of the initial grand design for a new theatre practice. The abstract style of the Lehrstücke proved to be forward-looking. As a utopia for the theatre, the project stimulated work that, since the 1960s, has taken different forms in both theatrical and paratheatrical practice. The spread of encounter workshops (self-awareness groups) since the '60s, despite having a different objective, has perpetuated the idea of self-sufficient role-play.

Formal affinities are evident in the abstract dramaturgy of Gertrude Stein and the aesthetic of Robert Wilson (repetitions, symmetry of the acts, singing). It is not surprising that Robert Wilson directed *Der Ozeanflug* [The Flight over the Ocean] with the Berliner Ensemble in 1998. The abstract dramaturgy of the Lehrstücke anticipates the later, fully developed theory of *Verfremdung* [alienation] and uses much sharper alienation effects than those of the large parable pieces. *Verfremdungseffekte* in the Lehrstücke refer not only to the *Gestus* of the singing and the music composed for the text. They also concern movements, which are not presented as action but as the report of action that has already taken place. Further, Verfremdung is achieved through role exchange. The composition is based on the montage of diverse elements: chorus, quoted dialogue, quoted movements and situations, aria-like solo numbers, commentaries, and so on. The diversity and flexibility of these loosely assembled elements is a distinguishing feature of this novel module-dramaturgy.

The 'modular' structure of the short pieces – they are constructed of symmetrical units – allows for shifts of elements, depending upon the play's arrangement. If one takes Brecht at his word, as expressed in his theory, then the Lehrstücke (completely apart from the fact that they were initially performed for the public) potentially constitute a theatre without an audience – that is, without passive spectators. Lehrstücke once more raise the issue of representation in the theatre: no characters, no roles with the call for identification, actions rather than an action – what is represented is the learning process.

The space of the Lehrstücke is a play space beyond a conventional dichotomy of the stage and the auditorium. In the ideal Lehrstück, performing and watching are two modalities of theatrical acting. *Erfahrungs*-theatre is the antithesis of *Erlebnis*-theatre.[1] For this reason, attempts to perform the Lehrstücke in the conventional theatre space are problematic, even if they were originally performed in such spaces – for example, *Die Maßnahme* [The Measures Taken] at the Berliner Philharmonie, 13–14 December 1930. Lehrstücke were once a subversive form of the alternative culture. The performance strategies used in *The Measures Taken* included the incorporation of the workers' chorus trained in classical repertoire (Bach, Händel), the use of bourgeois opera soloists, and a change of venue to a conventional concert hall (Berliner Philharmonie) with high admissions prices.[2] One can assume that the actual (not to be equated with the intended) learning process of the Lehrstücke – also in Brecht's time – referred more to the 'camaraderie of performance' than to ideological indoctrination. Today, any pedagogical effort in the performed Lehrstücke, if at all effective, refers to the ethos of artistic collaboration and not to indoctrination. The critical interrogation of the material in today's 'postideological era' is what distinguishes a Lehrstück from a conventional production.

Lehrstücke should be seen as works of aesthetic and ideological (in that order) dissidence. These works are still avant-garde and relevant; this is confirmed by looking at the music as well as the libretti and their dramatic form. I suspect, although I cannot prove, that they were much more effective as an act of artistic rather than ideological

---

[1] A rare instance of a notion which can be expressed more concisely in German than in English. Approximately: learning by playing versus being impressed by a play; experience versus impression; didactic theatre versus culinary theatre; *Lehrstück* versus spectacle; theatre for doers (active) versus theatre for spectators (reactive), etc. This connotatively rich dichotomy is fundamental for the Brechtian Lehrstück/*Schaustück* discourse.

[2] There were three Berliner workers' choruses: the Gemischte Chor Großberlin, the Schubert Chor, and the Fichte Chor. The popular tenor of the bourgeois repertoires, Anton Maria Topitz, was cast as the singer instead of Ernst Busch.

dissidence. The Brechtian Lehrstück project is a utopian plan under the conditions of compromise.

Lehrstücke are realized through scenic presentation and stage presence (the Gestus); in other words, through performance. The music locks out the freedom of improvisation and is not only a distancing but also a disciplining medium. In my experience with Lehrstück projects students often want to perform their own music, which I consider to be pedagogically legitimate and perhaps an elegant approach: self-devised discipline in the performance.

The central problem of the *Fatzer* material[3] and *Measures Taken* – spontaneity versus doctrine – becomes primarily artistic exercise in the performed presentation. Through the introduction of voice and music, the dogmatic edge of the writing is raised from the ideological to the aesthetic level of multimedia. So: Aestheticization of ideology with the medium of the Lehrstück? Style as the final determinant of the message? The aestheticization of ideology would become a disruptive factor in a pedagogy that is based on the Socratic method (*Meäutik*) of ascertaining the truth. But such a pedagogy is not Brecht's concern. Brecht's theory of the Lehrstücke is more radical than what was practiced in the productions of his lifetime, involving strategic and cultural political compromises. Their utopian radical core is the unrepeatable, autarkic metatheatre without audience, in which the performers function as actors and spectators. The performed Lehrstück coheres into a performance piece par excellence once the singing, *Sprechgesang* [Speech-song], quoted dialogue, orchestration, and choreographed movement (without intending a *Gesamtkunstwerk*) are united as a fully realized multimedia play.

Lehrstücke are sound poems with music, and their most rigorous guiding principles are composed according to the rule of homophony. The 'Yes' of the boy in *Jasager* [He Who Said Yes] is not abstractable from its performed recitation. It is in fact articulated with a childish alto voice in response to the basso profundo of the chorus. (The act of the agreement is relativized and made suspect through seduction and intimidation.)

Seduction and intimidation of the young by adults appears only at the level of presentation, that is, the performance – the performed text becomes multidimensional. The sentences that come across as theses lose their dogmatic call and become performance material wanting to be sung – the musicalizing and singing invalidating ideology. Danced ideological deviations from the party line (Fatzer's walks, the young comrade's break of discipline[4]) become a musical or choreographic event. Stepping out of the collective becomes a Dionysian dancer's step out of the chorus.

This movement of the anti-ecstatic Brecht toward Nietzsche's aesthetic (evident in performance only) at first comes as a surprise. But then one notices an astonishing parallel in the conception of the chorus. For Nietzsche, 'the dithyrambic chorus is a chorus of the

---

[3]Brecht's *Fatzer* material consists of over 500 pages of unpublished fragments, notes, and sketches from 1926–1929 stored in the Bertolt Brecht Archive in Berlin and in Harvard University's Houghton Library. They are from two incomplete play projects: a Schaustück version of 1927 and a Lehrstück version of 1929. Published for the first time in its entirety in volume 10 of *Werke* (BFA 10), Brecht had considered *Die Maßnahme* and *Fatzer* as the most formally advanced projects of his oeuvre.

[4]In *Fatzer*, four soldiers, radicalized by their experience of WWI, desert from the front and go underground. They expect that a general uprising of the people will put an end to their predicament. The revolution never comes and the isolated self-appointed commune becomes increasingly fanatical and internally divided through the opposition of an individualist Fatzer. Ultimately, Fatzer is killed by his comrades shortly before they die by the bullets of the legalists. Fatzer's deviations from the commune are represented naively as Fatzer's 'strolls'.

transformed, who have completely forgotten their civic past, their social status' (1972, 1:61). It corresponds exactly to the Brechtian notion of the control chorus in the Lehrstücke.

With the anti-ecstatic Brecht there is yet another similarity to Nietzsche, which is noticeable only in the practical work with a Lehrstück performer. The intended adept of the Lehrstück becomes a multimedia performer: He or she makes music, sings, and dances, like a Dionysian actor who has danced himself free from the chorus (Fatzer's walks and their interpretation by my Australian students are an example: Fatzer's monologue performed as a cowboy's song from a Western).

The way the Lehrstück was performed during Brecht's lifetime stood in contradiction to the radicality of its theory, which emphasizes a sharp contrast between the *Schaustück* [a play for the benefit of the audience] and the Lehrstück [for the benefit of the players]. The radical core of Brecht's utopian theory is the idea of an autarkic (self-sufficient) metatheatre, a utopian objective accompanied by a utopian ideology. Brecht's amateur players, members of the workers' choruses of the Weimar Republic, were formed by a culture which, through the liturgy of Protestantism (church singing) and the bourgeois 'house music', partly dissolved the contradiction between the professional and nonprofessional. Thus the musicians and the singers in the choruses were at that time adepts for whom this was not a principal occupation. But they understood enough about their hobby to be effective collaboratively. One must also remember the large number of small school brass bands that existed then. The instrumentation in *The Measures Taken* refers to these resources in the society at that period – Hanns Eisler's use of traditional forms, ecclesiastical modes, and brass players strong enough to assert themselves against the chorus.

The musical strategy of this Lehrstück was to win the singing workers over to the proletarian repertory by using the apparatus of the bourgeois music culture – the Philharmonie as performance venue, high admissions prices, casting a famous operetta tenor as a soloist, and piano accompaniment. The piano was considered a bourgeois instrument at that time, while the shawm orchestra was considered proletarian, beloved as much among the Communists as among the Nazis. It is necessary to know the historical background of the Lehrstücke, but this knowledge is not very helpful when working on Lehrstücke today, with different target groups and in a changed political and ideological context.

II

My theses regarding the Lehrstück are based on 25 years of experience in theoretical and practical work at major universities in four countries and on three continents. The target group was always college students, undergraduates as well as graduates – and the performance resulted mostly from the semester-long theoretical engagement with the material. My work on the university campuses was allowed to proceed under optimal conditions, with access to libraries, rehearsal spaces, and technical equipment for scenic production and documentation of the work. Yet there was no expectation to produce something judged as a 'success'. The spirit of the work was experimental. Students joined from various departments – drama, arts, modern languages, sciences – with theatre and German studies students rarely forming the majority. I understood my work with the Lehrstück to be a process in which at every stage one sought another way into the material (always *Measures* and the *Fatzer* material in translation), taking into account the results of the previous work.

In 1973, I worked on Eric Bentley's adapted English translation of *The Measures Taken* with CUNY (City University of New York) dance department students. Unfortunately, the rights to Eisler's music could not be obtained. The work developed in the direction of a danced oratorio – with strict, formal choreography and the text performed as a sound poem – and became a practical exploration of inwardly directed communication (what I call 'intrinsic communication').

The campus gymnasium was chosen as an optimal location for the rehearsals and performance. Bleachers served for the placement of the chorus whose speakers made a larger-than-life impression. Four female dancers played the roles of the agitators on a very small platform set in the middle of the gym. Sightlines between the dancers and the chorus ran from below to above in a diagonal line that ran over the heads of the 'invitees' sitting on the floor (we avoided the term 'audience'). In this way we hoped to integrate the guests into the communicative events of the play and to make them an expanded 'control chorus'. The New York work made evident the piece's potential as a movement score. Sprechgesang (Speech-song) and recitation took the place of the missing music, and the stiff style of the chorus formed the counterpoint to the composed movement pattern of the dancers. Thus the players' performative temperament was strongly expressed within the frame of a disciplining, self-contained, communicative structure, without any reference to outsiders.

In 1976 at Stanford University, I arranged the *Fatzer* Lehrstück fragments (an unpublished translation by myself, A. Leslie Willson, and David J. Ward) in a television studio, the result of semester-long work with the students (see Wirth 1978). About two dozen invited guests from the campus were allowed to interact with the performers, according to the rules of the performance. They could recite chorus fragments with the actors and were encouraged to ad-lib interruptions during the short dramatic scenes. Cast and guests were gathered in front of the music stands holding the text scores. The circle this formed became the actual performance space. It was an attempt to bring the guests and performers together in performance, another contrast to the New York experiment, where the guests were, in a manner of speaking, played *over* by the performers.

In 1977 in London, at Bedford College, using the *Fatzer* material, we attempted a form of collective autoperformance in an audiovisual studio, performed in the manner of a reading. The recorded material then became the topic of critical discussion. We then analyzed the poetic text as performance, which would barely have been possible without vocal participation.

A year later, at St Antony's College in Oxford, I confronted the students with the following question: Is a strictly structured performance without rehearsal and based on a computer-generated, randomly fragmented text possible? The guests, who didn't know the text, became performers, directed by the computer cards with simple movement requests and splinters of text (electronically produced random sentence fragments). This experiment confirmed the uncommon evocative power of Brecht's language as performance material. Despite the arbitrary and aleatory deconstruction of the play text, the unsuspecting performers were in a position to describe the idea of the deconstructed work in the subsequent questioning period. The Oxford experiment was a novel instance of a learning-theatre, derived from the Lehrstück and implicit in Lehrstück theory – without rehearsal and without an audience.

One year later, at the Freie Universität Berlin, the *Fatzer* fragments were the subject of a collective reading. The work was transferred from a seminar room into a rehearsal space in a fashion of 'mechanical speaking' (*Sprech–Maschine*). The participants, some of them sympathizers of the terrorist scene, were encouraged to bring their choice of props. So great was their desire to take part theatrically in the execution of a deviationist, individualist Fatzer, that some brought infantry helmets and guns. In contrast, the American students at Stanford three years earlier had regarded Fatzer's deviations as a slight offense, which at most could be punished with a parking ticket. The Lehrstück as performance thus opened ever new intercultural insights.

In 1987 at the Institut für Angewandte Theaterwissenschaft in Gießen, my students and I undertook the project of adapting the *Fatzer* material as a mixed form of radio-play and installation. There were no live performers. The tape-recorded voices of the arrangers were played endlessly for the random passersby, from a tape-loop cassette in a dark room. Once again the evocative value of Brecht's text was affirmed – sentences, screams, interruptions that force one to pause and reflect:

> hier ist nichts
> hier ist stille
> kein mensch, sie sind
> alle hin, die da waren;
> ich esse mit
> das ist die neue zeit.
> der denkende man sitzt in dunklen kammern
> mit dem gesicht zur wand.
> ich will nicht sterben
> ich bin fatzer.
> es war kein urteil
> es war die maßnahme [...].

(BFA 10:523)

> [here is nothing
> here is silence
> not a soul, they are all gone who were there;
> I eat with you
> this is the new age.
> the thinking one is sitting in a dark chamber
> with his face to the wall.
> I don't want to die
> I am fatzer.
> there was no verdict
> it was the measure taken (...).]

At the invitation of the Centre for Performance Studies at Sydney University, in 1994, in collaboration with the choreographer Emma Lew Thomas from UCLA, I arranged a student performance mined from the *Fatzer* material. We investigated the possibilities of choreographed movement in a play without an outside spectator; we called it intrinsic communication. The premise was that movement precedes language. The results of this workshop were videotaped and presented to the participants of an international German studies conference in a closed, one-hour performance debut. This experiment could be considered evidence that even in an area remote from European ideological discourse, the performance strategies of a Lehrstück lead to stimulating results (see Thomas and Wirth 1994).

III

In the last few years one could see productions of the Lehrstücke in Berlin, which have contributed to a renewed assessment of both the potential and the limitations of this theatre form. The Berliner Ensemble produced *The Measures Taken* (1997) using Eisler's full score, which had not been played in full since the piece was banned in 1993.

Only when one interprets the Lehrstücke as thesis pieces, ignoring that they are libretti, do these short pieces seem obsolete and to a certain extent compromised by the collapse of the ideology inscribed in them. Henning Rischbieter interprets *The Measures Taken* in the current Berliner Ensemble production as 'empathy with Stalinism' (1997).

The recent productions of the Lehrstücke are appearing under different circumstances. Today it is possible to free the Lehrstücke from the compromises of the past and to bring them up to the standard of, as I call it, the autarkic metatheatre. When you arrange the Lehrstücke as performance libretti and not as tools of indoctrination, their performative potential, like the revolt of the young comrade, breaks through all barriers of doctrine.

It is fundamentally wrong to produce the Lehrstücke on the stages of conventional theatres. Even worse is watching professional actors play the parts meant for amateurs, as in the Berliner Ensemble production. The chief merit of the Berliner Ensemble production is their brilliant execution of the very difficult vocal and musical score, which doesn't leave out a single note of Eisler's music. That is the work of the highly talented professionals in the chamber ensemble Neue Musik Berlin, the concert choir of the Staatsoper, 'Chorus anticus', and the music dramaturg Lucchesi.

The only amateur singer in the production was, paradoxically, the career actor of the Berliner Ensemble, Götz Schulte. Schulte, who was singing arias for the first time, was cheered as a star soloist by the audience at the premiere as well as by the critics. Regrettably, I saw the production again a month later and realized that the delightful naiveté of the actor had transformed into pretentious overacting. The naiveté, which Brecht had identified in his later work as the main aesthetic criterion of the theatre, had disappeared from the performance.

A counterpart to the production of *The Measures Taken* was the guest performance of *Der Jasager* [He Who Said Yes] of the Paul Dessau music school in Zeuthen. Under the musical direction of Sigrid Schella, and with an arrangement by Steffen Kaiser, this production displayed the naiveté that was missing from the Berliner Ensemble production of *Measures*. The casting of teenage students brought this Lehrstück arrangement to the intended players. An absolute amateur would probably not be capable of fulfilling the demands of the Weill score, but a student who is not yet a professional – yes! After a long intermission, the invited audience awaited the second Lehrstück on the program, *Neinsager* [He Who Said No]. But what was performed was the exact repetition of *Jasager*, only with an alternate cast of students. A very Lehrstück-like and quasi-postmodern reading (compare Robert Wilson's *Patio* two-acter) but one that leaves the question open as to what one could learn from this Lehrstück.[5]

IV

I see the future of the Lehrstück not on the professional stage, but rather at secondary schools and universities, as a practical demonstration of Brechtian theory. The Berliner Ensemble has collaborated with Berlin schools and the results could be seen on the

---

[5] Not until after I had written up these observations did I learn that this 'concept' that I had found so interesting had been the result of a performance accident. On that evening, the tape recorder with the cued 'Nein!' didn't work. Nevertheless every performance should be described the way it was presented.

Berliner Ensemble rehearsal stage: The *Lukullus* opera was worked on at the Walther-Rathenau school; *Jasager* and *Neinsager* at the Luise-Henriette school; and the above-mentioned *Jasager* on the mainstage of the Berliner Ensemble.

The question of what today's students can learn from the Lehrstück is as fundamental as it is tricky, especially when the genial poet styles a common-sense sentence from Lenin as high wisdom – 'klug ist nicht, der keine fehler macht, sondern/ Klug ist, der sie schnell zu verbessern versteht' [clever is not the one who makes no mistakes, rather/ Clever is the one who knows to quickly correct them] (BFA 3:644); and when a no less genial composer arranges this sentence as a vocal canon of seductive beauty. One can only learn from the lesson under the condition of absolute historical ignorance, for the total inability of the applied Marxism-Leninism to learn from its own mistakes, its dogmatic obstinacy, led to the bloodiest crime of the century.

Otherwise, one would have to answer that students today can only learn from the Lehrstücke *ex negativo* (Brecht, the dialectician, saw to this possibility in *Jasager/ Neinsager*). But then what about the aesthetic criterion of naivete, which seems to be constitutive of the beauty of these short pieces? Is *The Measures Taken* to be read as the anticipation of Stalin's show trials and *Jasager* as the anticipation of Nazi 'euthanasia'?

I would argue that the pedagogy of the Lehrstücke is clarified by the following consideration: that the transition from Kafka's central idea (the trial) to Brecht's central idea (the measure taken) is one of the most significant paradigm switches in the literature and political practice of this century.

All the same, the decision of the students at the Paul Dessau school, prompted by a lucky accident, to play the *Jasager/Neinsager* complex as a doubled *Jasager* version is the most reasonable response to the question. From the Lehrstücke, one can learn nothing of the ideological intent of the author, but much about the theatre. There is no better model for learning about the limits of theatrical representation than what can be gained from practice. As performance-generating material that allows the existential motivation of young people to be freely articulated within the framework of a strict transmedial play structure, the Lehrstücke can hardly be surpassed. The evocative power of their language and music are masterful. And while the solidarity learned is no longer proletarian – an anachronistic concept – artistic sensibility and the elementary camaraderie of the participants remain an important virtue to be transmitted to young people by the Lehrstück.

REFERENCES

Berliner Ensemble
1998   *Der Ozeanflug* [The Flight over the Ocean]. Directed by Robert Wilson; music by Hans Peter Kuhn. Premiere 17 January.
1997   *Die Maßnahme* [The Measures Taken]. Directed by Klaus Emmerich. Premiere 17 September.

Brecht, Bertolt
1988–1999   *Werke. Große kommentierte Berliner und Frankfurter Ausgabe* (BFA). 30 vols. Edited by Werner Hecht, Jan Knopf, Werner Mittenzwei, and Klaus-Detlef Müller. Berlin and Weimar: Aufbau and Frankfurt am Main: Suhrkamp Verlag.

Nietzsche, Friederich
1867–1977   *Die Geburt der Tragödie* [The Birth of Tragedy]. 15 vols. Edited by Giorgio Colli and Mazzino Montinari. München, Berlin, and New York: DeGruyter.

Rischbieter, Henning
1997   'Einfühlung in den Stalinismus'. *Theater Heute*, 11:10–11.

Steinweg, Reiner
1972   *Das Lehrstück, Brechts Theorie einer politisch-ästhetischen Erziehung*. Stuttgart: Metzler Verlag.

Thomas, Emma Lou, and Andrzej Wirth
1994   Fatzer: *BB/HM/RW Interface*. Videotape. Centre for Performance Studies, University of Sydney, edition UCLA.

Wirth, Andrzej
1978   'Brecht's *Fatzer*, Experiments in Discourse Making'. *TDR* 23, 4 (T80):55–66.

CHAPTER TWELVE

Review of *The Decision*

DURUS
TRANSLATED BY ROMY FURSLAND

There has already been much discussion of *The Decision*, the *Lehrstück* by Brecht and Eisler [also known in English as *The Measures Taken*]. The first performance at the Philharmonie resulted in a lively debate in our own camp, and it is not the least triumph of this innovative, formally impressive work of art, which challenges all parties to actively take up a political position, that it does not permit a passive, 'purely aesthetic' response.

We must say an emphatic 'Yes' to the second production in Berlin, even though we feel that the overall concept of the text is rather contrived – since it is based not on revolutionary praxis but on a purely cerebral engagement with revolutionary theory.

We must say 'Yes' politically, because the advantages of the play's overall impact (which is positive, from a propaganda point of view) largely outweigh the disadvantages of its ideological ambiguities. The shooting of the young, undisciplined comrade by his fellows, whose knowledge of theory is sound but who are reckless in repeatedly giving the young comrade difficult and illegal assignments, is not justified from the perspective of revolutionary praxis.

But *The Decision* uses this elaborate example to teach us something positive, something true, something crucial to the revolutionary movement in all countries: the fact that the Party's interests come before those of the individual and that a proletarian revolutionary, however sincere and passionate he or she may be, is only half a revolutionary without the clarity of revolutionary theory.

Bert Brecht (the author of *The Decision*) should take note, however, that a knowledge of Marxist-Leninist theory *alone* is not enough; that even the genius of a writer who has read all of Marx is no substitute for revolutionary experiences and putting in the legwork for the revolutionary cause.

Nevertheless, it is extremely interesting and important that we are now seeing the best bourgeois writers in Germany being gripped by Marxism as a revolutionary theory. In order to achieve a complete understanding of revolutionary theory, it is essential to take the next step into *revolutionary praxis*!

The staging of *The Decision* is of vital importance in terms of the workers' choir movement. This is the most ideologically mature and artistically accomplished full-length choral work for workers' choirs we have seen to date. No mere musical wallpaper. No sentimental Luddism with leitmotifs like 'Poor proletarian!', but instead a call to

---

Durus, '[Review of *The Measures Taken*]', in Monikà Wyss, *Brecht in der Kritik* (Munich: Kindler, 1977), pp. 134–6.

revolutionary action! A decisive message in favour of revolutionary theory, of Communism, of the Party.

In artistic, literary and musical terms, *The Decision* is an epoch-making work. It is comparable to the Marxist teaching play *For Soviet Power*, by The Red Megaphone, although it does not quite equal the achievements of this acting troupe in terms of their ideology and the consistency of their creative working methods.

It is important to note that *The Decision* is formally innovative and compelling, that it uses contemporary methods when it comes to form and artistic technique, and that it does not hold up aesthetic regressiveness as a 'revolutionary virtue' (like that earlier 'proletarian' oratorio *Battleship Potemkin*).

There is a dialectical interplay between the artistic form and the social content of an artwork, and the formal qualities of this still half-anarchistic play are sure to inspire other revolutionary working-class writers to produce more ideologically mature works.

The performances of the three proletarian choirs – Schubert-Chor, Gemischter Chor Groß-Berlin and Gemischter Chor Fichte, all brilliantly conducted by Rankl, were once again excellent. The actors Granach, Busch, Helene Weigel and Topitz all gave of their best.

It would be useful to have another version of the work, less musically demanding and requiring fewer singers, to make it easier to perform it widely in the provinces.

Durus
Die Rote Fahne, Berlin, 20 January 1931

Exile

Exile

CHAPTER THIRTEEN

Theses for Proletarian Literature

BERTOLT BRECHT
TRANSLATED BY ROMY FURSLAND

1) Fight by writing! Show that you are fighting! Powerful realism! Reality is on your side – be on its side! Let life speak! Do not violate it! Know that the bourgeoisie do not let it speak! But you can. You must. Find the places where reality is denied, pushed aside, painted over. Scrape off the paint! Contradict, instead of soliloquising! Inspire contradiction! Your arguments are the living practical and practised man and his life as it is. Be fearless: you are speaking the truth! If you are right in your conclusions and proposals, then you must be able to tolerate the contradictions of reality, explore difficulties in their formidable entirety, engage with them out in the open. Do everything you can to advance the cause of your class, which is the cause of all of humanity, but do not leave anything out because it does not fit with your conclusions, proposals and hopes; forego such a conclusion in any given case rather than foregoing the truth; but even in this case, insist that the difficulty you are illustrating in its formidable entirely must be overcome. You are not fighting alone – your readers will fight with you, if you can inspire them to fight. You are not the only one finding solutions: your readers will find them too.

2) Fight against your own poverty! As a writer, at your writing desk, you must emancipate yourself from the misery of your proletarian existence! You must be master of your experiences.

Brecht, 'Thesen für proletarische Literatur', in Brecht, *Schriften*, vol. 2 (Berlin and Frankfurt/Main: Aufbau and Suhrkamp, 1993), pp. 39–40.

CHAPTER FOURTEEN

Brecht's Epic Theatre as a Theatre of Exile

EHRHARD BAHR
TRANSLATED BY ROMY FURSLAND

Among Brecht scholars in the West, there is now a widespread view that Brecht was forced by the circumstances of his exile to largely abandon the form of epic theatre. The individual scenes in *Fear and Misery of the Third Reich* are said to have been 'conceived as naturalistic and traditional from the outset'. Brecht apparently acknowledged 'quite openly' that the one-act play *Señora Carrar's Rifles* featured elements of 'Aristotelian theatre, aimed at getting the audience to empathise with the characters in the play'. At the same time, however, Brecht is said to have been developing the theory of epic, non-Aristotelian theatre into an increasingly coherent concept. This obvious contradiction between theatrical theory and theatrical practice is explained by the fact that 'in the mid-1930s, Brecht subordinated everything else to the pressing political demands (of exile)'.[1] The rigid dramaturgy of the *Lehrstücke* during the avant-garde phase of 1927–1930 was allegedly abandoned for three reasons: firstly because Brecht's everyday political struggles in exile forced him to do so; secondly because he recognised the one-sidedness of the *Lehrstück* as a genre; and thirdly because by and large, naturalism was still the prevailing theatrical style in the countries where Brecht lived in exile.[2] This consensus in Western Brecht scholarship was first challenged by the *Lehrstück* debate of 1973. In 1971, Reiner Steinweg described Brecht's epic theatre as a backward step induced by his exile.[3] Other

---

Ehrhard Bahr, 'Brechts Episches Theater als Exiltheater', in Alexander Stephan and Hans Wagener (eds), *Schreiben im Exil: Zur Ästhetik der deutschen Exilliteratur 1933-1945* (Bonn: Bouvier, 1985), pp. 109–22.

[1] Reinhold Grimm, *Bertolt Brecht*, fully revised 3rd edition (Stuttgart: Metzler, 1971), 42–43.
[2] Ibid., 43. See also Ulrich Weisstein, 'Bertolt Brecht: Die Lehren des Exils' in *Die deutsche Exilliteratur 1933-1945*, ed. Manfred Durzak (Stuttgart: Reclam, 1973), 373–397, esp. 380–384; Jan Knopf, *Brecht-Handbuch: Theater: Eine Ästhetik der Widersprüche* (Stuttgart: Metzler, 1980), 417–424; Franz Norbert Mennemeier and Frithjof Trapp, 'Zur deutschsprachigen Exildramatik' in *Handbuch des deutschen Dramas*, ed. Walter Hinck (Dusseldorf: Bagel, 1980), 431–439, esp. 431–432; Ehrhard Bahr, 'Exildramatik' in *Deutsche Literatur: Eine Sozialgeschichte*, ed. Horst Albert Glaser. Vol. 9 (Reinbek: Rowohlt, 1983), 293–301.
[3] Reiner Steinweg, 'Das Lehrstück: ein Modell des sozialistischen Theaters: Brechts Lehrstücktheorie' in *Alternative* 78/79 (1971), 102–116. For a revision of his own opinion of 1971 see also Reiner Steinweg, *Das Lehrstück: Brechts Theorie einer politisch-ästhetischen Erziehung* (Stuttgart: Metzler, 1972), 210; and by the same author, 'Begriff und Erfahrung: Anmerkungen zur Lehrstücksdiskussion' in *Brechts Modell der Lehrstücke: Zeugnisse, Diskussion, Erfahrungen*, ed. Reiner Steinweg (Frankfurt: Suhrkamp, 1976), 448–449. For further discussion of the *Lehrstück* see also *Alternative* 91 (1973) and the bibliographical references in *Auf Anregung*

than this, however, there is broad agreement (with the exception of the *Lehrstück* debate) among Western critics of Brecht's exile drama, insofar as his theatrical theory and practice are viewed through the lens of his exile at all. Some of the most important studies do not even take into account Brecht's working conditions in exile and the subject matter and forms that resulted from them.[4] Brecht scholars in the GDR come to similar conclusions, albeit from completely the opposite angle: they treat Brecht's exile dramas of 1935–1947 as a transition into Socialist Realism.[5] In doing so, they regurgitate positions from the Marxist cultural policy of the late 1930s. Georg Lukács, in the famous Expressionism debate of 1938, found much to praise about Brecht's playlet *The Spy* from *Fear and Misery of the Third Reich* and declared that the dramatist was developing a 'diverse and multi-layered' realism.[6] In the eyes of the West, this categorisation of Brecht as a proponent of Socialist Realism is seen as a compromise with Aristotelian theatre. In *Linkskurve* in 1932, Lukács had rejected Brecht's avant-garde experiments with theatrical form.[7] Critics in the GDR have proceeded in a similar vein, reproaching the *Lehrstücke* with a lack of Socialist Realism and viewing them as, at best, a necessary precursor to Socialist Realism.[8]

In Brecht's theatrical theory and practice between 1933 and 1947, then, we have a corpus of exile literature which we can use as a model for analysing the phenomenon of an 'aesthetic of exile'. It is generally agreed that Brecht's dramaturgy was influenced by the conditions in which he lived in exile. This essay, in contrast to Brecht scholarship in general, will argue that at least the theory if not the practice of epic theatre was validated and broadened by the conditions and experiences of exile theatre (even if it did not originate in them). Indeed, many of Brecht's theoretical works on epic theatre were written in exile, such as *Buying Brass* (1939–1940), which is regarded

---

Bertolt Brechts: Lehrstücke mit Schülern, Arbeitern, Theaterleuten, ed. Reiner Steinweg (Frankfurt: Suhrkamp, 1978), 24–25. See also Petermichael von Bawey, *Rhetorik der Utopie: Eine Untersuchung zum ästhetischen Aufbau und argumentativen Zusammenhang der Lehrstücke Brechts* (Munich: Fink, 1981).

[4] See e.g. Klaus-Detlef Müller, *Die Funktion der Geschichte im Werk Bertolt Brechts: Studien zum Verhältnis von Marxismus und Ästhetik* (Tübingen: Niemeyer, 1967); Heinz Brüggemann, *Literarische Technik und soziale Revolution: Versuche über das Verhältnis von Kunstproduktion, Marxismus und literarischer Tradition in der theoretischen Schriften Bertolt Brechts* (Reinbek: Rowohlt, 1973). In Jan Knopf's research report, too, the exile period is not really mentioned (*Bertolt Brecht: Ein kritischer Forschungsbericht: Fragwürdiges in der Brechtforschung* [Frankfurt: Athenäum 1974]). One exception is Herbert Claas, *Die politische Ästhetik Bertolt Brechts vom Baal zum Caesar* (Frankfurt: Suhrkamp, 1977), 72–107. Only in discussions of Brecht's poetry is the exile period properly taken into account: see Peter Paul Schwarz: *Lyrik und Zeitgeschichte: Brecht: Gedichte über das Exil und späte Lyrik* (Heidelberg: Stiehm, 1978); Christiane Bohnert: *Brechts Lyrik im Kontext: Zyklen und Exil* (Königstein: Athenäum, 1982).

[5] See Werner Mittenzwei: *Bertolt Brecht: Von der Maßnahme zu Leben des Galilei* (Berlin/Weimar: Aufbau, 1965), 129–251; Ernst Schumacher, *Die dramatischen Versuche Bertolt Brechts 1918-1933* (Berlin: Rütten & Loening, 1955), 495–501; Werner Hecht, *Brechts Weg zum epischen Theater: Beitrag zur Entwicklung des epischen Theaters 1918 bis 1933* (Berlin/West: deb., 1962), 121–160; Ernst Schumacher, 'Stoff und Form in Leben des Galilei' in *Brecht: Theater und Gesellschaft im 20. Jahrhundert: 21 Aufsätze* (Berlin/West: deb., 1973), 201–241; Käthe Rülicke-Weiler, *Die Dramaturgie Brechts: Theater als Mittel der Veränderung* (Berlin/West: deb., 1976), 13–28.

[6] Georg Lukács, 'Es geht um den Realismus' in *Das Wort 3* (1938), No. 6, 112–138.

[7] Georg Lukács, 'Aus der Not eine Tugend' in *Linkskurve 4* (1932), No. 11/12, 15–24.

[8] See Mittenzwei, *Bertolt Brecht: Von der Maßnahme zu Leben des Galilei*, 119–126; Rülicke-Weiler, *Die Dramaturgie Brechts*, 20–22. On the reception of the *Lehrstück* debate in the GDR, see Werner Mittenzwei, 'Die Spur der Brechtschen Lehrstücktheorie: Gedanken zur neueren Lehrstück-Interpretation' in *Brechts Modell der Lehrstücke*, 225–254.

as 'Brecht's most important theoretical achievement'.[9] His *Short Organon for the Theatre*, of 1948, is just an abridged summary of the theatrical theory he developed in exile. Essentially, the *Organon* can already be seen as a 'formal regression' insofar as it points out the 'limited opportunities' for realising 'true, radical epic theatre in Germany'.[10]

The term 'epic theatre' is used here because Brecht's theatrical theory and practice in general have become known by that name, even though Brecht himself later preferred the terms 'anti-Aristotelian' or 'dialectical' theatre.[11] The term 'epic theatre' stems from Brecht's 1926 period of work and was used in print for the first time, to my knowledge, in 1927.[12] The 'Notes on the Opera *Rise and Fall of the City of Mahagonny*', from 1930, set out the schema of the dramatic and epic form of theatre. The term and the concept, then, were already in existence before Brecht went into exile. What we are dealing with here is the development and reinforcement of this theatrical theory in exile.

Brecht's statements about his exile dramas are contradictory. For this reason we will need to take a historical-dialectical approach, and look also at how the plays were received. In this regard, Walter Benjamin's observations on Brecht's epic theatre are of particular methodological importance, since Benjamin is one of the few critics to have understood the historical dialectic of an 'aesthetic of exile'. We know from Brecht's remarks on poetry that he was aware of the problematic nature of such an aesthetic. The poems he produced in exile were written in the knowledge that 'mere existence [...] has become a political issue'. For this reason, Brecht claimed, poetry inspired entirely by feelings was no longer viable: 'Our feelings (instinct, emotion) are completely silted up; they are in a state of constant opposition to our basic interests' (BB 19: 393).[13] For this reason, Brecht called for 'criteria arising from rationality' to be applied to the poetry of exile (BB 19: 393). Poets did not need to fear rationality; on the contrary, they should seek it out: 'They [should] know, at least, that feelings can be just as false as thoughts' (BB 19: 391). For the 'German Satires' of 1937, which Brecht had written for German Freedom Radio in Moscow, he considered unrhyming poetry and irregular rhythms to be essential:

> It was about broadcasting individual sentences to a distant, artificially scattered audience. These sentences had to be formulated as concisely as possible, and I wanted to make sure that interruptions (by the jammers) wouldn't matter too much. Rhyme didn't seem to me to be appropriate, because it can easily give a poem a self-contained

---

[9]Knopf, *Brecht Handbuch: Theater*, 452. See also Klaus Detlef-Müller, 'Der Philsoph auf dem Theater: Ideologiekritik und "Linksabweichung" in Bertolt Brechts *Messingkauf*' in *Zu Bertolt Brecht: Parabel und episches Theater*, ed. Theo Buck (Stuttgart: Klett-Cotta, 1979), 84–112; Hans Mayer, 'Dramaturgische Positionen oder der Messingkauf', ibid., 113–126.

[10]Knopf, *Brecht-Handbuch: Theater*, 458. The Brecht quote comes from *Bertolt Brecht: Arbeitsjournal*. Vol. 2. (Frankfurt: Suhrkamp, 1973), 912.

[11]See Knopf, *Brecht-Handbuch*, 394–396. The term 'non-Aristotelian drama' was developed by Brecht from 1933 onwards. See *Bertolt Brecht: Gesammelte Werke in 20 Bänden*. Vol. 1. (Frankfurt: Suhrkamp, 1967), 228–336 (edition Suhrkamp). Cited hereinafter e.g. as BB 15: 228-336. On the term 'dialectical theatre', see Brecht's early theoretical piece 'Die dialektische Dramatik' from 1931 (BB 15: 211-225). The term was then shelved, to be reintroduced in 1951 in 'Dialektik auf dem Theater' (BB 16: 867-941). See also Mittenzwei, *Von der Maßnahme zu Leben des Galilei*, 189–190.

[12]Knopf, *Brecht-Handbuch*, 395. See BB 15: 132.

[13]Brecht, *Gesammelte Werke in 20 Bänden*. Cited in the text hereinafter as BB with volume and page number.

feeling, make it pass the listener by. Regular rhythms with their smooth rise and fall don't grab the listener's attention enough either, and they force you to paraphrase, because lots of modern-day expressions don't fit into them: the intonation of direct speech was what was needed.

(BB 19: 403).

Brecht's statements about his exile dramas are not so clear-cut. As he noted in an entry in his *Journals* on 25 February 1939, he regarded *Life of Galileo* as a 'big step backwards' in technical terms, and the same went for *Señora Carrar's Rifles*. He called *Life of Galileo* 'too opportunistic' – in other words, too heavily tailored to being performed on the stages of exile countries and having a direct impact on exile audiences. Brecht felt that one would have to completely rewrite *Life of Galileo* in order to capture 'that [...] "breeze that comes from fresh coasts", that rosy dawn of science everything more direct, without the interiors, the "atmosphere", the empathy'.

At the time, Brecht described the *Fatzer* fragment and the *Bread Store* fragment, both from the pre-1930 *Lehrstück* period, as being 'of the highest technical standard'.[14] He invoked this period again later on when, in August 1956, just before his death, he was asked by Manfred Wekwerth about the 'form of the theatre of the future', and cited his 1930 play *The Decision*.[15] Conversely, Brecht noted in his *Journals* on 15 March 1939, while he was working on *The Good Person of Szechwan*, that this project would enable him to 'develop the epic technique and thus get back up to standard at last'. While working on *Galileo* he felt the lack of 'contact with a stage' to be a serious disadvantage, whereas with *The Good Person of Szechwan* he seems to have seen this same lack of contact as a liberation from the technical apparatus of the stage, and declared 'you don't have to make any concessions when writing for yourself.[16] For Brecht, then, exile meant either adapting to the theatrical situation and audiences in his countries of exile, or the theoretical anticipation of a stage and an audience well-schooled in 'epic theatre'. Brecht certainly seems to have recognised that exile drama needed Aristotelian empathy for tactical reasons related to the day-to-day political struggle, without believing he had to renounce the developments that had been achieved in 'epic theatre'. He was able to make a virtue of a necessity. The lack of a permanent stage in exile forced Brecht to take a break from writing plays, enabling him to concentrate on theatrical theory and anticipate the 'theatre of the future' in a dialectical leap forward. To some extent, this progress in theatrical theory was achieved as a result of setbacks in theatrical practice.[17] On 15 August 1938, in reference to the plays written for Slatan Dudow's stage, Brecht noted: 'Proletarian theatre in exile is keeping theatre going.'[18]

In this dialectic of progress and regression, Brecht was encouraged in particular by Walter Benjamin, who joined him in Danish exile in 1938. In his review of the first performance of eight scenes from *Fear and Misery of the Third Reich* in Paris, Benjamin wrote in *Die Neue Weltbühne* on 30 June 1939 that 'the theatre of emigration has to be in the business

---

[14]Brecht, *Arbeitsjournal*, Vol. 1, 41.
[15]Manfred Wekwerth, *Schriften: Arbeit mit Brecht* (Berlin: Henschel, 1973), 78.
[16]Brecht, *Arbeitsjournal*, Vol. 1, 41, 45.
[17]See Franz Norbert Mennemeier and Frithjof Trapp, 'Zur deutschsprachigen Exildramatik' in *Handbuch des deutschen Dramas*, 431–432.
[18]Brecht, *Arbeitsjournal*, Vol. 1, 22.

of political drama'. The political drama of the Weimar Republic, according to Benjamin, had been overtaken by events: 'The theatre of emigration must start afresh; not only its stage but also its drama must be rebuilt.' Unlike Georg Lukács, Benjamin saw Brecht's non-Aristotelian theatre as the right starting point, but thought Brecht had to begin again from the beginning: 'He is an expert in starting from scratch.' This, said Benjamin, was the mark of a true dialectician. Brecht was a practised dialectician: '... and a particularly dauntless one in his new plays, written for performance on the stages of exile'.[19]

However, Benjamin also acknowledged that epic theatre was not sufficiently well-established, and the circle of its initiates not sufficiently large, to be able to build upon it in exile. Benjamin suggested that the series *Fear and Misery of the Third Reich* was constructed in line with the rules of traditional dramaturgy, but justified this technical backward step by pointing out the play's effectiveness. The *Schutzverband Deutscher Schriftsteller* [Association for the Protection of German Writers] had lent its patronage to the production, which was hailed (by the exiles in Paris) as a landmark artistic and political event. Benjamin reported that the audience, 'after five years in exile, finally saw their shared political experience reflected on a stage'.[20]

Based on the experience of exile, Benjamin did, however, manage to convincingly highlight one of the basic categories of epic theatre within this otherwise naturalistic play. He addressed the idea (rejected by Brecht) of actors empathising with their characters and trying to identify with them. Benjamin pointed out that this traditional process of empathy could no longer happen in exile, if the actor was playing an SA man or a member of the Nazis' People's Court: 'no political activist can "empathise" with the murder of his or her comrades'.[21] In this way, a specific technique of epic theatre was given a new justification. Only through the experience of exile could the political and aesthetic necessity of this technique be conveyed. The 'kind-hearted' actor apostrophised by Benjamin, playing Iago in Shakespeare's *Othello* in pre-1933 Germany, would probably not really have understood the necessity of distancing himself from his role, but any actor in exile playing an SS officer in a Hollywood film post-1933 would have done. He would have understood Brecht's dramatic art perfectly.

The extent to which acting represents a special aspect of epic theatre in exile is evident from the poems Brecht wrote about actors in the years 1938–1941. There are almost forty poems in total, and one is even entitled 'The Actress in Exile'. Four poems are devoted to Helene Weigel in the role of Señora Carrar in Brecht's exile drama of 1937. This play too, as Brecht noted, was 'Aristotelian (empathy) drama'.[22] But Brecht sought to compensate for this drawback dialectically, by allowing 'actors like Weigel to generate seemingly total empathy in the spectators (they said excitedly: "She wasn't playing the fisherwoman – she *was* the fisherwoman")' whilst instructing those actors to simultaneously 'activate the spectators' critical attitudes'.[23] Brecht called Weigel's acting in *Señora Carrar's Rifles*

---

[19]Walter Benjamin, 'Das Land, in dem das Proletariat nicht genannt warden darf' in *Die neue Weltbühne* on 30 June 1938. Cited from Walter Benjamin, *Versuche über Brecht*, ed. and with an afterword by Rolf Tiedemann (Frankfurt: Suhrkamp, 1966), 44.
[20]Ibid., 46.
[21]Ibid., 47.
[22]BB 17: 1100. See Brecht's *Señora Carrar's Rifles*, ed. Klaus Bohnen (Frankfurt: Suhrkamp, 1982), 97.
[23]Ibid., 199; BB 15: 316. Brecht also tried to compensate for the drawbacks of empathy-based dramaturgy through documentary films or, as in *Fear and Misery of the Third Reich* (BB 16: 890-891) through intercalary scenes (BB 3: 1187-1193). It was a form of retrospective 'epicization'.

an 'example of applied dialectics'.²⁴ In the poem 'Description of H.W.'s Acting', he emphasised in particular the way she distanced herself from her role and its function:

> Although she showed everything
> That was necessary to understand a fisherwoman
> She did not completely transform herself
> Into that fisherwoman, but acted
> As if she was still engaged in contemplation
> As if she was constantly thinking: how does this bit go again?
> Even though you couldn't always
> Guess her own thoughts about the fisherwoman,
> She showed that she was thinking them,
> And thus invited others
> To think them too.
>
> (BB 9: 782)

Brecht's exile plays number almost twenty works, beginning with the second version of *Round Heads and Pointed Heads* from 1934 and ending with *The Caucasian Chalk Circle* from 1944 – and we might also include the adaptation *The Antigone of Sophocles* from 1947. After that, Brecht only ever produced reworkings (with one exception). The exile years were a creative phase not only in Bertolt Brecht's dramatic production but in German drama as a whole.²⁵ This fact is often ignored by West German literary criticism, and the cliché of the 'empty notepads' of exiled dramatists persists, despite the fact that it has long since been disproved by statistics. The number of German-language plays written in exile is currently estimated to be between 500 and 700, and records show that there were over 800 German-language productions in exile.²⁶

Brecht was, however, forced to make compromises with Aristotelian dramaturgy in many of his exile plays (bar a few exceptions). A progressive increase in epic elements can be identified between 1934 and 1944, but some of the plays were only staged as traditional productions in an illusionistic style (like *Fear and Misery of the Third Reich* in New York in 1942), whilst others had to wait till the end of the exile years for their premieres, like *Mr Puntila and his Man Matti* (first performed in Zurich in 1948) and *The Resistible Rise of Arturo Ui* (first performed in Stuttgart in 1958). The Zurich Schauspielhaus, which rendered outstanding services to German exile drama between 1933 and 1945, premiered both *The Good Person of Szechwan* and first version of *Life of Galileo* in 1943, although without concerning itself with epic theatre. *The Good Person of Szechwan* was interpreted as a tragedy, and *Life of Galileo* as a historical drama with a traditional hero. But in 1941, the Zurich Schauspielhaus developed a model for *Mother Courage and her Children* which Brecht adopted for the Berliner Ensemble in 1949. He retained the basic arrangement with Courage's rolling canteen wagon, as well as the principle of the revolving stage.²⁷ Swiss critics showed little understanding of epic theatre, however: they praised Brecht's

---

²⁴BB 16: 890-891.
²⁵Franz Norbert Mennemeier and Frithjof Trapp, *Deutsche Exildramatik 1933-1950* (Munich: Fink, 1980), 18–19.
²⁶Bahr, 'Exildramatik', 295.
²⁷Werner Mittenzwei, *Exil in der Schweiz* (Leipzig: Reclam, 1978), 373–375.

dramatic creativity.[28] The dialectic of progress and regression, then, is also evident within Brechtian theatrical practice, and there are several other examples of it.

The second version of *Life of Galileo* was particularly important. It was produced in English in Los Angeles from 1944–1947, in collaboration with Charles Laughton, and premiered on 30 July 1947 at the Coronet Theatre on La Cienega Boulevard. This production, directed by Joseph Losey and with Charles Laughton in the lead role, was more closely aligned with epic theatre than has hitherto been supposed. Credit is due to James K. Lyon for his reconstruction of the production, in which he maps out the various elements of epic theatre that featured in it.[29] Thanks to Brecht's essay 'Constructing a Role: Laughton's Galileo', we know plenty about the collaboration between the playwright and the actor. A single quotation suffices as evidence of the dialectic of progress and regression at the heart of this collaboration. Brecht and Laughton had agreed that the portrayal of Galileo should not lead the audience to 'sympathise, empathise or let themselves be swept along; instead, the audience should be encouraged to adopt a more critical and analytical attitude – an attitude of astonishment'. These maxims are in line with the principles of dramatic art in epic theatre. The following sentence, however, contains a dialectical concession; Brecht elaborates: 'Galileo should be portrayed as a phenomenon like Richard III, whereby the vitality of this alien figure elicits the emotion of approval in the audience.'[30]

In the second version, written in the shadow of the atom bomb and its deployment, Galileo was no longer supposed to be a rebel hero as he had been in the first version, but a villain like Richard III: his retraction had made him a social villain of science.[31] In the penultimate scene of the second version, Brecht gives his Galileo the famous lines: 'I have betrayed my profession. A man who does what I have done cannot be tolerated in the ranks of the scientific community' (BB 3: 1341). Laughton could not quite pull off this new version, with Galileo's cynical self-condemnation at the end, and neither could Ernst Busch in the Berliner Ensemble's 1957 production, as we know from Käthe Rülicke's dramaturgical notes.[32] The actors' admiration for the figure of Galileo was too great – they were unable to portray him as a 'scoundrel' who cynically condemns himself.[33] Although for this American premiere of the play Brecht was willing to permit the audience 'emotional acquiescence', he certainly did not want to invite sympathetic admiration or empathy. He had pinned his hopes on the V-effect of Galileo's vitality (i.e. gluttony) as demonstrated in the penultimate scene, where the protagonist seems more preoccupied with a roast goose liver than with the scientific conversation. But his high

---

[28]*Brecht in der Kritik: Rezensionen aller brecht Uraufführungen sowie ausgewählter deutsch- und fremdsprachiger Premieren: Eine Dokumentation*. Compiled by Monika Wyss with abridged and related texts by Helmut Kindler (Munich: Kindler, 1977), 203–212.

[29]James K. Lyon, *Bertolt Brecht in America* (Princeton: Princeton University Press, 1980), 184–201. See also Ernst Schumacher, *Drama und Geschichte: Bertolt Brechts* Leben des Galilei *und andere Stücke* (Berlin: Henschel, 1965), 196–204.

[30]*Materialien zu Brechts Leben des Galilei*. Compiled by Werner Hecht (Frankfurt: Suhrkamp, 1965), 47.

[31]Ibid., 37; 73–74; 106; 118. Linda L. Thomas has established that the dropping of the atom bomb on Hiroshima was not the direct cause of the changes Brecht made to the Galileo character, but the event's influence on his conception of the character is undeniable (see Linda L. Thomas, *Ordnung und Wert der Unordnung bei Bertolt Brecht* (Bern: Lang, 1979), 41–48).

[32]*Materialien zu Brechts Leben des Galilei*, 73–74; 122. See also Schumacher, *Drama und Geschichte*, 201; 297–301; 305–306.

[33]*Materialien zu Brechts Leben des Galilei*, 122.

hopes of the V-effect were not fulfilled – in Hollywood or Berlin. The historical subject matter, with its innate drama, resisted the acting style of epic theatre which Brecht felt had been developed in such an exemplary way in the *Fatzer* and *Bread Store* fragments.[34]

When it comes to the other aspects of the production, including the press reception, we have not been fully or accurately informed up to now. The picture painted by Martin Esslin in his book *Brecht: A Choice of Evils* is a misleading one, and has since been corrected by James K. Lyon.[35] In the set and the costumes, in Hanns Eisler's music and Lotte Goslar's choreography, elements of epic theatre were clearly in evidence. The production even used 'the Brecht curtain', the light half-curtain that became Brecht's trademark. As James K. Lyon shows, Brecht more or less took over the direction of the play, but managed to do so without offending the official director Joseph Losey. Conversely, Brecht did not hesitate to take on board suggestions and advice from Losey. This led, as Lyon remarks, to an 'unusually harmonious collaboration' under his direction, such as might not have been possible with Erwin Piscator or another German director in exile.[36] In the remaining roles Brecht had mainly cast younger, less experienced actors who had not yet had the method acting of the Stanislavsky school drilled into them. The Stanislavsky system, with its complete transformation of the actor into his or her character, was predominant in America and diametrically opposed to epic theatre. By giving parts to inexperienced actors, Brecht was able to implement epic theatre at least to some extent.[37] The different acting style was perceived by both the public and the press, at any rate, and the relationship to Elizabethan theatre was clearly recognised. A good half of the criticism was positive and enlightened. Epic theatre was mentioned by name and emphasised as an asset. The theatre management under the actor John Houseman, who is still well-known today, defended epic theatre by pointing out that Brecht was using it to try to escape the realistic theatre in Germany.[38] But the Broadway success that Brecht, against his better judgement, had hoped for until 1947 never materialised. In New York in December 1947, *Life of Galileo* (again with Charles Laughton in the lead role) was cancelled after seven days. Brecht had come out of exile and moved to Zurich in November 1947.

Though regression may have been the dominant force in Brecht's theatrical practice in exile, progress definitely dominated his theatrical theory. This theory identified theatre in exile as epic theatre *par excellence*: it used the experience of exile to drive forward the theory of epic theatre. This is particularly evident in *Buying Brass* (1937–1951), where the Dramaturg tells the Philosopher about the members of a theatre group 'who had all fled their homeland to escape the house-painter's [i.e. Hitler's] hordes and had a certain style of acting in common'. It will be immediately obvious to a Brecht expert that this is a reference to Slatan Dudow's exile theatre, which staged the first performances of *Señora Carrar's Rifles* and scenes from *Fear and Misery of the Third Reich* in Paris. The style of this theatre is apostrophised as the style of the theatre-making of the future, as envisaged by the Philosopher (BB 16: 602). In the dialogue of the First Night, the Philosopher had called for the theatre to be renewed by science, and in order to describe this new form (in stark contrast to traditional theatre) he had coined the word 'thaëter'. As a basic model

---

[34] Brecht, *Arbeitsjournal*, Vol. 1, 41.
[35] Martin Esslin, *Brecht: Das Paradox des politischen Dichters*, 2nd edition (Munich: dtv, 1970), 112–113.
[36] Lyon, *Bertolt Brecht in America*, 185–186.
[37] Ibid., 187.
[38] Ibid, 196–200.

for a scene in the 'thaëter', the epic theatre of the future, the so-called 'Street Scene', is introduced in the Second and Third Nights. The scene consists of the reconstruction of a road accident by witnesses and the people involved.

The three most important texts in *Buying Brass*, which draw on the experience of exile theatre to justify and develop the theory of epic theatre, are as follows: 'On the Theatricality of Fascism', 'The Actor's Speech About How to Portray a Little Nazi' and 'Weigel's Descent into Fame'. In 1935, in *Legacy of This Time*, Ernst Bloch had already pointed out the link between politics and aesthetics in Fascism. In *Buying Brass*, this link was now analysed in relation to the theatre; Brecht demonstrated how Fascism had carried over the bourgeois theatre of empathy into the political sphere – with the dictator as the lead actor. Karl, the Dramaturg in the dialogue of the Second Night, says:

> There's no doubt that the Fascists behave in a particularly theatrical way. They have a real flair for it. They themselves talk about 'direction', and they've borrowed a whole host of effects straight from the theatre: the spotlights and the accompanying music, the choruses and the surprises.
>
> (BB 16: 560)

Karl refers to the acting lessons Hitler received from the court actor Basil in Munich. From Basil Hitler learnt 'how to stride like a hero', 'how to swing your knees forward and press your foot firmly to the ground to make yourself look more majestic. He also learned how to cross his arms impressively and how to adopt a casual attitude'.

(BB 16: 561)

In this dialogue the Philosopher concentrates on an analysis of Hitler's speeches, explaining: 'We have to look at what he does when he wants his audience to empathise with him and say: Yes, we would have done the same thing. In short, when he presents himself as a "human being" and wants to persuade the audience to see his actions as simply natural and human, and thus to feel favourably towards him'.

(BB 16: 563)

Based on this analysis, the theatricality of Fascism is unmasked as the theatre of empathy. For Brecht, the theatricality of Fascism with its mass appeal was in the same tradition as the bourgeois theatre whose tried-and-tested props and stage effects Hitler had borrowed. Epic theatre, which saw its own political and aesthetic necessity justified in its confrontation with Fascism in exile, was entirely different.

In 'The Actor's Speech About How to Portray a Little Nazi', Brecht sought to harness the 'new methods' of epic theatre he had previously discussed – *not* in order to make the character of the little Nazi 'interesting' or 'render him unfathomable' but instead to 'generate interest in his fathomability'. Under no circumstances, says the Actor, would he have wanted to portray anything like 'a born Nazi', only the way in which someone *becomes* a Nazi:

> I had to portray every step he took as an explicable one, and at the same time I had to hint at a different step he could have taken, which would also have been explicable. People shouldn't be treated as if they can only behave 'this' way; they can always behave differently. The houses have fallen down, but they could still be standing.
>
> (BB 16: 569)

Epic theatre, as exile theatre, puts Brecht's theory of Fascism into practice by having actors portray the 'little Nazi' in a way that makes him explicable. The aesthetic portrayal is designed to enable a theoretical understanding of Fascism which, as Frank Dietrich Wagner powerfully puts it, 'proves itself to be a knowledgeable and practical antifascism'.[39]

The third text tells of 'Weigel's Descent into Fame'; in other words, how Weigel gives up the bourgeois theatre of empathy to focus on a proletarian audience. Brecht used the topos of the 'inverted world' in his political and aesthetic diagnosis of Weigel's acting career. The outcome of this ironically named 'descent' is illustrated by the following sentence: 'the art connoisseurs stopped coming, and the police turned up instead' (BB 16: 608). The second section of 'Weigel's Descent into Fame' describes exile theatre:

> Around this time the house-painter came to power and she was forced to flee the country. She knew no other language than the one nobody knew as well as she did. So she performed, only a few times, with small troupes [...] for other refugees. [...] Her efforts to perform for the many had led to her only being able to perform for the very few. When she did perform, it was only in plays that showed the horrors of the age and the causes of those horrors. The persecuted people who heard her may have forgotten their misery, but never the causes of that misery. And they always went away from her performances with renewed strength for their struggles. This was because Weigel [...] continued to perfect her art; she took her ever more significant art to ever deeper depths. In this way, once she had completely renounced and lost her former fame, her second period of fame began: a lowly fame, existing in the thoughts of a few persecuted people at a time when very many people were being persecuted.
>
> (BB 16, 609)

The theory of epic theatre as exile theatre could hardly be documented in a clearer or more moving way. Here, in the truest sense of the phrase, we have an 'aesthetic of exile': an analysis of Helene Weigel as an actor who sought to develop, hone and perfect her art under the conditions of exile and resistance.

In 1948, in the preface to his *Short Organon for the Theatre*, Brecht declared that the bourgeois aesthetic, 'the legacy of a depraved and parasitic class, is in such a woeful state that a theatre would gain both respect and freedom of action by changing its name to thaëter' (BB 16: 662). This 'thaëter' is epic theatre, which could only be developed and demonstrated in exile – and not in Germany during the years of the Nazi regime and the war. Brecht's *Short Organon* of 1948 was intended to serve as a theatrical foundation for the remigration of epic theatre, in two ways. In the narrower sense, the *Short Organon* was designed to contribute to the return of epic theatre to the field of the hitherto despised bourgeois aesthetic. As Brecht explained, it would be too difficult 'to represent the theory of theatrical *Verfremdung* outside of an aesthetic' (BB 16: 662). In the dialectical historical sense, however, the *Short Organon* represents the outcome of epic theatre as exile theatre and its remigration into a practice which did not always succeed in fulfilling the hopes of the exile years. The 'P type', the theatre as planetarium, as outlined by Brecht in *Buying Brass*, clearly exhibits utopian characteristics. As Brecht said of the Los Angeles production of *Galileo*, '[...] such productions must be viewed as examples of the kind of

---

[39]Frank Dietrich Wagner, 'Hitler und die Theatralik des Faschismus: Brechts antifaschistischer Diskurs' in *Zeitschrift für deutsche Philologie 101* (1982), 561–583; esp. 563, 576–581.

theatre that might be possible under different political and economic circumstances. With their successes and their failures, they are useful case studies for those who aspire to a theatre of important subject matter and worthwhile acting.'[40]

If we take seriously the idea of Brecht's epic theatre as exile theatre, we rediscover this crucial period of utopian anticipation whose dialectical historical fulfilment represents the 'theatre of the future'. As his last conversation with Manfred Wekwerth in August 1956 proves, Brecht pursued this project developed during the exile years right up until the end of his life.

---

[40]*Materialien zu Brechts Leben des Galilei*, 78.

CHAPTER FIFTEEN

Review of *Mother Courage and Her Children*

HANS OTT
TRANSLATED BY ROMY FURSLAND

The epic and balladesque visual drama *Mother Courage and her Children*, which draws on the chronicles of the Thirty Years War and on an awareness of historical materialism, is, in a nutshell, the best play yet by the German writer Bertolt Brecht – a politically committed, combative artist whose earlier work was rather relentless in its didacticism. Since column inches are rationed here and there is not enough space for an analysis of this logical yet moving, sad yet beautiful play with songs, we refer the reader to Peter Merin's essay 'The Work of Bert Brecht' as a useful introduction to Brecht before going to see *Mother Courage*. The essay appeared in the seventh issue of the fifth year (1935) of the magazine *Internationale Literatur*, which has since fallen victim to the war. Merin's analysis is a convenient way in to a deeper understanding of Brecht's epic drama (which is frequently interwoven with ballads). It also anticipates Brecht's huge potential as a writer.

Germany's new dramatic genius has never made it easy for himself. With the masterwork *Mother Courage* – whose date indicates that it is not a completely new work – this uncompromising dramatist, who is always on the side of the workers, always fighting for social equality, has convinced and surpassed his critics, who have proved themselves capable of learning.

Almost a decade ago, Bertolt Brecht set out his conception of the differing natures and techniques of the dramatic and the epic form of theatre. A very well-written essay, featured in the Schauspielhaus's programme for the *premiere* of *Mother Courage*, points to this conception of Brecht's (with one very apt caveat). In my personal view, the crucial step forward which inspires in us both delight and certainty is the fact that Brecht has managed to achieve a *fusion*, a homogenous blend of *the dramatic and the epic* – with ballads thrown in for good measure.

In short, what we are now seeing from this idiosyncratic poet and dramatist – who has always been a thorn in the side of those critics who focus solely on aesthetic and artistic concerns – is no longer just rationality, no longer just a *'Lehrstück'*, for which he practically held the German party-political patent and which he wanted to use as a form of monumental propaganda. Brecht's *Mother Courage* gives us both reason and emotion, technique and art, doctrine and life. My opinion is that, in line with the Brechtian credo of the dramatic and epic form of theatre, the scenes of wartime life which illustrate the

---

Hans Ott, '[Review of *Mother Courage and her Children*]', in Monika Wyss, *Brecht in der Kritik* (Munich: Kindler, 1977), pp. 210–12.

fate of Mother Courage and her children (whose deaths are preordained) give rise to the following epic-dramatic Brechtian theatre form.

This war play about the camp follower Courage, a character familiar to us from Grimmelshausen's *Simplicissimus* of 1669, not only narrates events but also embodies them on the stage.

It does not simply allow the spectators to be observers, but involves and implicates them in the characters' actions. The play inspires and requires them to become active participants; it elicits emotions and demands decisions. It conveys experiences and insights, and places the spectator *within* the plot and yet also outside of it. It achieves its effects through argument but also through suggestion. The alterable and the altered person is represented through the twists and turns of the plot in a way that makes clear what the world is like and what it could be like if people could rise above base instincts and disorder. In contrast to Brecht's earlier, purely 'cerebral' plays, this illuminated chronicle of a war, by depicting the lives and suffering of Mother Courage and her children, shows not only people's motives but also their instincts; it shows how human beings, with all their flaws, stand in their own way.

The only thing that remains entirely mechanistic are the fates of the characters; the first time Courage appears on stage in her canteen wagon (the main prop), she plays a fortune-telling game and reveals the black crosses that foretell the deaths of her children. We know in advance *what* will happen, but we are still on the edge of our seats as we watch the play's events unfold – proof of how well Brecht dramatises the epic, with what artistry he crafts the *'how'*. In this play of plays there are many different settings: a country road with a Swiss town in the background, military camps, a bombarded village, a copse just outside a town, a wintery street with a rectory, and a farmstead.

But it is always the same theatre: the theatre of war, everywhere and nowhere. And throughout the play, in a hundred different variations, in dialogues, monologues and ballads, we are told of the futility of *life at war*, and it is always the same cry, a phrase uttered by Mother Courage as she laments her children's fates: *War be damned!* This is the profound meaning of the epic-dramatic tale of Bertolt Brecht's Mother Courage and her children, a tale which aims to teach us where war ultimately leads. War eats its own children, even those who make a living from it and ostensibly benefit from it. For, as Mother Courage declares in her final song following the deaths of her three children by different fathers – her Eilif, her Swiss Cheese and her mute daughter Kattrin:

> With all its luck and all its danger
> The war is dragging on a bit,
> Another hundred years or longer
> The common man won't benefit.
> Filthy his food, no soap to shave him,
> The regiment steals half his pay
> But still a miracle may save him:
> Tomorrow is another day!
> The new year's come. The watchmen shout.
> The thaw sets in. The dead remain.
> Wherever life has not died out
> It staggers to its feet again.[1]

---

[1] Translation by John Willett in Bertolt Brecht, *Mother Courage and her Children*, translated by Michael Hofmann, songs translated by John Willett (London and New York: Bloomsbury Methuen Drama, 2006).

We were deeply impressed by the premiere at the Zurich Schauspielhaus, which is worthy of acknowledgement in its own right. The superb production by Leopold *Lindtberg* (director), Teo *Otto* (set designer), Paul *Burkhard* (musical director) and Ferd. *Lange* (technician) certainly met with the approval of the attentive audience, who were profoundly moved by the play. The script, the sensitive direction and the performances by Therese *Giehse* (Mother Courage), Erika *Pesch* (Kattrin), W. *Langhoff* (Eilif), K. *Paryla* (Swiss Cheese), W. *Steiner* (the Chaplain), and all the others, were greeted with a good five minutes of rapturous applause. Bertolt Brecht's Mother Courage is a warning to us in Switzerland too.

Hans Ott
Volksrecht, Zurich, 24 April 1941

Return to Germany/ Adaptations

CHAPTER SIXTEEN

Adaptations for the Berliner Ensemble

DAVID BARNETT

Bertolt Brecht is celebrated as a dramatist in his own right, but he was also involved in literary collaborations for the duration of his career as a writer. He gathered a group of friends around himself as a young man in Augsburg to exchange ideas and discuss their literary work, and the practice continued with different writers, directors and dramaturges until his death in 1956. Another form of collaboration, however, is to be found in Brecht's relationship with the work of other playwrights. His first full-length play, *Baal*, was a direct and critical engagement with Hanns Johst's *The Lonely Man*, yet, over the years, Brecht also developed more intimate relationships to source texts in the form of adaptations. His approach was not dictated by a standard approach but by complex responses to the dramatic material in question. Brecht's *The Life of Eduard II of England*, for example, was a radical dismemberment and reassembly of Marlowe's play, while Brecht preserved many important elements of John Gay's *The Beggars Opera* in *The Threepenny Opera*. *Round Heads and Pointed Heads* began as an adaptation of *Measure for Measure* before taking a completely different direction and leaving little more than a passing resemblance to Shakespeare's play. However, once Brecht had a theatre of his own, the Berliner Ensemble (BE), his approach to adaptation began to take its lead from a series of political and aesthetic principles, as we shall see below. The adaptations in this volume, which were written between the BE's first season (1949–50) and the last one Brecht would experience (1955–6), conform to these principles, but, as will become evident, their application did not lead to standardized output by any means. In order to understand this shift to a different, more focused form of adaptation, we need to appreciate what having his own theatre meant to Brecht and how this affected the work he sought to bring to it.

* * *

Brecht, together with his wife, Helene Weigel, and their children, had been in exile in a number of countries since the Nazis came to power in 1933. During this period Brecht had very little access to the theatre and instead devoted most of his creative energy to

---

David Barnett, 'Adaptations for the Berliner Ensemble', in Brecht, *Berliner Ensemble Adaptations* (London: Bloomsbury, 2014), pp. vii–xxiii.

writing plays, poems and theoretical texts. Having left the USA in October 1947, after a not untraumatic hearing at the hands of the McCarthyite House Un-American Activities Committee, he journeyed on to Zurich via Paris, and contemplated a return to active theatre-making. At this time, it was by no means certain that he would settle in the Soviet zone of Berlin. Although the Soviets had offered him incentives, he flirted with relocating to Salzburg and Munich but these plans came to nothing.

By late 1948 Brecht finally decided to return to Berlin, the site of his only major triumph to date, *The Threepenny Opera*. Yet the theatre in which it premiered under the direction of Erich Engel in 1928, the Theater am Schiffbauerdamm, was already occupied by a company under the leadership of Fritz Wisten. Indeed, there seemed to be no room at all in what would become East Berlin for Brecht and a new ensemble; it looked like he had arrived in Germany too late. So, with this lack of free space in mind, he sought to attach the new ensemble he proposed, at least for the short term, to an existing theatre. The East German government was planning to rebuild another major theatre, the Volksbühne, with a view to moving Wisten and his troupe there and allowing Brecht to return to the Schiffbauerdamm. Estimates concerning the building project were hopelessly optimistic, however. In the meantime, the BE, with Weigel as general manager and Brecht as artistic director, was supposed to spend just one season at Wolfgang Langhoff's Deutsches Theater. As it turned out, they remained there until 1953.

After much to-ing and fro-ing between the various institutions that ran Berlin before the foundation of the German Democratic Republic (GDR) on 7 October 1949, Weigel finally signed a contract with the Department of People's Education that brought the BE into existence on 1 September. The initial question that confronted the new company was what it was going to perform. Brecht certainly had enough plays of his own and, indeed, opened the new season on 12 November with *Mr Puntila and his Man Matti*. However, he was reluctant to turn his company into a vehicle solely for realizing his own dramas and wanted a greater mix, including contemporary and classic plays, that could make an active contribution to the cultural life of the city and its citizens.

While Brecht was interested in attracting other directors to work at the BE, he was also keen to develop his own theorized practice now that he had regular access to a proper stage. This he could not do alone and so he re-activated old contacts, such as Erich Engel and his school friend, the set-designer Caspar Neher. Yet these were collaborators of Brecht's generation, and one of the BE's missions was to test out and disseminate a new way of making theatre. Consequently, Brecht recruited a team of young assistants who were to learn from him, not by spending hours in the archive reading his unpublished theories, but by observing him at work, making suggestions, and reflecting on the work they observed in their own detailed and analytical rehearsal notes. Brecht created a circle of enthusiastic, committed theatre-makers with whom he could collaborate and advance his ideas. Yet the tasks he set them extended well beyond the rehearsal room.

In a bid to build the BE's repertoire, Brecht returned to the practice of adaptation, but also exploited the *process* of adaptation as a means of developing his young assistants. That is, he was able to focus his assistants' nascent interests and abilities by encouraging them to edit and, indeed, to adulterate existing texts while reserving his own place as editor-in-chief and writer of additional material. But the repertoire was not merely to comprise a collection of Brecht's favourite plays; Brecht was profoundly aware that he had opted to live in the first (and, as yet, last) socialist state on German soil and set about fashioning a repertoire worthy of that state. So, while he implemented ideas that had fermented during his long exile – from developing an active ensemble on stage to assembling a dynamic team he envisaged as able successors in due course – he did not neglect the material his predominantly young cast and crew were to perform. The adaptations, which would become something of a staple at the BE, were written in such a way that they would exemplify the social aims of the company, and these can be seen in the criteria Brecht set down for his young assistants.

* * *

The first text Brecht selected for adaptation was *The Tutor*, written by J. M. R. Lenz in 1774. Lenz was one of a disparate group of energetic young writers who would collectively be known as the 'storm and stress' movement, or *Sturm und Drang*. His dramatic output is marked by its bold themes and formal innovation; indeed his play *The Soldiers* can be read as a precursor to Brecht's epic theatre in that it regularly features scenes in which characters comment explicitly on the action rather than participate in it, like Brecht's narrators. *The Tutor*, a play that is today regarded as a classic of the 'storm and stress' period, was, in 1949, little-known and ripe for rediscovery. However, Brecht was not prepared to direct it as it stood and engaged his assistants in the process of adaptation. In the following extract, we can see the sort of tasks he set. This systematic approach to adaptation may have been implicit to his own practices previously but the overt statement of its tenets signalled a set of principles which informed both his thoughts about the nature of dramatic source texts and how they might be realized at the BE.

First, he asked his assistants to trim 30 minutes off the total running time. He then wanted them to:

2. establish clearly the central *Fabel* (the account of the real events) so that it is easily understandable, while retaining the elegance of the sequence of the scenes,
3. arrange the subplots around the central *Fabel* so that they illuminate and explicate the latter smoothly without interrupting it,
4. eliminate the untypical, accidental or purely pathological features in the motivation of the action and the characters.

The instructions point to several important aspects of an adaptation for Brecht. Items 2 and 3 put an unmistakable emphasis on clarity. The organization of the main plot and the subplot had to serve the purpose of drawing clear through-lines in the complicated course of events. Lenz, who, like other storm-and-stress playwrights, was influenced by Shakespeare, wanted to give his play the richness and liveliness associated with Shakespeare's dramas. Brecht, however, sought to impose order upon the various plots as a way of deepening the treatment of the central themes, rather than taking in too many extraneous meanderings, as he saw them. It should be noted, however, that this formal reorganization was not to interfere with the beauty of the play's flow. Brecht was not suggesting a utilitarian butchering of the play's form; instead he wanted to combine his aims with the qualities that made Lenz's play so attractive to him in the first place. This respect towards the unique appeal of all the source texts in this volume is one factor that prevented the adaptations from becoming mechanical or repetitive: each work had to be confronted on its own terms and only then could adaptation proceed.

Item 4 deals more specifically with issues concerning Brecht's political aims for the adaptation as the basis for a successful performance. The direction to eliminate certain elements again concerns itself with clarity. In addition, the three elements also tell us about the type of material that was not admissible in a text designed to engage the audience's critical faculties to the full. Eliminating the untypical meant that spectators could contemplate characters and events which were not in some way out of the ordinary but ones which would have concrete significance for them. Similarly, the accidental relied too much on chance to offer an audience material from which it could make meaningful connections about the world and the way it worked. Brecht maintained here that the representation of the world on stage had to be exemplary – it could not simply follow the foibles of everyday life but had consciously to aim to reproduce actions that were important and intelligible to an audience. If spectators were to learn anything, then exceptional or accidental material could not be included. The prohibition on 'pathological features' indicates another area Brecht deemed beyond the remit of a politically committed drama, in that such conditions were innate and thus unchangeable. While scholarly work has subsequently posited links between mental illness and the mechanisms of society, at that time, socialist states considered psychoanalysis and psychotherapy bourgeois and alien to working people.

The three items thus show how Brecht's formal adaptation process focused on offering material to the audience defined by its usefulness. The unswerving drive towards clarity should not, however, be mistaken for a desire to make things easy for the audience. Brecht's theatre was based on posing questions which only the spectators could answer. 'Clarity', then, involved articulating these questions as clearly as possible. The questions came in the form of on-stage contradictions. In *The Tutor*, for example, the audience was confronted with the central issue of why an intelligent tutor had to sell his services and demean himself in order to survive in the society of the time. Brecht thus sought to make the articulation of that difficult contradiction clear while the responses to it were complex and a matter for the audience.

Adaptation was not only a business that concerned the form of a play. Certain aspects of the original's themes were also important. For example, Lenz's play contains a reformist streak, suggesting that class and educational systems were capable of repair under feudalism. Brecht disagreed with this position and both deleted the first scene from Lenz's second act and rewrote the main voice of reform, Major von Berg, in order to expunge this suggestion from the play. As a Marxist, Brecht wanted to point to the failings of the system itself and suggest that only revolution was the appropriate solution. However, the accuracy of the depiction of feudalism and those involved in it should equally demonstrate just how difficult it would be to engineer such social and political upheaval.

Formal and thematic adaptation served to heighten the central theme of the play in Brecht's reading: the German 'misère'. Broadly speaking, this term refers to the German people's inability to bring about a successful social revolution, unlike the French in 1789. The Peasants' Revolt of the early sixteenth century and the bourgeois uprising of 1848 both came to nothing and the patchwork of German states retained their class-based hierarchy. Brecht also noted in the unpublished introduction to *Turandot* that even in the most terrible days at the end of World War Two, the German proletariat had not seized the moment and risen up against the Nazis. To Brecht, *The Tutor* was an object lesson in servility and deference to one's social 'superiors', and he wanted the production to use comedy as a way of pointing to this attitude with a view to overcoming it.

Adaptation was also much more than merely cutting and reworking the text into a finished product; it was an ongoing process that ran through rehearsals. Several drafts of

The Tutor exist and chart the ways in which practical work affected the architecture and feel of the new script. Rehearsal would reveal just how successful the current draft had been and the rhythm of lines, speeches, dialogues and scenes would change in accordance with the effects generated on stage. It is worth noting that this was an experimental process: actors were not required merely to perform what they found on the page but to plumb the text's depths and make discoveries which may not have been apparent to the adapters. The discoveries would then inform the next draft. The lack of a definitive end point for the script, for example, is betokened by the fact that Brecht wrote the epilogue to *The Tutor* very late in the day. Up until then, the cast had used the more general epilogue to *The Good Person of Szechwan*. This shows how the team were not working towards this end from the outset; on the contrary, the epilogue took the material developed previously and made its own concluding remarks.

* * *

I have dwelt on the adaptation of *The Tutor* at length because it offers a model for how the other adaptations in this volume also developed. The emphasis on clarity, the social rather than the individual dimension, and the idea that text can only be properly developed in rehearsal runs through the BE's work under Brecht's leadership. The one adaptation which did not make it to rehearsal in Brecht's lifetime was *Coriolanus*. As a result, the text we have is incomplete, especially, as Ralph Mannheim notes, around the battle scenes at the end of Act One. However, it should not be overlooked that rehearsal itself might well have revealed more about the initial adaptation and that the final version might have looked very different from the version Brecht in fact left after he stopped working on it in 1953. Indeed, when the BE finally staged the play in 1964, the directors Manfred Wekwerth and Joachim Tenschert spent much time with a battery of assistants adapting the adaptation. The final BE script contained roughly 10 per cent of material added after Brecht's death.

It was a logical progression for Brecht to move from Lenz to Shakespeare, and he said as much in a *Journal* entry of 22 December 1949. Brecht rated Shakespeare as the greatest realist of the bourgeois stage, yet realism here does not denote the faithful reproduction of everyday appearances, as is the case with plays by Chekhov, for example, or Arthur Miller. What Brecht meant was that Shakespeare understood how characters behaved and acted under the pressure of their historical situation – this was the 'reality' Brecht sought beneath surface appearances. The characters' language may, of course, be poetic and metaphorical – nobody actually talks like that. To Brecht, it was the attitudes towards reality encoded in such speeches that rendered them 'realistic'. Performing such realism was not easy and so *The Tutor*, inspired by Shakespeare's dramaturgy, offered the BE, and particularly its young actors, an opportunity to develop the skills demanded by Brecht's realistic theatre before the cast and crew confronted the master of the genre.

As much as Brecht admired Shakespeare, he still felt that there were characters and events that required further adaptation. The 'Study of the first scene of Shakespeare's *Coriolanus*' demonstrates the ways Brecht interrogated the material he found. The 'study' is not a verbatim account of a meeting, in which Brecht is represented by a 'B'; he rewrote it in order to emphasize certain salient points. B's role here is to stimulate dialogue by asking questions and making observations about the text as it stands. On occasion, he notes that Shakespeare was writing for a different kind of theatre, one of a class society. Brecht and the BE, on the other hand, were planning a production in a socialist state, and this shift of context provided the main reason for an adaptation. Brecht sought to undermine the prejudices against the working people of Rome that pervaded Shakespeare's time and to undermine the implicit dominance of the patricians. In response, the people's tribunes became more credible characters in their own right than mere intriguing politicians who have a personal problem with Coriolanus himself. The common people were also recast. Shakespeare's IV iii became Brecht's IV i, for example, and the scene was completely rewritten. Rather than making the banishment of Coriolanus the focus, two men, a Roman and a Volscian, consider how the world is safer without Coriolanus, but they are more concerned with their common social plight away from the tribal wrangles. The workers of this world most certainly unite, because they understand that they share a common set of problems defined by their place on the lower rungs of the social ladder.

The last scene also presents a very different finale: rather than the dramatic murder of Coriolanus at the hands of Aufidius and his men, the audience is returned to a more tranquil and understated setting, the Roman Senate. Life goes on and the politicians are going about their legislative business when news of Coriolanus' death arrives. Menenius asks that the vanquished general's name be inscribed in the Capitol but the politicians continue their meeting. The family is also denied the honour of wearing public robes of mourning for ten months, a decision that inverts the ending of Shakespeare's play. This final scene is also interesting in that it features senators, a consul, and the tribunes. That is, the defeat of Coriolanus and the relegation of his importance has not suddenly led to social revolution: the noble senators are still present in the legislature. However, the tribunes are the ones who reject the two proposals to memorialize the man who ultimately betrayed Rome, despite his victories earlier in the play. Power is shifting, but is not in the tribune's hands yet.

Brecht was also troubled by the figure of Coriolanus himself because he represented one of Shakespeare's 'great individuals'. These characters appeared to be imbued with character traits that resisted social categorization, that is, they were seemingly 'given' naturally, something Brecht found difficult to accept. Instead he read Coriolanus as a specialist in war who overestimated his own value. Viewing himself above and apart from society, he mistakenly believed he was indispensable. Brecht showed how the people of Rome went on to arm themselves against further attack from the Volscians under Coriolanus in order to point out Coriolanus' more peripheral status. His tragedy in Shakespeare is his pride; in Brecht he falls because of his individualism, a category which is social as well as personal. He fails to realize that the upper echelons of Roman society indulge him his individualism when he is in favour but that the people, in the form of the tribunes, reject it when he fails to play his role in the political process. Brecht thus retained the element of tragic pride but re-contextualized it in the power networks of Roman society.

* * *

The social element also provided the focus when Brecht and Benno Besson adapted Anna Seghers' *The Trial of Joan of Arc at Rouen, 1431*. The original radio play mostly emphasized the trial, yet the adapters sought to bring in the on-stage audience far more prominently as a way of creating a fuller picture of French society under English rule. Besson, who directed the production, acknowledged that this was his first show in which he clearly understood the way socially defined contradictions manifested themselves on stage and changed as events changed. The new script thus allowed him to construct contradictions, resolve them and develop them with new ones. Indeed, the expansion of the crowd scenes led to experiments with the staging, in that Besson used approaches taken from Stanislavsky in order to individualize the representative crowd more 'realistically'. The BE found that Stanislavsky could be integrated into the BE's working methods as long as the focus of the work remains social rather than psychological. The individuality brought out from the members of the crowd emphasized details of their social origins and attitudes, and made plain how these factors altered as new information and relationships emerged in the light of the trial.

Don Juan initially started as a project commissioned by another theatre, the Volkstheater Rostock. Besson had been out of favour at the BE because he had lost the rehearsal notes to *The Tutor* and was invited independently of Brecht to direct any play of his choice. Having been involved in the adaptation process at the BE, he chose Molière's play because he considered it formally weak in comparison to the rest of the French playwright's *oeuvre*. He was particularly concerned by the way the action seemed to drag in the original's final two acts and so he conflated them into what is the final act of the adaptation, Act Four. Elsewhere we notice again the introduction of new characters and situations in a bid to expand the social reach of the play.

Besson reported that he and Brecht's long-standing collaborator Elisabeth Hauptmann started translating and adapting the text when Brecht got wind of the project and that Brecht then took a leading role. A transcript of a meeting that Brecht chaired, which appears to be verbatim rather than the edited text on *Coriolanus* discussed above, again shows how actively Brecht sought to problematize the texts staged by the BE. In this discussion, he particularly focused on what comedy meant in *Don Juan*, but rather than offering his own theses, he employed an interrogative mode, persistently posing questions to tease out the meaning of the genre in the context of the Don Juan myth, which is usually considered tragic. His constant questioning did not settle on the answers given by his collaborators but used them only to probe further.

Again the central figure proved problematic and Brecht was keen to process the reviews the production garnered in Rostock in order to correct some of its perceived flaws and to improve upon them. Brecht objected to the position that Don Juan's atheism was in some way progressive. He preferred to view it as a mark of Don Juan's decadence in a decadent court, an absence of faith rather than the militant championing of a cause. Again, social contradiction is central to Brecht's thought: Don Juan's hedonism makes him lazy, and his hedonism is an index of the state of the court in pre-revolutionary France. Brecht wanted Besson to bring out these aspects as comic and laughable. This Besson did when he directed the play afresh as the curtain-raiser when the BE finally moved to the Theater am Schiffbauerdamm in early 1954. That Brecht chose to open the new venue with a play written by another dramatist and directed by one of his assistants and not himself shows how he was happy not to hog the limelight but to promote the talent of others. Brecht certainly played a major role in both the adaptation and the direction. As he told Besson afterwards, he was happy to help, but he would have staged the production quite differently and so he wanted Besson to take the credit as sole director.

Brecht followed up the success of the adapted *Don Juan* with another comedy, taken from a different tradition. George Farquhar's Restoration Comedy *The Recruiting Officer* formed the basis of *Trumpets and Drums*. One of the most obvious changes is historical: Farquhar's original settings taken from his own time, the beginning of the eighteenth century, shift forward to the American War of Independence, much later that century.

This decision appears to have been taken in a bid to make the action more accessible for the German audience. Spectators would have found it easier to understand the tensions associated with imperialism, although this could have led to a political issue concerning the positive portrayal of the Americans at a time when they played the role of imperialist aggressor in GDR cold-war propaganda.

As it happened, this was not the case. Instead, the ruling Socialist Unity Party (abbreviated in German to 'SED') had more pragmatic concerns. As John Willett notes in 'Adapting Farquhar', the main work on the adaptation took place between March and April 1955, yet the play was only premiered in September. The reason for this was that the cultural functionaries were concerned that the play, which has a critique of press-ganging as its theme, could be construed as pacifist. The Federal Republic of Germany was remilitarizing and founded the *Bundeswehr* a month after the premiere, and the GDR followed suit in 1956 with the formation of the *Nationale Volksarmee* (National People's Army). The SED thus viewed pacifism as a position that undermined the planned establishment of its armed forces and did not want its most famous theatre producing work that could be interpreted as critical of the policy. In the period between adapting *The Recruiting Officer* and putting it on the stage, the BE set about insulating the text from any charge of pacifism by focusing its critique on the issue of *imperialist* warmongering and the lengths to which the British would go to fight their war of subjugation, rather than as a blanket condemnation of military action.

* * *

This, however, was not the only occasion on which the SED intervened in the BE's plans regarding adaptations. Indeed, adaptations were much contested because of their implication in a major aspect of GDR cultural policy. The SED viewed the GDR as the inheritor of a progressive German tradition and used this usurped authority as a way of distancing the GDR as a socialist republic from the catastrophe of Nazism. The way in which this political definition of the nation affected culture was in the treatment of the German cultural heritage. Productions of classic works were obliged to emphasize positive aspects in the plays in order to connect the present with those chosen and preferred parts of the past. It is thus not a little peculiar that the SED neither publicly nor privately censured *The Tutor*. Staging the 'misère' pointed out, after all, a deep-rooted historical inability of the German people to shape history in its own interests, and the production's ironic happy ending would not have protected the BE against the charge of pessimism. To Brecht, on the other hand, the play and its ending were an example of a 'negative example', one in which the audience was confronted with the parody of an ideal with a view to suggesting its own improvements. The lack of pointers towards a brighter future would not have sufficed as a valid conclusion to the authorities, who banned Hanns Eisler's *Johannes Faustus* in 1953 for its negative portrayal of Faust, the SED's most cherished figure from the German canon.

The question then arises as to why the SED did not move against *The Tutor* in 1950. It is likely that three main factors led to the production failing to register with the SED's cultural organs. First, *The Tutor*, as already noted, was not that well known. It would have been difficult to raise the Party's hackles if it could not refer to an official line on the play. Similarly, the audience would have encountered performances 'afresh' with few, if any, preconceived notions about the play, its themes or its forms. That Brecht and his collaborators had made great changes may not have been all that noticeable, especially given the second item in the list of tasks for the adapters: that the play should retain 'the elegance of the sequence of the scenes'. Second, the production was a great success. Audiences and reviewers alike praised its precision, its beauty, its lightness and its humour. The young ensemble had demonstrated how well it could function as a unit, and the production's critique of an oppressive society was lively and engaging, not leaden and propagandistic. Third, the SED itself was uncertain how to wield its new power. The regime was still in a process of bedding down and culture was administered by a range of different agencies, ranging from the Central Committee, through the recently established Ministry of People's Education, down to more local Berlin authorities. It is possible that the Party was not confident enough to launch an attack on a work that was at once unfamiliar and remarkably popular.

The same could not be said of *Coriolanus*. By 1951, the SED was firmly in control and had turned its opinions on the cultural heritage and other aspects of cultural policy into dogma. The Party officially adopted positions on various cultural matters at a conference held between 15–17 March 1951. After this date, it sought to impose its will more heavy-handedly, and, in a meeting in August 1951, it banned further work on the Shakespearean adaptation. The combination of the world's most famous dramatist, whom the Germans had been calling 'our Shakespeare' since at least the eighteenth century, and a protagonist, who had certain affinities to Stalin, was enough to alert the Central Committee to the potential dangers of a production. Brecht did continue to work on the play, but kept the further adaptation quiet, partly for political reasons, partly because he could not secure a suitable male lead for the eponymous hero.

Another BE adaptation, not included in this volume, also came in for official criticism. In 1951, the company staged a fusion of two plays by Gerhart Hauptmann that featured the same lead character, one each side of the interval. *The Beaver Coat* is a full-blooded comedy, *Red Hen* a tragi-comedy; their joining did not make for great theatre, and the production was not well received despite the much-lauded performance of one of Germany's most accomplished actors, Therese Giehse, in the main role of Mother Wolffen. The SED was not concerned about the success or failure of the production; it found the process of adulterating two classic plays by transforming them into one evening's theatre at odds with its ideas on the purity of the cultural heritage and sought to remove the mongrel from the repertoire. In this case, however, the SED was beaten to its goal by Hauptmann's estate which unknowingly shared the Party's view and withdrew the rights after a mere fourteen performances. The estate explicitly objected to the act of adaptation because it had only granted permission for what it called a 'dramaturgical arrangement' of the material.

It is telling that the BE's most controversial production in this early period of GDR history was deliberately kept 'un-adapted'. The BE staged Goethe's *Urfaust*, the early drafts of what would become the first part of *Faust*, in 1952 in Potsdam and 1953 in Berlin. After the diktats on *Coriolanus* and other works scheduled for the BE, Brecht was naturally wary. Nonetheless, he supervised the *Urfaust* production, which was directed by assistant Egon Monk, and approached it in much the same way he would any other production. That is, he mined it for contradictions and conferred on it a lively new reading, away from the orthodoxies of the day. The first production, which portrayed Faust as a charlatan and seducer, was initially praised in the local press but a letter from the Party group at the theatre that hosted the production was merciless in its critique of how the BE had betrayed the German cultural heritage. An adaptation would have merely given the Party more grist to its mill, in that Brecht would have been accused of 'perverting' the text to suit his ends. The preservation of the original text meant that he was only working with the material he found. The second attempt to stage the play in Berlin was deliberately toned down, in the light of the public criticism. Faust no longer had the negative traits that he had had in Potsdam; his tragic contradiction was predicated upon the position that he had to engage in a pact with the devil in order to pursue his more progressive ends. This radical shift in interpretation could not, however, save a production already sullied. The head of the Deutsches Theater, Wolfgang Langhoff, did not allow *Urfaust* to be performed to audiences as an evening show, and consigned it to matinees. After seven of these passed, and with no prospect of entering the normal repertoire, the production vanished, never to be seen again, although, ironically enough, young film-maker Hans-Jürgen Syberberg captured some of the rehearsals on his 8mm camera in 1953.

The Trial of Joan of Arc and *Don Juan* did not attract any adverse criticism. One can only speculate about why this was the case, but *The Trial* was, like *The Tutor*, a little-known work, and it was written by Anna Seghers, a socialist writer of impeccable credentials. Brecht's additions were not controversial – they mostly expanded the crowd scenes to involve the Party's hero of choice, the common people. *Don Juan* was being rehearsed on one of the most traumatic days in the GDR's history: 17 June 1953. This was the day when workers went on strike and protested against the SED's economic policies. With support from the West, the protests became an uprising in which the masses on the streets called for the removal of the SED from power. Soviet tanks rolled into Berlin and order was restored, yet the SED was given the bloodiest of noses and was forced to dilute its hard-line position on a variety of fronts. What followed for the cultural sector was something of a thaw. It is difficult to know whether *Don Juan* would have attracted censure in the first place – Molière was not as problematic as Goethe or Shakespeare, and to call a possibly progressive aristocrat decadent was hardly incendiary. It is more likely that the authorities felt severely restricted in their ability to intervene and this particular play offered so little offence that it would not have been worth criticizing the work.

* * *

Adaptations, it would seem, were an important part of the BE's repertoire, yet the BE's two attempts at *Urfaust* raise an important question regarding the necessity of adaptations at Brecht's theatre at all. With the SED firmly applying pressure to *Coriolanus*, Brecht decided to trust his own approaches to making theatre rather than risk a ban on a play he considered important. Brecht's stagecraft was concerned with activating the audience and he developed a range of ideas and practices to achieve this. At their base was the desire to do away with a harmonic union of signs transmitted from the stage to the auditorium. For example, Brecht did not necessarily want lines about, say, happiness to be delivered in a happy voice, or for music to tell the same story as a song's lyrics. Similarly, an actor's body could articulate something different from what he or she was saying. Such moves were designed productively to unsettle the spectators and ask them why the theatre was saying two different things at once. In short, Brecht was keen for his audience to question what it saw and heard, and to ask what might be motivating it. And with his customary emphasis on the social, contributory factors tended to emanate from society rather than the characters.

So Brecht had envisaged modes of performing which criticized or at least modified the material being performed. His theatre of juxtaposed signs deferred ultimate interpretation to the audience. Performance was thus taking on some of the qualities identified in the adaptation discussed above: it pointed to areas one might consider questionable and invited constructive responses. Brecht said as much shortly before his death in 1956: 'if I were putting him [Shakespeare] on today, it is only small changes I would have to make in the production, changes of emphasis'. Sadly, we do not know how Brecht would have directed *Coriolanus* or any other classic play after this pronouncement, but perhaps he had realized by then that the stage could offer a forum for creative challenges to dramatic works to dislodge the centrality of the written adaptation. Regardless of this late position, the BE continued to adapt plays, including those by Brecht that were as yet unperformed, such as *Arturo Ui* and *The Days of the Commune*.

Whether Brecht planned to shift from adapting texts to staging them more radically will never be known. The adaptations in this volume, however, give a clear sense of Brecht's theatrical interests and the directions he sought to pursue upon arriving back in Germany and taking control of an ensemble of his own. The need to make socially useful theatre runs through the adaptations, and the dramaturgical 'corrections' he introduced point to a need to readjust older plays for a more complete picture of society represented on stage. From a new role for the common people to the relativisation of seemingly autonomous central characters, the plays give the audience more to consider in terms of the interaction between the individual and society. This expansion of the social palette was matched by an almost iron resolve to achieve clarity on stage. The social contradictions could not be blurred or mistaken for something else, otherwise the audience would not be able to make informed decisions. The adaptations strove to include only salient material. This did not mean that society was in some way reduced to simple tensions; rather the adaptation process was concerned with bringing out the complexities of society in a clear fashion. Merely observe the dynamic modulations that run through the crowd scenes in *The Trial of Joan of Arc*, for example, to understand how changes in situation affect different social strata in different ways.

The adaptations draft a vision of socially committed drama to act as a corrective to plays that suggest we are prisoners of our psychology and unable to influence our environment. Brecht and his collaborators set about probing the texts in question to expose how people got trapped in the seemingly unchangeable structures of society and to ask in whose interests such structures functioned. Hasty, the eponymous tutor, is no fool but finds himself suffering at the hands of a system loaded against him. While he can hardly be said to triumph at the play's conclusion, the audience, armed with more knowledge about the social set-up, can speculate about how Hasty and others like him might seek to escape their fate.

The BE was a hothouse that produced innovative ways of conceptualizing and realizing theatre. The adaptations in this volume represent one of the strands Brecht developed to change the theatrical landscape of Germany. While they are one of many, they endure today as documents that reflect important directions for a new kind of theatre. And while reading them is one thing, they also invite theatre-makers to take up their challenge and realize productions that present a world which may not be easy to change, but is changeable all the same.

CHAPTER SEVENTEEN

Review of *Mother Courage and Her Children*

GERHARD WAHNRAU
TRANSLATED BY ROMY FURSLAND

1949 The Berliner Ensemble performs Mother Courage
(Deutsches Theater, East Berlin, 11 January 1949)

This is a discussion of the 200th performance on 3.4.1954 at the Theater am Schiffbauerdamm

Directed by Erich Engel, Bert Brecht
Set design: Teo Otto, Heinrich Kilger
Music: Paul Dessau

Five-and-a-quarter years have passed since 11 January 1949, when this 'chronicle of the Thirty Years War' had its Berlin premiere at the Deutsches Theater. Since that day the Berliner Ensemble have performed Bertolt Brecht's play 200 times, an astounding number for such a serious drama. That alone is a good reason to revisit this production, which was a landmark in the post-war history of Berlin theatre – perhaps its most significant achievement to date. A new review is also needed because almost all the roles have been recast over the past five years. Of the original actors only Helene Weigel, Angelika Hurwicz and Gert Schäfer remain (Schäfer originally played a young soldier, and now plays the General). And finally, we need to take a fresh look at the production now that it has moved from the Deutsches Theater to the Berliner Ensemble's own Theater am Schiffbauerdamm.

The directors Erich Engel and Bertolt Brecht had tailored their production to the large stage at the Deutsches Theater, where the set was designed by Heinrich Kilger with just a few pieces of scenery, props and texts. Against the vast grey horizon which, in its endlessness, served as a symbol of desolation, the production had something visionary about it. The actors playing the people who had died in the war stood on this expanse of stage like silhouettes against a backdrop of eternal hopelessness. The unique effect created by the production did not come directly from the actors. It was reflected first off the horizon, which acted like a huge concave mirror in the centre of which the words and gestures of the actors were caught, concentrated, intensified and broken up, to be beamed in a wide spectrum across the audience. The much smaller stage at the Schiffbauerdamm

---

Gerhard Wahnrau, '[Review of *Mother Courage and her Children*]', in Monika Wyss, *Brecht in der Kritik* (Munich: Kindler, 1977), pp. 216–18.

and the lack of the rounded horizon have, in some respects, significantly altered the emphasis of the production. Indirect effects have given way to direct ones.

And these effects are inescapable. In the smaller theatre, the audience and the actors come face to face – everything about the actors' performance is direct and immediate, meaning that the production has even more of that 'Brechtian style' (which has fascinated us ever since the *Threepenny Opera*) than its predecessor. The audience no longer merely witnesses a depiction of horror, poverty, vice; they are within touching distance of it and perhaps even, one might argue from an artistic point of view, a little too close to it. But perhaps this helps Brecht, as the writer, achieve his aim – of making the audience actively observe what is happening on stage – in an even more powerful way.

At the same time, the transfer of this production from one stage to another is an interesting contribution to Brechtian model theory. It is beyond the scope of this review to address the issue, but it is worth noting that this production could be used as an example on which to base a meaningful discussion of this important topic.

Just like on the first day (in both a chronological and an artistic sense), Helene Weigel plays Mother Courage and Angelika Hurwicz plays Kattrin. They have not grown with their roles over the years for the simple reason that their performances the first time were unsurpassable. Indeed, it is a compliment to both actresses, particularly the younger Angelika Hurwicz in the exceedingly difficult and risky role of mute Kattrin, to say that they are still 'the same as on the first day'. Helene Weigel performs with the same restraint, simplicity and authenticity as she did back then. Not a single gesture is superfluous; she never overacts, or tries to showcase her own talent. And Angelika Hurwicz is still the same mute, suffering creature – but without ever becoming a dumb animal, which is one of the risks of the role if certain delicate nuances are handled wrongly.

The Cook is now played by Ernst Busch. He is not, as Paul Bildt was, a wreck of a human being, a chuckling toothless old man who clings on to the past and tries to play the dashing ladies' man. Ernst Busch's Cook really *is* this smooth operator, a man who knows exactly what he wants and what he is capable of. For him, the job of cook beside a general's tent is not a last refuge but the best and quietest place in which to sit out the war. Despite this very different interpretation of the role, Busch still manages to portray the character's development into the resigned man we see at the end of the play. And he gives a harrowing rendition of 'The Song of Home'. Erwin Geschonneck is now playing the Chaplain. His interpretation of the role also differs from Werner Hinz's. Hinz's Chaplain was a squalid creature, a degenerate intellectual to whom juggling with Bible quotations came as naturally as deviousness, cowardice and bootlicking. Geschonneck's Chaplain is more primitive, more animal. He is an example of a man who took up a vocation without a calling, proof of the fact that – to borrow a metaphor from his own *métier* – Saul does not become Paul simply by virtue of dressing like him.

When Busch and Geschonneck appear on stage together with Helene Weigel and Angelika Hurwicz (who stays mainly in the background), this is still unique and unparalleled theatre. One example among many is the magnificent scene in which the three declaim the hymn 'A Mighty Fortress is Our God'.

Alongside them, the rest of the Ensemble do not have it easy. Five years ago the production was a major theatrical event partly because its minor roles and bit parts were played – with the exception of a few talented up-and-coming performers – by well-known and important actors. It brought together an ensemble of big names. Since then the Berliner Ensemble has trained up its own tribe of mostly young actors. They strive for that characteristically Brechtian style which calls for actors to appear on stage 'in a double guise' (see the *Short Organon*, Section 49). This means that they must not only inhabit their role but also stand outside of it and continually observe themselves. The efforts of all the actors to embody this double entity, from which the performance as a whole arises, is unmistakeable. The diversity of the roles makes it impossible to know to what extent each individual performer is doing justice to his or her task. Brecht's 'staccato style' calls for the actors to be completely present from the word go: there is no time for slowly 'warming up' or getting into one's stride. His 'punchlines', which are also truths, must be fired out by the actors 'from a standing start'. This is difficult, and not every actor is able to master it straight away. In this regard the directors still have work to do, particularly in the cases of Ekkehard Schall (Eilif) and Georg August Koch (the Sergeant). But these relatively minor issues should not stop us from praising the coherence of the production. It is, as before, an exemplary ensemble performance. In every scene, one perceives the sincere efforts of the individual actors to do justice to one of the greatest dramatic works of our time. And the fervent efforts of young people are worth no less than the consummate talents of experienced ones.

Gerhard Wahnrau
Theater der Zeit, East Berlin, May 1954

CHAPTER EIGHTEEN

Review of *Coriolanus*

FRANZ SCHONAUER
TRANSLATED BY ROMY FURSLAND

1964 Premiere in East Berlin (Theater am Schiffbauerdamm 25 September 1964)

Directors: J. Tenschert, M. Wekwerth
Set design: Karl von Appen
Music: Paul Dessau

Of all Shakespeare's great tragedies, that of the Roman general Coriolanus, believed to have been written in around 1607, has always been one of his least performed plays. This is not due to a lack of stageability, but rather to a sense of embarrassment and discomfort about a drama whose stark, brutal message is not rendered more palatable by any poetic flourishes or heady celestial music.

Brecht's preoccupation with Shakespeare dates back to the year 1920; the young playwright from Augsburg read *Antony and Cleopatra* with great enthusiasm, and the older playwright translated and reworked *Coriolanus* for his own theatrical ends. In between came a long dialectical process of engagement with the figure and the work of the English dramatist.

It is no surprise that Brecht seized upon *Coriolanus* for the programme of his 'epic theatre'; what is more surprising is that this was the only Shakespeare play he adapted in this way. Brecht was working on the play in 1951/52, and the trajectory and aims of his experiment emerge clearly from notes he wrote at the time. Brecht declares: 'It is not necessary – nor, given Shakespeare's genius, is it possible – to disregard or even simply to soften the tragedy of pride. It may be that Coriolanus sees his own death and downfall as a price worth paying to give free rein to his exorbitant pride. But ultimately society pays the price too; Rome pays the price, and is nearly brought down. And as far as the hero is concerned, society is interested in another aspect which affects it directly: the hero's belief that he is irreplaceable. Society cannot submit to this belief without risking its own downfall. That places it in inevitable conflict with this hero, and the nature of the performance must permit and indeed enforce this.'

Brecht's reworking does not exactly use 'force' on Shakespeare's *Coriolanus*, but it does aim to produce a contemporary adaption that serves the purposes of Brecht's ideology. Where the Shakespearean model ends with the hero being murdered by the Volscians and then glorified after his death, Brecht ends his version with a meeting of

---

Franz Schonauer, '[Review of *Coriolan*]', in Monika Wyss, *Brecht in der Kritik* (Munich: Kindler, 1977), pp. 396–8.

the Roman Senate which, following opposition from the people's tribunes, rejects calls to immortalise Coriolanus's name on the Capitol. Society (which Brecht understands as the plebeians) has come of age, and has not only dispensed with the hero but – far more significantly for its future political development – no longer even feels the need to commemorate him. The second, scarcely less important, element emphasised by Brecht's adaptation concerns the attitude of the plebeians and their tribunes to Coriolanus and his patrician supporters. In a deviation from Shakespeare, the people of Rome, faced with impending attack by the Volscians, demand that they be allowed to appoint tribunes to represent their interests in the Senate. And unlike in Shakespeare's play, Brecht's Coriolanus is not elected to the consulship because he reveals himself, when questioned about his manifesto by the tribunes, to be an enemy of the people.

These are significant interventions which transform Coriolanus from a tragic hero into a class enemy of whom the people, through their representatives, make a political example. Given that Brecht's play has such a clear ideological bent, it was always going to be interesting to see how the adaptation would work on stage.

Apparently initial rehearsals did take place in 1953, but plans for a production were shelved after the author's death, particularly since the adaptation was not entirely complete. Not until the spring of 1963 did the Berliner Ensemble revive the project. It is safe to say that the unusually long period of experimentation and rehearsal (even by the Ensemble's standards: the official rehearsals went on for eight months!) has definitely paid off. The premiere at the Theater am Schiffbauerdamm (now 'am Bertolt-Brecht-Platz') was proof of this. It showed, throughout the performance of over three hours, that the spirit of the greatest theatre theorist and practitioner of our times is alive and well, and demonstrated in a truly breathtaking way what a thoroughly trained troupe can achieve, without ever constraining the individual actor.

This time too, nothing was left to chance; everything was thought through and perfectly executed, right down to the tiniest detail. In this theatre even the technical equipment and stage machinery are treated as an aesthetic effect and a crucial element of the play. And the performance itself? Anyone whose enjoyment of theatre has waned after watching one too many West German 'rush job' productions will be glad to rediscover the unadulterated pleasure in the dramatic experience which this play affords. The lengthy script was split up by the directors (Manfred Wekwerth and Joachim Tenschert) into twenty-seven short scenes performed in rapid succession, which brought dynamism to the performance and prevented any moments of inertia or tedium. The production places particular emphasis on its crowd scenes and large-scale choreographic demonstrations; more than any other feature of the play, they are a persuasive example of what Brecht wanted people to understand by 'gestic expression'. Alongside the crowd scenes there were a great many individual masterstrokes of acting and staging, which merit our deepest admiration.

It is also important to note that the directors, for all their overt ideological bias, did not update the play so drastically as to turn the Roman general Coriolanus into a modern war criminal in hock to monopoly capitalism; the greatness he is imbued with by Shakespeare was retained. There was not a single weak link among the actors. Noteworthy individual performances included Ekkehard Schall's barbaric Coriolanus and Wolf Kaiser as the artful orator and Senator, Menenius Agrippa.

Franz Schonauer
Kölner Stadtanzeiger, 30 September 1964

Fragments

fragments

CHAPTER NINETEEN

The Making of a Document: An Approach to Brecht's *Fatzer* Fragment

JUDITH WILKE

In the *Fatzer* fragment (1926–1930) Brecht develops his own concept of the document in response to the increasing popularity of documentary drama and literature in the 1920s. He plays with the conventional meaning of this term and especially with the common understanding of authenticity. As early as 1926 Brecht outlines his idea of the document as an artifact or even a fake that would become 'authentic' only by provoking conflicting commentaries. In the context of *Fatzer* the document is reflected as a theatrical potential, vacillating between true or false, real or fictitious. Its meaning depends on the audience, which is obliged to enact and discuss it. Thus, Brecht favors the idea of a theatre where the spectators would be able to take part in the making of documents, embodying thereby a revolution of the theatrical process itself.

Fatzer is a fragment in progress. Brecht worked on it from 1926 to 1930, covering over 500 pages with numerous drafts of the story, dramatic scenes, chorus parts, theoretical notes and bits of sentences barely decipherable. Spread out over different folders and notebooks, parts of this material might also belong to other projects and fragments of that time, when Brecht wrote most of his *Lehrstücke* and plays such as the *Dreigroschenoper* (Threepenny Opera). The story of *Fatzer* is set in World War I, taking place at the battlefield and in the industrial area of the 'Ruhrgebiet' behind the front. Together with Fatzer as their leader, four deserters try to survive in hiding, waiting for a revolution that doesn't occur. This situation remains the focus for Brecht's examination of Fatzer, the egotist, who endangers the group in order to get his own way until finally his comrades decide to execute him. Although he had published parts of it in the first number of the *Versuche* essays in 1930, Brecht did not complete the play *Untergang des Egoisten Johann Fatzer* (The Downfall of the Egotist Johann Fatzer). And as if he had wanted to demonstrate the failure of his project and of its dramatis personae, he put the remaining fragments on file and called them the 'Fatzerdokument' (BFA 10:1116).

In the context of *Fatzer*, Brecht developed his own concept of the document in response to the increasing popularity of documentary drama and literature in the 1920s. Using this

---

Judith Wilke, 'The Making of a Document: An Approach to Brecht's "Fatzer" Fragment', *TDR* 43: 4 (1999), pp. 122–8.

term, he plays with its conventional meanings 'certificate', 'record', or 'piece of evidence', exposing them to a certain ambiguity between true and false, real and fictitious. However, this ambiguity has a part in Brecht's rhetoric of the 'document' itself. It is interesting to know that Brecht intensified his work on *Fatzer* in 1927/28 during the time of his collaboration with the newly founded theatre of Erwin Piscator. He participated in the dramatic preparation and also in the staging of various productions: *Rasputin, die Romanows, der Krieg und das Volk, das gegen sie aufstand*; *Die Abenteuer des braven Soldaten Schwejk* by Jaroslav Hašek; and *Konjunktur* by Leo Lania. For the 1929/30 season Piscator even intended to produce *Johann Fatzer* (Piscator 1979:233). Obviously Brecht received an important stimulus from this cooperation, but in the following years he formulated an alternative model, especially in the theory and practice of the Lehrstücke. According to his comments in 1928, the revolutionary demands of documentary drama were counteracted by the restriction of documentary techniques to the depiction of history. In Brecht's opinion the directors of this theatre were the last advocates of a bourgeois, naturalistic theatre, *Morgenluftarrangeure*, who had failed in the necessary revolution of the theatre itself (BFA 21:234). In contrast to Piscator's theatre and its use of historic events – which were staged as reality using films, reports, and photographs – Brecht developed his idea of the document as an artifact that would become 'authentic' only by provoking conflicting interpretations.

Especially in the *Fatzer* fragment Brecht outlines a dialectical concept of document and commentary:

> Zum Fatzerdokument gehört das [sic] Fatzerkommentar. Das Fatzerkommentar enthält zweierlei Anleitungen für die Spieler: solche, die die Darstellung, und solche, die den Sinn und die Anwendung des Dokuments betreffen.
>
> (BFA 10:515)
>
> [The Fatzer commentary belongs to the *Fatzer* document. The *Fatzer* commentary contains two sorts of instructions for the actors: those concerning representation and those concerning the meaning and application of the document.][1]

This short remark seems to suggest a hermeneutic model that distinguishes the play's action from its explanation, according to the traditional relation between a text and its commentary. And it seems natural that the document needs the commentary in order to be understood properly. But in Brecht's use of this hierarchical model 'Dokument' and 'Kommentar' no longer indicate a chain of supplementary materials, but an interruption and a discontinuity of meaning, which is handed over to readers and audience. So the fragments of the 'Fatzerkommentar' by no means interpret the dramatic material. Far from constantly referring to the story of *Fatzer*, they contribute to a particular 'stratum' of the fragment, in which general questions of pedagogy, rhetoric, criticism, and theatre are discussed (see Wilke 1998). While the commentary itself takes on the function of a document that requires or provokes interpretation, Brecht constructs the 'Fatzerdokument' as an artifact – or even a fake – that produces a reality through commenting on it.

As early as 1926, even before the differentiation of document and commentary, Brecht envisaged a procedure that he called 'anlegung von dokumenten' (BBA 813:41). At that time he also made a polemic against contemporary works of literature: instead of being valuable as documents (*Dokumentwerte*) they were devastated by psychology. In his short

---

[1]All translations by author, unless otherwise noted.

text, *Kleiner Rat, Dokumente anzufertigen* (Short advice on Producing Documents), he draws the conclusion out of this observation:

> Praktisch gesprochen: wünschenswert ist die Anfertigung von Dokumenten. Darunter verstehe ich: Monographien bedeutender Männer, Aufrisse gesellschaftlicher Strukturen, exakte und sofort verwendbare Information über die menschliche Natur und heroische Darstellung des menschlichen Lebens, alles von typischen Gesichtspunkten aus und durch die Form nicht, was die Verwendbarkeit betrifft, neutralisiert.
>
> (BFA 21:165)

> [In terms of practice: the making of documents would be very welcome. That means: monographs of important persons, outlines of social structures, precise and immediately usable information about human nature, and heroic descriptions of human life, everything seen from typical points of view and, concerning its usability, not neutralized by form.]

Through his paradoxical demand to make up documents, Brecht subverts the idea of an unquestionable authenticity of documents in general. And as an artifact the document meets the requirements of an 'immediate usability'. This particular combination of an increased relevance to a present situation and an unlimited validity for the future demands the viewpoint of a chronicler and a poet, who produces the 'document' as a utopian model of history. In the theoretical draft 'Die dialektische Dramatik' Brecht describes the historical task of his own generation of new dramatists:

> [Die junge Dramatik hatte] das Bewußtsein einer vorwiegend historischen Aufgabe. Sie sah eine große Zeit und große Gestalten und fertigte also Dokumente davon an. Dabei sah sie doch alles im Fluß.
>
> (BFA 21:437)

> [(The young dramatists) were conscious of a mainly historical task. They saw a great age and great figures out of which they produced documents. And yet they saw everything in a state of flux.]

Anticipating a future observer, this contradictory or perhaps dialectic perspective also determines Brecht's work on the *Fatzer* fragment, especially when he comments on his own writing. Shortly after declaring the fragment to be a document, valid material and a testimony for the next century, he decides to destroy the 'whole play': 'Das ganze Stück da ja unmöglich, einfach zerschmeißen für Experiment ohne Realität! Zur "Selbstverständigung"' (10: 1120). [Since the whole play is impossible, it should just be thrown away as an experiment without any reality! For 'self-understanding'.]

Because a mere copy would not be sufficient for the representation of reality, Brecht understands the document as a construction and invention, as expressed in his remarks in the *Dreigroschenprozeß:* 'Die Wirklichkeit war im Prozeß zu konstruieren' (BFA 21:460) [The reality had to be constructed in a process]; 'Die eigentliche Realität ist in die Funktionale gerutscht' (21:469) [The actual reality has slid into a functional sphere]. According to these observations Brecht valued the photomontages produced by John Heartfield as slices of reality much more highly than any newspaper photograph because the technique of montage provides the pictures with an element of commentary and also of writing. On the other hand Brecht calls into question the objective value of documents when he writes (in his judgement of a competition for 400 young poets in 1927): 'Alle großen Gedichte haben den Wert von Dokumenten. In ihnen ist die Sprechweise des Verfassers enthalten, eines wichtigen Menschen' (21:191). [All great poems have the quality of documents. They contain the author's way of speaking, that is the speech of an important person.] Even the speech of an important person doesn't guarantee an objective truth, as pointed out in the text *Kleiner Rat, Dokumente anzufertigen*:

> Ich habe jetzt, noch druckfeucht, Frank Harris' Selbstbiographie gelesen: es ist ein anziehendes Buch, viel interessanter als fast alles, was gegenwärtig an Romanhaftem produziert wird. Es ist ein wirkliches Dokument, obwohl es das Beste ist, was ein ungeheurer Lügner zustande bringen konnte.
>
> (BFA 21:163)
>
> [I have read now the recently published autobiography by Frank Harris: an attractive book, much more interesting than almost everything fictional which is produced nowadays. It's a real document, although it is the best that an enormous liar could bring about.]

So the 'real document' is an enormous lie. Just in documenting a magnificent fake it becomes effective – like Peachum's beggars in the *Dreigroschenoper*, who succeed by forging the most authentic testimonies of their misery, wounds, and diseases.

In the *Fatzer* fragment the 'document' is a construction rather than a depiction. Its testimony refers to something that lies beyond representation. Particularly with regard to the experiences of soldiers on the front in World War I, testifying itself became an unsolvable problem.[2] Similar to the unconscious traces of a traumatic experience, the artificial documents of the 'inexplicable' in *Fatzer* are only traces that demand reading, repetition, and interpretation. In a short note Brecht describes the chorus sections as parts of the document: 'Die Chöre/ zum Dokument gehörend' (10: 1134) [The Choruses/ part of the document]. But these choruses themselves appear as commentators on documents, testifying unbelievable events:

> ZWEI CHÖRE
> Aber als alles geschehen war, war da
> Unordnung. Und ein Zimmer
> Welches völlig zerstort war, und darinnen
> Vier tote Männer und
> Ein Name! Und eine Tür, auf der stand
> Unverständliches.
> Ihr aber seht jetzt
> Das Ganze. Was alles vorging, wir
> Haben es aufgestellt
> In der Zeit nach genauer
> Folge an den genauen Orten und
> Mit den genauen Worten, die
> Gefallen sind. Und was immer ihr sehen werdet, am
> Schluß werdet ihr sehn, was wir sahn:

---

[2] In his essay 'Der Erzähler', Walter Benjamin remarks that World War I had produced an inability to communicate experiences, indicated also by the war literature of the late 1920s (1980, 2:439).

Unordnung. [...]
Und aufgebaut haben wir es, damit
Ihr entscheiden sollt
Durch das Sprechen der Wörter und
Das Anhören der Chöre
Was eigentlich los war, den
Wir waren uneinig.

(10:477)

[TWO CHORUSES
But when everything had happened there was
disorder. And a room
that was completely destroyed and inside
were four dead men and
a name! And a door on which was
something incomprehensible.
But now you see
the whole thing. Everything that happened we
have set up in time according to exact
sequence at the exact words that
were spoken. And whatever you may see,
in the end you will see what we saw:
disorder. [...]
And we have constructed it so that
you should decide
by speaking the words and
listening to the choruses
what was really going on, for
we disagreed.]

(translated by A. Leslie Willson, Andrzej Wirth,
and David J. Ward)

Remains of a catastrophe, arranged like ciphers in a tableau: a room, completely destroyed with four corpses lying around, a name and something incomprehensible written on the door. This emblematic image itself already demonstrates the necessity for the failure of any attempt to understand. And the choruses, confessing their own disagreement concerning what they have seen, hand over this first and last picture to the spectators to let them decide what had happened – like the agitators in *Die Maßnahme* or like the demonstrator in the street scene in *Der Messingkauf*. In reconstructing the fatal incidents as something incomprehensible the choruses reject any responsibility. Hence, the meaning of the document depends on the audience, which is obliged to enact and discuss it. There is still something akin to a utopian hope in this gesture. It delivers the responsibility of interpretation to the audience instead of ending in conclusions, definite results, and moral advices. However, the openness of this chorus part reveals the theatrical potential of Brecht's document itself.

The stage as a place of spectacle and demonstration allows a particular action to gain the same reality as a historical document. This idea is developed in a commentary text of the *Fatzer* fragment:

> Wann ist der Gang des Fatzer durch die Stadt Mülheim eine Wirklichkeit – obwohl kein Mann Fatzer durch die Stadt Mülheim gegangen ist?
> Antwort: Wenn genügend viele, genügend gute Leute [...] ihn als wahrhaftig erkannt haben.
>
> (10:516)
>
> [When becomes Fatzer's walk through the town of Mülheim a reality – although no man Fatzer did walk through the town of Mülheim?
> Answer: When a sufficient number of sufficiently good persons [...] have acknowledged it as truthful.]

The acknowledgement of the walk of a dramatic character as a 'real' document depends on the audience and needs to be perceived and invented by 'a sufficient number of sufficiently good people'. From this point of view, Brecht understands theatre not only as a collective experience but also as a cognitive process based on the interdependence of production and reception, acting and watching. In his theory of the Lehrstücke he develops the idea of a theatre mainly for its producers, which includes an audience that is no longer restricted to an act of passive consumption. But in the context of *Fatzer* these ideas are also connected to the circumstances of writing:

> Der Zweck, wofür eine Arbeit gemacht wird, ist nicht mit jenem Zweck identisch, zu dem sie verwertet wird. So ist das Fatzerdokument zunächst hauptsächlich zum Lernen des Schreibenden gemacht.
>
> Wird es späterhin zum Lehrgegenstand, so wird durch diesen Gegenstand von den Schülern etwas völlig anderes gelernt, als der Schreibende lernte. Ich, der Schreibende, muß nichts fertig machen. Es genügt, daß ich mich unterrichte. Ich leite lediglich die Untersuchung und meine Methode dabei ist es, die der Zuschauer untersuchen kann.
>
> (10:514)
>
> [The purpose of the making of a work is not identical with the purpose of its use. So the *Fatzer* document is made at first for the writer's instruction.
>
> When later on it becomes a subject of instruction the students will learn by it something totally different from that which was learned by the writer. I, the writer, don't have to finish something. It is enough that I instruct myself. I am only leading the examination and it is my method which can be examined by the audience.]

Producing the 'Fatzerdokument' Brecht struggles with the fact that an author cannot restrict the interpretation of his works to his original intentions. While refusing to finish his work, he still tries to determine its possible functions. Adding these reflections to the corpus of the document itself, he subverts his own position as a playwright and conveys his personal doubts and questions to a future audience. Although Brecht insists on the role of a 'leader', he at the same time favors a 'collective reading'. Prevalent in *Fatzer* is the idea of a theatre where the spectators – as actors, readers, or writers – would be able to take part in the making of documents, embodying thereby a revolution of the theatrical process. Thus, the *Fatzer* fragment envisages a performing art dependent on the dynamics of watching and acting between reading and examination, document and commentary.

REFERENCES

Benjamin, Walter
1980   'Der Erzähler'. In *Gesammelte Schriften*. Vol. 2, edited by Rolf Tiedemann and Hermann Schweppenhäuser, 438–65. Frankfurt am Main: Suhrkamp Verlag.

Brecht, Bertolt
n.d.   Bertolt Brecht Archive (BBA). Berlin.
1988–1999   *Werke. Große kommentierte Berliner und Frankfurter Ausgabe* (BFA). 30 vols. Edited by Werner Hecht, Jan Knopf, Werner Mittenzwei, and Klaus-Detlef Müller. Berlin and Weimar: Aufbau and Frankfurt am Main: Suhrkamp Verlag.

Piscator, Erwin
1979   *Das Politische Theater*. Reinbek bei Hamburg: Rowohlt.

Wilke, Judith
1998   *Brecht's Fatzer-Fragment: Lektüren zum Verhältnis von Dokument und Kommentar*. Bielefeld: Aisthesis Verlag.

Poetry: City Poems

From *Ten Poems from A Reader for Those who Live in Cities*
'Part from your friends at the station'

I

Part from your friends at the station
Enter the city in the morning with your coat buttoned up
Look for a room, and when your friend knocks:
Do not, o do not, open the door
But
Cover your tracks.

If you meet your parents in Hamburg or elsewhere
Pass them like strangers, turn the corner, don't recognise them
Pull the hat they gave you over your face, and
Do not, o do not, show your face
But
Cover your tracks.

Eat the meat that's there. Don't stint yourself.
Go into any house when it rains and sit on any chair that's in it
But don't sit long. And don't forget your hat.
I tell you:
Cover your tracks.

Whatever you say, don't say it twice
If you find your ideas in anyone else, disown them,
The man who hasn't signed anything, who has left no picture
Who was not there, who said nothing:
How can they catch him?
Cover your tracks.

See when you come to think of dying
That no gravestone stands and betrays you where you lie
With a clear inscription to denounce you
And the year of your death to give you away.
Once again:
Cover your tracks.

(That is what they taught me.)

Translated by Frank Jones[1]

---

[1]BFA 11, p. 157; *Poems*, pp. 131–3.

CHAPTER TWENTY

The Poet in Berlin: Brecht's City Poetry of the 1920s

DAVID MIDGELY

The city was not an altogether new theme in German poetry in the 1920s. The processes of industrialisation and urbanisation had left their mark on literary writing in the German-speaking world, as elsewhere, in the course of the nineteenth and early twentieth centuries. The perception of the modern city as the site of a depersonalised and dehumanised cultural condition is familiar to us from the writings of Rilke, as it is from those of Eliot; and in the poetry of Georg Heym and others, written in the years immediately before the First World War, the impulse to disrupt and overcome the processes of depersonalisation and dehumanisation expresses itself in imagery which demonises the urban world. But at the same time as industrialisation and the commodification of human creative effort were being interpreted as dehumanising tendencies, it was also recognised that the very abstraction of human and economic relations in the city was creating the conditions which provided new kinds of personal freedom and individual opportunity. In a famous essay of 1903 on the effects of urbanisation on intellectual culture, the sociologist Georg Simmel noted on the one hand the tendency for city life to reduce human relations to a system of commercial transactions and calculations, and on the other hand the differentiation and refinement of mental responses that comes with increasing specialisation of social and economic functions in the city.[2]

There are, however, certain senses in which the poetic treatment of the city underwent intensification in the 1920s and, partly as a consequence of a new intimacy with the life and language of the city, something qualitatively new entered into German poetry. Brecht's city poetry of the 1920s illustrates both sides of the picture. The world of human relations he depicts has definitely become abstracted and depersonalised, human individuals have become interchangeable and in obvious senses commodified. But at the same time, that abstraction of relations poses a new challenge to poetic expression, a challenge to identify and articulate the precise nature of such abstracted relations and their implications for the lives of the individuals who inhabit this city environment.

Brecht grew up in the small provincial town of Augsburg, and before he ever went to Berlin he contemplated the atmosphere of the big city as something alien and threatening,

---

David Midgely, 'The Poet in Berlin: Brecht's City Poetry of the 1920s', in Tom Kuhn and Karen Leeder (eds), *Empedocles' Shoe* (London: Methuen, 2002), pp. 89–106.

[2] Georg Simmel, 'Die Großstädte und das Geistesleben', reprinted in *Dos Individuum und die Freiheit* (Frankfurt am Main, 1993), pp. 192–204.

but also as the mode of social organisation which would undeniably dominate the world of the future. In a diary entry of 1921, which pre-dates his experience of Berlin (although he did have first-hand experience of Munich by that time), he muses on the challenge the city presents to the literary writer, and he does so in terms which are still strongly influenced by the stories of colonial adventure and pioneering conquest which he had absorbed in his youth and which provided the subject matter for some of his early ballads:

> When I considered what Kipling did for the nation that is engaged in 'civilising' the world, I made the historic discovery that nobody up till now has actually described the big city as a jungle. Where are the heroes, the colonisers, the victims of the metropolis? Its hostile atmosphere, its stony hardness, its Babel-like confusion, its poetry, in short, is something that has yet to be recorded.[3]

Brecht, at the age of twenty-three, was approaching the issue of city life in heroic vein, as a subject which appeared to defy the capacity of poetic convention to voice its characteristic hardness, hostility and confusion, in a manner comparable to the way Kipling had expressed the idiom and the tensions of imperial conquest. In the course of the 1920s, Brecht made a number of attempts to present the world of the modern city in dramatic form, ranging from *Im Dickicht der Städte/In the Jungle of Cities* to *Aufstieg und Fall der Stadt Mahagonny/The Rise and Fall of the City of Mahagonny*, but it has to be said that the representation of city life in those projects remains rather sketchy and in any case subordinated to the main issues Brecht is dramatising: in the one case, the notion of human existence as a struggle between vital potencies; in the other case, the perception of human society as ultimately subordinated to the demands of commercial exploitation.

What I want to argue about Brecht's city poetry, particularly as it develops in the mid-1920s, is that on the one hand it represents a more *modest* attempt to capture specific aspects of human relations in the city, and that on the other hand it leads to the development of an important *technique* for exposing the role of specific forms of discourse in the urbanised human society with which he is concerned. The technique I have in mind is not something that Brecht develops single-handedly; it is related to a trend in poetic writing in Germany after the First World War which belongs to what may loosely be called the 'cabaret' tradition of modern German poetry, and which achieves some of its most striking effects by combining phrases drawn from the various familiar idioms of the public world. Both Kurt Tucholsky and Erich Kästner worked within that tradition in the 1920s, but its real pioneer is Walter Mehring, and it is from Mehring's work that I want briefly to illustrate my point, before examining the senses in which Brecht's city poems also represent a productive development of that tradition.

Mehring genuinely wrote for cabaret performance, as Brecht, generally speaking, did not – although the two of them probably met up for the first time when Brecht was briefly engaged to perform two of his ballads in Trude Hesterberg's 'Wilde Bühne' [Wild Stage] cabaret in Berlin in January 1922.[4] When the theatre impresario Max Reinhardt sought to revive the pre-war tradition of literary cabaret in 1919, he recruited Walter Mehring off the street, as it were, where Mehring had been demonstrating with the Dadaists against the very bourgeois culture that Reinhardt might have been said to stand for, and

---

[3]BFA 26. p. 236.
[4]*See* Werner Mittenzwei, *Das Leben des Bertolt Brecht* (Frankfurt am Main, 1987), vol. i, p.165; Peter Jelavich, *Berlin Cabaret* (Cambridge, Mass., 1993), p. 150.

put him to work inside the theatre. More precisely, Reinhardt employed Mehring as the 'conférencier' in his 'Schall und Rauch' [Sound and Smoke] cabaret, which operated as the late-night parodistic appendage to the mainstream repertoire of the Deutsches Theater. The text that Mehring wrote to open the show invokes a special kind of political role for lyric poetry, which explicitly adumbrates the sort of poetic effects I have in mind. After some ironic opening remarks about the esoteric character of this particular cabaret, Mehring invokes the precedents of classical antiquity – presenting the show as a satyr play, to follow the great historical tragedy that has just come to an end, namely the First World War – and goes on to suggest that the appropriate way for the artist to respond to a world that is dominated by the hackneyed phrases of nationalist fervour and Utopian socialism is to cultivate a lyrical virtuosity that asserts its command of 'political dialectics' in its manipulation of the various idioms of public life: the jargon of pimps and prostitutes as well as the argot of diplomats and the gobbledegook of politicians.[5]

Mehring's cabaret verses – which were published under the title *Das Ketzerbrevier / Heretic's Breviary* in 1921, several years before Brecht's *Hauspostille / Domestic Breviary*, and which parallel the blasphemous effects of Brecht's collection – are often stunning in the way they confront the bustle, the *razzmatazz*, the economic frenzy and the political platitudes of the post-war world with the debunking street-wisdom of the Berlin vernacular. The effects are often impossible to capture in translation, which is probably why Mehring's verses are little known outside the German-speaking world. But I have chosen a relatively accessible example to illustrate my point. 'Des Tippelkunden Frühlingslied' / 'Tippler's spring song' uses the persona of a Berlin drunkard to convey a sense of undeluded alienation between the human individual and the ordered world of the city, and hints at the close association of church and state in the regulation of human lives. It is characteristic of the cabaret-style tradition of the 1920s, incidentally, that the refrain – in this instance, the allusive use of the proverbial phrase about the mills of God grinding slowly, but exceedingly small – takes on a variety of complexions as it reappears in the context provided by each new stanza in turn.

> Kommt der erste Frühlingstag an,
> Wird so schwach een'm,
> Und denn macht man
> Raus auft's Kaff.
> Wenn sich aus de sand'gen Kuhlen
> Blätter puhlen,
> Würmer spulen,
> Stehste baff!
> Und denn liegt man sich zu aal'n, wo
> Mang die kahlen
> Letzten Häuser
> Gottes Mühlen
> Langsam mahlen.

---

[5]*See* Walter Mehring, *Großes Ketzerbrevier* (Munich, 1975), pp. 146–8. For a fuller account of Mehring's contribution to German poetic writing in the 1920s, *see* Hans-Peter Bayerdörfer, 'Weimarer Republik', in *Geschichte der deutschen Lyrik vom Mittelalter bis zur Gegenwart*, ed. Walter Hinderer (Stuttgart, 1983), pp. 439–76.

Bürgers samt Familienkette
Stiebein fette
Und adrette
Fein mit Ei!
Ob een'm unter dunst'ge Kiepen
Lause piepen
Wanzen ziepen,
Einerlei!
Jeder looft zur rechten Schmiede
Hundemiede!
Gottes Mühlen
Mahlen langsam!
Und solide!

Stochert man im weichen Mülle,
Jibbts die Hülle
Und die Fülle,
Hat man Schiß;
Manchmal find't man einer Schneppe
Blut'ge Schleppe,
Blonde Zöppe
Und Jebiß!
Für die Toten is's nich wichtig!
Jeld bringt's tüchtig!
Gottes Mühlen
Mahlen langsam!
Aber richtig!

Schließlich land't man treu und wacker
Ausjebaggert
Uff'm Acker,
Sacht nich: meff!
Leichenschauhaus zahlt die Rente
Und verwendt dir
Zu Zemente,
Altes Reff!
Nächstes Jahr deckt's Jroß-Stadtpflaster
Deine Laster!
Denn wo Gottes
Mühlen mahlen,
Wächst keen Jras mehr!

[When the first spring day arrives, you go all weak, and then you take yourself off out. As the leaves sprout and the worms crawl out of the sandy hollows, you're dumbstruck! And then you stretch yourself out where, among the last bare houses, the mills of God slowly grind.

The burghers with their families in tow strut along in their finery. If lice or bugs chirp out from under their steaming hampers, who cares? Each one trapezes home to his allotted place, dog-tired. The mills of God grind slow – and proper!

If you poke around in the rubbish (and there's all sorts to choose from), mind how you go; sometimes you find some old slapper's blood-stained dress, her blonde plaits, and her teeth! It doesn't matter to the dead. It still brings in the cash. The mills of God grind good and proper.

Finally, like a real gent, you end up clapped-out in the graveyard, you've breathed your last! The morgue'll pay your pension now, and turn you into cement, you old soak! Next year the city streets'll cover up your sins! For where the mills of God grind – the grass never grows!]

The sardonic jollity that we find in Mehring's verses is perhaps closer in mood to the songs Brecht wrote for the *Die Dreigroschenoper/The Threepenny Opera* than to his city poetry, although in this poetry we find Brecht, too, confronting the bleakness of a depersonalised society and articulating the tactical responses of individuals to particular conditions of urban life. The common feature in the poetry of Brecht and Mehring that I want to emphasise is the deployment of forms of everyday diction in constellations, which trigger insights into particular dimensions of the social world. The text in which Brecht arguably comes closest to the style of poetic composition pioneered by Mehring is one which was intended for the *Threepenny Opera*, but was not performed in the original production because the actress who was to sing it found it altogether too provocative; it is the 'Ballade der sexuellen Hörigkeit' / 'Ballad of sexual obsession', which is composed almost entirely of stock phrases used to characterise social attitudes and relationships, including some of an overtly sexual nature. But it is with the broader aspects of Brecht's experimentation in poetry, which speaks the language of everyday life, that I am concerned here.

Between 1921 and 1927, Brecht accumulated a considerable number of poems that evoke characteristic experiences of urban populations, and from among these he decided to include just ten in the 1930 collection *Aus einem Lesebuch für Städtebewohner/From a Reader for Those who Live in Cities*. Unlike the *Domestic Breviary*, in which the notion of the fleetingness of human existence is set in a cosmic dimension and which often express vitalistic and hedonistic responses to a sense of metaphysical emptiness, these poems focus on concrete social situations as the product of human actions and human attitudes. Some of them adopt an overtly instructional tone, whether in an encouraging manner – 'Die Städte sind für dich gebaut'/'The cities were built for you'[6] – or in a spirit of admonition:

> If you had read the papers as carefully as I do
> You would have buried your hopes
> That things may yet get better,[7]

Others evoke nightmarish experiences of the transience, impersonality and alienation of human relationships, in a city environment:

> The woman I slept seven years with
> Greets me politely on the landing and
> Passes by
> Smiling,
> [...]

---

[6] GW, p. 277; *Poems*, p. 141. Page references in this paragraph are to Bertolt Brecht, *Gesammelte Werke* (Frankfurt am Main, 1967), in which the arrangement of the poems by Elisabeth Hauptmann gives a more immediate sense of the range of Brecht's city poetry than the new BFA edition, which recognises only those poems as 'belonging' to the *Reader* project which Brecht himself expressly assigned to it.
[7] GW, p. 282; *Poems*, p. 144.

> It seems
> I have moved out. Someone else
> Is living here now and
> Doing so in
> My linen.[8]

Sometimes, the poem simply consists in the (studiously presented) imitation of an everyday utterance:

> I told him to move out.
> [...]
> When he came back the same night
> His bags were downstairs. That
> Shook him.[9]

It might imitate the brutal manner of an overseer addressing his workforce: 'Fall in! Why are you so late? Now / Just a minute! No, not you!'[10] Or it might stylise the emotional impulses of a situation into an almost theatrical speech with strong rhetorical effects, as in the insistent repetition of syntactical structures which prepares the way for the image of revenge in the following example:

> I know you all want me to clear out
> I see I eat too much for you
> I realise you've no means of dealing with people like me
> Well, I'm clearing out
> [...]
> When I come back
> Under a rougher moon, my friends
> I shall come in a tank
> Talk through a gun and
> Wipe you out.[11]

What is technically interesting about this group of poems in general is the way that fragmentary indications of the character of human situations in the city are constructed out of the discourse of city-dwellers themselves. What is fascinating about the *Reader* in its narrow sense is firstly the way it is deliberately organised, and secondly the manner in which everyday discourse is used in interaction with other specific poetic effects.

Before examining individual poems, it is worth setting the record straight about the rhetorical principles at work in the collection. In a recent book, Helmut Lethen presents Brecht's *Reader*, amongst other publications of the 1920s, as the expression of a 'doctrine of behaviour', a 'Verhaltenslehre'.[12] In an effort to construct a general theory of cultural change in Germany after the First World War, however, Lethen treats the text as if it were a direct and transparent expression of the author's attitude; with that aim in mind, he denies the ironic character of Brecht's *Reader* poems.[13] It is in fact perfectly easy to

---

[8]GW, p. 281; *Poems*, p. 143.
[9]GW, p. 288; *Poems*, pp. 146–7.
[10]GW, p.277; *Poems*, p.141.
[11]GW, pp. 293ff; *Poems*, pp. 127–8.
[12]Helmut Lethen, *Verhaltenslehren der Kälte. Lebensversuche zwischen den Kriegen*, (Frankfurt am Main, 1994).
[13]Lethen, *Verhaltenslehren*, pp. 175–8. For a full account of my reservations about Lethen's argument, *see* my article 'Vom Lebenswandel in der mechanisierten Gesellschaft. Zu neueren Tendenzen in der Theoretisierung der

show how the presentation of ideas in Brecht's poems relates to the techniques which, in the classical tradition of rhetoric, combine to achieve an ironic effect: *simulatio* and *dissimulatio*. The effect we are dealing with in Brecht's case is akin to that of 'Socratic irony', which is to say that the significance of an utterance is initially kept hidden in order that it may be more deeply appreciated when it is revealed.[14] The way this typically occurs in the *Reader* poems is that the individual text simulates a speech situation (which may superficially resemble an act of instruction or advice, or the declaration of an attitude), and this speech situation is given a sense of context only in the last line (which typically appears in brackets). The effect can be a quite startling dislocation of the expectations created within the body of each text. The first poem sounds like a set of instructions to the reader on how to adjust to living in the city, until we arrive at the last line and are told, 'Das wurde mir gelehrt' [That is what I have been taught].[15] The second describes a seemingly singular moment in which an individual becomes alienated and isolated from the group with which he has apparently been used to working, but ends with the words, 'Das hast du schon sagen hören' [You have heard this said before]. And the third consists of a brutal and unadorned announcement that we want to take over your house, denounce you when they come looking for you, and even make you disappear like smoke up the chimney. But then we read, 'So sprechen wir mit unsern Vätern' [This is how we talk to our fathers]. It is also consistent with the rhetorical concept of dissimulation, incidentally, that this contextualisation is itself only brought about in vague or reticent terms. It is as if the author knows more than he is giving away; he alludes to the social dimension of the attitude the poem is expressing, but leaves the anticipated readers of the collection to puzzle over how best to make sense of the information they are given, in the light of their own experience, which is to say, their experience as city-dwellers.[16]

In other words, the manner in which Brecht presents city experiences in these poems is closely related to what he meant by the term *Gestus* [gesture] as he later applied it to his plays. There, the idea is that each scene points to a particular aspect of the social relations depicted in the play without necessarily making it verbally explicit; here, in the *Reader*, the effect is to isolate and point to a particular kind of social attitude, and to the manner in which it is linguistically constructed. This, Brecht is saying, is the way someone speaks in a certain situation. It is only in the final poem that we encounter an overt expression of intention in the manner of a direct communication from author to reader, and even here we are not given a key to what the collection as a whole signifies; rather, it is to the *manner of speaking* we have heard in the collection, and to what that signifies, that our attention is drawn:

> When I speak to you
> Coldly and impersonally
> Using the driest words

---

kulturellen Entwicklung im Zeitraum der Weimarer Republik', in *Schwellen. Exkursionen der Literaturwissenschaft*, ed. P. Möbius, N. Saul und D. Steuer (Würzburg, 1999), pp. 177–84.

[14]See Gert Ueding and Bernd Steinbrink, *Grundriß der Rhetorik: Geschichte, Technik, Methode* (Stuttgart, 1986), pp. 291ff.

[15]I am following the 1938 version of this text, which I interpret as a clarification of intentions on Brecht's part, as I explain below.

[16]For fuller discussion of the rhetorical effects in these poems, see Franz Norbert Mennemeier, *Bertolt Brechts Lyrik: Aspekte Tendenzen* (Düsseldorf, 1982), p. 97; R V. Brady, 'Aus einem Lesebuch fir Städtbewohner. On a Brecht Essay in Obliqueness'. *German Life & Letters*, 26 (1972), pp. 160–72; Peter Whitaker, *Brecht's Poetry* (Oxford, 1985), p. 53.

> Without looking at you
> (I seemingly fail to recognise you
> In your particular nature and difficulty)
>
> I speak to you merely
> Like reality itself
> (Sober, not to be bribed by your particular nature
> Tired of your difficulty)
> Which in my view you seem not to recognise.[17]

The collection, we are being told, is intended to *sound like* the harsh and unfeeling reality, which constitutes the life of the city. But the significance of the *content* of individual poems, the sense in which they do indeed reflect something of that 'reality' of city life we need to recognise, remains for the reader to extract by an act of interpretation.

There are just nine poems in the 1930 collection apart from the one just quoted, and on close inspection it is possible to see relations of both similarity and contrast between them. There are implicit connections between the poignant discovery of one's own superfluity in the second poem and the aggressive assertion of the interests of the young generation over those of the old in the third; between the fourth poem, which mockingly evokes the disciplined avoidance of stress, and the fifth, which presents someone who is determinedly overcoming her own fickleness; and between 6, 7 and 8, which describe varieties of response to failure or catastrophe. The ninth is the well-known and much anthologised poem which presents four different ways in which a man is offered a bed for the night, whereby the mode of address in each instance carries the markers of a particular kind of social relationship, from something that resembles family hospitality, albeit of a brusque kind, to the business-like attitude of the whore. The resonance between the situations evoked in the individual poems – and indeed between the various linguistic registers employed within them – is, however, left to speak for itself. If the collection provides instruction for city-dwellers, then it does so, as Philip Brady has argued, indirectly and obliquely.[18] The requirement to interpret these poems by acts of inference is built into the composition of the collection. But when we examine the specific effects of individual poems, then it also becomes apparent how the *Reader* poems stand in a relation of tension – both with Brecht's own earlier poetry and with the general trend of the 1920s which I have highlighted. I should like to demonstrate this point with reference to the first and the fifth poems in the collection.

Readers familiar with Walter Benjamin's commentaries on Brecht's poetry will know that Benjamin interprets the first of the *Reader* poems – quoted at the head of this essay (p. 90) and also known under the title 'Verwisch die spuren' / 'Cover your tracks' – as expressing a conscious political strategy. He construes the furtiveness of the behaviour described in the poem as that of an underground agitator, and relates it to the position of the Communist as an 'exile in his own country'.[19] Benjamin explicitly relates his interpretation to the actual experience of exile from National Socialism after 1933, but he may have been encouraged in this view by the original wording of the last line, 'Das wurde mir *gesagt*' [That is what they said to me], which does indeed carry the implication of deliberate instruction. That impression is, however, significantly altered by the change which Brecht made to that last

---

[17]BFA 11. p. 165; *Poems*, p. 140.
[18]Brady, loc. cit.
[19]Walter Benjamin, *Versuche über Brecht* (Frankfurt am Main, 1981), pp. 80ff

line in 1938,[20] precisely at the time when Benjamin was visiting him in Denmark and writing his commentaries. The wording of the new version, 'Das wurde mir *gelehrt*' [That is what they taught me], leaves open the possibility of interpreting the body of the poem as a set of conclusions drawn from experience, rather than as an explicit set of instructions.

There are, to be sure, clear overtones of political activity elsewhere in the collection. Poems 7 and 8 in particular evoke the experiences of being on the run and receiving political instruction. But even if the final stanza of 'Part from your friends at the station' contains lines about being betrayed and given away, the context in which these lines appear creates difficulties for a political interpretation. This first poem in the collection ostensibly provides a guide to survival tactics – keep yourself to yourself, mingle with the crowd, don't commit yourself – but it does so in terms which point beyond such seemingly practical guidance. For a start, the emphatic repetition of imperative verbs in stanzas 1 and 2 lends a peculiarly insistent pathos to the injunctions to keep the door shut and not to show your face: 'Do not, o do not, open the door' and 'Do not, o do not, show your face'. This is not the language of sober instruction or rational deduction, but rather suggests a strongly emotional response, even a panic response. In stanza 3, we might note, the urban environment is presented, not as the hard reality whose language we should learn (as the final poem indicates), but as a landscape that is there to be grazed without concern for the consequences, a site for satisfying the appetites of the individual, however anonymous he has become: 'Eat the meat that's there. Don't stint yourself.' If we put this injunction to consume in the here and now alongside the intimation of positively embracing death at the end of the poem, then we are not all that far from the vitalistic evocations of human endeavour and of ultimate absorption into the natural world that we find in the 'Choral vom Manne Baal' / 'Hymn of Baal the great' or the 'Ballade von des Cortez Leuten' / 'Of Cortez's men' in the *Domestic Breviary*.[21] But there is a particular twist to the presentation of the notion of death in this instance, which takes us, if anything, further away from Benjamin's political interpretation.

If, as initially appears to be the case, this poem offers advice to a newcomer on how best to protect himself in the city, then what sense should we make of stanza 5, in which even the moment of death is presented as an occasion to erase the traces of individual existence, to avoid having a gravestone which advertises your name and betrays you by displaying the date of your death? If we apply the expectations of traditional rhetoric to this element in the poem, and try to account for it as a case of *amplificatio* – as the deliberate exaggeration of something self-evidently repugnant – then we find the poem's apparently serious advice on how to adjust to the demands of city life collapsing into absurdity.[22] A more plausible suggestion is that death is evoked in the manner of the baroque *memento mori*.[23] The fact that this motif is presented here as an intentional action for which we should prepare – 'Sorge, wenn du zu sterben *gedenkst*' [Be careful when you come to think of dying] – might perhaps be seen as an assimilation to the speech situation of instruction which the poem is apparently imitating. But however we view it, the introduction of this motif of the anticipation of death gives the poem an impetus running beyond the framework of preparation for living in the city. It is

---

[20]BFA 9, p. 350.
[21]BFA 11, pp. 107–8; BFA 11. pp. 84–5.
[22]See Mennemeier, *Bertolt Brechts Lyrik*, p. 97; Whitaker, *Brecht's Poetry*, pp. 42ff.
[23]*See* Hans-Thies Lehmann, 'Schlaglichter auf den anderen Brecht', *Das Brecht-Jahrbuch*, 17 (1992), 1–13 (p. 10).

an allusion to death which might reasonably attract the comment which Brecht himself made with respect to the prominence of the death theme in the *Badener Lehrstück/ The Baden-Baden Lesson an Consent*, when it was published in the same volume of the *versuche / Experiments* as the *Reader* collection in 1930: 'Dem Sterben ist im Vergleich zu seinem doch wohl nur geringen Gebrauchswert zuviel Gewicht beigemessen' [Too much emphasis is put on dying, given its negligible usefulness].[24] The precise manner in which it is introduced in the poem also makes it difficult to view the motif in this instance as an example of the knowledge of death providing a sense of the framework for an *ars Vivendi* in the here and now, which has been seen as characteristic of Brecht's poetry of the early 1920s.[25] When viewed in conjunction with the intimations of pathos in earlier stanzas of 'Part from your friends at the station', moreover, the death motif here seems to carry the implication of an emotional impetus, which is not consistent with the logic of an instruction to avoid identification, but which runs on, as it were, in *parallel* to it and aims at the total effacement of personal identity: don't open the door, don't show your face, save nothing for the morrow, don't take responsibility for anything, leave no sign of your existence behind you after your death. This sense of emotional impetus at least lends credence to one aspect of Lethen's interpretation of the poem, when he comments: 'Das Ich ergreift die Flucht nach vorn – wo der Tod wartet' ['The lyric 'I' flees ahead into the future – where death awaits'].[26]

What I want to suggest about this poem, then, is that it articulates two parallel lines of argument, which find their common theme – their slogan, so to speak – in the refrain 'Cover your tracks'. One of them aims at public communication, and consists in the rhetorically disciplined presentation of survival tactics, which the final line of the poem identifies as a summary of experiences learned from the environment. The other expresses emotional responses to that environment of a personal and intimate nature, and tends ultimately to a total obliteration of self. I am sceptical about the possibility of drawing any conclusion of a general nature from the presence of this latter motif, as Lethen does, whether in relation to the personal psychology of Brecht or to the cultural climate of Germany in the 1920s. But I do see it as evidence that both the personal character of lyric poetry in its traditional sense and themes which are characteristic of Brecht's personal career as a poet are carried forward, in the *Reader* poems, within the envelope of a poetry which is becoming more obviously orientated towards intervention in the social domain. The precise implications of that development in Brecht's poetry become clearer if we now consider the fifth poem in his sequence alongside the first.

The dominant theme of the fifth poem is self-overcoming. The sentiments voiced are those of a woman who is determined to take advantage of whatever favourable opportunities present themselves to her, and to assert herself against whatever holds her back. She has fought against drink, drugs and sexually transmitted disease, and by implication she has also fought against the self-contempt which expresses itself in the recurrent phrase, 'Ich bin ein Dreck' [I'm dirt]. Like the drunkard of Walter Mehring's song, this is someone with an intimate knowledge of life at the bottom of the heap. But unlike Mehring's drunkard, she is not simply resigned to being ground down and turned

---

[24]BFA 3, p. 26.
[25]See Horst Jesse, *Die Lyrik Bertolt Brechts von 1914–1956 unter besonderer Berücksichtigung der 'ars vivendi' angesichts der Todesbedrohungen* (Frankfurt am Main, 1994), p. 15.
[26]Lethen, op. cit., p. 173.

into 'cement' at the end of her life. The self-image which supplants her self-contempt in the final stanza is that of the 'hard mortar' with which cities are built. It is an image of a substance that is as common as dirt, but which is capable of hardening to provide the binding force that will hold a structure in place. The self-evident seriousness of this poem is further highlighted by its position in the sequence of Brecht's *Reader:* it is preceded by one which ironises a keep-young-and-beautiful routine, and it is followed by one which exposes the self-deluding character of the effort to put a bold front on commercial failure.

But what is remarkable about this poem in its context is not the theme of self-overcoming in itself, nor the way it makes explicit those elements in the woman's own make-up which *need* to be over-come, but the precise terms in which her programme of self-overcoming is evoked. Her self-contempt relates to her recognition that the best she can expect of her own nature is 'weakness, treachery and degradation'. She can resolve to throw off the drink and the drugs when she sees what they are doing to her, but the self-assertion on which she prides herself takes place in the terrain of her own sexuality. In stanza 4 she responds to the recognition of her diseased state by seeing it as a challenge to recover her sexual allure:

> Who
> Would ever have thought a woman like me
> Would ever make men crazy again –
> I began again at once.

She is manifestly trying to put herself in control, but it is a self conceived in terms of sexual assertiveness, and that remains the measure of her achievement, even as she notes that to assert herself in this way requires the exercise of emotional self-control and the suppression of warmth and receptivity towards the men in her life:

> I have never taken a man who did not do
> Something for me, and had every man
> I needed. By now I'm
> Almost without feeling, almost gone dry
> But
> I'm beginning to fill up again, I have ups and downs, but
> On the whole more ups.[27]

When, in the following stanza, she speaks of controlling the impulse to display her jealousy of sexual rivals, then it is precisely the external display of emotion that she wants to avoid, rather than the emotion itself. The impulses which govern her sense of purpose in life are, again, those which we find celebrated in Brecht's earlier poetry; they are those of the human organism seeking, above all, the gratification of its vital urges in life.

There is a clear dialectical tension between the first and the fifth poem in the *Reader:* where the one draws out a trajectory of self-effacement, the other describes a programme of self-assertion. But there is also a dialectical tension within the fifth poem itself. It evokes a social force which sees its time as having come and which adopts the self-discipline necessary to assert itself, but it also shows that social force to be ultimately driven by the demands of the flesh. Through these internal tensions, it again throws light on the relationship between two conceptions of poetry which vie with each other within

---

[27]*Poems*, p. 136.

the framework of the *Reader*. The first poem remains ambiguous, I suggested, because the personal emotional theme is not integrated with the ostensible public purpose, but runs in parallel to it, and because the two themes meet only in the refrain 'Cover your tracks'. In the fifth poem, the tension between the personal and the public is effectively resolved, not only because the woman's life story is made public in the act of telling, but because the trajectory of that personal life is one of competent integration into the social world. This is the sense in which I see the fifth poem as epitomising the impetus behind the composition of the *Reader* as a whole. It retains a sense of the tension between personal motivation and the demands of the social world, but it also shows the character of the social world being constituted out of the impulses of individuals. By combining the articulation of personal impulses with the rhetorical demands of the public domain, we might say, Brecht's city poetry shows the elements of individual experience through which the development of the social world will have to be effected, and indeed that such development cannot be effected other than through personal experience.

Exile Poems

CHAPTER TWENTY-ONE

'Visit to a Banished Poet': Brecht's *Svendborg Poems* and the Voices of Exile

TOM KUHN

> The man who finds his homeland sweet is still a tender beginner; he to whom every soil is as his native one is already strong; but he is perfect to whom the entire world is an exile.
>
> (Hugh of St Victor, *Didascalion III*, 20)

Brecht's close contemporary, the German philologist and critic Erich Auerbach – who spent the years of his exile from 1936 an outcast from Nazi Germany in Istanbul – cites these words from the writings of a twelfth-century mystic in a late reflection on culture, humanity and nationality: 'perfectus vero cui mundus totus exilium est'.[1] In this essay I shall investigate the significance of exile for Brecht and for his lyric voice. I shall reflect on the relationship between, on the one hand, the cultural context and the tradition of exile, and, on the other, the poet's own personal and political reality. Ultimately I shall suggest that, however inappropriate to Brecht any concept of 'perfection' might be, it was indeed in exile and because of exile that Brecht achieved the characteristic literary persona which is familiar to his readers, and in particular to readers of the *Svendborg Poems*. This is in itself not a new thought. After all, Brecht had his own ironic exilic credo, which we may set alongside that of Hugh of St Victor: 'The best school for dialectics is emigration.'[2]

Tom Kuhn, '"Visit to a Banished Poet": Brecht's Svendborg Poems and the Voices of Exile' in Ronald Speirs (ed.), *Brecht's Poetry of Political Exile* (Cambridge: Cambridge UP; 2000), pp. 47–65.
[1] Erich Auerbach, 'Philologie der Weltliteratur', in: *Weltliteratur. Festgabe für Fritz Strich* (Bern, 1952), p. 50. Hugh of St Victor was, coincidentally, an upholder of the dialectic method (admittedly one very different from that of Hegel or Marx).
[2] *Flüchtlingsgespräche* (BFA xviii, p. 264). Discussions of Brecht and exile are many. With reference to the poems, see in particular Helmut Brandt, 'Funktionswandel und ästhetische Gestalt in der Exillyrik Bertolt Brechts', in Alexander Stephan and Hans Wagener (eds.), *Schreiben im Exil* (Bonn, 1985), pp. 123–44.

I

The condition of exile has an ancient association with the intellectual and the poet. Brecht thematises just such a 'tradition of exile' in the *Svendborg Poems* themselves. In 'Besuch bei den verbannten Dichtern' [A visit to the banished poets] he mentions Ovid, Euripides and Chinese poets of the eighth and ninth centuries, as well as more recent European models. The story of the preceding poem of the collection, 'Legende von der Entstehung des Buches Taoteking auf dem Weg des Laotse in die Emigration' ['Legend of the origin of the book Tao-Tê-Ching on Lao-tsû's road into exile'], dates back to the sixth century B.C. There is, then, an ancient and international, even universal, dimension to this understanding of exile: exile is less a punishment for wrongdoing than the site of virtue, justice and authenticity – set apart from all base material concerns and from the abuse of power by the state. That this was also, to some degree, Brecht's own understanding is made evident in a gently ironic open letter of 1942 to Karin Michaëlis, whose friendship had been of great importance to Brecht and his family during their exile in Denmark and who herself had now been forced from her homeland by the spreading war:

> Dear Karin,
>
> I don't suppose you are very surprised to find yourself in exile; I myself would be rather more surprised if you were not in exile – given your love of truth and your rage at injustice. The history of our own literature doesn't number so many exiled writers as for example that of the Chinese. We can only excuse that by remarking that our literature is still very young and insufficiently cultivated. The poets and philosophers of China were, I am told, accustomed to go into exile rather as ours go to university. It was simply the done thing.[3]

There is, whatever Brecht may maintain, also a specifically German dimension to the idea of exile, although it is one which he chooses to underplay. In 'A visit to the banished poets' he mentions only one German writer, Heine. Yet the paths of exile in modern German cultural history were not something other contemporaries could overlook. The whole precarious negotiation of culture and political power since the eighteenth century had given many a German writer cause, at some time or another, to forsake his *Heimat* and to seek refuge abroad, even if it were only in a close neighbouring state. German anti-fascist exiles were wont to invoke, with greater or lesser justification, such a range of names as Schiller, Büchner, Grabbe, even Theodor Storm, amongst a host of others. Exile could seem quite a German phenomenon. Indeed it has even been suggested that, in the German tradition, exile is the proper condition of authentic culture. For many German intellectuals of the left, by the beginning of the twentieth century, and certainly in the Weimar Republic, things had come to such a pass that at least half of German culture was reckoned to be permanently in *metaphorical* exile. The attitude many writers adopted even long before 1933 was one of critical alienation from what they saw as an establishment national culture. As Johannes R. Becher later put it: 'We'd lived for years already in exile.'[4] Those who styled themselves in cultural opposition could perhaps even feel at home in this particular homelessness.

---

[3] 'Geburtstagsbrief zum 23. März' [1942], BFA xxiii, 9 (my translation).
[4] The last line of a poem by J.R. Becher entitled 'Exil', see e.g. *Lyrik des Exils*, ed. Wolfgang Emmerich and Susanne Heil (Stuttgart, 1985), p. 154.

In addition to the German aspect there is also a specifically 'modernist' aspect to exile. In the earlier part of this century poets and writers seem almost habitually to have sought a period of 'exile': the Irish went to America and Paris, the Americans came to London and Europe, the Eastern Europeans came west, the Western Europeans at least went south. Indeed, if one were to draw up a list of great poets of the twentieth century one would find that they nearly all spent extended periods away from 'home'. The displacement from a home culture became an important component in their aesthetic make-up. As James Joyce puts it in *A Portrait of the Artist as a Young Man* of 1916 (chapter 5),

> I will not serve that in which I no longer believe whether it call itself my home, my fatherland or my church: and I will try to express myself in some mode of life or art as freely as I can, using for my defence the only arms I allow myself to use, silence, exile, and cunning.

Despite familiar echoes across the writings of such various exiles, Brecht's own strategies of 'cunning' and his personal experience of exile were clearly very different from those of Joyce.[5] Not all exile, and not all that has been termed exile, is the same. There are essential differences between exile to a truly alien nation, culture and language, and any variety of inner emigration, internal exile, or 'exile' to a neighbouring province – not to mention all the classes of an exile more metaphorical than real. There is also a sometimes uneasy distinction to be drawn between enforced banishment and willing emigration. Amongst the German exiles after 1933 there was a lively debate about these categories and their terminologies. Brecht himself comments in one of the *Svendborg Poems*:

> Immer fand ich den Namen falsch, den man uns gab: Emigranten.
> Das heißt doch Auswanderer. Aber wir
> Wanderten doch nicht aus, nach freiem Entschluß
> Wählend ein anderes Land. Wanderten wir doch auch nicht
> Ein in ein Land, dort zu bleiben, womöglich für immer.
> Sondern wir flohen. Vertriebene sind wir, Verbannte.
> Und kein Heim, ein Exil soll das Land sein, das uns da aufnahm.
>
> (BFA XII, 81)

> I always found the name false which they gave us: Emigrants.
> That means those who leave their country. But we
> Did not leave, of our own free will
> Choosing another land. Nor did we enter
> Into a land, to stay there, if possible for ever.
> Merely, we fled. We are driven out, banned.
> Not a home, but an exile, shall the land be that took us in.
>
> (WM, 301)

There may have been degrees of coercion and of reluctance, but it is clear that most of the refugees from National Socialist Germany were genuine political exiles. In this they were different from many of the modernist poets (Eliot, Auden, Pound) who were, by and large, émigrés rather than exiles.

---

[5] 'List' (cunning) is the most important strategy of political art in Brecht's classic essay, 'Five difficulties in writing the truth' (1935).

There are also important differences between the anti-fascist exiles and the figures in the cultural tradition which Brecht invokes in his poems. Brecht was, in reality, part of a mass enforced political exile, whereas Euripides, Heine and Lao-tsû were half-reluctant, lonely émigrés. He found himself in flight with many others, and he shared their experiences to a degree. So although cultural history might have appeared to offer comforting analogies and precedents, the proponents of Germany's critical and modernist anti-state culture were in fact far less well fitted for exile than, for example, the Chinese sages to whom Brecht makes such fond allusion. Brecht had notably more baggage, both material and intellectual, than he gives Lao-tsû in his poem,

> Und er packte ein, was er so brauchte:
> Wenig. Doch es wurde dies und das.
> So die Pfeife, die er immer abends rauchte
> Und das Büchlein, das er immer las.
> Weißbrot nach dem Augenmaß.
>
> (BFA xii, 3a)
>
> And he packed up what he would be needing:
> Not much. But enough to travel light.
> Items like the book that he was always reading
> And the pipe he used to smoke at night.
> Bread as much as he thought right.
>
> (WM, 314)

or than he ascribes by implication to himself, in 'Gedanken über die Dauer des Exils' ['Thoughts on the duration of exile'] or 'Zufluchtsstätte' ['Place of refuge'].[6] These poems appear to depend on an image of the cultural emigrant or hermit-wanderer that has been familiar at the very least since the Middle Ages. Real physical exile and banishment, when they came to the representatives of German left-liberal culture in the twentieth century, proved far more traumatic than this.

Brecht's own biography and the more general coordinates of the exodus from Nazi Germany are now fully documented and can be read about elsewhere.[7] Briefly: for much of the period we are concerned with the exile appeared to be predominantly one of middle-class artists and intellectuals and of the politically active. All the same, by 1938 about half a million (nearly 1 per cent of the population) had fled Germany. The refugees from anti-semitic persecution swelled to a flood only after 1935 and more especially after 1938.

---

[6] For a tragi-comical account of Brecht and his anything but light baggage as an exile, see Peter Weiss, *Ästhetik des Widerstands* (Frankfurt am Main, 1983), pp. 310–19.

[7] Of the biographical works about Brecht, Harald Engberg, *Brecht auf Fünen. Exil in Dänemark 1933-1939* (Wuppertal, 1974; originally *Brecht pa Fyn*, Odense, 1966), although now dated, is devoted exclusively to Brecht's time in Denmark. Werner Mittenzwei, *Das Leben des Bertolt Brecht, oder der Umgang mit den Welträtseln* (Berlin and Weimar, 1986), 2 vols., is the fullest general biography. Of the many books on the German exile, *Die Künste und die Wissenschaften im Exil 1933–1945*, ed. Edith Böhne and Wolfgang Motzkau-Valeton (Gerlingen, 1992) attempts a general picture by way of essays on the various arts and academic disciplines. Sections in *Exil in der Tschechoslowakei, in Großbritannien, Skandinavien und Palästina*, ed. Ludwig Hoffinann and others (= *Kunst und Literatur im antifaschistischen Exil 1933–1945*, vol. v) (Leipzig, 1980, 1987), and essays in *Deutschsprachiges Exil in Dänemark nach 1933. Zu Methoden und Einzeterbnissen*, ed. Ruth Dinesen, Birgit S. Nielsen and others (Copenhagen and Munich, 1986), give the specific national context for Brecht's own situation in the 1930s.

Many of the persecuted were never to return home. The experience left three generations of victims devastated by loss and death, and with permanent psychological scars; and it left the better part of German culture – liberal, humanist, socialist, modernist, not to say Jewish – beaten into submission, sacked and ruined, or in panicked retreat. Brecht himself suffered, in his own family and amongst his closest circle, the losses and the horrors which are a ghastly commonplace of these years. And yet – and this is the extraordinary paradox which we have to confront – in the terms of his own literary oeuvre and in the development of his aesthetics, the years of exile proved quite exceptionally productive.

The significance for Brecht's literature of the move into exile is often underestimated. Where it tends to be taken more seriously is in discussion of Brecht's development as a dramatist and dramatic theorist. For Franz Carl Weiskopf, however, who wrote one of the earliest accounts of German literature in exile, the dramatists and the lyric poets were, in contradistinction to the novelists and essayists, the real 'problem children of the emigration' – for reasons so obvious I need not elaborate them here.[8] Brecht himself commented apropos of the first edition of the *Svendborg Poems* on the irony of writing 'something so unprofitable as antifascist poems'.[9]

II

Before the *Svendborg Poems* Brecht had already published one book of poems in exile, the *Lieder Gedichte Chöre* [Songs, Poems, Choruses] of 1934, which make no particular reference to exile. However, here, in the Svendborg collection, the situation and perspective of exile are thematised centrally. Although a couple of the poems were actually written in the 1920s and not in exile at all, Brecht originally proposed to publish the new collection under the title *Gedichte im Exil* [Poems in Exile]. He went so far as to suggest that a book containing these poems, scenes from *Fear and Misery of the Third Reich* and three (unspecified) essays could form his definitive literary statement about the exile.[10] As the collection now stands, all of the poems, whenever and wherever they were individually written, are framed by the motto: 'Geflüchtet unter das dänische Strohdach, Freunde' ('Refuged beneath this Danish thatched roof, friends'), and by the final section (VI) of the collection, where all the poems make explicit reference to exile. The whole collection is rounded off by 'Verjagt mit gutem Grund' ['Driven out with good reason'] and 'An die Nachgeborenen' ['To those born later']: 'Gingen wir doch, öfter als die Schuhe die Länder wechselnd / Durch die Kriege der Klassen' ('For we went, changing countries oftener than our shoes / Through the wars of the classes') (BFA xii, 87; WM, 320). This final poem, Brecht's most resonant poetic testament, addresses posterity specifically from the experience of exile. The many poems between the opening motto and that concluding statement were of course written in various circumstances and for various purposes and

---

[8] F.C. Weiskopf, *Unter fremden Himmeln: Ein Abriß der deutschen Literatur im Exil 1933-1947* (Berlin, 1948), p. 27.
[9] Letter to the American Guild for German Cultural Freedom, dated June 1939 (BFA xxix, 147).
[10] Letter to Wieland Herzfelde, 7 June 1938, *Nachlaß Herzfelde*, quoted in BFA xii, 351. The earlier plans for a collection involved a very slightly different selection of poems. For the details, see BFA xii, 351–4, and Christiane Bohnert, *Brechts Lyrik im Kontext. Zyklen und Exil* (Königstein/Ts, 1982).

publics, and they assume a very wide variety of voices and roles. Nonetheless, the collection as a whole establishes firmly, and crucially, a perspective of exile.

In the context of the displacements and disruptions of his own biography, Brecht seems always to have sought at least some sort of *poetic* home for himself, a base from which his lyric voice could explore its range and his poems could draw their sense of rightness and rootedness. For Brecht this sense of place is very often associated with trees and with water. So too in Svendborg. The Svendborg Sound and the now famous 'Baum im Hof' ('the tree in the yard') may be compared to the river Lech and the chestnut-trees the young Brecht knew in Augsburg, or the pines and poplars he later saw around the lakes of Buckow. All three place-names feature in titles Brecht gave to collections of poems, and all three are set up there as places away from the hurly-burly of the political and cultural centres. As Brecht wrote to Walter Benjamin about Svendborg, 'the world is coming to an end *more quietly* here'.[11] In Svendborg, the pseudo-idyll of 'Sund und Laubwerk' (the water of the Sound and the foliage of the trees) provides a background against which the 'blutige Gesichte' ('deadly visions') (BFA xii, 7; WM, 320) of political reality intrude with all the more violence and urgency. Brecht wrote comparatively little about his land of exile, but he did take care to establish, at least in his poems, a provisional but quite precise sense of locality. It is not exactly a place to settle. The doors of the house are there 'to escape by', not entrances through which to come home – in 'Place of refuge' as in Villon's question in 'A visit to the banished poets': 'Wie viele / Türen hat das Haus, wo du wohnst?' ('How many / Doors has the house where you live?') (BFA xii, 83 and 35). But it has the essentials. It is a place for waiting and watching from – the attitudes of waiting and watching which pervade the 'Deutsche Kriegsfibel' ['German War Primer']. The Sound separating Fyn from its neighbouring islands (and, not far beyond, from Germany) is an important part of this creation of a lyric perspective: it is a figure both of distance and separation, and yet of relative proximity. The fact that Brecht did indeed spend a large part of the 1930s living on Fyn is ultimately less important for these poems than the symbolic import for the poet of living on a small and marginal island, apart, but not that far, from the European mainland. When Brecht looked out over the sea, his posture was literally and symbolically 'with his face turned towards Germany'.[12] For Brecht – or for Brecht's poems, wherever they were actually written – it was useful to define a place and a point of view on the periphery, a periphery even of exile. It was from here that Brecht could develop his self-image as an observer and as a writer. Gradually, a real situation was transformed into a far-reaching metaphor.

When Walter Benjamin received the new collection in 1938 he noted the 'contrast between the *political* and the *private* poems'.[13] Other commentators have tried to distinguish between poems which deal with a generalised myth of exile and those which speak of Brecht's own situation.[14] Brecht himself seemed to underline the notion of an authentic personal voice when, as he was compiling the *Hundert Gedichte* [One Hundred Poems] in 1951, he gave the poems of section VI a heading: 'Personal' ('Persönliches').

---

[11]Letter dated Skovsbostrand per Svendborg, 22 December 1933 (BFA xxviii, 395), italics original.
[12]As Rudolf Leonhard characterised the posture of the literary exiles, in *Der Gegen-Angriff*, 15 February 1936. The island is itself an ancient symbol of isolation, the very word derived from the Latin 'insula'.
[13]Diary note in Walter Benjamin, *Gesammelte Schriften*, ed. Rolf Tiedemann and Hermann Schweppenhäuser, vol. VI (Frankfurt am Main, 1985), p. 538.
[14]See, e.g., Peter Paul Schwarz, 'Legende und Wirklichkeit des Exils. Zum Selbstverständnis der Emigration in den Gedichten Brechts', *Wirkendes Wort 19* (1969), pp. 267–76.

Unlike most of the rest of the *Svendborg Poems* apart from the motto, these final poems are full of mentions of a first person who can easily be associated with Brecht. They include a number of references to the concrete physical details of Brecht's own refuge in Svendborg: the oar holding down the thatched roof, the tree in the yard, the arm of the sea which Brecht could see from his window and in which the family used to swim, and so on:

Zufluchtsstätte

Ein Ruder liegt auf dem Dach. Ein mittlerer Wind
Wird das Stroh nicht wegtragen.
Im Hof für die Schaukel der Kinder sind
Pfähle eingeschlagen.
Die Post kommt zweimal hin
Wo die Briefe willkommen wären.
Den Sund herunter kommen die Fähren.
Das Haus hat vier Türen, daraus zu fliehen.

(BFA xii, 83)

Place of refuge

An oar lies on the roof. A moderate wind
Will not carry away the thatch.
In the yard posts are set for
The children's swing.
The mail comes twice a day
Where letters would be welcome.
Down the Sound come the ferries.
The house has four doors to escape by.

(WM, 302–3)

Yet, when we look a little closer, these details seem in fact extraordinarily sparse, almost token trappings of any biography in a foreign land. The point is that he has shelter, a simple roof, any roof would do. The image of the oar may well have derived from a real, local observation, but it has taken on a quite new significance by its use and placing in the poem.[15] And was the tree a chestnut, as in 'Thoughts on the duration of exile'; or was it not a plum-tree, as in the children's song 'Der Pflaumenbaum' ['The plum-tree']; or again perhaps a pear-tree, as in the later 'An die dänische Zufluchtsstätte' ['To the Danish refuge']?[16] Could not that bit of sea be almost any channel with its boats? And so on.

Other German poets in exile suffered painful identity problems which are only too evident in their poems. Much of German exile poetry is peopled with lonely foreigners, shelterless hermits, loners without families or friends, suffering an alienated and hopeless non-existence in an atmosphere of cold and night. My point is simply this: with those

---

[15] It was actually a sort of wooden frame with which the thatch, following the Danish custom, was secured at the top, called in Danish the 'Åre' (or pl.'Årer, Årerne' = German 'Ruder', oars). Christiane Bohnert has suggested, taking the oar literally, that it becomes a symbol of movement and activity, temporarily misplaced by the experience of exile (Bohnert, *Lyrik im Kontext*, pp. 76 and 136).

[16] BFA xii, 82, 21 and 99. In fact there are, to this day, quite a variety of trees in the garden and around the house in Svendborg. A large mature chestnut (the sapling which Brecht describes watering?) overshadows the house at the back.

very few, almost homely tokens Brecht's poems avoid that miserable voice and achieve for themselves an identity, even quite a comfortable one. The lyric subject in the *Svendborg Poems* is a construction, almost a mask; the biography of 'Driven out with good reason' is more important for its stylisation than for its accuracy. It is not that the biography of the politically exiled poet manifests itself in the text; rather, the tenuous coherence of the text is manufactured by reference to a constituted 'exile' persona and place. In the context of the collection, it is from the comparative security of this unrevealing, almost self-denying fictive identity that the apparently impersonal, political poems may also achieve their particular force. The 'personal' and 'political', so-called, are mutually dependent. Moreover, it is in the articulation of a stylised, non-personal condition of exile that Brecht makes all-important contact with other exiles, with the tradition of the exiled intellectual, and even with a myth of exile. Having once insisted on the particular and historical distinctions, in 'Über die Bezeichnung Emigranten' ['Concerning the label emigrant'], for example, Brecht re-builds an image of a generalised and ahistorical exile – which, for his writing at least, will prove extremely productive.

III

The real meeting between Brecht's fictive poetic 'self' and the myth of exile occurs not so much in the last section of the *Svendborg Poems* as amongst the earlier 'Chronicles', above all in the poem 'A visit to the banished poets' (BFA xii, 35–6).[17] Here, in the company of Dante (with whose spirit Brecht enjoyed a long and lively debate) and in a poem with clear echoes of the *Divine Comedy*, an unnamed third person is introduced in a dream to leading representatives of banished and proscribed literature, across the world and across the ages. This is elevated company. To some extent, evidently, exile is a distinction.

The poem enacts an unbalanced dialogue with literary history, in which the silent modern newcomer is bombarded with advice from all sides, but there is no agreement. Direct speech predominates. We are told in the opening lines that 'disputation and laughter' issue from a neighbouring hut, that of the banished teachers. It transpires, however, that this is not something to *distinguish* the bickering teachers from the lofty poets, but rather to *associate* the two. What we hear from the poets, as the conversation warms up, is exactly that: disputation and laughter. These are positive signs to Brecht of an active, critical and yet 'friendly' engagement. The poets have become teachers too – as Brecht aspired to become. Their teaching carries us, not into a world of easy answers, but, predictably, into debate, into dialectics.

On the other side of the imbalance, in the person of the modern poet, the poem presents us with one of those ambivalent moments of self-denial and self-assertion which are typical of Brecht.[18] No name is mentioned for the dreamer who here steps into the hut of the banished poets of past ages; and the first of the ghosts to speak, Ovid, addresses the visitor in terms which draw attention to his unstable self and threaten his (anti-fascist) exile-identity: who knows if he won't some day return – 'Und ohne daß andres sich ändert / Als du selber' ('Even if nothing has changed / Except yourself')? The line division underpins the threat. The poem's clamour of interjections rises from a whisper to a rowdy

---

[17]BBA 425/128 makes it clear that Brecht originally intended to place this poem in the last section of the collection.
[18]Another famous example is the poem 'Ich benötige keinen Grabstein' ['I need no gravestone'] of about 1933 (BFA xiv, 191–2; WM, 218).

exchange and then subsides, and the poem ends, again emphatically: 'Der Ankömmling / War erblaßt' ('The newcomer / Had turned pale'). He has perhaps not only blenched, but also 'faded', paled into insignificance in the contemplation of his fate and of his tradition. The ghostly presence of the living amongst the vigorous dead is not only a nice inversion, it expresses also the poet's anxious awareness of the vigour of his predecessors' achievement.[19] Despite the welcome accorded by the distinguished assembly, the new poet does not speak. Yet, and this is surely important, Brecht's own personal situation and works are hinted at in almost every one of the remarks of the great poets. Villon all but quotes the poem 'Place of refuge' from section VI of the *Svendborg Poems*. Others comment on such 'Brechtian' obsessions and strategies as entertainment, instruction and censorship, the naming of injustices while keeping an eye on one's own material well-being, and so on. Euripides' recommendation to 'take a rogue for your lawyer' is reminiscent not only of the Azdak of *The Caucasian Chalk Circle* (not yet written, but long mulled over), but also of Brecht's own experience in the so-called 'Dreigroschenprozeß' (the trial about the film rights to the *Threepenny Opera*). In the very act of self-denial, the poem reasserts a powerful sense of a 'self'.

The associations with a Brechtian 'voice' are underlined further by a number of connecting links with the neighbouring poems in the collection. Perhaps the most striking is the use of the comparative adjective 'irdischer' ('more worldly') to describe Villon's intervention. 'Irdisch' is a key word in both 'Der Schuh des Empedokles' ['The shoe of Empedocles'] and 'Gleichnis des Buddha vom brennenden Haus' ['The Buddha's parable of the burning house']. The recognition and dissemination of concrete truths about earthly reality was Brecht's overwhelming preoccupation – as he liked to remind himself with the Hegelian-cum-Leninist motto, 'Die Wahrheit ist konkret' ('Truth is concrete'), attached to a beam in the house in Svendborg. In 'A visit to the banished poets' the word has one further association: 'irdisch' here means not just 'worldly' but also 'of *this* world'. Although Villon is long dead, his earthy profanity propels him back towards the world of the living, while at the same time the living dreamer-poet all but slips into the realm of the dead.

The poem subverts and asserts not only the conventions of the subject and its concerns, but also those of that other traditional function of the lyric: the *memoria*. On the one simple level the poem commemorates the work and the posture of some of the great political poets of the past. In the final lines, however, a cry is heard from a darker corner of the hut. In hushed tones Dante introduces 'the forgotten', those who cannot be a part of the cheerfully argumentative community of the tradition and yet still lurk in its hidden corners. The poem thus stages both the act of remembering and that of forgetting. The forgotten are remembered here too, precariously.[20] So Brecht resists the very tradition on which the poem seems to depend. He discovers that the impression, drawn from cultural history, of an endless succession of great truth-telling poets languishing in banishment, may in part be an illusion; the cycle can be interrupted. As so often with Brecht, history and the tradition can be re-told – but this time his conclusions seem far from encouraging.

---

[19]One is reminded of another great modernist (émigré) poet, T. S. Eliot, who reflects, in 'Tradition and the Individual Talent' (1919), on the 'process of depersonalisation and its relation to the sense of tradition'.

[20]As Anthony Phelan makes clear, it is by no means Brecht's only poem about memorials and forgetting, nor even the only one in this collection; compare, for example, 'Die Teppichweber von Kujan-Bulak ehren Lenin' ['The carpet weavers of Kuyan-Bulak honour Lenin'], 'Die unbesiegliche Inschrift' [The invincible inscription] and 'Grabschrift für Gorki' ['Epitaph for Gorki'] (BFA xii, 37–9; WM, 174; BFA xii, 39–40; BFA xii, 60/WM, 269). Survival and endurance (Dauer) are lasting preoccupations of Brecht's writing.

He steers us back towards his own historically specific exile. The final feared experience of the text is not so much that it will not be able to measure itself against that awesome tradition, but that it will not live at all.[21] For a moment, a real psyche and a real fear seem to intrude, chillingly, into the poem. Ruth Berlau, one of Brecht's long-time assistants, remembers that in Denmark Brecht did indeed once ask her to learn his poems by heart, fearful of just this dark corner of forgetfulness.[22] 'A visit to the banished poets' is perhaps, despite the lightness of the earlier exchanges, one of the pessimistic low-points of Brecht's lyric project in exile.[23]

On the other hand, the poem itself implies a way of evading the clutches of oblivion. The stress on teaching is the key. Poetry will die if it is lost and forgotten. But teaching, in Brecht's sense, requires no text, for it lives on in those who are taught. It is the *readers* who must 'prevail and escape persecution'. As in other poetological poems, those of exile especially, Brecht's text is not a monument to the author and his situation, nor to the poets mentioned here; instead the situation (and here the confrontation with tradition) is exploited as itself a creative opportunity. The processes become the stuff of the poem. It is appropriate that we arrive at no fixed position. Instead we are left suspended in a dialectics of presence and absence, of memory and oblivion, and of teaching and learning – a dialectics which might, if all goes well, continue to resonate through our present readings and into a future of further creative potential. Hope lies with the readers as much as with the poets.

IV

The voice of National Socialist culture was undialectically propagandist, but it was also a collective voice. The artist spoke, supposedly, in the name of the 'Volk' or the 'Gemeinschaft'. Fascist poetry saw the almost complete suppression of the lyric subject in community songs, marching songs, communal hymns of celebration in praise of the 'Führer' and of 'Deutschland', and in the bogus 'Volkspoesie' of 'Blut und Boden' ('Blood and soil') nature poetry. Most German exile poetry took, understandably, an opposite course, and asserted the individual at the expense of all community. The loss of community was after all the condition of exile. Max Herrmann-Neiße spoke of exile poems as a 'monologue': 'Doch hier wird niemand meine Verse lesen, / ist nichts, was meiner Seele Sprache spricht' ('But no one here will read my verses, / and nothing speaks the language of my soul').[24] For Brecht, however, that monologic voice was simply not an option. He had always understood poetry as a dialogue in a social context. Where that context is anti-fascist exile, the society is so ruptured that communication may seem scarcely possible. 'Lyric poetry like this', he wrote later in his *Journal*, 'is a message in a bottle' (*Journals*, 218; BFA xxvii, 80).[25]

---

[21]'Erblassen' or 'erbleichen', in poetic diction, can even mean 'to expire': the thought that his works might not endure imperils the poet's very existence. This is the point at which he almost steps across, to join the dead.
[22]Ruth Berlau, *Brechts Lai-Tu. Erinnerungen und Notate*, ed. Hans Bunge (Berlin, 1987), P. 275.
[23]It is a relatively late poem in the *Svendborg Poems*, written against the background of the National Socialist advances of 1938.
[24]'Ein deutscher Dichter bin ich einst gewesen', cited from Emmerich and Heil (eds.), *Lyrik des Exils*, p. 234.
[25]It is arguable that by this time the dialogic project was beginning to fade, as Brecht felt himself increasingly isolated in his Californian exile.

One of the major tasks, then, was to construct a sense of society and community in which the dialectical pedagogy of his poems could be heard and could make sense. And Brecht cautiously does just that. In the poems of Section VI of the Svendborg collection a 'we' and a 'you' are as prominent as an 'I': 'Unruhig sitzen wir so, möglichst nahe den Grenzen / Wartend des Tags der Rückkehr' ('Restlessly we wait thus, as near as we can to the frontier / Awaiting the day of return') (BFA xii, 81; WM, 301) or 'Tag um Tag / Arbeitest du an der Befreiung / Sitzend in der Kammer schreibst du' (BFA xii, 82) ('Day after day / You work for the liberation. / You sit in your room, writing') (BFA xii, 82; WM 302). Long before we come to the future with 'Ihr, die ihr auftauchen werdet aus der Flut ...' ('You who will emerge from the flood ...') of 'To those born later', we have the much more immediate second person plural (addressed to those who had stayed in Germany) of the last two poems of the 'German War Primer' (BFA xii, 87, 14 and 15). And the whole of section IV consists of addresses, appeals, pleas, words of praise and even epitaphs, some referring apparently to Brecht's own experience and some as explicit role-poems. Together these pronouns and forms of address begin to imply an international community of anti-fascists at home and abroad, some already fallen in the struggle, but most still well and truly living. It is no grand, triumphant collective, like that of fascism (or, for that matter, of Stalinist Socialist Realism); rather it is a modest, fragmented collection of individual voices. But it is a sketch of a dialogic Community, nonetheless, and that is crucial.

The community draws its strength and finds its meaning in relation, not only to anti-fascism, but also to Brecht's eclectically international vision of a cultural tradition. Unlike that of the Nazis themselves, indeed unlike that of his fellow exiles, there is little specifically German about Brecht's sense of cultural place. He had never associated closely with a national culture, either as upholder or as critic, and so he did not now feel the need to discover an 'other Germany', as so many others strove to do. His 'Chronicles' invoke stories of the exiled intellectual and of proletarian solidarity from all over the globe, to underline the general potential of the experience and the international nature of the struggle. From the relative privilege of the marginal exile he had chosen to construct, Brecht investigates all kinds of corners of alien cultural history and the humanist tradition. His inclination, even from long before 1933, to discover a whole 'other culture', a set of alternative traditions and alternative readings of traditions, seems immeasurably sharpened. In exile we find Brecht more willing to recognise cultural traditions as something to engage with, and not just something to tease and trespass upon. He finds allies, not only, as one might have predicted, in Lenin and Gorki, but also in Voltaire, Shakespeare and Dante. Moreover, as he sets about cautiously mapping the unstable coordinates of his own cultural place, he starts to investigate, in a poem such as 'Fragen eines lesenden Arbeiters' ['Questions from a worker who reads'], the whole issue of the relationship between people, nations and classes, and their culture. The very particular engagement with tradition which is such an important part of the *Svendborg Poems* can then perhaps be seen, in part at least, as a product of the perspective of exile.

The securing of a geographical and cultural place from which to speak, the establishment of a community in which dialogue is meaningful, and the investigation of his own and others' relationships with their culture and traditions – all this draws Brecht to consider, not merely the situation of artists and poets and their various publics, but also of teachers and sages and their pupils. In 'A visit to the banished poets', as we have already remarked, the banished teachers live in the adjacent hut. They live in the adjacent poems too. The motto of the whole collection has set the tone: here is a teacher and student at one and the same time, sending thoughts and advice to colleagues, and promising that once all this is over he will go back to school (BFA xii, 7). Issues of knowledge and communication, teaching and learning, crop up all over the place, especially in sections III and IV, and of course in the last poems of the whole collection. These are fragments of precisely that active involvement in a pedagogic process (teaching *and* learning) which is characteristic of Brecht – rather than the one-way didacticism of which he is often accused. Gorki is described as 'Der Lehrer des Volkes / Der vom Volk gelernt hat' ('The people's teacher / Who learned from the people') (BFA xii, 60; WM, 269). Along with Gorki and Lenin come such surprising teachers as 'Gothama, the Buddha', Empedocles, and of course Lao-tsû.

Exile is not the only thing the figure of Lao-tsû has in common with the lyric persona of the *Svendborg Poems*. There is also the central point of the Lao-tsû poem, the mutual interdependence of teacher and pupil: 'Denn man muß dem Weisen seine Weisheit erst entreißen' ('For a wise man's wisdom needs to be extracted') (BFA xii, 34; WM, 316). There is the poverty and simplicity in the affectionately ironic characterisation of Lao-tsû's surroundings and of his belongings; and there is the reflective loneliness engendered by Lao-tsû's separation from the struggles to which his thoughts are directed. Lao-tsû's place in Brecht's private network of theorists of change, and of teachers and taught, is underlined in an echo of Lenin's words in the line, 'Doch wer wen besiegt, das interessiert auch mich' (Who triumphs over whom, that interests me too) (BFA xii, 33). This was how in 1921 Lenin had stated the problem of the conflict of capitalism and Soviet power: 'Wer – wen?' ['Who – whom?'].[26] The mention of the shoe in the last line of the first stanza suggests a further set of associations. There are a great many shoes in the *Svendborg Poems*, from that of Empedocles in the preceding poem to the 'torn shoes' of 'Concerning the label Emigrant' and the oft changed shoes of 'To those born later'. Putting on your shoes is a preparation for a journey or, as here, for an exile – that age-old condition of poet and thinker. Yet this is an exile which brings with it not just impoverishment and disorientation, but also moments of opportunity. It is the moment of going into exile which provides the occasion for the writing of Lao-tsû's great work. The work itself becomes testimony, not to the genius of the individual sage who was its author, but to the processes which led to the effective introduction of his teaching into the world.

> Aber rühmen wir nicht nur den Weisen
> Dessen Name auf dem Buche prangt!
> Denn man muß dem Weisen seine Weisheit erst entreißen.
> Darum sei der Zöllner auch bedankt:
> Er hat sie ihm abverlangt.
>
> (BFA xii, 34)

> But the honour should not be restricted
> To the sage whose name is clearly writ.
> For a wise man's wisdom needs to be extracted.
> So the customs man deserves his bit:
> It was he who called for it.
>
> (WM, 316)

---

[26] Lenin, Werke, vol. xxxiii (Berlin, 1962), p. 46. Compare note in BFA xii, 368.

Just as in 'A visit to the banished poets', it is not the authority of any one or more of the great writers of the past that prevails, but rather the processes of debate that the 'newcomer' has stimulated by his arrival. Brecht's poems aspire to a similar effect.

V

The voice of 'Brecht-the-poet' seems sometimes almost utterly submerged in this network of other voices and traditions. Then it re-emerges, recognisable and more personal once more, as the voice of one who aspired to join these lonely exiled teachers, in need of learning and in search of readers and disciples. It is perhaps from the fleeting recognitions of the personal and the reminders of a real historical situation that the *Svendborg Poems* derive their most urgent and emotional appeal. Yet it is only from the constructed perspective of the exiled sage – one self-stylisation in the whole series of self-stylisations which characterise Brecht's biography, from *enfant terrible* to 'revered classic' – that the poems of Svendborg have become possible at all. A great many of the achievements of this collection, and of the features which set Brecht apart from other exile poets, can be explained in terms of the very particular modulations of this voice or perspective: perhaps we should call it, as Brecht might have done, a 'Haltung' or posture. It is by this that Brecht avoids despair or self-indulgent pathos; by this that he overcomes the purely monologic expression of much literature in exile; and by this that he escapes the common obsessions of German exile poetry with memory, loss, language, and fragments of *Deutschtum*, Others in exile were often left struggling merely to hang onto their damaged sense of self and purpose. Brecht, on the other hand, fashioned a semi-personalised mythic poetic exile out of a real political fate, and achieved a hugely productive fictive identity. The purposeful communicative voice of the *Svendborg Poems* is a striking one in the canon of modern lyric poetry. It came about very specifically as a voice of exile.

But we can go further than this. The real experience of exile was devastating, and Brecht speaks elsewhere of the privations and impoverishment. In these poems, however, exile emerges also, not as a setback, where new boundaries and hindrances rise up like mountain-ranges, as for so many of the anti-fascist victims, but rather, as for Lao-tsû, as an opportunity to journey across the world's cultural borders and to achieve a sort of liberated homelessness. Brecht was perhaps, after all, not burdened by so much metaphorical baggage as it appeared at the outset. I would not suggest he did anything so trite as to discover 'his true home in exile'.[27] The house of exile, we remember, has 'four doors to escape by'; it is a mere staging post for further travels. Rather, he (re-)discovered, in new ways, the strangeness, not just of his homeland, but of the whole world: 'he is perfect to whom the entire world is an exile'.[28]

The context for the quotation from Hugh of St Victor at the head of this chapter is supplied by a theology in which nowhere on this earth could be 'home' for the true believer: the world is a place of exile, from the Garden of Eden and from fulfilment in the life beyond. That may make it seem a singularly inappropriate motto under which to talk

---

[27]As Ulrich Weisstein suggests in his otherwise stimulating essay, 'Bertolt Brecht. Die Lehren des Exils', in Manfred Durzak (ed.), *Die deutsche Exilliteratur* (Stuttgart, 1973), p. 392.
[28]The association with Erich Auerbach is made the more interesting by Auerbach's own masterpiece, *Mimesis. Dargestellte Wirklichkeit in der abendländischen Literatur* (1st edn Bern, 1946), another reassessment of tradition and cultural place, a classic intellectual product of exile perhaps.

about an arch-materialist like Brecht. But perhaps Brecht's self-image has, after all, less in common with the aesthetically displaced modernist poet-émigré, and more to do with the sage-pilgrim of medieval legend. Brecht's political ideology, moreover, may even supply a context analogous to medieval theology.

In the *Svendborg Poems*, although Brecht mentions in passing the possibility of return, there is none of the nostalgia for the home country which we find in the writings of other German exiles. Indeed, Germany seems at least as odd and as unhomely as anywhere else. As we have seen, the landscapes and cultural traditions invoked in these poems are either those of exile, or are so sketchy as to be 'anywhere', or else they are explicitly drawn from all over the world. Clearly, Brecht did not want to return to Germany as it had been before he left, nor yet as it was now, while the global struggle between socialism and the forces of capitalism and fascism remained unresolved. Brecht's real interest is in how Germany *will be*. His path out of exile – at least as it is implied in this collection – is into the post-revolutionary promised land. His place in exile is defined, finally, not by anything geographical or cultural, but by his understanding of the political goal:

> Das Ziel
> Lag in großer Ferne
> Es war deutlich sichtbar, wenn auch für mich
> Kaum zu erreichen.
>
> (BFA xii, 86)

> Our goal
> Lay far in the distance
> It was clearly visible, though I myself
> Was unlikely to reach it.
>
> (WM, 319)

Until that goal is reached the entire world can provide only a surrogate, exile existence. The future perspective, this Utopian perspective which is rarely so explicit in Brecht's work, proves absolutely essential to the sense of purpose and of historical place of the *Svendborg Poems*. Thoughts of an undialectical perfection, glimpsed from exile, touch Brecht after all more closely than Ziffel's 'school for dialectics' in the *Flüchtlingsgespräche* [Refugee conversations] might imply. It is the hope of future salvation which drives a poem like 'Der große Oktober' [The great October]. And it is with thoughts of a time when fraternity will govern men's affairs that Brecht closes his collection – an address from exile, not to Germany, but 'to those born later', that is to say: after the flood in which he will have perished (the biblical image is no accident), and after, or beyond, the banishment which gave him both the need to speak and the voice with which to speak.

Sonnets

Two sonnets, after Brecht

On seducing angels
Angels aren't for ravishing – unless it's quick.
Just drag him straight into the entrance hall
Shove your tongue right down his throat and stick
Your finger up him, turn him to the wall
And when he's good and moist, lift up his gown
And fuck him. Should he groan as if in pain
Hold him hard, bring him on: once and again
That way he'll lack the strength to strike you down.

Remind him that he has to move his bum
And tell him he can go ahead and touch
Your balls, that he must just let go and come
While earth and sky are slipping from his clutch-

But while you're fucking don't look in his face
And see his wings unruffled, feathers stay in place.

Michael Morley[1]

When I'd brought the pair of them the news
that up among the living nowadays
no one actually gets killed since ownership

had been abolished, the man
who certainly wasn't her husband
lifted his hand attached by chains to her hand,

looked at her, then asked, 'If no-one can
own anything, then nothing can be stolen, right?'
I nodded, but saw that at his touch she turned

bright red. He noticed too. 'I haven't seen that happen,
not since the first guilty moment when our lips …
So now you mean there's not the slightest risk?'

And off they went, the chains that bound them tight
then seemed to weigh no more than paperclips.

Jamie McKendrick[2]

---

[1]Compare BFA 15, p. 193, 'Über die Verfuhrungvon Engeln'. In an excess of naughtiness, Brecht signed this and another poem, 'Sauna und Beischlaf'/'Sauna and copulation', both of 1948, with the name 'Thomas Mann', but he made no attempt to publish them. The German poem may read rather differently from the above: the word for angel, 'der Engel', is a masculine noun; the use of the masculine pronoun does not necessarily imply a homosexual encounter.]
[2]Compare BPA 14, p. 417. Brecht's poem is prefaced by an explanation: 'The Augsburger walks with Dante through the hell of the departed. He speaks to the inconsolable souls and reports that on earth some things have changed.' The reference is to the story of the adulterers, Paolo and Francesca, in Dante's *Inferno*.]

CHAPTER TWENTY-TWO

Brecht's Sonnets

DAVID CONSTANTINE

There are nearly seventy finished sonnets in Brecht's collected poems; another six or seven unfinished; and half a dozen more poems that have fourteen lines but may not strictly be called sonnets.[3] The earliest of his sonnets date from 1913, the latest from 1948.[4]

Brecht had periods of sonnet writing, the first in 1913 when, as a beginner in lyric poetry, he did what most would have done then and tried the sonnet. In his journal on 20 May 1913 he wrote: 'The following is an attempt at a sonnet'. The sonnet thus produced was 'Die Gewaltigen' / 'The mighty',[5] He wrote another five that year, and a poem of fourteen lines but no sonnet rhyme-scheme, called 'Der Narr' / 'The fool'. Formally these early sonnets are interesting in their mixing of metres and their frequent variations in lengths of line. 'Emaus' / 'Emmaus' indeed is, as to form, the least conventional, most experimental sonnet in Brecht's entire *œuvre*. Designated a sonnet in his diary,[6] it is set out as six very long lines and two hemistiches. The long lines rhyme halfway and as they finish, so that an almost conventional scheme (abba cddc efg egf) is there to be discovered. Chiefly these early sonnets advocate a zest-ful and even violent engagement

---

David Constantine, 'Brecht's Sonnets', in Tom Kuhn and Karen Leeder (eds), *Empedocles' Shoe* (London: Methuen, 2002), pp. 151–74.

[3] Identifying poems as sonnets or as drafts for sonnets and keeping a tally is difficult through the five volumes of the collected poems. Two sonnets 'Über das Böse' / 'On wickedness' and 'Über die Gedichte des Dante'/ 'On the poems of Dante' feature twice (BFA 11, p. 123 and 13, p. 341; 11, pp. 190 and 269) in slightly differing forms. 'Unfinished' may mean wanting half a line ('Sonett vom Erbe' / 'Sonnet on the legacy', BFA 14, p. 422) or wanting several lines ('Und als ich dringend fragte' / 'And when I urgently enquired', BFA 13, p. 326, or 'Als wir so lang getrennt wie vordem nie' / 'Longer apart than ever before', BFA 14, p. 332). It is also likely that Brecht would have altered things before any publication and in that sense several more may be thought unfinished. The fourteen-liners but not strictly sonnets are: 'Der Narr' / 'The fool' (BFA 13, p. 50), 'Die Schneetruppe' / 'Snow unit' (p. 76), 'Und als sie wegsah' / 'And when she looked away' (p. 145) and 'Schlechter Vorgang' / 'Bad occurrence' (BFA 14. p. 385). 'Als ich den beiden' / 'When I had told them both' (p. 417), though associated with the Studies, is more terza rima than sonnet. 'Schmalhans' / 'Slim Jim' (p. 385), unfinished, seems to be heading towards sonnet-form. Brigitte Bergheim has undertaken a similar general appraisal of Brecht's sonnets, which was drawn to my attention at a late stage in the work for this piece: 'Die Sonette Bertolt Brechts', in Theo Stemmler and Stefan Horlacher (eds), *Erscheinungsformen des Sonetts* (Mannheim, 1999), pp. 245–70. She identifies seventy-two sonnets. In other respects, her conclusions differ notably from mine.

[4] He seems to have written none after his return to Germany, Elisabeth Hauptmann noted that he was not the author of 'Lied der neuen Erde' / 'Song of the new earth'. 1955 (BFA 15, p. 494).

[5] BFA 13, p. 409. He was consciously trying out other forms as well. *See* his note on a poem, Heimat / 'Homeland', written next day: 'This is an attempt at a ballad. I still haven't mastered the style!'

[6] BFA 13, p. 413.

with life, already rather in the manner of the hard men and the pirates of the *Hauspostille/ Domestic Breviary*. Thus 'the mighty', in the poem of that name, 'go through dense grey fog/In their fiery eyes the crimson glow/Of spilt blood – but with clear consciences / They stride towards judgement';[7] and have young Eugen Berthold's approval.

Two other fourteen-line poems, 'Die Schneetruppe' / 'Snow unit' (early 1915) and 'Und als sie wegsah' / 'And when she looked away' (1919), complete the tally of Brecht's early dealings with the sonnet form. The first, dedicated to Brecht's Uncle August and published in the local newspaper, the *Augsburger Neueste Nachrichten*, fuses Nietzschean vitalism with the non-combatant's enthusiastic patriotism: 'You die then as though drunk on the noblest kind of giving/ In the deepest, most triumphant sense of divine life'.[8] The second, arranged in its rhymes 5+4+5, is fit to be sung by Baal:

> Der Himmel war wie Milch. Ich dachte kühl.
> Und lachte mit den Gliedern, die ermattet waren.
> Und dann war nichts zu tun. Ich bin von früh
> Bis spät den Mississippi abgefahren.
>
> [The sky was like milk, I was thinking coolly.
> And laughed with my limbs that were fatigued.
> And then there was nothing to do. From early
> Till late I sailed down the Mississippi.][9]

So much for Brecht's earliest sonnets. Brecht himself did nothing further with them. But he made the rest of his sonnets, written between the mid-1920s and 1948, into a considered, distinctive and coherent part of his whole lyric work. He gathered many of them into titled collections, in fair copy. And nearly all of the sonnets left over after that gathering do seem to 'belong to' one or another of those collections. These are the collections:

(i) *Die Augsburger Sonette*, 1925–7. Contains twelve sonnets, but of a further twelve written in the same period, ten are similar in tone and subjects and could be added to those collected.[10]

(ii) *Sonette and Englische Sonette*. There are thirteen sonnets in the first collection, three in the second, written in 1932–5 and all addressed to Margarete Steffin. Five or six more, written 1937-40), might be added to them.[11]

---

[7]BFA 13, p. 9.
[8]BFA 13, p. 76.
[9]BFA 13, p. 146.
[10]The collection contains one poem, 'Lehrstück Nr. 2. Ratschläge einer älteren Fohse an eine jüngere' / 'Didactic Piece No. 2. An old whore's advice to a younger whore', which is not a sonnet but which is consonant with its context in subject and tone. The first sonnet in the collection, 'Über Mangel an Bösem' / 'On the lack of wickedness', is a reworking of the uncollected sonnet 'On wickedness'(BFA 13, p. 341). The two uncollected sonnets of these years which don't obviously fit with those collected are 'Sonett vom Sieger' / 'Sonnet on the victor' (p. 320), whose subject is pointless combat in the manner of *In the Jungle of Cities*, and 'Das zehnte Sonett'/ 'The tenth sonnet' (p, 394), which, from first drafts in 1927, only evolved into a sonnet for publication in 1929. The fragment And when I urgently enquired' (p. 326), perhaps of 1925–6, is unlike the other sonnets of that time. It is, for one thing, more politically engaged.
[11]'19, Sonett' (1937; BFA 14, p. 354), 'Das 21. Sonett' (c.1938; p. 418), and 'Sonett Nr. 19' (1939; p, 437) are certainly for Steffin; 'Und nun ist Krieg' / 'And now it's war' (1939; p. 437), almost certainly; 'Über die Untreue der Weiber' / 'On the faithlessness of women' (c. 1937; p. 384), quite possibly. 'Über induktive Liebe' / 'On

(iii) *Studien* (*Studies*). These are eight sonnets on literary and artistic subjects, six of them written in 1938. Another five or six sonnets, written around that time, might be added to them.[12]

Of those four (effectively three) collections only one, the last, *Studies*, was published in Brecht's lifetime: in 1951, in *Versuche* (*Experiments*), volume 11.

Of Brecht's total sonnet *œuvre* after 1919 (about seventy, if we include the unfinished and the fourteen-line poems not strictly sonnets), most (fifty-four or thereabouts) were either gathered by him into definite collections or 'belong' in one or other of those collections. And nearly all of the few strays, written outside the main periods of sonnet-writing, in tone and/or subject are drawn to the collections. For example 'Empfehlung eines langen, weiten Rocks' / 'In favour of a long, broad skirt' (around 1944), 'Über die Verführung von Engeln' / 'On seducing angels' and 'Saune und Beischlaf' / 'Sauna and copulation' (both 1948) would be quite at home among the *Augsburg Sonnets*.[13] That is of *some* interest. We can say that the sonnet seemed to Brecht suitable for certain, quite restricted kinds of poetic undertaking.

I make that point – an obvious one – to emphasise how conscious Brecht was of the character and usefulness of different poetic forms, and how adept he was at exploiting them. He wrote ballads, chorales, music-hall songs, marching songs; psalms, epigrams, odes, elegies, idylls; he wrote in iambics, trochaics, hexameters, free verse; he rhymed when it suited him, didn't when it didn't; he wrote lyrically, reflectively, at length and with brevity; he wrote poems of lament, of grief, of rage, of celebration. That tribute is by no means exhaustive. The variety of his poetic craftsmanship is astonishing. I can't think of a poet who paid more and such close and unprejudiced attention to the poetic forms and possibilities placed at his disposal by tradition, by his own and by other languages' traditions.

Brecht was, to put it mildly, a contradictory man, and as such he needed things to contradict. Dozens of poetic forms and traditions served him in that way. But contradiction does not necessarily annihilate the thing it contradicts. The contradiction I have in mind (Brecht's sort, I think) draws its lifeblood out of the continuing life of what it contradicts.

---

inductive love' (c.1938; p. 425) seems to belong with the *Studies*, but could also be addressed to Steffin. The fragment 'Longer apart than ever before' (1936; p. 332) also looks to be for her and is very likely the beginnings of a sonnet.

[12]'Über die Gedichte des Dante auf die Beatrice' / 'On Dante's poems to Beatrice' was written in 1934 and included, as 'Das zwölfte Sonett' / 'The twelfth sonnet', in the *Sonnets* for Margarete Steffin. The sonnet on Lenz's *Der Hofmeister* / *The Tutor* was written in 1940. Brecht wrote or worked at half a dozen further sonnets on literary and artistic subjects in or around 1938. All may be associated with the *Studies* but only one of them, 'Über den Tod des Dichters Thomas Otway' / 'On the death of the poet Thomas Otway'(BFA 14, p. 424), is both finished and strictly a sonnet. 'When I had told them both' (p. 417) is fourteen lines of terza rima, appropriately since its subject is drawn from Dante. The others are: 'Du zarter Geist' / 'You gentle spirit' (p. 420). on Nietzsche, unfinished; 'Kritik an Michelangelos "Weltschöpfung"'/'Criticism of Michelangelo's "Creation"' (p. 420), probably unfinished, and a response to it, '(Vermutliche) Antwort des Malers' / 'The artist's likely reply', doubtless to be in sonnet form, was only sketched out; 'Sonnet on the legacy' (p. 424), an important poem, wanting half a line. 'An einen befreundeten Dichter' / 'To a poet friend' (p. 417), is a sonnet addressed, around 1938, to Johannes Becher. It warns him that his sonnets on the subject of Germany have lost touch with reality.

[13]BFA 15, pp. 117–18; p. 193. 'Finnische Landschaft' / 'Finnish Landscape' (1940; BFA 12, p. 110) was taken into the *Steffinsche Sammlung*/ *Steffin Collection*). 'Der Erbe' / 'The heir' (unfinished, around 1940; BFA 15, pp. 29–30) and 'Sonett in der Emigration' / 'Sonnet in emigration' (1941; p. 48) deal with survival in exile, the latter straightforwardly, the former cryptically.

If this is a dialectic, it is not one that resolves itself into a synthesis. The desired or at least the achieved effect (the truth of the writing?) lies actually in the antagonism, in the continuing struggle of diction and contradiction. That applies to these sonnets, applies to us in our reading of them (our relationship with them), and may, I think, also be the truth of the particular relationship out of which many of them came, that with the brave and poetically gifted Margarete Steffin.

It will be helpful, thinking about contradiction, to consider the 'Sonett vom Erbe' / 'Sonnet on the legacy':

> Als sie mich sahn aus alten Büchern schreiben
> Saßen sie traurig mürrisch bei mir, die Gewehre
> Auf ihren Knieen, und folgten meinem Treiben
> Gehst du bei unsern Feinden in die Lehre?
> Ich sagte: ja. Sie wissen, wie man schreibt.
> Und zwar die Lüge, sagten sie, die Lüge,
> Ich freute mich der Rüge
> Sie standen auf : ich sagte hastig: bleibt!
> Das sind die Leute, die uns
> Die uns das Brot in dünne Scheiben schneiden
> Und ihres Volkes Schlägern raten: schlagt es!
> Was können sie dich lehren? Sagte ich: zu schreiben.
> Und was zu schreiben? Sagte ich: ihr sagt es
> Sie schneiden euch das Brot in dünne Scheiben.
>
> [in the room with me, their guns across their knees,
> When they saw me writing out things from old books
> They followed my doing with sad and sullen looks:
> Are you taking lessons from our enemies?
> Yes, I answered. They know how to write.
> Write lies, they said, write lies, indeed they do.
> I liked this setting me straight.
> They rose to leave. In haste I said: Don't go.
> These are the people who ---------
> Who cut the loaf thin when they cut for us
> And counsel those who beat the people: Do!
> What can you learn from them? I said: To write.
> Write what? I answered: What you said:
> They cut the bread thin when they cut for you.]
>
> *Translated by* David Constantine[14]

Written around 1938 and not quite finished (it wants the rest of line 9 and perhaps some adjustment of the rhyme scheme in the sestet), the poem was probably intended for the *Studies*. Indeed, its title would serve for that whole collection and for other associated sonnets of the time whose subject, and practice, is present dealings with the culture of the past. The question of the legacy – whose is it? what to do with it? – was critical among German exiles in the 1930s, was so again in the GDR, and of course always is critical to

---

[14]BFA 14, p. 424.

any writer orientating himself or herself in tradition. 'Sonnet on the legacy' is one such self-orientation, but it also and properly, given the writer's real circumstances, addresses the further question: what can the writer do for and alongside the combatants in their common struggle? And it asserts that, for the struggle, you can learn the craft of writing even from the enemy.

The sonnet form itself stands in an interesting relationship to both those issues. Sonnets have been written in the languages of Europe for seven hundred years. Any writer using the form engages, consciously or not, with that long tradition and the best writers by the force of their own sonnets alter it. In his 'Sonnet on the legacy', Brecht acknowledges the tradition he belongs in, reflects on his own relationship with it, and enquires whether that particular tradition – the sonnet – can be made to serve his present needs. That specific dialectic is part of, or representative of, the larger one that the writer must engage in with all 'the legacy'.

Might the sonnet be useful in the struggle? 'Kohlen für Mike' / 'Coal for Mike' (1926)[15] was offered in the wish that it might, in its own way, be as materially helpful as the lump of coal thrown over the fence by Mike's comrades to his widow. Brecht in exile wanted to write poems that would be of material help in the struggle against Hitler. In 'Sonnet on the legacy', he stands in the same relationship to the armed fighters as he did to the brakemen in 'Coal for Mike', wanting to help, with a poem. He wrote only one sonnet to serve in that way: 'Vorschlag, für den Krieg mit Hitler schießbare Radioempfangsgeräte zu bauen' / 'Suggestion that for the war with Hitler radio receivers be manufactured that could be fired from guns'. Written, like 'Sonnet on the legacy', in or around 1938, addressed to the workers of the Soviet Union and probably intended, like the *German Satires*, for the Free German Radio, the poem proposes an action akin to the writing and polemical dissemination of poetry, namely bombarding the misguided German workers with little radios from which would issue arguments likely to convert them:

> Suggest they should ally themselves with you.
> Tell them the reasons. Shell them with the reasons.
> Many a one may be struck and come over to you.[16]

Again the association, in wishful thinking, of the poem with the more material aid or instrument: coal, rifles, artillery, radios. It is the wish that poetry should be, as Seferis says it is, 'strong enough to help'.[17] The question is always, of course: in what way is poetry best suited to help?

That is the only sonnet serving as the poet in 'On the legacy' hopes his verse will serve, as a weapon in the struggle.[18] Quite simply, Brecht did not think the form suitable for that particular purpose. The looser forms of the *German Satires* worked far better.

'Sonnet on the legacy' is an apologia for Brecht's irrepressible love of all manner and variety of writing. Certainly, he learned and borrowed everywhere, and very often from 'the enemy'. This sonnet suggests that his appropriation of models and traditions always had the committed purpose of serving the struggle. What he learned from the enemy,

---

[15] BFA 12, p. 40; Poems, p. 123.
[16] BFA 14, p. 425.
[17] George Seferis, *Days of 1945–51: A Poet's Journal* (Cambridge, Mass., 1974), p. 134.
[18] But see also 'Vorschlag, die Architektur mit der Lyrik zu verbinden' / 'Suggestion that architecture should be joined with lyric poetry' (1935; BFA 14, p. 301), a sonnet proposing that the workers in Moscow should decorate their Metro with poems. The formality of the sonnet suits the proposal, and again there is the wish that poetry should have its place in the midst of the more material work of the soldier-builders.

he could use against them. Needless to say, in spirit and in practice he was far less strict than that. And 'Sonnet on the legacy', depicting him at his most committed, is written in a form, the sonnet, which of all forms was the one he wrote in nearly always at his least committed. Most of them, even including the *Studies*, have to do with sex and many are pornographic. He had in mind to present the *Augsburg Sonnets* under the caption 'Meine Achillesverse' / 'My Achilles verses';[19] which is to say, punning on 'Achillesferse' / 'Achilles' heel', that he viewed their subject as his weakness and the sonnet as the form most suitable for indulging it. He wrote to Helene Weigel in August 1927 that he was writing pornographic sonnets 'as always when I'm doing nothing and on my own'.[20] Taken together, the sonnets are the least pointedly political genre in his poetic *œuvre*, though all but the first half-dozen post-date the *Domestic Breviary*. Many do have political point, of course; but they achieve it in a peculiarly equivocal way. Indeed, his most usual practice in the sonnets is to contradict the self – the committed comrade – who appears in 'On the legacy'. It is in the sonnets that he is at his most personal, sensual, selfish, quixotic and intractable. The form seemed to him suitable for trying out the least politically aligned aspects or versions of his complex and contradictory character.

Brecht's dealings with his models were always independent. He was never overwhelmed by them. Usually his dealings were critical, often they were actively hostile. His radically blasphemous appropriation and abuse of breviary, psalm and chorale in the *Domestic Breviary* is a good example. There is something of that tension in every poet's independent dealings with traditional pre-existent forms, indeed with poetic form altogether. A phrase of Hölderlin's – 'liebender Streit' [loving quarrel][21] – may be used to describe that coming together of free creative spirit with tradition and with the necessary shaping constraint of a particular form. In Brecht's case the quarrel is scarcely ever loving. Most often it is violent, and his self-assertion is an act of insult.

Brecht was not by any means a radical transformer of the sonnet *form*. Among his contemporaries, Rilke and Anton Schnack were much more adventurous, as was, among his predecessors, the seventeenth-century poet Gryphius. One hallmark of Brecht's sonnets (and of much of his other poetry too) is minimal punctuation; but his only repeated formal transgression – after the experiments and uncertainties of the very earliest attempts – is the line that exceeds the iambic pentameter by one or more feet. This occurs so frequently, and in sonnets which are otherwise regular in their rhymes and pentameters, that it reads rather like a signature. For example, line 5 of 'Was ich von früher her noch kannte, war' / 'Things I remembered from those past days were': 'Drum weiß ich nichts von ihr als, ganz von Nacht zerstört' / 'So all I know of her, by night undone'. Or line 4 of 'Die Opiumraucherin' / 'The opium smoker': 'Und: daß sie nur den dritten Teil vom Leben braucht' [And two-thirds of the time she won't be living].[22] He rhymes very obediently and fully; works in quatrains and tercets (with some licence in the arrangement of the tercets); or (less often) in quatrains and a concluding couplet.[23] Altogether, in the sonnets, he is strikingly less casual, careless, disrespectful

---

[19]BFA 13, pp. 190 and 468.
[20]BFA 11, p. 325,
[21]Line 6 of the poem 'An Diotima' ('Komm und siehe die Freude um uns...').
[22]BFA 13, p. 302; *Poems*, pp. 113 and 114.
[23]Tercets rhyming eff egg, as in BFA 11, pp. 190 and 196, do, of course, give a concluding couplet, but Brecht sets them out as tercets, as he does also the rhyme scheme efe fgg, for example, at pp. 125 and 189. Thus, he never emphasises the finality of a concluding couplet, but rather conceals it.

towards the chosen form than he is, when it suits him, in the very varied poems of the *Domestic Breviary*. His contradiction lies more in tone and register, in the mixing of tones and registers, and in subject and cast of mind; and this sort of contradiction is actually enhanced by his conforming to the sonnet's traditional requirements. Often the words are so packed into the prosody, in a way so sovereign, forceful and knowing, the lines seem on the verge of detonating: 'Wenn sie dies läs, sie wüßt nicht, wer es ist' [Nor would she see herself when reading this];[24] 'Gab's wenig Lust, ist auch der Gram gering' [Where lust was slight the grief is trivial too], 'Gekonnt ist gut, doch allzu schlimm: gemußt' [Good if one can; but too bad if one must].[25] Fitting the words into iambic pentameters unleashes their energy. That energy, released by form, is also its contradiction.

Obscenity is a more obvious contradiction. There was plenty of pornography in sonnets before Brecht – in the German baroque and in the Italian Renaissance (notably Pietro Aretino) – but usually of a rather polished kind. Obscenity itself is 'enhanced' by being fitted into an elegant, demanding and highly respected traditional form. Brecht – very self-consciously – pitches it low, as if to offend against the decorum, or pseudo-decorum, of the genre. Examples abound, but 'Sonett über einen durchschnittlichen Beischlaf' / 'Sonnet on a middling sort of copulation', 'On seducing angels' and 'Sauna and copulation' all seem particularly to revel in making obscenities of thinking, tone and language rhyme and scan.[26] In the case of the latter two, the last in his sonnet œuvre, written in Zürich in 1948, Brecht's offensive intention is further indicated by his having signed them 'Thomas Mann'. Brecht's obscenity is complex and interesting and I shall say more about it with reference to the *Augsburg Sonnets* and those to Margarete Steffin. But first a word on another aspect of Brecht's contradictory relationship with the sonnet form.

The sonnet is suitable for great clarity. It has a pleasingly lucid, intelligent procedure. It is a good medium for clear exposition, fine discriminations, development, turn and a point. Quite often, adopting and adhering to that form – quatrains and tercets, quatrains and a couplet, in regular metre, with full euphonious rhymes – Brecht gives you something of considerable intellectual and moral difficulty. He leaves you perplexed. Clear form is belied by what is being done in it. For example in 'Sonett Nr.1. Über Mangel an Bösem' / 'On the lack of wickedness'.[27] In the language of sport ('rounds', 'final spurt'), as though it were a matter of stamina, the poem laments our inability to bring forth decisively wicked people. The human race and the earth go on whatever we do. The opinion is very self-assured (line 2: 'as we know'), and its utterance laconic and throwaway, but our difficulty as readers lies more in our having to adjust to a bizarre opinion formally articulated. The regularity and clarity of the first line are very disorientating.[28]

The *Augsburg Sonnets* (the above poem is the first of them) overlapped in their composition with the poems of the *Reader for Those who Live in Cities*. Unlike them in form, they often resemble them closely in tone and in their mode or procedure. The *Reader*, in its lovelessness, pitilessness, treachery and alienation and in the flat brutality and the sarcasm of the language and in the impoverishment of its poetic forms, cries

---

[24]BFA 13, p 302; *Poems*, p. 114.
[25]BFA 11, p. 187; *Poems*, p. 213.
[26]Auden does the same in the poems (five sonnets and a chorale) that he wrote in German in 1930 after his months in Berlin. *See* my 'The German Auden: Six Early Poems', in *Auden Studies* I (Oxford, 1990), pp. 1–15.
[27]BFA 11, p. 123.
[28]*See also* 'The tenth sonnet' (BFA 13, p. 394) and 'Sonett Nr. 14. Von der inneren Leere' / 'On inner emptiness' (BFA 11, p. 127).

out to be contradicted. That is what I mean by its procedure. It demonstrates through the negative the need for radical humanising change. Humane dealings are actually fetched to the imagination, as a desperate need, through their very absence. Several of the *Augsburg Sonnets* work like that. A man presents himself living badly, his relations with his fellow human beings are contemptuous and loveless. The tone of voice is sardonic. In the poems of the *Reader* free verse, stripped of ornament, minimal and cryptic, is a highly appropriate medium. But so is the sonnet, as a contradiction. Its urbane form is insulted in the urban jungle. Its shapeliness, its harmonies, are denied by the tone and by the material; but they answer back, and perhaps help the reader do the same. 'Sonett Nr.6. Ein Mann bringt sich zu Bett' / 'A man gets himself to bed', 'Sonett Nr.12. Vom Liebhaber' / 'The lover' and 'Sonett über schlechtes Leben' / 'Sonnet on the subject of living badly' are good examples.[29] We see people living badly, in shapely form, in rhyme, in steady metre, in foul language, in a cynical bearing. The sonnet has been in use in many different societies in seven centuries. This is how it looks, this is what it does (says Brecht) in our own time and place.

A particularly bad thing in the sonnets of 1925–7, as in the poems of the *Reader*, is how men and women deal with one another. There is a moment of pity (or is it only fear?) in 'Entdeckung an einer jungen Frau' / 'Discovery about a young woman'.[30] The lover, or client, notices grey in the woman's hair when, like lovers in the traditional 'morning song', they separate after the night together. But the usual tone of the male persona is brutally, sardonically, reductively exploitative. These poems are quite loveless. They have to do with sex, and the best to be hoped for there is improved technique. Thus: 'Forderung nach Kunst' / 'Need for art' and 'Sonnet on a middling sort of copulation'.[31] It is not, I think, prudery that is offended by these sonnets, but humanity. And the offence is calculated and deliberate, in the spirit of Baudelaire's 'Hypocrite lecteur, – mon semblable, – mon frère!'[32] and of Brecht's own almost gleeful insistence on the details in 'On the infanticide Marie Farrar': 'so men may see what I am and you are'.[33]

The moral of the poems (their politics) is this: Life in the cities under capitalism is alienated and deformed. No life worthy the name can survive. They say: See how we live in the social order we have created. They excite revulsion, which is a strong form of contradiction. We are required to answer back, with a better idea of man and a better practice.

Of course, the specific disgust (at what capitalism does to human relations) may verge on or become an absolute cynicism and disgust at the nature and state of humanity under whatever system. The artist George Grosz went that far, I should say, in his *Ecce Homo*, and his friend Brecht, in the 1920s, seems quite near it.

Brecht in real life, especially in his dealings with women, seems not to have been any nicer than the male persona in his *Augsburg Sonnets*. He was, by many accounts, exploitative, sexist, boorish, faithless, ruthless, devious, selfish, cruel and mercenary. He seems quite often to have acted as the living proof of his thesis that true human relations under capitalism are impossible. He said once – or is said to have said – that he was not a

---

[29] BFA 11, pp. 125 and 127; *Poems*, p. 151. BFA 13, p. 306.
[30] BFA 11, p. 312; *Poems*, p. 114,
[31] BFA 13, pp. 312 and 341.
[32] The last line of 'Au Lecteur', which is the opening poem of *Les Fleurs du mal*.
[33] *Poems*, p. 91.

poet or a dramatist but 'a teacher of behaviour'.[34] His method, in this endeavour at least, seems to have been more Stanislavsky than Epic. I mean he lived the part. That is one way of understanding him: as the conscious embodiment of the contradictions wrought in humanity by capitalism.

Another possibility is that he and Baal are one flesh.

Of *Baal*, Brecht said (looking back on it) that the play might present all sorts of difficulties to people who had not learned to think dialectically.[35] He meant (I think) that just as the play itself came out of contradiction – the contradiction of the 'soft' play by Hanns Johst – so too Baal's behaviour is to be understood as countering other people's: Mech's for example, who wants, figuratively speaking, to turn him into matchsticks. But should Johanna, Sophie and Eckart have been countered just as ruthlessly? Baal was, Brecht noted in 1938, 'der Sichausleber', the man who lives himself out; but also 'der Andreausleber', the man who lives other people out.[36] His behaviour asks for their antagonism, in very self-defence. He requires them to answer with a countering, self-asserting energy. His way of being in the world must conjure up in others the means of their own equal engagement with him. You might say, putting the best possible slant on it, that he incites them into a robust self-realisation, against him or by means of him. In practice, they cannot answer back with sufficient force. Taking the phrase seriously, we may say *they cannot live up to him*. The perpetual provocation, challenge, threat of Baal's way of living (and of Brecht's perhaps) is, appropriately enough, how the poems work too. We are required to answer back, in defence of a more humane behaviour. Brecht, then, is the teacher of behaviour, dialectically. Poetry is very often an experimenting with possible ways of being in the world and of dealing with one another. Those ways don't have to be pleasant or agreeable. You might even say that it takes courage to try out what is offensive. Brecht is unusually thorough and pitiless (on himself and on us) in trying out attitudes and personae, so that he seems at times to be conducting experiments in the worst possible self. Most people, even the writers among them, are rather more concerned about how they look. Perhaps in his living, certainly in much of his poetry, Brecht shows off himself as badly as he could; and does two things in doing so: asks us are we very much better and cries out for contradiction.

Brecht's sonnets to Margarete Steffin, written between 1932–3 and 1939, are particularly interesting, first because she did answer back, and secondly because, though some are as brutal as any from Augsburg, others are very different – even, indeed, loving.

When Steffin died, of tuberculosis, in a Moscow clinic in June 1941, Brecht mourned her as his collaborator and comrade in the struggle against Hitler and for Communism:

My general has fallen
My soldier has fallen
My pupil has gone away
My teacher has gone away
My nurse has gone
My nursling has gone.[37]

---

[34]John Fuegi, *The Life and Lies of Bertolt Brecht* (London, 1995), p. 310.
[35]BFA 23, p. 241.
[36]BFA 26, p. 323.
[37]BFA 15, p. 45; *Poems*, p. 364.

Later, in America, where she was to have joined him, he wrote that without her he felt quite at a loss; as though his guide had been taken from him just as the desert began.[38] But of the sonnets only one, 'Und nun ist Krieg und unser Weg wird schwerer' / 'And now it's war; our path is growing steeper',[39] addresses her purely in that spirit and in those terms. Two others – 'Sonnet No. 19' and 'The 21st sonnet'[40] – allude strongly to a difficult way that has to be travelled together, and one other, 'The tenth sonnet',[41] presents her as fellow-worker in the cause *and* as lover, resisting and complying in both capacities. But in all the rest, nearly twenty, there is scarcely a mention of work or any public purpose, and the sonnet serves as it very often has, for utterance between two lovers, personal and peculiar to them and accessible and valuable to other readers by virtue of poetic form.

Brecht, as is well known, liked poetry to be useful, and he liked friends to be useful too. He viewed them as bridges and graded them according to their load-bearing capacity. He wrote:

> bridges can bear more or less weight. there are friends you can drive a thousand-ton goods train over, others can carry a bus and most a pram. but bridges that can bear a pram are still bridges (just so long as you don't drive over them in a small motor car because then they collapse and you get Weltschmerz).[42]

He expounded this theory or principle in a discussion concerning Margarete Steffin. She was a bridge over which a thousand-ton goods train might pass. Very candidly, that is how he mourned her in 1941:

> Once the stage was reached where a not unkindly Death
> Shrugged his shoulders and showed me her lungs' five ravaged lobes
> Unable to imagine her surviving on the sixth alone
> I rapidly assembled 500 jobs
> Things that must be dealt with at once and tomorrow, next year
> And in seven years' time from now
> Asked endless questions, decisive ones
> Unanswerable except by her
> And thus needed
> She died easier.[43]

We could say he used her; but anyone meaning that wholly critically should remember the urgency of their personal circumstances 'in Year Nine of the flight from Hitler',[44] and the value, incontrovertible as they saw it, of the cause they were both serving. Also acknowledge that being used in such a cause, being called upon, needed ('beansprucht'), might be enobling and empowering rather than demeaning. It might be that through which a self is made authentic. Naturally, people needed and used in that way forfeit their freedom. Brecht said so, as something they both understood, in 'Sonnet No. 19', a poem

---

[38]*Journal*, 1.8.1941.
[39]BFA 14, p. 437; *Poems*, p. 345.
[40]BFA 14, pp. 437 and 418; *Poems*, p. 330.
[41]BFA 11, p. 189.
[42]Margarete Steffin, *Konfutse versteht nichts von Frauen. Nachgelassene Texte* (Berlin, 1991). p. 352.
[43]BEA 15, p.45: *Poems*, pp, 364–5.
[44]Ibid., p, 364.

admitting their need for one another: 'Du weißt es: wer gebraucht wird, ist nicht frei' [You know whoever's needed can't go free].

Still, using people, particularly women, is the fault Brecht is most often accused of, and it runs through the sonnets to Margarete Steffin as it does through the *Augsburg Sonnets*; the vital difference being that in those to her it is challenged and countered by the writer himself, and by her replies. 'To use a woman' is an obsolete English locution meaning to have sex with her. It bears about as much contempt and misogyny as any locution could be made to bear. That tone and attitude prevail in the *Augsburg Sonnets* – 'Daß ich stets höre, wenn er sie gebraucht '/ 'That I always hear it when he uses her'[45] – and he tries them in some of the Steffin sonnets too. Possession and commodification in the fifth and seventh sonnets,[46] for example. Then in the ninth,[47] reducing his own involvement to the bare minimum ('Ich geb nicht mich, ich geb dir einen Schwanz' [I don't give me, what I give you's a cock]), he becomes fearful she might learn the lesson and cease caring who she is with. In 'The sixth sonnet' he shows himself as typical of his sex and the sex at its worst:

> Und besser ist: kein Gram als: viele Lust
> Und besser als verlieren: sich bescheiden.
> Der Männer Wollust ist es: nicht zu leiden.
> Gekonnt ist gut, doch allzu schlimm: gemußt,
>
> [Better to feel no grief than too much lust.
> And better than to lose, to be resigned.
> There's pleasure in not being hurt, men find.
> Good if one can; but too bad if one must.]

But admits 'Natürlich ist das eine schäbige Lehre' [Of course that is a pretty shabby moral], and the sonnet ends rather lamely but also more humanely:

> Ich meine nur: wenn einer an nichts hinge
> Dem stund auch keine schlimme Zeit bevor.
> Indessen sind wir nicht die Herrn der Dinge,
>
> [I only mean that unattached and free
> One may avoid a lot of suffering.
> Meanwhile we can't command what is to be.][48]

Several of the sonnets adopt the very Brechtian structure of teacher and pupil. The ninth again: 'Als du das Vögeln lerntest, lehrt ich dich/So vögeln, daß du mich dabei vergaßest' [When you learned how to fuck I taught you to/Fuck so that you forgot me doing it].[49] Steffin was sexually experienced but not, by her own account, sexually awakened.[50] So the man in these sonnets thinks of himself as the woman's teacher in the art of love. In that teaching there is an edge of extra pleasure (for him) when what he teaches her comes as a shock. Thus in his calling the thing by its common name:

---

[45]BFA 11, p. 127,
[46]BFA 11, pp. 187 and 188.
[47]Ibid., p. 188.
[48]BFA 11, p. 187: *Poems*, pp. 213–14.
[49]BFA, p. 1S8.
[50]See *Konfutse*, p. 204.

Als ich schon dachte, daß wir einig wären
Gebrauchte ich, fast ohne drauf zu achten
Die Wörter, welche meinten, was wir machten
Und zwar die allgemeinsten, ganz vulgären.
Da war's, als ob von neuem du erschrakst
Als sähst du jetzt erst, was das, was wir machten, sei
In vielen Wochen, die du bei mir lagst
Lehrt ich von diesen Wörtern dich kaum zwei.
Mit solchen Wörtern rufe ich den Schrecken
Von einst zurück, als ich dich frisch begattet
Es läßt sich länger nunmehr nicht verdecken:
Das Allerletzte hast du da gestattet!
Wie konntest du dich nur in so was schicken:
Das Wort für das, was du da tatst, war

[Already thinking we were of a mind
I used – and it was almost without knowing –
The words whose meaning was what we were doing
The commonest such words, the vulgarest kind.
All over again it shocked you through as though
Till now you had not seen what thing we did.
In many weeks of you with me in bed
Of words like that I scarcely taught you two.
But with these words I summon up the shock
Afresh of my first fleshly knowing you.
It can't be hidden any longer now:
Of all a lady's favours you kept not one back.
How could you make yourself common as muck?
The word for what it was you did was][51]

The shock of the word revives the first shock and pleasure of the thing itself. It may be difficult to imagine any such shock in the words nowadays, but Lawrence, in 1927–8, in *Lady Chatterley's Lover*, knowing full well their power to offend, tried to recover them for the language of tenderness between a man and a woman in love. He wrote: 'I always labour at the same thing, to make the sex relation valid and precious, instead of shameful. And this novel is the furthest I've gone. To me it is beautiful and tender and frail as the naked self is'.[52] So Mellors instructs Connie in the use of the taboo words, in a tone very different from Brecht's in the sonnets to Steffin. There is more than a touch of vindictiveness in Brecht, as though he were forcing her to see that she is no better than he is, that he and she are companions in something base. Henry Miller's male characters, in his *Tropic of Cancer* (1934) and *Tropic of Capricorn* (1939), take a similarly vengeful pleasure in ascertaining that sexual feelings are keen in women too. As though women

---

[51]'Das dritte Sonett' (BFA 11, p. 186); here translated by David Constantine. See also the thirteenth (p. 190), in which he etymologises on the missing word. The sonnet fragment 'Longer apart than ever before ...' takes an anxious interest in the woman's vocabulary during an absence.
[52]In a letter to Nancy Pearn, 12 April 1927. See *The Collected Letters of D. H. Lawrence*, edited by Harry T. Moore, 2 vols (London, 1962) ii, 972.

lived in hypocrisy, and must be made to own up to their sexuality, and so humiliated. Steffin responded to some such triumphant experiment in a poem remarkable for its candour and generosity. It begins:

> Als er mich zum ersten Male fragte
> Ob ich naß sei, dacht ich: Was ist das?
> Als er fragte, ob er nachsehn sollte
> Schämte ich mich sehr. Ich war ja naß.
>
> [When he asked me for the first time
> Was I wet, I thought to myself: What's that?
> When he asked should he look
> I was very ashamed. Because I was wet.][53]

That poem is one in an ongoing dialogue. Brecht actually altered the third person to the second on his copy, so: 'When you asked me for the first time ...'. Indeed, he seems to have written in the hope that she would always answer his sonnets with sonnets of her own, thus inviting their qualification or contradiction.[54] Only one such definite pairing has survived. His poem is affectionate enough, but her greater dependence (using his words, appropriating his characteristic longer line) and her vulnerability are evident. As she said in her sonnet 'Als der Klassiker am Montag dem siebenten Oktober 1935 es verließ, weinte Dänemark' / 'When the Classic Poet left Denmark on Monday 7 October 1935, Denmark wept': 'I shall be very alone and I shall love you'.[55] What she suffered, she expressed in several of her prose writings too. And noted with a terrible resignation: 'Naturally he is not to blame. He's always told me that he has the conscience of a lump of ice.' That comes in a piece beginning, like the fifth of Brecht's poems from the *Reader for Those who Live in Cities*,[56] with the words 'Ich bin ein Dreck' [I'm dirt].[57]

But in fairness, and to finish more encouragingly, it must also be said that among Brecht's sonnets to Margarete Steffin there are half a dozen in which tenderness and unselfish concern prevail and the man is shown as quite unable to live by the 'shabby moral' he offered in 'The sixth sonnet'; that is, he suffers from her absence, wants her near. Those two elements jostle in 'Fragen' / 'Questions', and in 'The eleventh sonnet'[58] thoughts of his dressing her warmly against the cold winter mix naturally with thoughts of undressing her, so 'mit sehr kalten Wintern' [with very cold winters] rhymes fitly with 'für den (geliebten) Hintern' [for your (beloved) bottom]. Sex then as in 'Liebesgewohnheiten' / 'Love habits'[59] – is a shared and equal enjoyment and their secret and incongruous way of alluding to it (the secret word, oddly enough, was the south German greeting 'Grüß Gott', in letters between them abbreviated to GG) gives them, even in the company of strangers, a peculiarly charged intimacy in a place apart. Sonnets very often have that

---

[53]*Konfutse*, p. 202.
[54]*Konfutse*, p. 312.
[55]*Konfutse*, p. 206. Properly set out, the initial letters of title and poem read: 'ADE GRÜSS GOTT BIDI' ['Farewell God Greet You Bidi']. 'Grüß Gott' was their 'word' and Bidi was a pet name for Brecht.
[56]BFA 11, p. 160.
[57]*Konfutse*, p. 181.
[58]BFA 11, p. 195; p. 189.
[59]Ibid., p. 196.

privacy, and reading them is like being let into secrets. Then the details become legendary. The little wooden and ivory elephants Brecht sent Steffin from cities he was in without her have that status. Thus in the lovingly anxious '21st sonnet' (they are 'our guardian beasts'), and in the '19th',[60] when they reprove him for not writing her a letter. To them, as to others among the emigrant's few belongings – the mask, the scroll, the little radio – an unbearable poignancy soon attaches. After she was dead, he wrote:

> I often see GRETE with her things that she was forever packing into her suitcases. The portrait on silk, painted by Cas; the wooden and ivory elephants from the different cities I was in...[61]

In 'Sonnet No. 19', urging her not to abandon him (at times he seems to have thought of her illness as a rival, to whom she might give in), Brecht wrote: 'Remember we're surrounded yet by night'.[62] (His sonnet 'Der Orangenkauf' / 'Buying oranges', one of the three *English Sonnets*, is a luminous moment in that darkness (see below, pp. 173). Much poetry, writing it and reading it, is an act of realisation. Something dawns, is made concretely clear. That happens here. The man comes through a pea-souper in Covent Garden into a luminous space, the cart, the lamp, the shining oranges. And that sight is a realisation of what he was unconsciously looking for or wanting. Focusing then so suddenly on that concrete presence, he focuses on her, the absent woman. Oranges are her usual and characteristic treat, and so the best bearer now of his love for her. He does what he always would do, in a loving habit: fishes for the money to buy them. Then comes another dawning: 'Du bist ja gar nicht da in dieser Stadt' [Of course you are not anywhere in this town]. In a regular iambic pentameter, in ordinary language, comes a realisation of pathos at the moment of disillusioning and disappointment (*Enttäuschung*). The love-gift cannot be the oranges, but is the poem instead, luminous as the oranges, standing in for them, *pis-aller* and recompense; and lasting beyond the lovers it first went between. The poem is in its own way concretely effective, stands to the oranges as 'Coal for Mike' stands to the lump of coal, for the lover and comrade Margarete Steffin.

Brecht, so often using the sonnet to experiment with the worst in himself (and in his readers, and in the citizens of any dehumanising social order), in these few at least shows a better possibility. But showing one face or the other, all his sonnets have a Utopian potential. They may conjure up their own contradiction, or realise it themselves in love and self-forgetting, man and woman equal as lovers and comrades. The moral power of poems lies in that agility.

---

[60]BFA 14, p. 418; p, 354; *Poems*, p. 275.
[61]*Journal*, 16.3.1942.
[62]BFA 14, p. 437; *Poems*, p. 330.

Later Poetry

CHAPTER TWENTY-THREE

Brecht in Buckow: *The Buckow Elegies*

KARL H. SCHOEPS

'Die Mühen der Gebirge liegen hinter uns
Vor uns liegen die Mühen der Ebenen.'[1]

In 1948, when Brecht settled down in the German Democratic Republic after his return from exile, the hated Nazi regime had been defeated, and at least one part of the former German Reich was on the road to socialism. But there were hosts of other problems to be solved in the Soviet occupation zone, and, after October 1949, the German Democratic Republic. The land was devastated, the people demoralized and generally hostile toward both the Soviets and socialism. The new government of the GDR did not enjoy great popularity; lack of money, manpower, and capital in addition to stiff reparations to the Soviet Union made reconstruction a very difficult task.

Brecht, however, was optimistic. For him, even a form of socialism imposed by the Soviet occupation forces was better than no socialism at all – as was the case in West Germany. He hoped that his work, largely written in exile and untested before a German audience, would contribute to the moral, cultural, and political reconstruction of Germany society – and with that he meant the whole of Germany, both East and West. Immediately upon his return he began his restless activities, disregarding personal health and well-being; he died – prematurely – on August 14, 1956.

His first task was to assemble a superb cast for the premiere of his masterpiece *Mother Courage and Her Children*, a cast that was to form the nucleus for the famous Brecht theater, the Berliner Ensemble. The first performance of this play about war and war profits took place on January 11, 1949, in the Deutsches Theater, Berlin. On their way to the theater, people had to make their way through the ruins of the once glamorous city. Would they ever learn? Brecht sincerely hoped so.

Brecht loved work, activity, and the company of people. But soon the hectic life in Berlin became too much for him. He began to look for a nearby retreat, which he found in the small town of Buckow in the province of Brandenburg ('Mark Brandenburg'), about an hour's drive to the east of Berlin.

Karl H. Schoeps, 'Brecht in Buckow: *The Buckow Elegies*', *Germanic Review*, 61, 4 (1986), pp. 168–76.
[1] Quote taken from Brecht's poem 'Wahrnehmung' in Bertolt Brecht, *Gesammelte Werke in 20 Bänden* (Frankfurt/Main: Suhrkamp, 1967), vol. 10 (Gedichte 3) 960. The page numbers in the text refer to this volume. In the following notes this edition is quoted as *Gesammelte Werke*.

At first glance, Buckow looks like an idyllic place. In February of 1952, Brecht and his wife, Helene Weigel, bought a piece of property near Buckow. On February 14, 1952, Brecht noted in his *Arbeitsjournal*:

> mit helli in buckow in der märkischen Schweiz landhäuser angesehn. finden auf schönem grundstück am wasser des scharmützelsees unter alten großen bäumen ein altes, nicht unedel gebautes häuschen mit einem andern, geräumigeren aber ebenfalls einfachem haus daneben, etwa 50 schritte entfernt. etwas der art wäre erschwinglich, auch im unterhalt. in das größere haus könnte man leute einladen.[2]

The larger house had previously belonged to a sculptor who had his two-story-high studio on the lake side of it. Now Helene Weigel tastefully furnished it with selected pieces of antique furniture.

In his *Arbeitsjournal* Brecht gives us quite a romantic description of his country home:

> vor meiner tür ist eine ecke, gebildet von einem demolierten gewächshaus und einer andern mauer. es gibt gras und tannen, wilde rosenstöcke an den mauern, ich habe einen dünnen wirtsgartentisch und die bank dazu aufgetrieben, mit eisernen beinen und den resten eines weißen anstrichs, sehr elegant.[3]

There was a jetty leading through reed to the waters of the lake, but Brecht hardly ever used it; since he was no great friend of physical exercise, he left the swimming to others. Today the former boathouse is used to store Mother Courage's wagon from the memorable Berlin premiere of 1949. The larger house now serves as a museum, the 'smaller' one is occupied by the Schalls (Brecht's son-in-law Ekkehart Schall, a leading actor at the Berliner Ensemble, and Brecht's youngest daughter Barbara).

In Buckow Brecht again found the time and the proper frame of mind to read one of his favorite poets, something he had not been able to do for a long time. As he jotted down in his *Arbeitsjournal* on July 15, 1952: 'haus und umgebung in buckow ist ordentlich genug, daß ich wieder etwas Horaz lesen kann.'[4]

Yet despite the pleasant surroundings, Buckow did not mean total relaxation for Brecht. It was here in Buckow that he worked on his last plays, such as *Coriolanus* and *Turandot*. Here he discussed Hanns Eisler's *Faust* opera with the composer, a close friend of his. Erwin Strittmatter, a budding East German writer, visited him in his country house to obtain help and advice for his play *Katzgraben*. Long hours were spent in preparing productions with actors and associates from the Berliner Ensemble. And it was here in Buckow that he wrote the 'Buckow Elegies'.

While still in exile, Brecht wrote in his poem 'An die Nachgeborenen' about those dark times: 'was sind das für Zeiten, wo / Ein Gespräch über Bäume fast ein Verbrechen ist / Weil es ein Schweigen über so viele Untaten einschließt!' (*Gesammelte Werke*, 9: 723). Now that the horrors are over, he rediscovers nature in Buckow. As Hugo Dittberner and Klaus Schuhmann pointed out, nature, so prominently featured in Brecht's early works,

---

[2]Werner Hecht, ed., *Bertolt Brecht Arbeitsjournal* (Frankfurt/Main: Suhrkamp, 1973), 2: 973 (February 14, 1952). In the following quoted as *Arbeitsjournal*. Brecht – and others after him – falsely call the lake Scharmützel Lake; its real name is Schermützel Lake. Lake Scharmützel is much larger and about 20 miles south of Buckow.
[3]*Arbeitsjournal* 986 (August 30, 1952).
[4]*Arbeitsjournal* 982.

receded into the background with his conversion to Marxism and his struggle against fascism, only to reappear again in the 'Buckow Elegies' as a central motif.[5]

In one of his 'Buckow Elegies', Brecht introduces us to the flower garden in his country seat:

> Am See, tief zwischen Tann und Silberpappel
> Beschirmt von Mauer und Gesträuch ein Garten
> So weise angelegt mit monatlichen Blumen
> Daß er vom März bis zum Oktober blüht.
>
> (p. 1008)

When he was still in California, Brecht described gardens in quite a different manner. They appear artificial ('Nachdenkend über die Hölle', p. 1009), dry ('Vom Sprengen des Gartens'), or shortly before destruction and decay, as Charles Laughton's garden:

> Leider ist der schöne Garten, hoch über der Küste gelegen
> Auf brüchiges Gestein gebaut. Erdrutsche
> Nehmen ohne Warnung Teile plötzlich in die Tiefe.
>   Anscheinend
> Bleibt nicht viel mehr Zeit, ihn zu vollenden,
>
> (p. 886)

In Brecht's view, Laughton's garden became a political metaphor for crumbling capitalism. Do the 'Buckow Elegies' now signify a retreat from politics into a private sphere? Does Brecht's idyllic country seat in bucolic Buckow mean a return to nature? In his readings of Horace he surely did not overlook the second epode, 'In Praise of Country Life', where Horace describes the joys of country life ('Beatus ille, qui procul negotiis ...'):

> Happy the man, who far from town's affairs
> The life of old-world mortals shares;
> With his own oxen tills his forebears' fields,
> Nor thinks of usury and its yields ...
> What joy, beneath some holm oak old and grey
> or on thick turf, one's limbs to lay;
> While streams past toppling banks roll down their flood,
> And the birds croon in every wood,
> And fountains murmur with their gushing streams
> Sounds that shall soothe to sleep and dreams.[6]

Even the poplar tree, which plays such a prominent role in Brecht's 'Buckow Elegies', is also part of Horace's country idyll, and we can be sure that Brecht was quite aware of it:

> His business is round poplars tall to twine
> The ripe young layers of the vine.[7]

---

[5]Hugo Dittberner, 'Die Philosophie der Landschaft in Brechts "Buckower Elegien." In *Text & Kritik. Sonderband Bertolt Brecht 2* (Munich: Boorberg, 1973): 54–65 and Klaus Schuhmann, *Untersuchungen zur Lyrik Brechts* (Berlin, Weimar: Aufbau-Verlag, 1977) 126.
[6]*The Complete Works of Horace*, Everyman's Library, (London: Dent, n.d.) 113.
[7]Horace 113.

We can certainly assume that Brecht also was aware of Horace's sixth satire, in which, as the title reads, 'he sets the conveniences of a country retirement in opposition to the troubles of a life in town.' In fact, the first few lines of this satire might even seem to serve as a proper description of Brecht's country home: 'This was [ever] among the number of my wishes: a portion of ground not overlarge, in which was a garden, and a fountain with a continual stream close to my house, and a little woodland besides; [...] O rural retirement, when shall I behold thee?'[8] Did Brecht, then, model his 'Buckow Elegies' after Horace's pastoral poetry?

For a long time many critics have indeed seen the 'Buckow Elegies' as an example of a new Brecht who turned away from politics and toward celebration of nature. For Thomas O. Brandt, Brecht has become something of an impressionist on the shores of the Schermützel lake, especially in his poem 'Rudern, Gespräche', describing two men talking to each other while paddling two canoes into the sunset. According to Brandt, this poem 'shows perfect harmony of man, motion and nature, a noiseless lifting and lowering of paddles under a still evening sky'.[9] Brandt discovers a similar picture of harmony in 'Der Radwechsel', another poem of the 'Buckow Elegies'. In this poem Brecht describes his feelings of impatience while he watches the driver of a car change a wheel. For Brandt, this poem expresses a 'hopeful view of the unity of all that is good, true and beautiful'.[10]

According to Alexander Hildebrand, Brecht's 'Buckow Elegies' are written in an 'Altersstil' (old-age style, whatever that means) dealing with small things easily overlooked and symbolizing eternal and basic human problems with memories prevailing over factual and contemporary realities.[11] Even in 1982 Franz Norbert Mennemeier still believes that the pervading mood of the 'Buckow Elegies' is one of distance from the demands of current politics ('Tagespolitik'); in his view, the prominently featured garden is a symbol of the 'desired happy cooperation between man and nature' and an expression of 'a universal philosophical interest'.[12]

For Günter Grass, too, the 'Buckow Elegies' are proof of Brecht's withdrawal into a private and exclusively esthetic sphere. In his largely unsuccessful play *The Plebeians Rehearse the Uprising*, Grass tries to portray Brecht as a mere esthete and stage revolutionary who ignores the real uprisings of the East Berlin workers in June of 1953. Rather than join the protesters in the streets, Brecht prefers to remain in his theater and rehearse the people's uprising in his adaptation of Shakespeare's *Coriolanus*. In order to make his case, Grass uses ample quotations from the 'Buckow Elegies' in this play. In a discussion on the esthetics of revolution he has with his assistant Erwin, the Boss (as Grass calls Brecht in this play) considers abandoning his work on *Coriolanus* altogether. Instead, he wants to write poems: 'Short intimate poems. With trees in them. Maybe silver poplars.'[13] To avoid painful discussions with workers, the Boss would prefer to read Horace. In a clear reference to the Buckow Elegy 'Tannen' the Boss asks himself in Grass's play: 'What do pines look like in the morning?'[14] Finally, at the end of the play,

---

[8]Horace 204, 206.
[9]Thomas O. Brandt, *Die Vieldeutigkeit Bertolt Brechts* (Heidelberg: Stiehm, 1968) 57–58.
[10]Brandt 86.
[11]Alexander Hildebrand, 'Bert Brechts Alterslyrik'. *In Merkur* vol. 10, no. 10 (1966): 952.
[12]Franz Norbert Mennemeier, *Bertolt Brechts Lyrik. Aspekte und Tendenzen* (Düsseldorf: Bagel, 1982) 210 and 56.
[13]Günter Grass, *The Plebeians Rehearse the Uprising. A German Tragedy*, trans. Ralph Manheim (New York: Harcourt, Brace & World, 1966) 13.
[14]Grass 71.

the Boss gathers his papers and withdraws into the country: 'I've rented a house on a lake with poplars around it. I could watch people rowing. Knocking themselves out. Or read Horace again. We can always fall back on books.'[15]

Actually, it may have been Brecht himself who lured the critics down the primrose path when he chose the term 'elegy' for his cycle of Buckow poems. The term 'elegy' usually evokes a mood of melancholy lament, of loss or death, often in connection with a pastoral and idyllic setting. At first glance, Schiller's definition of the elegy seems to apply to Brecht's elegies. In his essay on 'Naive and Sentimental Poetry' Schiller deducts the elegiac mood from the contrast between the ideal and reality. A poet can react in two ways to this contrast: either in a satirical way or in an elegiac fashion. But then Schiller proceeds to separate the elegy completely from the realm of reality: 'The content of poetic lamentation can therefore never be an external object, it must always be only an ideal, an inner one; even if it grieves over some loss in actuality, it must first be transformed into an ideal loss.'[16] As we shall see, however, Brecht's elegies have a great deal to do with reality. As he did on numerous other occasions, Brecht simply inverted Schiller's definition of the elegy, just as his play *Saint Joan of the Stockyards*, for example, is in many ways a *Gegenentwurf* (counter version) to Schiller's Saint Joan play (*The Maid of Orleans*, 1801); he places Schiller's idealism on a materialistic base. In the same vein, Brecht's 'Buckow Elegies' could be considered a counter version to other famous elegies in German literature such as Rilke's 'Duino Elegies' and Goethe's 'Roman Elegies'. The contrast in setting alone must have stirred Brecht's sense of contradiction: the small town of Buckow in the province of Brandenburg, 'the dust bowl of Germany', as it was called, versus exotic Duino and worldly Rome.

In 1942, in exile in California, Brecht had already written a series of poems he called elegies, the so-called 'Hollywood Elegies'. Here, the tone is satirical throughout, expressing his distance from and distaste for the 'American way of life'. The personal 'I' of the poet is rarely used in these poems. They reflect Brecht's attitude of distance toward California; he always felt like a stranger amid the California of rags and riches. Brecht's attitude in the 'Buckow Elegies' is quite different. The poet himself speaks directly in many of the poems, thus indicating that he now has more personal ties to the environment in which he lives. There is some satire, but mostly the tone is one of deep personal concern. The 'Buckow' and the 'Hollywood Elegies' are nevertheless similar in form. Some contain not more than four lines, thus bearing more resemblance to epigrams than to traditional elegies. Also in contrast to traditional elegies, both groups of poems deal with the present rather than the past. The 'Hollywood Elegies' express Brecht's reaction to life in California; the 'Buckow Elegies' reflect Brecht's attitudes and opinions about the contemporary situation in the German Democratic Republic. It is the purpose

---

[15] Grass 109. Other critics do not see any poetic merits whatsoever in the 'Buckow Elegies'. Having read 'Der Radwechsel', Clemens Heselhaus is reminded of a Kurt Schwitters title: 'Banalities from the Chinese.' (Clemens Heselhaus, *Immanente ästhetische Reflexion. Lyrik als Paradigma der Moderne*, Poetik und Hermeneutik, vol. 2 [Munich: 1966] 324.) Hanna Arendt is even more outspoken in her condemnation of Brecht's later poetry: 'What concerns us here is the sad fact that Brecht's poems from his last years, including the "Buckow Elegies", are not worth much, with only one exception, Brecht's poem "Die Lösung."' (Hannah Arendt, *Benjamin. Brecht. Zwei Essays* [Munich: Piper, 1971] 69–70.)

[16] Friedrich von Schiller, *Naive and Sentimental Poetry* and *On the Sublime*. Two Essays, trans. Julius A. Elias (New York: Ungar, 1966) 127.

of this article to examine more closely Brecht's frame of mind as reflected in the 'Buckow Elegies' at that particular stage in the development of the GDR.

Buckow did indeed provide Brecht with a place from which he could view events with more distance than he had in Berlin, but it was by no means a retreat from politics. In the same vein, Brecht's readings in Horace were by no means uncritical; the Greek poet's self-indulgent satisfaction annoyed him: 'die zufriedenheit des horaz mißfällt mir mehr und mehr.'[17] In Buckow he also discussed the difficult political situation of the GDR with long-time friends such as Jakob Walcher, an old communist of the Luxemburg-Liebknecht-Lenin school.[18] The 'Buckow Elegies' reflect Brecht's political concerns of the times in a highly artistic way; they allow us a rare glimpse into Brecht's mood after the terrible events of the workers' uprisings of June 17, 1953, in the German Democratic Republic, which nearly toppled the communist Ulbricht government. As an entry into his *Arbeitsjournal* August 20, 1953, shows, the events surrounding the uprisings affected him very deeply: 'buckow. TURANDOT. daneben die BUCKOWER ELEGIEN. der 17. juni hat die ganze existenz verfremdet.'[19] Brecht never once doubted that the German Democratic Republic was the more progressive of the two German states that emerged from the remnants of the former German Reich in 1949. But the events of June 17, 1953, were a severe blow to his confidence in the re-education of the German people and some of the policies of the GDR government as well. It is only in recent years that scholars have discovered that in the 'Buckow Elegies' Brecht attempted to cope with these fears and apprehension, although some Western critics now attempt to stylize Brecht as a Marxist martyr who suffered silently the indignities of an abhorrent SED regime and surely would have escaped to the West had he lived longer.[20]

The nature metaphors in the 'Buckow Elegies' do not amount to a praise of nature but serve to convey political meanings. In a speech he gave in 1956 before the Fourth Congress of German Writers (the GDR writers' association), Brecht made it quite clear that he had no intention of withdrawing into a private world with the epigrammatic forms of his later poetry: 'Die kleine Form gestattet ein direktes Sichengagieren im Kampf.'[21] This statement also applies to the 'Buckow Elegies'.

The twenty-three 'Buckow Elegies' we know today were written between July and November 1953. But it was not before 1980 that the complete cycle was accessible to readers in East and West Germany; Brecht himself published only six poems (in *Versuche* 13 and *Sinn und Form* 6, 1953). In 1964 twenty-one poems were published with Insel Publishers, and the last two poems appeared in *Sinn und Form* 5, 1980. Most of the poems were simply too controversial in the GDR to be published in 1953 or shortly thereafter.

---

[17]*Arbeitsjournal* 986 (August 30, 1952).
[18]See Klaus Völker, *Bertolt Brecht. Eine Biographie* (Munich, Vienna: Hanser, 1976) 373; James K. Lyon, *Bertolt Brecht in America* (Princeton: Princeton University Press, 1980) 277; *Arbeitsjournal* 744, 849, 886; and Bertolt Brecht, *Briefe* (Letters), ed. Günter Glaeser (Frankfurt/Main: Suhrkamp, 1981) 706, 708. In 1951 Walcher lost all official positions in the GDR purges of those communists who had spent their exile years in western countries. See Völker 375.
[19]*Arbeitsjournal* 1009.
[20]See Peter Bödeker's interpretation of 'Die Lösung' in Walter Hinck, ed., *Ausgewählte Gedichte Brechts mit Interpretationen* (Frankfurt/Main: Suhrkamp, 1978) 130.
[21]*IV. Deutscher Schriftstellerkongress. Protokoll I. Teil* (Berlin, 1965) 160. Quoted from Jürgen Link, *Die Struktur des literarischen Symbols* (Munich: Fink, 1975) 124.

Before the poems are analyzed in some detail, it is necessary to discuss Brecht's direct references to June 17, 1953. They help to clarify allusions to them in poetry.

Brecht was not really shocked by the uprisings of the workers. For him, the workers remained 'die aufsteigende klasse' – despite all their lack of direction and pitiful helplessness ('in aller ihrer richtungslosigkeit und jämmerlicher hilflosigkeit'). 'deshalb empfand ich den schrecklichen 17. juni als nicht einfach negativ.'[22] He felt that the workers' demonstrations were justified because of a number of wrong economic measures taken by the government: 'Die Demonstrationen des 17. Juni zeigten die Unzufriedenheit eines beträchtlichen Teils der Berliner Arbeiterschaft mit einer Reihe verfehlter wirtschaftlicher Maßnahmen.'[23] What really shocked him was the reappearance of fascist elements, long thought to have vanished, who tried to misuse the dissatisfaction for their own bloody purposes. 'Organisierte faschistische Elemente versuchten, diese Unzufriedenheit für ihre blutigen Zwecke zu mißbrauchen.'[24] Apparently, Brecht's fears were not unfounded. Among the 'freedom' shouters in the streets of the city of Halle was, for example, a certain Erna Dorn. She formerly had been the commander of the Ravensbrück concentration camp; now some sympathetic demonstrators had freed her from prison.[25] The situation in East Germany was so critical that Brecht feared it might come to a new catastrophe: 'Mehrere Stunden lang stand Berlin am Rande eines dritten Weltkrieges.'[26] For a long time, Brecht's attitude toward the SED regime was hotly debated in the West, especially after *Neues Deutschland*, the official SED newspaper of the GDR, published only the last sentence of Brecht's letter to the then head of state Walter Ulbricht, in which Brecht expressed his sympathy for the SED. In the meantime, we know that Brecht's view was much more complex, neither that of total approval nor total disapproval. His letter to his publisher Peter Suhrkamp of July 1, 1953, is probably the best summary of his views. After describing the uprising itself, Brecht concludes:

> Lieber Suhrkamp, machen wir uns nichts vor: Nicht nur im Westen, auch hier im Osten Deutschlands sind 'die Kräfte' wieder am Werk. Ich habe an diesem tragischen 17. Juni beobachtet, wie der Bürgersteig auf die Straße das 'Deutschlandlied' warf und die Arbeiter es mit der 'Internationale' niederstimmten. Aber sie kamen, verwirrt und hilflos, nicht durch damit.
>
> Die Sozialistische Einheitspartei Deutschlands hat Fehler begangen, die für eine sozialistische Partei sehr schwerwiegend sind und Arbeiter, darunter auch alte Sozialisten, gegen sie aufbrachten. Ich gehöre ihr nicht an. Aber ich respektiere viele ihrer historischen Errungenschaften, und ich fühlte mich ihr verbunden, als sie – nicht ihrer Fehler, sondern ihrer Vorzüge wegen – von faschistischem und kriegstreiberischem Gesindel angegriffen wurde. Im Kampf gegen Krieg und Faschismus stand und stehe ich an ihrer Seite.[27]

This clear and balanced statement on Brecht's part should put to rest all speculations about Brecht's attitudes to the GDR state: he was neither a hardened Stalinist nor a

---

[22] *Arbeitsjournal* 1009 (August 20, 1953).
[23] Bertolt Brecht, *Gesammelte Werke* 20: 326.
[24] Brecht, *Gesammelte Werke* 20: 327.
[25] See Ernst and Renate Schumacher, *Leben Brechts* (Berlin: Henschelverlag, 1978) 271.
[26] Brecht, *Gesammelte Werke* 20: 327.
[27] *Letters* 697.

dissident or secret sympathizer with the West. His letters in particular show his constant and sincere endeavors to influence policies in a constructive manner. There is no reason to assume that Brecht only guarded his own positions with shrewdness and cleverness, as Martin Esslin seems to suggest.[28]

The general feeling of dissatisfaction that erupted on June 17 also encompassed writers and artists, despite the privileges the state granted them: 'Vor dem 17. Juni und in den Volksdemokratien nach dem XX. Parteitag erlebten wir Unzufriedenheit bei vielen Arbeitern und zugleich hauptsächlich bei den Künstlern. Diese Stimmungen kamen aus einer und derselben Quelle. Die Arbeiter drängte man, die Produktion zu steigern, die Künstler, dies schmackhaft zu machen. Man gewährte den Künstlern einen hohen Lebensstandard und versprach ihn den Arbeitern.'[29] Instead of regarding everything as a means to an end, Brecht suggested: 'Wir müssen das Produzieren zum eigentlichen Lebensinhalt machen und es so gestalten, es mit so viel Freiheit und Freiheiten ausstatten, daß es an sich verlockend ist.'[30] Needless to say, Brecht's ideas found no echo in higher echelons at that time.

In Buckow, Brecht also talked to average citizens in order to learn more about the difficulties of everyday life in the GDR. In September of 1953, for example, he had a long conversation with a plumber who complained about the shortage of materials and labor, the bloated bureaucracy, the Russians, and the limitation of free speech.[31] Traces of the recent German past, openly visible on June 17, were still threatening behind an uneasy calm. On July 7, 1954, Brecht noted in his *Arbeitsjournal*:

> das land ist immer noch unheimlich. neulich, als ich mit jungen leuten aus der dramaturgie nach buckow fuhr, saß ich abends im pavillon, während sie in ihren zimmern arbeiteten oder sich unterhielten. vor zehn jahren, fiel mir plötzlich ein, hätten alle drei, was immer sie von mir gelesen hätten, mich, wäre ich unter sie gefallen, schnurstracks der gestapo übergeben ...[32]

In an article on 'Kulturpolitik und Akademie der Künste' that appeared in *Neues Deutschland* on August 12, 1953, Brecht noted the lack of a socialist consciousness among the people in the GDR: 'Große Teile der Bevölkerung sind noch tief in kapitalistischen Vorstellungen befangen.'[33]

This, then, is the historic background for the 'Buckow Elegies'. What Brecht expressed straightforwardly in articles, diary notes, and letters is clad in artistic form in the poems. The events of June 17, 1953, caused Brecht to take stock of the political achievements of the new GDR society and to reflect his own position and function in it as a writer.[34]

---

[28]Martin Esslin, *Brecht. A Choice of Evils* (London and New York: Methuen, fourth edition 1984) 169.
[29]Brecht, *Gesammelte Werke* 20: 327.
[30]Brecht, *Gesammelte Werke* 20: 328.
[31]*Arbeitsjournal* 1010 (September 12, 1953).
[32]*Arbeitsjournal* 1017.
[33]Brecht, *Gesammelte Werke* 19: 543.
[34]After years of comparative neglect, the 'Buckow Elegies' began to attract more attention since the mid-1970s with books by Jürgen Link, Klaus-Bernd Vollmar, and Nosratollah Rastegar (Jürgen Link, *Die Struktur des literarischen Symbols*; Klaus-Bernd Vollmar, *Ästhetische Strukturen und politische Aufklärung*, Bern, Frankfurt/Main: Lang, 1976; Nosratollah Rastegar, *Die Symbolik in der späteren Lyrik Brechts*, Bern, Frankfurt/Main: Lang, 1978). But as Jan Knopf has pointed out in his *Brecht Handbuch. Lyrik, Prosa, Schriften* (Stuttgart: Metzler, 1984) and in his *Brecht Journal* (Frankfurt/Main: Suhrkamp, 1983) those books contain too much theoretical speculation to be of great value – despite some correct insights. (Ulrich Weisstein, incidentally, arrives at the same

The only poem with a direct reference to June 17, 1953, is 'Die Lösung'. It was Brecht's answer to the secretary of the Writers' Union, Kurt Barthel, generally known as Kuba, who, in an article published in *Neues Deutschland* on June 20, 1953, had severely criticized the workers for their actions. Kuba warned that the workers now had lost their government's confidence and could only win it back with increased efforts. Brecht suggests another solution in this poem: '… Wäre es da / Nicht doch einfacher, die Regierung / Löste das Volk auf und / Wählte ein anderes?' (p. 1010).

Kuba was also one of the most loyal party poets who never tired of singing songs of praise for Stalin and his policies. He and his ilk are the target in the poem 'Die Musen', in which Brecht satirizes their blind and fawning obedience: 'Wenn der Eiserne [i.e., Stalin] sie prügelt / Singen die Musen lauter. / Aus gebläuten Augen / Himmeln sie ihn hündisch an' (pp. 1015–16). These are the only two bitingly satirical poems in the cycle. Needless to say, they were not published at the time they were written.

As Thiele and Hartinger clearly demonstrate, the poem 'Die Lösung' is far from being a devastating criticism of the East German SED regime by a disillusioned Brecht, as many critics would have it.[35] It cannot be denied, however, that 'Die Lösung' also contains a good deal of criticism of misguided policies on the part of functionaries isolated from the people. Both Raimund Gerz and Dieter Thiele point to parallels between 'Die Lösung' and the *Turandot* play which Brecht wrote at the same time as the 'Buckow Elegies' (although first plans for *Turandot* date back to 1930).[36] In *Turandot* Brecht castigates unscrupulous intellectuals ('Tuis') who lend their services to any cause.

Brecht recognized that mistakes had been made but he believed that party officials, cultural functionaries, and writers might fare best by frank admission of mistakes, thus regaining the confidence of the people. In his article 'Kulturpolitik und Akademie der Künste' Brecht warned of the grave dangers of hiding the truth: 'Schönfärberei und Beschönigung sind nicht nur die ärgsten Feinde der Schönheit, sondern auch der politischen Vernunft.'[37] One of his favorite lines was 'Die Wahrheit ist konkret', and in this vein Brecht admonishes his political friends in the elegy 'Die Wahrheit einigt': 'Freunde, ich wünschte, ihr wüßtet die Wahrheit und sagtet sie!' (p. 1011). The poem repeats the message of his article on cultural policies. Brecht strongly felt that

---

conclusion in his review of Jürgen Link's book *Die Struktur des literarischen Symbols* in *Monatshefte*, vol. 70, no. 2 [1978]: 207–11.) To date, Jan Knopf's own writings on the 'Buckow Elegies', together with respective chapters on these poems in books by Dieter Thiele (*Bertolt Brecht. Selbstverständnis, Tui-Kritik und politische Ästhetik* [Frankfurt/Main, Bern: Lang, 1981] 68–116) and Christel Hartinger (*Bertolt Brecht – das Gedicht nach Krieg und Wiederkehr* [Berlin: Brecht Zentrum der DDR, 1982] 242–322), offer the most convincing interpretations – next to a small number of articles dealing with individual poems such as articles by Theodore Fiedler 'Brecht and Cavafy' in *Comparative Literature* vol. 24, no. 3 (1973) on the poem 'Bei der Lektüre eines spätgriechischen Dichters' or Gerhard Seidel's article in Sinn *und Form* vol. 32, no. 5 (1980) presenting two more 'Buckow Elegies' to bring the total number of poems belonging to this group to twenty-three. Thiele discusses the 'Buckow Elegies' in the context of the relationships between the artist-intellectual and the socialist state. The East German critic Hartinger interprets the 'Buckow Elegies' in a wider political context that goes far beyond the events of June 17, 1953. All of these critics offer new departures for a more productive interpretation of the 'Buckow Elegies'.
[35]See Thiele 70–76, Hartinger 260–72. Even Brecht's relationship with Kuba was not always so bad. In a letter to Willi Bredel dated Nov. 22, 1951, he wrote of Kuba: 'Ich schätze ihn sehr.' See *Letters* 666, letter no. 676. However, one should also bear in mind that in this very same letter, Brecht politely declines to write an afterword to a volume of Kuba's poems, which Bredel had requested from Brecht.
[36]See *Gesammelte Werke 5*, notes, p. 3. Raimund Gerz, *Bertolt Brecht und der Faschismus* (Bonn: Bouvier, 1983) 171. In quoting a passage from *Turandot* similar to the last two lines in 'Die Lösung', Thiele even goes so far as to suggest fascist tendencies in Kuba's argumentation. See Thiele 76.
[37]Brecht, *Gesammelte Werke* 19: 541.

particularly in times of crisis the naked truth is vastly preferable to rosy-colored cover-ups as expressed in so many official decrees and stereotyped works of socialist-realist literature. In the middle of August of 1953, Brecht sent this poem to Paul Wandel, the secretary of the Central Committee of the Socialist Unity Party (SED), hoping to effect change. ('Wandel', by the way, means change. Surely the meaning of the name was not lost on Brecht.) In an accompanying letter he warned of the dangers of neo-fascism: 'Lieber Genosse Wandel, ich schicke Dir ein Gedicht, das ich nicht veröffentlichen will, sozusagen zu innerem Gebrauch. Die Wahrheit, die wir unserer Arbeiterschaft sagen sollten, ist meiner Meinung nach: daß sie in tödlicher Gefahr ist, von einem neu erstarkenden Faschismus in einen neuen Krieg geworfen zu werden; daß sie alles tun muß, die kleinbürgerlichen Schichten unter ihre Führung zu bringen. (Wir haben unsern eigenen Westen bei uns!) Kurz, wir dürfen nicht wieder den Kopf in den märkischen Sand stecken! Dein Brecht. Buckow, Mitte August 53.'[38]

Another poem in the cycle of 'Buckow Elegies' closely related to 'Die Wahrheit einigt' is the poem 'Bei der Lektüre eines spätgriechischen Dichters'. As Theodore Fiedler has pointed out, the source for this poem is by no means 'a Troy novel, Strabo, or Pausanias' as Edgar Marsch assumes,[39] but Brecht's near contemporary Greek poet Constantin Cavafy (1863-1933), whose poems – in a German translation by Helmut van den Steinen – were published in 1953 by Brecht's West German publisher Suhrkamp.[40] In the often (mis-) quoted letter to Walter Ulbricht of June 17, 1953, Brecht hoped: 'Die große Aussprache mit den Massen über das Tempo des sozialistischen Aufbaus wird zu einer Sichtung und zu einer Sicherung der Sozialistischen Errungenschaften führen.'[41] Brecht felt that a realistic assessment of resources and capabilities was essential for the construction of a new socialist society rather than piece-meal reforms by unrealistic planners and the false optimism based on a false analysis of the situation ('Richteten die Troer Stückchen grade, Stückchen' – the expression 'Stückchen' appears three times in this short poem of six lines!).

In the context of writer and society, the poems 'Bei der Lektüre eines spätgriechischen Dichters', 'Die Lösung', 'Die Musen', and 'Die Wahrheit einigt' represent a good deal of literary criticism in addition to their political criticism. Brecht himself never wore the rosy-colored glasses of narrow-minded socialist realism. As his own difficulties with such works as *Lucullus* demonstrated, he himself was often the target of those narrowly conceived policies, and he continually argued for more realism and greater artistic freedom: '*Nur Stiefel kann man nach Maß anfertigen.*'[42] Again in a letter to Paul Wandel, written 'deeply troubled' ('in wirklicher Sorge') in August of 1953, Brecht demanded that the state-controlled supervisory board for the arts ('Kunstkommission') be abolished immediately: 'Eine Aufrechterhaltung der Kunstkommission würde keinesfalls als Festigkeit, sondern nur als Sturheit betrachtet werden, als Unnachgiebigkeit nur gegen die Vernunft. [...] Was wir jetzt brauchen, ist eine besondere Entfaltung der Produktivität der Kunst, die soviel tun kann, wenn man sie läßt (und klug führt).'[43]

One of Brecht's criticisms of party policies was that much of the central planning was done without due consideration for the wants and wishes of the people. In 'Große Zeit,

---

[38]*Letters* 701, letter no. 733.
[39]Edgar Marsch, *Brecht-Kommentar zum lyrischen Werk* (Munich: Winkler, 1974) 358.
[40]See Theodore Fiedler, 'Brecht and Cavafy', *Comparative Literature*, vol. 25, no. 3 (1973): 240–46.
[41]*Letters* 693, letter no. 725.
[42]*Gesammelte Werke* 19: 545.
[43]*Letters* 699–701, letter no. 732.

vertan' he illustrates this with an example taken from the construction industry. Here we should keep in mind that the uprising of June 17, 1953, started with a peaceful protest of the construction workers in East Berlin's 'Stalinallee' (Stalin Avenue, now Karl Marx Avenue). In this poem, Brecht asks in the last two lines: 'Was sind schon Städte, gebaut / ohne die Weisheit des Volkes?' (p. 1010).

Brecht also included himself in his reflections and criticisms. Did he, the privileged artist, do everything he could to help improve the lot of the common man in the socialist workers' and peasant state? His use of distorted nature images seems to express doubts. In 'Böser Morgen' he awakens from bad dreams in which he saw fingers, worn and broken, pointing at him, accusingly. 'Unwissende! Schrie ich / Schuldbewußt' (p. 1010). The beautiful poplar trees now look to him like old harridans; the clear lake like a foul puddle of dishwater. Here we have a very rare glimpse of Brecht, the man, who usually hides behind his work. This admirable admission of possible personal failings earned him many vicious attacks from the West. Western critics frequently point to this poem as Brecht's own admission of guilt for not having actively supported the workers on that fateful June 17, 1953.[44] But how could he have done so when he saw the justified complaints of some workers being distorted by fascist elements? In the struggle against fascism he unequivocally supported the SED, as we have seen. Hartinger's interpretation seems much more to the point: Brecht felt that he as a writer had not done enough to openly oppose the Stalinist terror ('broken fingers').[45] Brecht's dilemma was, of course, that the necessary debate of Stalinist methods could not take place during the struggle against fascism,[46] nor after 1945 in the cold war period when such a debate only would have served to provide ammunition for the 'class-enemy'. Other poems in the Buckow cycle clearly referring to Stalin help to support Hartinger's view.

Another poem that can be seen in the same context as 'Böser Morgen' is 'Die Kelle'. It is another dream scene in which the poet sees himself confronted with a difficult situation, although in this poem the poet's commentary is lacking – unlike 'Böser Morgen'. The speaker of the poem ('ich') sees himself as a bricklayer, but before he can begin to build, his tool ('Kelle') is destroyed by a shot. If we take the 'ich' of the poem to be Brecht, the writer, the poem could again be seen as an expression of Brecht's struggle to come to terms with his relations to the workers (his inability to use the trowel) – similar to 'Böser Morgen'.[47] On the other hand, the poem also signifies the interruption of the construction of socialism by violence, perhaps even the danger of war ('Schuß').

'Der Radwechsel', far from praising the unity of all that is good, true and beautiful as Brandt would have it, is Brecht's attempt to define his position in a changing world, especially after June 17. The poem reports how the poet watches the driver of a car changing the wheel.[48] Although he does not like either the place he came from or his destination, he watches with impatience. The wheel evokes the medieval concept of the wheel of fortune with man being a helpless victim. In Brecht's poem, however, the wheel

---

[44]See, for example, Peter Paul Schwarz, *Lyrik und Zeitgeschichte. Brecht: Gedichte über das Exil und späte Lyrik* (Heidelberg: Stiehm, 1978) 118–19, and Edgar Marsch, *Brecht–Kommentar zum lyrischen Werk* 356.
[45]See Hartinger 300–11.
[46]Brecht, for example, never published his views in the so-called debate on realism (or expressionism) in the thirties when Georg Lukács' Stalinist views prevailed in the journal *Das Wort*. See Hans-Jürgen Schmitt, ed. *Die Expressionismusdebatte* (Frankfurt/Main: Suhrkamp, 1973).
[47]See also Thiele 99.
[48]As Jan Knopf points out, the original version of this poem has 'Strassenhang' (slope next to the road) instead of 'Strassenrand' (roadside). Knopf prefers the more ambiguous first version. See *Brecht Journal* (1983) 93–96.

is the object and the driver the active force. The dynamic force of the poem and the impatient wish to move on are checked by the skeptical view of the past and present policies ('Ich bin nicht gern, wo ich herkomme. / Ich bin nicht gern, wo ich hinfahre' [p. 1009]). There is uncertainty about the future course of GDR policies. Yet impatience to move on suggests cautious optimism. Besides, one could argue, a defective wheel is only a minor damage; the essential object, the car, is still intact. 'Der Radwechsel' obviously recalls the earlier poem of 1949, 'Wahrnehmung', especially its last two lines: 'Die Mühen der Gebirge liegen hinter uns / Vor uns liegen die Mühen der Ebenen' (p. 960).

The idea of change, a key concept in Brecht's work, also underlies the 'Buckow Elegies'. The various poems express disappointment about lack of change, unwillingness to change, hope for change, and first signs of change. An indicator for Brecht's skeptical mood at the end of 1953, however, is the motto of the elegies:

> Ginge da ein Wind
> Könnte ich ein Segel stellen.
> Wäre da kein Segel
> Machte ich eines aus Stecken und Plane.
>
> (p. 1009)

Apparently there is no wind, and that means there is no motion, no change. By the same token, however, there is apparently a sail, allowing for the possibility of motion. The motto and 'Der Radwechsel', the poem immediately following the motto, express the same idea: the dissatisfaction with stagnation and eagerness to move on, to make changes, to progress. At that point in history, Brecht only experiences motion in a dream. In the poem 'Eisen' he sees a vision of a mighty storm sweeping away the inflexible iron parts of a scaffolding, leaving only the flexible wood unscathed. The reference to the construction workers' protests and inflexible Stalinist bureaucrats is obvious ('Stahlinist' – in German: 'Stahl' = steel, iron).

As Brecht indicates in 'Tannen', the fir trees he sees early in the morning still look like copper, as they did fifty years ago. But two world wars have since changed Germany and him. As he expresses in the poem 'Beim Lesen des Horaz' he was one of the few survivors of the 'black waters' of the 'flood' – the black S.S. hordes of Nazi Germany. In this sense the poem 'Beim Lesen des Horaz' is directly connected with 'An die Nachgeborenen', written in Danish exile in Svendborg around 1938 when he feared that he and other anti-fascists might 'go under' in 'the flood':

> Ihr, die ihr auftauchen werdet aus der Flut
> In der wir untergegangen sind
> Gedenkt
> Wenn ihr von unseren Schwächen sprecht
> Auch der finsteren Zeit
> Der ihr entronnen seid.
>
> (*Gesammelte Werke* 9: 724)

'Beim Lesen des Horaz' has been interpreted in various ways: as a counter poem to Horace, who expected salvation from the gods in Ode I, 12; as an expression of Brecht's mood after June 17, 1953; or as surviving the revolution.[49] The reference to fascism

---

[49] See Thiele 87–93.

seems much more plausible, especially since a number of 'Buckow Elegies' deal directly with the fascist past, as we shall see.

As he did in his *Arbeitsjournal*, Brecht also describes in some of the 'Buckow Elegies' how ominous remnants of the past threaten the new German state which he had chosen as his home. The one-armed man in the undergrowth in the poem 'Der Einarmige im Gehölz' initially arouses our compassion. With great effort, plagued by heat and mosquitoes, the man goes about his laborious task of collecting firewood in the woods. Apparently he lost one arm in the war and now he has to combat the post-war shortages. But then he raises his arm to probe for rain. Immediately the poem takes on a new meaning. The gesture of the raised arm reminds the poet of the hated Nazi salute: 'Die Hand hoch / Der gefürchtete SS-Mann' (p. 1013). Thus the poem becomes a metaphor for Brecht's apprehensions that underneath the surface of post-war Germany the threat of fascism is still alive. As he noted in his *Arbeitsjournal*, June 17, 1953, confirmed his worst fears, when former Nazis were openly visible in the streets of Berlin and other cities.

In the poem 'Vor acht Jahren' Brecht goes on to ask about the attitudes of the average citizen. The mailman, the electrician, the butcher's wife appear to be peaceful inhabitants of Buckow now. But what were they thinking and doing only eight years ago, before 1945? Do they have something to hide? If so, what? Have they changed their habits and their ways of thinking?

Other poems describe some habits still extant from times past. There is the Prussian commando-tone Brecht castigates in 'Gewohnheiten, noch immer' in which 'Mit schriller Stimme / Ertönt das Kommando: Zum Essen!' (p. 1011). In the poem 'Heißer Tag' the poet sits in his summer house, typewriter on his knees. Out on the lake he sees a child rowing a nun and a priest: 'Wie in alten Zeiten, denke ich / Wie in alten Zeiten!' (p. 1011) – religion again appears as an exploitive power.

Compounding the internal threats is the external danger of war: in the poem 'Der Himmel dieses Sommers' the poet sees a bomber high above the peaceful rowing boats on the lake. External and internal dangers are actually linked through similar images in the two poems 'Der Himmel dieses Sommers' and 'Gewohnheiten, noch immer'. In the latter poem, it is 'Der preußische Adler / Den Jungen hackt er / Das Futter in die Mäulchen' (p. 1011). In the former poem, the people in the rowing boats look up to the bomber 'Von weitem / Gleichen sie jungen Staren, die Schnäbel aufreißend / Der Nahrung entgegen' (p. 1015).

External threats and internal problems are also the subject of a poem belonging to the 'Buckow Elegies' first printed in *Sinn und Form* in 1980 (vol. 32, no. 5) entitled 'Lebensmittel zum Zweck':

An Kanonen gelehnt
Teilen die Söhne Mac Carthys Schmalz aus.
Und in unendbarem Zug, auf Rädern, zu Fuß
Eine Völkerwanderung aus dem innersten Sachsen.

Wenn das Kalb vernachlässigt ist
Drängt es zu jeder schmeichelnden Hand, auch
Der Hand seines Metzgers.[50]

---

[50]Quoted from *Sinn und Form*, vol. 32, no. 5 (1980) 1091.

Brecht clearly alludes to the masses of people who left the GDR for greener pastures in the West because they felt that the GDR did not take care of their economic needs. They are lured by the 'economic miracle' and false promises ('Schmalz') to the West, only to become victims in a possible new hot war instigated by Western cold war politicians.

Economic difficulties are also the subject of the poem 'Die neue Mundart', like 'Lebensmittel zum Zweck' first published in *Sinn und Form* in 1980.

> Als sie einst mit ihren Weibern über Zwiebeln sprachen
> Die Läden waren wieder einmal leer
> Verstanden sie noch die Seufzer, die Flüche, die Witze
> Mit denen das unerträgliche Leben
> In der Tiefe dennoch gelebt wird.
> Jetzt
> Herrschen sie und sprechen eine neue Mundart
> Nur ihnen selber verständlich, das Kaderwelsch
> Welche mit drohender und belehrender Stimme gesprochen wird
> Und die Läden füllt – ohne Zwiebeln.
>
> Dem, der Kaderwelsch hört
> Vergeht das Essen.
> Dem, der es spricht
> Vergeht das Hören.[51]

Like the poems 'Die Lösung' and 'Große Zeit, vertan', this poem decries the isolation of some functionaries who have risen to high office forgetting their humble origins and the needs of the people. It is also a critique of language, the functionary's lingo, the 'Kaderwelsch' as Brecht calls it in German ('Kader' = cadre = party elite; a word play on 'Kauderwelsch' = gobbledygook). As in 'Die Lösung', one is tempted to see another example of Tui criticism in this poem.

Yet despite all threats, there are Brecht's visions and hopes for a new life worthy of human beings in a new order of society. The poem 'Bei der Lektüre eines sowjetischen Buches' shows confidence that nature's forces will be tamed for the benefit of the people. The book Brecht reads describes how near Stalingrad, where once death and destruction raged, a new dam will provide the waters bringing life to the arid plains. The previously mentioned poem 'Rudern, Gespräche' is indeed a highly poetic work of art. Yet, as Klaus-Bernd Vollmar pointed out,[52] it does not present an impressionist idyll as Brandt assumed. In this poem, both canoeists are equally occupied with paddling. At the same time, they are talking with one another. Both activities are linked together by a syntactical chiasmus: 'Nebeneinander rudernd / Sprechen sie. Sprechend / Rudern sie nebeneinander' (p. 1013). There is perfect harmony between man and nature and between the two men. This poetic metaphor has political significance; it is a perfect metaphor for perfect harmony between theory and practice and for an ideal collective. Thus, this poem provides a striking contrast to the reactionary situation in 'Heißer Tag', where a child has to row two well-fed adults, and the nature imagery in 'Der Einarmige

---

[51] Quoted from *Sinn und Form*, vol. 32, no. 5 (1980) 1091.
[52] Vollmar 107.

im Gehölz' and 'Der Himmel dieses Sommers', where nature images are used to express political dangers.

In all poems of the 'Buckow Elegies', human relations are Brecht's central concern. Nature imagery is not used as an end in itself, but as a metaphor and a semiotic system to express political and social relationships. In the romantic period of German literature in the late eighteenth and early nineteenth centuries, nature was seen as an escape from the bondage of human society. Nature imagery stood for individual freedom and independence. Brecht, on the other hand, uses nature imagery to express social concerns. Thus, the poem about his flower garden in Buckow quoted at the beginning of this article has significance only in relation to his activities as a writer, as the second stanza makes clear. The flower garden is a symbol for creativity, productivity, and change. As Brecht sees it, nature's only significance is in relation to man; it is subservient to man. In the poem 'Der Rauch', the idyllic house, the trees, and the lakes would be dreary without a sign of human activity: the smoke coming from the chimney. As he states in the poem 'Laute', the only sounds that count are those of people ('Aber den ganzen Sommer durch höre ich / Da die Gegend vogellos ist / Nur Laute von Menschen rührend. / Ich bin's zufrieden' [p. 1014]). When Brecht calls the Buckow region 'birdless' – which it certainly is not – he does not only indicate that his primary concern is with people, not with nature. He also seems to reject implicitly the bucolic nature image Horace projects – especially the line 'And the birds croon in every wood' from the second epode 'In Praise of Country Life' quoted earlier in the article. Here we have another proof that Brecht's nature imagery serves a new and non-traditional purpose; it presents a counter version to Horace.

The 'Buckow Elegies' show people, including the poet himself, in a particular historical time, as defined and limited by particular historical circumstances. This emphasis on social situations and historical relations presented in artistic forms connects the collection of Buckow poems with Brecht's other works. There are also similarities in structure. Although the poems are interrelated through similar themes and images, they do not form an inflexible and closed entity. Most of them are artistic gems that in their epigrammatic shortness comprise a vast net of connotations and associations. When certain groupings of poems are suggested in the interpretations attempted above, it was done in the full knowledge that other groupings are equally possible. The poems have a multi-faceted relationship to each other that operates on many different levels. Small wonder that the 'Buckow Elegies' have attracted more attention in recent years. Like his plays, they are intended to raise questions and to start a thought process. Finally, they provide us with Brecht's personal concerns in a time of great personal and historic crisis in the GDR of 1953.

Prose: The Novels

CHAPTER TWENTY-FOUR

The Anti-Aristotelian Novel: Brecht's Contribution to the Novel of Classic Modernity

KLAUS-DETLEF MÜLLER
TRANSLATED BY ROMY FURSLAND

It was not only the drama of the twentieth century that Brecht changed fundamentally with his epic theatre. He also effected innovations in the area of prose fiction that have so far been rather neglected. Here too the word he used to describe his procedure was 'anti-Aristotelian'. The aim is to counter empathetic reception and to develop narrative possibilities that do not depend on individual characters. The Threepenny Novel *and* The Business Affairs of Mr Julius Caesar *will be used here to show how this is feasible in theory and fruitful in practice.*

1

One of the most striking characteristics of Brecht's satirical narrative style in his *Threepenny Novel* (BFA 16) is that the characters are sometimes not responsible for the thoughts attributed to them. The war invalid Fewkoombey, for example, reflecting on Polly's situation, thinks that it is a good thing abortion is against the law and hence prohibitively expensive, otherwise no woman would ever be so unmaternal as to condemn her child to existence in a world of pervasive and ineradicable misery, as he sees it. In fact, though, the point of these reflections – so apt and logical in the objective horizon of the character – is that they are not really his thoughts at all, for they are followed by: 'This was more or less what the soldier would have thought, if he had been thinking. But he didn't think: he was trained to be disciplined' (BFA 16: 74). Similarly, a lofty and impassioned speech is attributed to the 'Beggar King' Peachum following a failed business deal. Peachum compares his misfortune with that of the most tragic heroes of Greek antiquity – but the speech is followed by the caveat that he would have spoken this way 'if he had been well-educated' (BFA 16: 97). He is not, however, so he cannot articulate his feelings in the way

---

Klaus-Detlef Müller, 'Der nichtaristotelische Roman: Brechts Beitrag zum Roma der klassischen Moderne', in Robert Gillett and Godela Weiss-Sussex (eds), *'Verwisch die Spuren!'. Bertolt Brecht's Work and Legacy. A Reassessment* (Amsterdam: Rodopi, 2008), pp. 13–32.

ascribed to him. Who is speaking here, then, in the guise of the characters who are unable to express themselves in a way that suits the narrative context? Clearly it is the (satirical) narrative voice, which does not, however, distance itself from the characters but remains within their restricted horizons (which are criticised by the narrative constellation) and thus uses their voices. In a broader sense, therefore, it is the narrated situation and its simultaneously subjectively biased and objectively instructive perception which literally becomes speech here.

Both monologues are highlighted in the text of the novel through italicization. The use of this typographical distinction for the thoughts, reflections, speeches and dreams of the characters in the novel, for some of the linguistic articulations which are attributed to them or which merely *could* be attributed to them, is one of the most important and probably the most striking stylistic feature of the novel. It is not used simply to force certain passages on the reader's attention in a didactic way, because sometimes the italicised text is parenthetical and unimportant, and, conversely, some sections which *are* particularly important are not italicised. This is not a mistake on Brecht's part, as Bernd Auerochs assumes,[1] but evidence of the function of this approach.

Walter Benjamin described the italicised passages as 'a collection of speeches and aphorisms, confessions and pleas' which is 'quite unique. It alone would ensure the work's long-term relevance. Nobody has ever uttered any of the things that are written there, and yet they all talk that way'.[2] Brecht emphasised to his collaborator Margarete Steffin, who had not understood the method, how important it was: 'The accidental, crude, abrupt nature of the moral considerations is intentional'.[3] And he gave the publisher specific instructions about how the novel should be printed, explaining that it was important to convey the impression 'that something is being *quoted*, that certain maxims and sayings are being *presented*'.[4] 'The italicised passages must have the character of quotations – in other words, the reader must associate them with quotations. […] The reader must think: "Why has the typeface suddenly changed?"'.[5] A provisional and incomplete answer, based on the conclusions established thus far, might be that Brecht is working with a new combination of character, narrated situation, narrative voice and narrative style as well as a new orientation towards the recipient's consciousness of reality. If this is more than a singular formal experiment, the method implies a new and different aesthetic of the novel.

And Brecht does indeed mount a determined opposition to the bourgeois realistic novel right from the start, as early as the 1920s. This includes the bourgeois novel of classic modernity (which he rejects as historically obsolete) as well as bourgeois drama. Both are, in his view, founded on Aristotle's poetics, which in effect understands epos and tragedy as parallel forms of literary imitation. The Aristotelian method, according to

---

[1] Bernd Auerochs, *Erzählte Gesellschaft: Theorie und Praxis des Gesellschaftsromans bei Balzac, Brecht und Johnson* (Munich: Fink, 1994), 153.
[2] Walter Benjamin, 'Brecht's *Dreigroschenroman*' in WBGS III, 440–449. Here 445–446. See also Klaus-Detlef Müller, *Brecht-Kommentar zur erzählenden Prosa* (Munich: Winkler, 1980), 185–185; Auerochs, *Erzählte Gesellschaft* (see footnote 1), 153–158; Wolfgang Jeske, *Dreigroschenroman. Entstehung* in BFA 16: 396–414. Here 403–404; Klaus-Detlef Müller, 'Die Aktualität von Brechts *Dreigroschenroman*' in *Bertolt Brecht und das modern Theater. Jahrbuch der Koreanischen Brecht-Gesellschaft* 5 (1998), 51–72. Here 69–71.
[3] Bertolt Brecht, letter to Margarete Steffin, 19.8.1933. BFA 28: 379.
[4] Bertolt Brecht, letter to the publishing house Allert de Lange, 26.8.1934. BFA 28: 433 (emphasis in text).
[5] Bertolt Brecht, letter to the publishing house Allert de Lange, 1.9.1934. BFA 28: 435.

Brecht, demands empathy and identification from the recipient,[6] as well as an uncritical acceptance of mimesis and the illusions it creates. One of its most important prerequisites is the portrayal of '"free" individuals' as acting subjects.[7] This, in particular, is outdated: 'individuals cannot be granted much more space in books, and most importantly they cannot be given a different status in books than in reality.'[8]

This viewpoint is not a new one, of course, but describes a basic tendency of the classic modern novel which developed as a symptom of the 'crisis of narration' in Germany. It is based on the realization that the world of the novel – i.e. the perception of the world in the novel – can no longer be constructed by one central character, or even by an ensemble of independent characters, because in this increasingly reified and abstract reality, a self-determined identity is not even remotely possible any longer and individual actions have become meaningless.[9] In his opposition to novelistic representation based on autonomous individuality, Brecht is part of what is actually quite a mainstream current of thought within the history of the genre – although Brecht, as we will show, updates it in a radical way and finds new solutions based upon it.

Brecht also sees the traditional structure of the epic world as Aristotelian and thus designed to make the reader empathise and identify:

> The bourgeois novel still always creates 'a world'. It does this for purely idealistic reasons, based on a worldview, on the more or less personal, but at any rate individual, views of its 'creator'. Within this world, of course, all the details are perfectly coherent – the same details which, detached from their context, would not for one moment seem authentic compared with the 'details' of reality. We learn only as much about the real world as we learn about the author, the creator of the unreal world – meaning, of course, that we learn only about the author and not about the world.[10]

The apparent coherence of such fictional constructs arises from the fact that their elements are evenly distributed, so that through 'general abbreviation and

---

[6] See Bertolt Brecht, '[Kritik der "Poetik" des Aristotles]', BFA 22.1: 171–172, where empathy is also described as a kind of religiosity, and as such outdated.

[7] See Bertolt Brecht, 'Thesen über die Aufgabe der Einfühlung in der theatralischen Künsten', BFA 22.1: 175–176. Here 175.

[8] Bertolt Brecht, '[Über Georg Lukács]', BFA 22.1: 483–487. Here 485. The polemic is directed against Georg Lukács' understanding of reality.

[9] Even Thomas Mann, whom Brecht abhorred, confronts his character Hans Castorp (the protagonist of *The Magic Mountain*, who is explicitly described as 'average') with an essayistically presented inventory of contemporary trends which are difficult to convey and which Castorp is not intellectually capable of understanding; in the rarefied and artificial atmosphere of the Swiss tuberculosis clinic, he is both fascinated and disconcerted by them. In *The Sleepwalkers*, Hermann Broch shows how the narrated subjects become the victims of uncomprehended cultural fictions which, once established, develop a life of their own – unbeknownst to the characters – and determine their behaviour. In *Berlin Alexanderplatz*, Alfred Döblin made the city of Berlin the protagonist of the novel, and used the story of Franz Biberkopf merely as an auxiliary construction, one which shows only the vaguest interest in the conventions of the genre and which simultaneously devalues them through its balladesque gestus. Robert Musil overtly conceptualises the central character of his novel as being 'without qualities', thus denying him any kind of identity that might make it possible for the 'eternal artifice of the epic' to tell a story based on the course of a character's life (Robert Musil: *The Man Without Qualities* [Hamburg: Rowohlt 1952, 649–650]). And Franz Kafka, in *The Castle*, shows that the all-determining reified order has become so intangible that it makes any concept of a subject impossible from the outset.

[10] Bertolt Brecht, 'Der Dreigroschenprozeß. Ein soziologisches Experiment', BFA 21: 448–514. Here 465.

deformation [...] the impression of logic' emerges.[11] This, of course, calls for a specific response mode from the reader; and the writer's 'own world', which 'does not need to coincide with the other', is designed with this response mode in mind: 'empathy (generated by suggestion) [...] with the artist and, via the artist, with the characters and events'.[12]

From the point of view of the individual and within the horizon of individual experiences as the basis of the empathy technique, reality – the 'entire social causal complex', as Brecht specifies[13] – is no longer representable, certainly not as a reality that can be changed and controlled, the kind of reality Brecht wants to see as the object of an active, intervening art. Hegel's definition of epos and also of the epic work of art as the representation of the entirety of a world in which an individual act takes place is absolutely compatible with Brecht's conception of literature, if we understand the world in its entirety as extra-aesthetic reality which takes shape in a specific, and in this respect individual, sequence of actions, i.e. organised into a plot. The characters are then exemplary representatives of the whole social complex, if not by any means autonomous individuals. The actual subject matter is reality itself, viewed as a totality – not restricted by aesthetic pressures but in its historical specificity. And this applies not only to the novel but also to drama, which is why Brecht described his theatre as epic theatre; in other words, as theatre committed to the viewpoint of epic totality. Many of the principles of his theatrical theory, therefore, also apply to his novel-writing. This is especially true of the anti-Aristotelian approach.

Reality as Brecht experiences it in the first decades of the twentieth century is determined by the universal 'reification of human relationships'; art, too, can no longer be organised on the basis of experience and framed within the horizon of the individual: 'Someone who reflects only those parts of reality that can be experienced is not reflecting reality itself'.[14] Above all, however, the outdated subject- and experience-oriented model of representation hinders the choice of representative subject matter. Brecht illustrated this in an ironic way using the example of a jealous pilot: a jealous man flying a plane is a suitable subject for a discussion of jealousy, but not for a discussion of flying.[15] The new 'major subjects', however, are what Brecht is interested in. He gives the examples of 'war, money, oil, railways, parliament, wage labour, land',[16] some of which define Brecht's novels. In the 'huge seascapes' of traditional novel-writing, they feature in the background at best – as 'forces of nature, fateful powers, monolithic in their encounters with human beings'.[17] They are deemed unpoetic, although Brecht knows very well that they can only become the subject of literature in the context of character-based plots; in other words, as specific shadings of the generality they indicate.

Brecht illustrated the way in which traditional narratives would deal with the new subjects in a short but important note entitled 'On the Aristotelian Novel'. He uses an example based on the justice system:

---

[11] Bertolt Brecht, 'Notizen über realistischer Schreibweise', BFA 22.2: 620–640. Here 627.
[12] Bertolt Brecht, 'Über experimentelles Theater', BFA 22.1: 540–557. Here 551.
[13] Bertolt Brecht, 'Übergang vom bürgerlichen zum sozialistischen Realismus', BFA 22.1: 460–462. Here 461.
[14] Brecht, 'Dreigroschenprozeß' (see footnote 10), 469.
[15] Bertolt Brecht, '[Benutzung der Wissenschaften für Kunstwerke]', BFA 22.1: 479–480.
[16] Bertolt Brecht, 'Die großen Gegenstände', BFA 22.1: 480–481. Here 480.
[17] Ibid., 481.

> Let's assume that it [the Aristotelian novel] is constructed around the statement:
> Justice is unjust (1),
> because of the novel form, this immediately becomes:
> A judge is unjust (2),
> and in a plot, this becomes (because of the novel form):
> A judge does something unjust (3).[18]

The problem for the author who is interested in the new objects of inquiry is that the novel form necessitates the concretisation of the general statement (1) which the author is actually interested in; but this concretisation does not illustrate the general statement. Because if 'all judges are committed to justice and, by being committed to justice, act in an unjust way', then they are not acting as individuals. But if they are not committed to justice, then the statement that justice is unjust is at least selectively disproved by their actions. 'If judges are unjust and not committed to justice and if justice is unjust, then *this* general statement cannot be tackled by the Aristotelian novel with a plot.'

The consequence of this syllogistic refutation of the form of the Aristotelian novel is the call for a 'non-Aristotelian mode of novel-writing'[19] which, however, is not to be understood merely as a representational technique but also as a change in the function of literature. The aim should be to 'make statements about phenomena which permit operations with these phenomena, and to establish practical statements, i.e. operational phrases'. Like epic theatre, the anti-Aristotelian novel should not only reflect reality but also enable and incite practical, world-changing actions by giving an insight into reality's laws. This sounds like didacticism, but Brecht (almost) always stressed that instruction in an aesthetic medium must be entertaining and thus subject to the highest aesthetic standards. He observes these principles himself in the *Threepenny Novel*, as demonstrated below.

2

The subject of the novel is the capitalist economy, which is understood in line with Marxist doctrine (though this is interpreted very freely). In *The Threepenny Opera* the economy was only a marginal theme, addressed as part of the Peachum storyline (which Brecht largely added onto Gay's original), but it increasingly came to the fore in further reworkings of the material. This, then, is a major subject, one which is topical and entirely prosaic, but is conveyed with a keen sense of art. This is made possible mainly by the novel's satirical writing style and narrative irony. As a satirist Brecht modelled himself, by his own admission, on Jonathan Swift and particularly on Swift's *A Modest Proposal* (1729), of which he said the following:

> Jonathan Swift wrote a pamphlet suggesting that, to help make the country more prosperous, the children of the poor should be salted and sold as meat. He set out precise calculations to show that you can save a great deal of money if you will stop at nothing to do so. Swift was playing dumb. He defended a certain way of thinking

---

[18]Bertolt Brecht, 'Über den aristotelischen Roman', BFA 21: 538–539.
[19]Bertolt Brecht, 'Über ein nichtaristotelisches Romanschreiben', BFA 21: 541.

(which was actually abhorrent to him) with great passion and rigour on an issue which revealed the full extent of its callousness for all to see.[20]

As in Swift's work, the satire in the *Threepenny Novel* is not a character satire – given the supposed insignificance of individuals and their behaviour, this would be too trivial – but rather (to use Bernd Auerochs' very apt term) a satire of a system.[21] It poses a problem for the narration which arises from one of the defining principles of satire, that of norm and deviation. Character satire as a common literary model illustrates a behaviour which is questionable and wrong according to the (usually ethically motivated) standards shared by both the narrative voice and the recipient. It criticises the agents of this behaviour and attacks their morals by making them look ridiculous: satire, according to Jürgen Brummack's generally accepted definition, is 'aesthetically socialised aggression'.[22] Such a normative point of reference seems to be absent from the *Threepenny Novel*, even if it is undoubtedly present for the construction of the novelistic world according to the Marxist social model. But this point of reference is not communicated by the narrative voice as knowledge, and it does not, or does not yet, have any significance for the world in which the reader lives, so it cannot be used to generate a consensus. There are norm violations, certainly, but only apparent ones. Ideas about morality and the justice system do feature, but they appear only as the products of a system which legitimises itself through them and thus creates that appearance of order which ensures its survival. And this means that, in cases of conflict, they are ineffectual and are sacrificed as a matter of course. They have the function of an alibi, and have an affirmative effect. For this reason the novel does not want to find consensus with them; on the contrary, it is designed to criticise them.

Brecht declared the 'DEMONSTRANDUM OF A THREEPENNY NOVEL', i.e. the narrative intention of the book, to be: 'the petty criminals are just as bourgeois as the petty bourgeoisie, the upper classes are just as criminal as the petty criminals'.[23] With the category of the criminal, a particularly authoritative norm seems to have been introduced. At the same time, however, it is rendered null and void because no distinction is drawn. For the purposes of the satire of the system, the capitalists' business deals are criminal and the activities of the petty criminals are conformist; they do not differ or deviate at all, but are rational and even necessary within this system – necessary for survival, to be precise. Equating business with crime is a striking proposition, as bold and simple as vulgar-Marxist propaganda. Brecht was well aware of this, and satirically put paid to the objections he fully expected from critics by including in the novel an apologia for the 'crude thinking' which he says 'comes very close to reality' and therefore has a bad reputation (BFA 16: 173).[24] The important thing, however, is the way in which this thesis becomes evident in the novel.

The novel features three business deals of differing quality, which intersect with each other over the course of the novel and by the end of the novel have all merged into one: 1.

---

[20]Bertolt Brecht, 'Fünf Schwierigkeiten beim Schreiben der Wahrheit', BFA 22.1: 74–89. Here 85.
[21]Auerochs: *Erzählte Gesellschaft* (see footnote 1), 170.
[22]Jürgen Brummack, 'Zu Begriff und Theorie der Satire' in *Deutsche Vierteljahrsschrift für Literaturwissenschaft und Geistesgeschichte* 45 (1971). Particularly research papers, 275–377. Here 282.
[23]BBA 295/11. See also Dieter Schlenstadt, 'Das Demonstrandum des *Dreigroschenromans*' in Brechts *Tui-Kritik. Aufsätze, Rezensionen, Geschichten*, ed. Herbert Claas and Wolfgang Fritz Haug (Berlin: Argument, 1976), 150–175 (Argument special issue 11); Müller, *Brecht-Kommentar* (see footnote 2), 134–185.
[24]See also Benjamin, 'Brechts *Dreigroschenroman*' (footnote 2), 445–447.

the entirely legal begging syndicate run by Jonathan Peachum who, in order to exploit the haves' guilty consciences regarding the have-nots, trains and equips professionals (a little like the actors in Aristotelian theatre) to dress up as beggars and successfully appeal to the compassion of those who secretly know that they themselves are the cause of the poor's misfortunes;[25] 2. the shipping venture of the broker Coax, which Brecht borrows from the depiction of Cornelius Vanderbilt, 'the foremost mercantile pirate and commercial blackmailer of his day', in Gustavus Myers' *The History of the Great American Fortunes*,[26] and integrates into the novel as a typical example of economic criminality; and 3. the rise of the petty criminal Macheath, alias Mack the Knife, to the position of bank manager and head of a chain of retail stores. The third plotline is the most important, and the other two are subsumed into it.

In *The Threepenny Opera*, Mackie Messer says in his parting speech at the foot of the gallows:

> Ladies and gentlemen, you see before you the vanishing representative of a vanishing class. We petty bourgeois artisans, who work with humble jemmies on the cashboxes of small shopkeepers, are being swallowed up by big business, which is backed by the banks. What is a picklock to a bank share? What is the robbing of a bank to the founding of a bank? What is the murder of a man to the employment of a man?[27]

The new Macheath of the *Threepenny Novel* goes down precisely the route described here, which not only makes criminality less dangerous (because it does not lead to the gallows) but also a great deal more profitable. He may not found his own bank, but he does go from bank robber to bank manager and is, in many respects, a man who employs others and lives off the surplus value of their work. As the most criminal of the three businessmen brought together by the novel, he proves to be the most cunning: Coax the broker overplays his hand by trying to cheat and ruin the partners in his business ventures, commercially murdering them, so to speak. As a result, Macheath, Polly and Peachum, each of their own accord, feel compelled to actually kill him, meaning he is sent to his death by his own kind and not by the real victims of his criminal dealings (a turn of events he had thought would be quite logical[28] and which is in fact circulated as the official version of his death). And Peachum, though capable of concluding Coax's lucrative shipping deal to his own advantage, does not have the wherewithal to produce the kind of 'Napoleonic plans' (BFA 16: 152) attributed to Macheath – he is too pessimistic and fearful, and is forced to admit defeat by his son-in-law. Macheath has followed the advice of his friend, Police Chief Brown: 'Why go down the illegal route? [...] It's a bad idea. A businessman doesn't break and enter. A businessman buys and sells. And he gets the same results. [...] Work with the banks, like all the other businesspeople do! It's a different kettle of fish!' (BFA 16: 146–147). But what does 'wherewithal' signify here, and what

---

[25]See BFA 16: 23: 'In response to the progressive hardening of hearts, the businessman J.J. Peachum had opened a shop where the wretchedest of the wretched could purchase all the accoutrements they needed to appeal to an ever more obdurate public'.
[26]Gustavus Myers, *Geschichte der großen amerikanischen Vermögen* (Berlin: S. Fischer, 1926), 269. Brecht praises the German translation as one of the best books of 1926: [*Die besten Bücher des Jahres 1926*], BFA 21: 176.
[27]Bertolt Brecht, *Die Dreigroschenoper*, BFA 2: 229–322. Here 305.
[28]"'It's incredible, really," he thought, "that they don't just knock us down where they find us. After all, there aren't very many of us"' (BFA 16: 301).

are these 'Napoleonic plans'? At the end of the novel, Macheath is praised as a great man and a forward-looking business leader, at which he permits himself a striking confession:

> I make no secret of it: I have worked my way up to where I am today. [...] I started small, in a very different milieu from this one. By and large, however, my activities have always been the same. People tend to accredit a man's rise to his ambition or to some grand, elaborate plan. But to be honest, I had no grand plan. I was always just trying to keep myself out of the poorhouse.
>
> (BFA 16: 374)

The novel is narrated in such a way that the reader is able to confirm this as a rather euphemistic but basically accurate statement. Macheath's actions have been logical and, in light of the laws of this economic order, perfectly sensible. In every situation he has done the right thing by being willing to take risks, although without following a grand plan. The novel is not, therefore, the story of a social climber, or even the satirical revelation of a remarkable career. And Macheath is not a great individual but a well-functioning agent of the economic system: the real protagonist of the novel is the economy. Its laws determine the possibilities of the plot and the not-at-all autonomous behaviour of the characters. Even in its choice of subject matter, then, the novel is already anti-Aristotelian.[29]

The nub of the satire lies in the fact that it is a petty criminal who moves up in the world to become a big business leader. The formal model of the crime novel thus comes into play as the genre 'responsible' for such objectivity. Brecht is writing a threepenny novel, after all, not a penny dreadful – but he is committed to a narrative tradition which, in its ironic emphasis, does not lay claim to its aesthetic standard through psychological approaches and empathetic reception but which makes demands of the intellect, even if these demands are considered trivial. He sees the advantage of the crime novel in his 'healthy' schema:

> It is crucial that the plot is not developed based on the characters but that the characters are developed based on the plot. We see people's acts in a fragmented way. We are kept in the dark about their motives and have to deduce them in a logical manner. Their interests are assumed to have a decisive effect on their acts – and we are talking almost exclusively about their material interests. They are what we are looking for.[30]

The 'way a writer designs a crime novel is influenced by science' and only gives pleasure when 'causality functions in a satisfactory way'.[31] Uncovering the connections is the detective's job, but also the reader's. The genre therefore calls for active reception.

In the *Threepenny Novel*, however, unlike in the schema of the detective novel, the protagonists' actions are not concealed, so they do not need to be deduced using clues. Ulf Eisele concludes from this that, in contrast to the general consensus among scholars

---

[29] On this subject, Brecht observed ironically in a commentary, 'Über die Darstellung von Geschäften im Drama' (BFA 21: 376–377): 'Today, when a writer writes a dramatic work (or a novel) featuring business dealings, that writer has to contend with the fact that the people who would understand something of the play's (or book's) subject matter will not read it and the people who would read it will not understand anything of the subject matter. [...] One of the main arguments [...] against the depiction of business dealings in art [...] is [...]: art is too serious to concern itself with something as menial as business transactions'.
[30] Bertolt Brecht, 'Über die Popularität des Kriminalromans', BFA 22.1: 504–510. Here 505.
[31] Ibid., 506 and 507.

which sees it as a special variant of the genre, the *Threepenny Novel* is not a crime novel at all.³² No detective is required here because there is nothing to conceal and because the legal system has no interest in punishing the criminal acts which enable the system to function. This is true, but does not rule out the use of techniques usually reserved for the detective novel, and that is what we are dealing with. For the most criminal elements in the novel are not the unlawful actions of the protagonists but the conditions which facilitate and motivate those actions, and which are the main target of the satire of the system. Here too, to quote Brecht's famous statement from the *Threepenny Lawsuit*, 'actual reality has slipped into the functional' (BFA 21: 469). The reader's job, then, is to identify the real circumstances that lie behind the apparent ones, without the help of a detective within the novel. To a certain extent the reader must become a detective on his or her own initiative. The principle of detective work is also intrinsic to the novel, however, in that the competing protagonists must constantly try to see through each other's scheming in order to be able to act and thus expose the hidden causality.

It is also crucial to the satirical bite of the narrative that the protagonists are all able to identify each other as criminals. Peachum's inquiries about Macheath yield the following insight: 'Somehow this life was sliding backwards, down into the underworld. There was a time, not very long ago, when the methods of this successful gentleman had been cruder, simpler, easier for the courts to understand' (BFA 16: 112). His appearance is correspondingly ambiguous, as his business rival Aaron observes: 'for a crook he was pretty bourgeois, but for a bourgeois he was pretty crooked' (BFA 16: 178). Conversely, Macheath realises during his negotiations with the businesspeople that he is in the company of criminals:

> They're trying to cheat me? I do everything I can to get on the straight and narrow, I refrain from any kind of violence, I follow the rules slavishly or at least fairly closely, I turn my back on where I came from [...] and my first experience here in these higher echelons is of people trying to rob me! Is this supposed to be more moral than what I used to do? It's less so! We simple crooks are no match for these people.
>
> (BFA 16: 140)

During his negotiations with the merchants, he feels as though 'he had fallen in with a gang of highwaymen' (BFA 16: 181), and describes their practices thus: 'So first robbery and then murder. On the highway it's the other way around – murder comes first' (BFA 16: 238). And once he has reached the finishing line and is negotiating with other banks in his capacity as a bank manager, he realises:

> They're just waiting for their chance to strike a deal. [...] All this haggling disgusts me, a former gangster! Here I sit, quibbling over percentages. Why don't I just take my knife and stab them with it if they don't give me what I want? [...] All this hiding behind judges and court bailiffs is so undignified! It's demeaning. Enough to make you lose all self-respect. But you don't get anywhere these days with simple, natural, unpretentious street robbery. It no more resembles today's business practices than a sailing ship resembles a steam ship.
>
> (BFA 16: 358)

---

³²See also Ulf Eisele, *Die Struktur des modernen Romans* (Tübingen: Niemeyer, 1984), 210–256. Here 219ff.

Consequently, he has to acknowledge that he must become a burgher if he wants to take bigger prey. This does not constitute a rejection of criminality, but in submitting to the laws of economic rationality he is opening up new opportunities for himself:

> He was beset by a real thirst for solidity. A certain amount of honesty and contractual fidelity – of human reliability, pure and simple – was essential in major business deals! Or else why would honesty be so highly valued, he wondered, if it wasn't really necessary? The entire middle class was built upon it, after all.
>
> (BFA 16: 222)

Thus something like a norm or a standard is introduced into the satire of the system after all, albeit in the form of a useful ideology which in no way dictates people's actions and does not commit the police, the courts or the church to anything at all. It is above all an ingenious artistic device on Brecht's part to select as the protagonist of a novel which centres on the equivalence of business and crime, of respectable burghers and gangsters, a criminal who discovers to his astonishment that his decision to shift his activities over to the right side of the law changes nothing whatsoever. Macheath's journey of discovery enables Brecht to satirically expose the criminality of business, given that Macheath is a specialist in all things criminal. The perspective generated in this way makes the events of the novel strange and at the same time makes clear that acting in accordance with the standards of individual and social bourgeois morality would not be expedient under the circumstances. Only those who act in an immoral and criminal way are acting rationally, by simply adapting to the opportunities available to them.

What is thereby made visible, in satirical affirmation, are the laws of value-added production. They are ideologically justified by the Biblical parable of the talents, in which the servants are supposed to use the talents entrusted to them to generate a profit.[33] The servant who does not turn a profit is punished. The parable is endorsed by the novel and only outside of the novel, in the Epilogue, is there something approaching a refutation of it, in the form of the soldier Fewkoombey's dream.[34] The dreaming character is the detective's means of discovery in the crime novel. Fewkoombey, in his existential distress, has the desire to understand his circumstances but not the intellectual or mental capacity to do so. So he dreams, partly about his own circumstances and thus without consequences. And Fewkoombey himself is then sacrificed for the crimes (now declared a scandal) of those who successfully generate a profit from their talents; he is 'sentenced to death and hanged, in the presence and to the applause of a large crowd of small traders, seamstresses, invalid soldiers and beggars' (BFA 16: 391). Thus, paradoxically, the judgement of a corrupt justice system is applauded by the victims of the system themselves.

Like the thoughts expressed in the italicised passages, the dream cannot actually be ascribed to the character to whom the narrative voice attributes it. Instead, it is the objective content of the situation which is articulated here. In reified reality, the characters are functional mediums for the reflection of the narrated subject matter, which is objectively interpreted by them without what is said being overtaken by their subjectivity. In this way the anti-Aristotelian novel solves the problem arising from the fact that, in this modern,

---

[33] Luke 19, 12-28; also Matthew 25, 14-30.
[34] See also Klaus-Detlef Müller, 'Die Fewkoombey-Handlung als Erkenntnismedium' in *Bertolt Brecht. Epoche – Werk – Wirkung*, ed. Klaus-Detlef Müller (Munich: Beck, 1985), 195–197.

abstract world, characters are no longer available to the novel-writer[35] – and yet the novel still needs characters. In Brecht's work these characters are not independent individuals who invite identification and empathy and can be understood via introspection. At most, they function as character masks who give information about reality without having to account for it. The narrative voice which attributes this information to them must align itself with them: it shows how the useful social ideology is effortlessly used and abused by businesspeople, the justice system and the church, and it shows the petty bourgeoisie's self-destructive belief in ideology and the deluded behaviour of the lower classes who welcome the thing that destroys them. The narrative gestus, then, is mimicry of everything that is wrong with the world, a contradiction that is resolved by irony and satire.

3

It is difficult to determine whether satirical representation is obligatory for the anti-Aristotelian novel,[36] but it does define Brecht's other two novel projects, at any rate: the fragmentary *The Business Affairs of Mr Julius Caesar* (BFA 17: 163–390) and the drafts for the *Tui-Novel* (BFA 17: 9–161). It enables a writing style that engages with representationalism but also maintains a distance that makes things strange and thus eliminates the gestus of direct instruction from the commentary function which is so fundamental to Brecht's functional understanding of literature, in favour of an entertaining approach.

With the *Caesar* novel Brecht enters the realm of the historical novel, which was highly regarded among exile authors. The project can be traced back to a plan for a play whose subject matter he describes in a letter to Karl Korsch as a 'Threepenny history'.[37] At the same time, however, he declares that he is deviating from common practice by not aiming to bring it up to date: 'I don't want to do an allegorical play; conditions were so different in antiquity. […] The difficulty: Caesar nevertheless represents progress, and the inverted commas around progress are extremely difficult to dramatise'.[38]

I cannot devote much space here to an examination of the quite remarkable depiction of Roman history contained in the novel; I will discuss it only insofar as the narrative approach justifies and determines it or, conversely, arises from it. The praxis of the

---

[35] See also Bertolt Brecht, 'Gibt es noch Charaktere für den modernen Romanschriftsteller?', BFA 21: 132–133.
[36] In the context of the so-called realism debate, following what was for him an intolerable criticism of the *Threepenny Novel* by Alfred Kantorowiczs – who judged it an 'idealistic book' – Brecht writes a letter to Johannes R. Becher in early/mid-January 1935 objecting to the theory (completely absurd, in Brecht's eyes) that 'the entire genre of satire is excluded [from realism], because it is not realistic' (BFA 28: 478). For Brecht, Swift and Cervantes are realistic authors, as is Hašek.
[37] Bertolt Brecht, letter to Karl Korsch in late October/early November 1937, BFA 29: 58. Brecht has no problem switching between genres and mediums, since dramatic representation and narrative are already part of epic theatre. The same goes (in the same thematic field) for epic narration and film: a film exposé for the director William Dieterle (see Bertolt Brecht, *Journal*: 8.4.1942, BFA 27: 80–81) is turned, without major changes, into one of the most fascinating of the *Tales from the Calendar*: 'Caesar and his Legionnaire' (BFA 18: 389–404). See also Müller, *Brecht-Kommentar* (see footnote 2), 343–346. In both cases the epic form is limited by the fact that it will be either difficult or impossible to realise in theatre and film, but this does not make it a compromise.
[38] BFA 29: 57. In a letter to Karl Korsch in April 1938, he retracted this opinion as a result of the work he had done on the novel: 'Certain "positive" aspects of Caesar, which initially I did not want to simply overlook as a preconception, soon went up in smoke when I started to study them further. The question "positive for whom?" made everything clearer' (BFA 29: 92).

anti-Aristotelian novel is different here from that of the *Threepenny Novel*. And the justification in the surviving paratexts is more explicit, because Brecht wanted to argue the case for his views on the novel: he had been put on the defensive in the so-called realism debate, which was rather absurd given that Brecht – compared to the dogmatic stance of Georg Lukács and his disciples – was advocating by far the more modern view.

In this context Brecht reflects on the concept of the 'artistic act':

> If I choose a particular narrative position (or to put it better: if I am compelled to adopt a particular narrative position), then only very specific effects are available to me, my material is organised in line with that perspective, my verbal and visual resources are all allocated in a specific direction, drawn from a specific pool; a certain amount (and no more) of my readers' imagination is available to me, I can make use of their experiences to such-and-such an extent, their emotions are aroused in such-and-such a way, etc. The narrative position is not, of course, a coherent, constant, non-contradictory thing.[39]

In the *Caesar* novel, the narrative position as such is not a coherent one like in the *Threepenny Novel*; the book is narrated by various characters with different interests, and consequently from different perspectives. The satire arises from the confrontation of these different points of view in a quasi-objective form, more on the level of the *histoire* than that of the *discours*.

The primary narrative voice is identified as the young scholar who, twenty years after Caesar's death, wants to write his biography and starts to conduct research and collect material for it. He starts from an already consolidated view of the founder of the empire as one of the great men of history, even though he knows that his 'idol' (BFA 17: 171) systematically curated his own image for posterity and that this image does not therefore represent historical truth. The planned biography, however, proves impossible to write because the sources and the information provided by Caesar's contemporaries not only confound the scholar's expectations (i.e. his research hypothesis) but even call into question the possibility of writing biographical historiography per se. By actually presenting the reader with the documents being examined by the scholar, the novel gives an account of a failed attempt at a biography. Brecht is here pursuing an early observation on the theory of the novel which he published under the title 'A Little Piece of Advice About Producing Documents' and in which he describes the autobiography of the 'egregious liar' and snob Frank Harris as 'much more interesting than almost anything currently being written in the way of novels' (BFA 21: 163–165. Here 163).

In the *Caesar* novel, shifting the narrative focus to the reproduction of the documents means that the scholar as the narrative voice is relegated to the margins, and essentially left with only one – admittedly vital – mediating function. The most important fictitious documents are the diaries of Caesar's secretary Rarus, which are in the possession of the banker Mummlius Spicer. But Spicer refuses to grant access to the diaries until the scholar concedes, more in jest than in earnest, that economic details such as lists of corn prices could provide evidence of historical facts. The records are particularly instructive from this point of view, since 'this Rarus was concerned with the business side of the ventures, and you know that side of things doesn't much interest our historians. They haven't a

---

[39] Brecht, *Journal*: 7.12.1939, BFA 26: 349.

clue what short selling is'.[40] Spicer sells (!) the information only on condition that he is allowed to add his own annotations to the material; these annotations depart further and further from Rarus's records from the third book onwards. Spicer becomes increasingly enthusiastic about the project. And in the later, unfinished books, which would have dealt with the Gallic War, his memories would have become the most important source. Ironically, however, it is precisely the (initially only feigned) interest in the business affairs of Julius Caesar which scuppers the planned biography and feeds into Spicer's sarcastic report on the Roman economy in the final years of the Republic. The subject of the narrative also moves towards the problems of historiography, as a result of which the novel becomes increasingly self-reflexive.

This brings two more characters' perspectives into play. The lawyer Afranius Carbo, who is working as a legal adviser to a trust, is very excited about the project: 'The concept of empire! Democracy! Ideas of progress! At last, a book written in a scholarly way which both the common man *and* the man in the City can read' (BFA 17: 192). He complains of a lack of historical sense which has meant that the opportunity has been missed 'to paint commerce itself, and its ideals, in the best light. The great, democratic ideals!' (ibid.) 'We've forgotten that we are plebeians. You are, Spicer is, and I am. Don't say it doesn't matter anymore. That in itself is the great achievement: the fact that it doesn't matter anymore. That's all Caesar's doing.' (BFA 17: 196). It is ironic, again, that a historical work is hereby envisaged which the scholar does not want to write because he is following a 'literary plan' (BFA 17: 192), but which does actually end up being produced in the form of a novelistic account of the failed project – even if it is in the shape of documents with a very different message from that which Carbo was expecting.

A different viewpoint again is provided by the poet Vastius Alder, who is himself introduced as a garrulous aesthete and who in turn describes Caesar from the perspective of a pointedly sarcastic satire:

> A great man [...] the kind of figure historians need. The man of the people and the man of the Senate. The kind of person that is copied from one book to the next over thousands of years. [...] I doubt [...] whether a poet who was inclined to write about him would be able to manage more than a couple of lines. [...] As far as poetry is concerned, the man we are talking about is something Brutus stuck his sword into. You can say it a thousand times: the founder of the empire, a dealer on a global scale! He doesn't take on a patina, this dealer.
>
> (BFA 17: 303–304)

Alder's written-down monologue is many times the 'couple of lines' he granted the poet on the subject of this 'dealer', and he feels compelled, as Spicer contemptuously observes, to 'write down his prattle straight away' (BFA 17: 306).

Another disappointment awaits the scholar when he meets one of Caesar's former legionnaires, from whom he hopes to learn something of the army's 'reverent adoration for the great general' (BFA 17: 188). (The scholar feels that Spicer's statements did not do justice to 'the real Caesar'). The laconic remarks of the veteran – who only saw the general twice, from a long way off, in Gaul – do not give him much more to go on. When asked what Caesar looked like, the legionnaire simply says 'spent' (BFA 17: 191). The

---

[40]Bertolt Brecht, *Die Geschäfte des Herrn Julius Caesar*, BFA 17: 169.

narrator can only lament 'people's inability to see greatness for what it is' (ibid.) What he fails to notice is the fact that the legionnaire's reluctant testimony about his living conditions is already included in its entirety in an exemplary tale of plebeian life, and thus confirms what the subsequently reproduced documents attest to as historical truth.

The documents and the testimony of contemporary witnesses, then, do not supply any material for the biography of one of the great individuals of history, but they do provide evidence for a depiction of an important phase in Roman history which refutes the prejudices of contemporary and later historiography and also takes issue with them. Caesar is the protagonist of the novel but he is not its subject; the world of the novel does not revolve around him. He appears in a strict extrospection, in a perspective which Brecht called cinematic: 'the individual motivations of the characters are omitted, and their inner lives are never the main cause and seldom the principal result of the plot; characters are seen from the outside'.[41] The narrative voices are separate from Caesar; there is no introspection at all, no opportunity to empathise and no attempt to use the quirks of his personality or his subjective motivation to justify his behaviour. In this sense, *The Business Affairs of Julius Caesar* can be described as an anti-Aristotelian novel. Brecht applied the principle of desubjectification, which is founded in a modern conception of reality, to the historical material, making it the object of a materialist understanding of history. This, admittedly, caused problems when it came to the novel's reception. Even Walter Benjamin and Fritz Sternberg, 'very highly qualified intellectuals' who were familiar with Brecht's intentions and his writing style, did not, as Brecht wrote in his *Journal*, 'understand the book and they urged me to put in more human interest, more of the old novel!'.[42] Although he could not help but regard this as absurd and in conflict with his chosen novelistic form, he did mention in his work notes that 'the characters need to be clearer – almost all of them do. Rarus needs to contribute to small-town gossip' (BFA 17: 364).

This would change nothing about the overall concept, however. In a fragment from the fourth book, Rarus is told he would be the ideal person to write a 'biography of the celebrated Julius', a very special type of 'biography of businesspeople and [...] their representatives'. Rarus' objection that such a biography would not give an impression of Caesar's character is rebutted with the observation: 'No other account would be able to make a character out of your Julius. [...] Your master is not an individual, but merely the most visible part of a powerful, pernicious entity which is constantly changing its appearance' (BFA 17: 371–371).

Brecht privately acknowledged the problems that had been identified with the novel project. In his *Journal*, he states: 'The entire "Caesar" concept is inhuman. On the other hand, inhumanity cannot be represented without also giving an idea of what humanity looks like', and not from a modern-day perspective but within the historical era itself, whereby the narrated events are effectively 'a cold world' and can therefore only take shape within a 'cold work'.[43] It is important to avoid the impression that 'things had

---

[41]Brecht, *Dreigroschenprozeß* (see footnote 10), 465. See also: Bertolt Brecht, 'Glossen zu Stevenson', BFA 21: 107–108.
[42]Brecht, *Journal*: 26.2.1939, BFA 26: 331.
[43]Brecht, *Journal*: 25.7.1938, BFA 26: 314–315.

to happen the way they did', a common idea which has 'turned historiographers into fatalists'.[44]

The solution to this problem of representation, according to Brecht, is a satirical writing style[45] which has to be 'naturally funny'.[46] This has stylistic consequences:

> The Rarus sections necessitate a poor style, if poor style is understood to be inelegant, careless and stilted. 'Beauties' are in the structural line. [...] The Spicer sections allow for better reflections, and the satirical element is more direct, whereas the structural element has an impoverishing effect.[47]

If Spicer, like Carbo and Alder, is a satirical voice, he is not one designed to orient the text towards a norm accepted by the reader, such as the 'humanity' referred to by Brecht. Instead, he is a lawyer who serves business interests in the City. As the son of a freed slave, he was initially the court bailiff responsible for Caesar – this alone is a relationship ripe for satire – and once Caesar's debts have reached gigantic proportions, Spicer (in his role as a banker) becomes his manager, and in the Gallic War his overseer, so that Alder is justified in calling Caesar Spicer's 'employee' (BFA 17: 306). Spicer is also the reader and censor of Caesar's *De bello Gallico*: 'I went through the manuscript very thoroughly [...] I don't think there was anything interesting left in it' (BFA 17: 376).

The satire arises, therefore, from the contrast between the glorified image of Caesar and lived reality. Spicer admits that Caesar has stature, but what he understands by this is something rather singular:

> Don't think [...] I don't see him as a great man. [...] I do see him as a great man, one of the greatest. He's exactly what great men are like. [...] Once you set him on the right track, he got on with things very proficiently. [...] You said he has no character, but who does in politics? [...] To me, the greatest thing about Caesar was always the fact that he had no opinions whatsoever.
>
> (BFA 17: 384)

The satirical voice integral to the novel, then, does not set itself up in opposition to Caesar and the inhuman aspect of the 'cold world', but justifies both from the perspective of the interests they represent. The satire is therefore objective, as in the *Threepenny Novel* and Swift's *Modest Proposal*. It provokes the reader, who, however, is by no means called upon to take Caesar's side against Spicer's destructive sarcasm, but must distance himself from them both by realising that they are two sides of the same coin. Like in the *Threepenny Novel*, the protagonist's success in the *Caesar* novel is not the result of a 'grand plan', but the consequence of a constellation in which Caesar is actually much less autonomous and less free than Macheath. He is not the subject, but the largely dependent medium of the events in the novel.

---

[44]Brecht, *Journal*, ibid. 23.7.1938, ibid., 312. See also Brecht's working note 'Fatalismus der Deterministen', BFA 17: 386–387.
[45]In a letter to the American Guild for Cultural Freedom, Brecht mentions a 'satirical novel [...] with a strictly historical foundation' (BFA 29: 110–111. Here 111). In a note, he writes of the *Caesar* novel: it 'is a historical novel, it calls for an extensive study of Roman history. It is satirical' (Bertolt Brecht, 'Über den formalistischen Charakter der Realismustheorie', BFA 22.1: 437–445. Here 437).
[46]Bertolt Brecht, letter to Martin Domke on 19.11.1937, BFA 29: 61–64. Here 63.
[47]Brecht: *Journal*: 21.9.1939, BFA 26: 349–350.

4

It may be a little dubious to claim that two literary texts and a series of theoretical statements constitute their own genre. Brecht did not manage to produce a third example: the (overly) ambitious *Tui-Novel*, which was a long time in the planning, never made it past the fragment stage, and remained a collection of elaborated materials. The 'formal difficulties' (BFA 22.1: 438) remained unsolved, and the drafted models proved to be manifestly unsuitable or unfeasible. The surviving drafts are a brilliant satirical *Verfremdung* of the history of the Weimar Republic, though without specific insights or intrinsic aesthetic value. The fragment lacks a central plot, and it lacks striking characters. Although the autonomy and independent significance of such characters is systematically disputed by the anti-Aristotelian novel, they are clearly indispensable to its ability to tell a story.

If I stand by the term 'anti-Aristotelian novel' (which was actually introduced fairly casually by Brecht), it is because of the unique profile of the *Threepenny Novel* and *The Business Affairs of Mr Julius Caesar* in the history of the genre of the classic modern novel. Challenging the concept of the autonomous individual as the subject of a novel is, as previously mentioned, not original – almost all important authors start from the same assumption – but in Brecht's work it is not a matter for reflection and introspection as it is with these other authors, but the representative principle of the novelistic universe. The consequence of this, however, is that the narrative voice gains in importance, not as a character but as an organisational principle and implicit commentator. Here Brecht is applying the epic gestus of his theatrical theory to the epic genre and at the same time adopting an 'avant-garde' position in the controversy with Georg Lukács. Given its specific profile, the anti-Aristotelian novel seems to me to represent an important contribution to the novel of classical modernity.

The Short Stories

CHAPTER TWENTY-FIVE

The Subject Herr Keuner: Towards a Brechtian Ethics

SONIA ARRIBAS

1. MARXISM AND ETHICS

Although the Marxist idea according to which the determination of subjective life by material life (i.e. by the economy) has been historically fundamental to Leftist movements, politics, theory and art, it is also true that today a great amount of Leftist theory and politics does not want to deal directly with economic problems, and concentrates instead on cultural, identity or 'merely political' issues.[1] In fact, today a great deal of Leftist theory and politics reject Marxism altogether, and with this rejection also goes a great part of its intellectual and artistic inheritance, including of course that of Brecht's corpus. According to this contemporary understanding, then, Brecht's Marxism is to be erased or put aside as if it didn't exist or as if it were a failure of his that we are supposed to bracket –or at most consider his personal mistake.

The tenor of contemporary criticisms of Marxism generally underlines how it collapses the irreducible autonomy and contingency of political, symbolic, ethical and subjective life into the objectivistic metalanguage of the economy. The individual is always and necessarily inserted in a wider context (the social and the economic); and this wider context, when fully taken into account, does not leave any space for the wealth of the individual, for her ethical life, for her responsibility, for the complexity of life. This is a problem that is seen to pervade the entire tradition of Marxism, starting obviously with Marx. It is thus argued that Marxism dangerously tends to a very strong reductionism that prevents any correct explanation of subjectivity, particularity and multiplicity, and the ways in which these express themselves in history via contingency, free play, and creativity. Historical materialism, so the argument goes, enacts inexorable and abstract laws of history as if these were capable of being formulated scientifically, the consequence being that no space is left for the theorization of the possibility of random events, the singular agency of subjects, or the expression of discursive differences and modes of

---

Sonia Arribas, 'The Subject Herr Keuner: Towards a Brechtian Ethics', *Brecht Yearbook*, 35 (2010), pp. 2–23.

[1] I use the expression 'merely political' following Marx, 'Introduction to A Contribution to the Critique of Hegel's Philosophy of Right', *Deutsch-Fratnzösische Jahrbücher* (February 1844). Reprinted in www.marxists.org/archive/marx/works/1843/critique-hpr/intro.htm (March 2009).

existence.[2] This is its purported scientific and mechanistic flaw, the claim according to which Marxism explains away real history in its construction of all-encompassing and deterministic cause-effect laws of history, where no accidents and lived experience are allowed to be perceived at all. But it also amounts to its metaphysical inclinations, the fact that it tends to see all social reality through the lenses of class analysis, as if the only real and existing subject were the proletariat, destined to appropriate history through its praxis. Ernesto Laclau has termed this problem of Marxism its 'Platonic cave of class reductionism'.[3] In its stubborn emphasis on class, Marxism was wrong in that it didn't conceive of other forms of identity formation besides class (e.g. gender, race, nation, etc.); in that it only conceptualized the working class in terms of production, and not in terms of symbolic or other kinds of historical experience;[4] and, finally, in that it ended up having a naïve faith in the missionary and revolutionary role of the proletariat: it expected that once the proletariat had learned of its subjective position and implication in the capitalist mode of production, this self-consciousness would ineluctably and radically transform history.

More specifically, as pertains to the contemporary rejection of Brecht's Marxist affiliation, which is what primarily interests us here, it is usually claimed that his lack of a proper account of subjective wealth is clearly noticeable in his disdain for humanist concerns. This disdain is concomitant to his modernist appraisal of scientific experimentation and economic production, and to his belief in useful scientific and economic knowledge. Thus, Brecht is depicted as someone who believes in a form of artistic creation that simply mirrors technical skill, as both are rooted in the collective and emancipatory development of industrial production.[5] It should be stated, however, that nobody affirms that Brecht fell prey to the belief in a historical (economic or technological) force that would achieve a predetermined revolutionary goal.[6] Rather, his problem has something to do, according to his critics, with his incapacity to properly theorize the subject. Indeed, it was another Marxist, Georg Lukács, who already pointed at how Brecht's characters were merely abstract functions in a formal dialectical method of class struggle: disembodied, not really individualized figures totally emptied out of psychological traits.[7] This tendency to abstraction is certainly compatible with what other critics have perceived as his contempt for individual or personal issues, which vanish to nothing in the face of his paramount concern with the collective (be it the factory, the army, or the government) or with the

---

[2]For a very good summary of poststructuralist criticisms of Marxism, see Barbara Foley, 'Marxism in the Poststructuralist Moment: Some Notes on the Problem of Revising Marx', *Cultural Critique* 15 (Spring 1990): pp. 5–37.

[3]Ernesto Laclau, *Politics and Ideology in Marxist Theory: Capitalism-Fascism-Populism* (London: New Left Books, 1976), p. 12.

[4]Jean Baudrillard, *The Mirror of Production*, trans. Mark Poster (St. Louis, Mo.: Telos Press, 1975).

[5]See Eugene Lunn, 'Marxism and Art in the Era of Stalin and Hitler: A Comparison of Brecht and Lukács', *New German Critique* 3 (Autumn, 1974): pp. 12–44,

[6]Engels and Bebel wrote in the 1890's that the revolution could be foreseen scientifically, and this became the main premise of orthodox Marxism. See David McLellan, *Marxism after Marx. An Introduction* (Boston: Houghton Mifflin, 1979), pp. 31–32.

[7]Georg Lukács, 'Reportage or Portrayal', in Rodney Livingstone ed. *Essays on Realism*, trans. David Fernbach (Cambridge, MA: MIT Press, 1981), pp. 45–75, and Georg Lukács, 'Aus der Not eine Tugend', *Marxismus und Literatur: Eine Dokumentation in drei Bänden*, ed. Fritz Raddack, 2 (Reinbeck bei Hamburg: Rohwolt, 1969), pp. 166–177.

belief in a collectivist orientation.[8] In fact, as Marc Silberman contends, 'Brecht insisted, of course, on a political and sociological definition of class as the primary or hegemonic articulation of subject identity,'[9] with the consequence that he was sometimes unaware of 'a much more complex intersecting of needs, demands, fears, and desires'.[10]

So even if Brecht himself conceived of his work as a 'new, social and antimetaphysical art',[11] his alleged use of an epistemological model of 'false consciousness' as applied to the subject could be easily criticized as falling prey to metaphysics. That Brecht *only* used a model of false or reified consciousness for his ideological critique of culture is an argument that is repeated, even by those commentators who are generally very sympathetic towards his work.[12] What this model usually entails is a clear-cut differentiation between an ideological bourgeois consciousness, absolutely and illusorily embedded in a false representation of the economic base, and the real active consciousness of the proletariat.[13] It is metaphysical to the extent that proletarian subjectivity is seen as more authentic and ontologically more aware of the actual conditions of existence than its counterpart, bourgeois morality, but also in that the economic base is established as having ontological priority to the ideological superstructure, which serves as a disguise of real material interests, and which is supposed to float substanceless on top of the base. Not only juridical and state institutions and practices, but also subjective claims to universal morality or individual ethics are seen, according to this model of false consciousness, to be part of the ideological framework of the capitalist mode of production that illusorily presents itself as independent, without acknowledging its ultimate determination by the real material conditions of production.[14]

It should also be emphasized that these readings of Brecht's Marxism that we are briefly putting forward here need to be located and understood historically, according to the different stages and political contexts of the reception of his work after his death. To grasp the different constellations of ideas about Brecht in this period, I will just very quickly divide it into three moments (1960s, 1970s, and 1980s–1990s); and will only refer

---

[8]Lunn, 'Marxism and Art in the Era of Stalin and Hitler', p. 27. See also Marc Silberman, 'A Postmodernized Brecht?' *Theater Journal* 75.1 (March 1993): pp. 1–19, here 19.
[9]Ibid., p. 11.
[10]Ibid., p. 10.
[11]Bertolt Brecht to Jean Renoir, in John Willett, ed., *Bertolt Brecht Letters*, trans. Ralph Manheim (New York: Routledge, 1990), p. 249.
[12]Lunn, 'Marxism and Art', p. 26. Also see Renate Rechtien, 'Relations of Production? Christa Wolf's extended engagement with the legacy of Bertolt Brecht', in *Bertolt Brecht Centenary Essays. German Monitor 41*, ed. Steve Giles and Rodney Livingstone (New York: Rodopi, 1998), pp. 196–210, here p. 201.
[13]This is the way David Bathrick describes Brecht's appropriation of Karl Korsch's Marxism: David Bathrick, 'The Dialectics of Legitimation: Brecht in the GDR,' *New German Critique* 2 (Spring 1974), pp. 80–103, here p. 102. Similarly, Bathrick also reviews some other critics of Brecht, such as Helmut Holzauer postulating that Brecht is an 'Aufklärer', who 'never goes beyond common utilitarianism just as one can speak at best of his crude historical materialism'. Ibid., p. 94.
[14]This is indeed what Karl Korsch writes about false consciousness, precisely in relationship to the explanatory metaphor of the base and the superstructure, as employed by Marx in the Preface to 'A Contribution to the Critique of Political Economy' (Moscow: Progress Publishers, 1977). Reproduced in www.marxists.org/archive/marx/works/1859/critique-pol-economy/preface.htm (March 2009). See Karl Korsch, *Marxism and Philosophy* (New York: Monthly Review Press, 1970). Reproduced in www.marxists-org/archive/korsch/1923/marxism-philosophy.htm (March 2009). Korsch's explanations did serve Brecht in his approach to Marx, but -as we will see later – Brecht moved beyond the metaphysical implications of the use of the architectonic metaphor of base-superstructure.

to the artistic and philosophical reception, without properly addressing wider historical and political issues of the last 50 years. Stephen Mulke reminds us that in the 1960s Brecht's Marxist model was praised by the student movements, and taken as the main reference and source of inspiration by play and film writers such as Max Frisch, Peter Weiss, Rainer Werner Fassbinder and many others.[15] This appropriation was not without certain distancing, for, as Jane Shattuc has also argued,[16] Brecht was considered by some of these new cultural movements part of the 'old Left', i.e., the established Left that was accepted by the Left in power (the SPD in the FRG and the SED in the GDR). Although he himself a great follower of Brecht's *Verfremdungseffekt*, Fassbinder declared that his own alienation techniques were stylistic, as opposed to Brecht's, which were merely intellectual.[17] This was not entirely disconnected to Lukács' earlier claims that Brecht's *Verfremdungseffekt* tried to mistakenly bring together the method of science with that of aesthetics, and thus ran the risk of 'excessive conceptualization, of being connected from Signal System I to Signal System 2'.[18] In France, Roland Barthes had been praising Brecht since the 1950s and proclaimed that the only political theater that was taking place at that time in Europe was the one developed by the German author. In his view, it was a theater that tried to connect to the people, that owed its inspiration to historical materialism in its view of the world as class struggle, but that, contrary to any deterministic view of history, it never tried to reduce individuals to mere pawns on a chessboard, or mere signs of a historical algebra.[19] Also in France, Louis Althusser published an article on Brecht in his book *On Marx* in which he discussed Brecht's method as a critique of psychological identification and ideology,– where ideology includes morality, politics and religion.[20]

Hannah Arendt had of course a very different perspective on Brecht. In the chapter dedicated to him in her book *Men in Dark Times*, she clearly displays great admiration for his poetry, his innovation in the German language, and even for certain traits of his character (such as his lack of self-interest, or his love of anonymity, – but even in this respect she qualifies her praise, as she thinks of these as a gift he possessed which easily turned into a curse). She also recognizes the difficult times that he had to live through, not only during the exile period in Denmark and America, but also when he finally settled in the GDR and had to constantly maneuver to maintain his political independence, and to keep his art autonomous. But all in all Arendt cannot but think of Brecht as a poet who naively went beyond the limits that are assigned to poets, as he committed the worst possible mistake in being a Marxist and following the doctrinarian communist ideology. Her overall reading is to separate completely one Brecht, the exceptional witness of an epoch of darkness and catastrophe, from another Brecht, the trivial Marxist who supported the communist variety of totalitarianism.[21]

---

[15]Stephan Mahlke, 'Brecht ± Müller: German-German Brecht Images before and after 1989', *The Drama Review* 43.4 (1999): pp. 40–49, here p. 41.
[16]Jane Shattuc, '«Contra» Brecht: R. W. Fassbinder and Pop Culture in the Sixties', *Cinema Journal* 33.1 (Autumn 1993): pp. 35–54.
[17]Ibid., p. 37.
[18]Georg Lukács, 'On Bertolt Brecht', *New Left Review* 1/110 (July-August 1978): pp. 88–92, here p. 92.
[19]Roland Barthes, *Oeuvres completes. Tome I. 1942-1965* (Paris: Seuil, 1983), here p. 754.
[20]Louis Althusser, 'Piccolo Teatro: Bertolazzi and Brecht. Notes on a Materialist Theater', in *For Marx* (New York: Pantheon, 1969): pp. 129–151.
[21]Hannah Arendt, *Men in Dark Times* (New York: Harcourt, Brace and World, 1968).

In the 1970s, and certainly due to Heiner Müller's well-deserved rise, it was generally accepted that Brecht had introduced a very important new angle into theater that had to be pursued by the new generations of writers. However, what was felt as Brecht's orthodox Marxism was seen to impose a very rigid and conventional structure onto the writing process, one that didn't allow for new experimentations. Müller stated that the only way to remain faithful to Brecht was by strongly criticizing him. He thus argued that instead of attending to the essential contradictoriness of the social, Brecht's Marxism just tried to offer very quick ethical solutions. And this was more so the case in parables such as *Geschichten vom Herr Keuner*, which were seen to be very rigid in that they adhered to fixed systems of reference, at least in comparison with another master of parables, Kafka and his suggestive alienating effects.[22] Müller hence tried to develop Brecht's conception of gestus, but now in order to show contradictions at a micrological and subjective level, leaving open and mainly undecided the path of action of the characters, thus eliminating from his work what was characterized as Brecht's dialectical machine of readymade solutions.

Stephan Mahlke argues that, except for a few names, Müller's image of Brecht still dominated in the 1980s and 1990s, and especially since 1989.[23] During this period, Brecht tended to be condemned on moral grounds, that is, as the last representative, in art, of the dangers of a highly ideological and even totalitarian epoch. What was to be rescued in Brecht, partially following Müller, was the non-Marxist Brecht, i.e. the great creator of the *Verfremdungseffekt*, – now merely understood as an example of sophisticated humor and postmodern irony – , or as the theorist of *Gestus*, – merely tantamount to Nietzschean or Artaudian figures of excess. One great exception that we should obviously keep in mind is Fredric Jameson's critique of this outlook in *Brecht and Method*,[24] which steered clear of any culinary and not-useful (Brecht's words, of course) reading of Brecht, and never renounced his Marxist allegiance.

Now, if these are the main coordinates from which Brecht's Marxism has been received and analyzed, it should come as no surprise the difficulty that one encounters today when trying to study the more specific Marxian ethics that could follow from his approach. There is obviously no space in this article to discuss in depth the wider issue of Marxism and ethics, although above I have already pointed at a few problems. The relationship between Marxism and ethics has been extensively investigated by Marxists and non-Marxists alike, although today not with the same intensity as it was done till the 1980s or early 1990s. This is certainly because of the crude problems that we have already mentioned with respect to Marxism in general, but also as a consequence of the global political situation since 1989. For the sake of argument, I will just roughly distinguish between three extreme, but quite generalized, positions that have been traditionally

---

[22]Ibid. pp. 43–4, and Heiner Müller, 'Fatzer ± Keuner', in Frank Hörnig, ed., *Schriften. Werke* Vol. 8, (Frankfurt am Main: Suhrkamp, 2005): pp. 223–231. Müller also denounces Brecht's paternalism, which he interprets as functional with respect to DDR politics.

[23]Mahlke, 'Brecht ± Müller', pp. 47–8. The main exception is Einar Schleef's 1996 production of *Herr Puntila und sein Knecht Matti*. The dominating tendency is represented by Hans-Thies Lehmann, 'Schlaglichter auf den anderen Brecht', in *The Other Brecht I* (Madison: University of Wisconsin Press, 1992); and Joachim Fiebach, 'Bilder der Großen Kapitulation. Brechts Dekonstruktionspotential', in Marc Silberman, ed., *drive b: brecht 100* (Berlin: Theater der Zeit, 1997). See also the controversial biography: John Fuegi, *Brecht & Co. Sex, Politics, and the Making of the Modern Drama* (New York: Grove Press, 1994).

[24]Fredric Jameson, *Brecht and Method* (London: Verso, 1998).

advanced with respect to the relationship of ethics and Marxism. We will see below that they share very crucial presuppositions, all of which need to be criticized.

The three positions on Marxism and ethics are: (1) Marxism guarantees that a fully socialist society entails an entirely moral and ethical individual. This is the radical position of Lukács in 1919, which is based on the belief that such a society is possible at 'the point at which individual and class interests converge' and due to 'increased production, a rise in productivity and a corresponding strengthening of labour discipline'.[25] It has its origin in Marx's own claim, put forward in the 1844 *Economic and Philosophical Manuscripts*, according to which in a communist society individual being and human species being would coalesce in the full development of their capacities. As the above quote makes clear, it entails a very deterministic view of productivity as the motor of social change.[26] Lukács adds to this utopian view the idea that in such a society there would be no need for legality, which he understands as merely compulsive and restrictive with respect to the individual and collective goal of freedom.

(2) Marxism and morality are incompatible. Marxism shows that any claim to abstract universality–in the form of human rights, for instance – forms part of the ideological and superstructural framework of society. This is, for instance, Steven Lukes' thesis, based on his reconstruction of Marx's views about morality in *The German Ideology* (with Engels), the *Critique of the Gotha Programme*, and some passages in *Capital* in which Marx criticizes Proudhon's abstract views of equality and justice.[27] According to Marxism, Lukes maintains, any conception of abstract universality in the form of rights or obligation, as valid for all members of society, and as autonomous of particular interests is necessarily ideological. And by ideological he means 'spurious' and 'illusory': 'They serve to conceal the real function of principles of Recht, which is to protect the social relations of the existing order.'[28] Marxism's main task, therefore, is to unmask and unveil this self-portrayal of morality by showing the real bourgeois interests that it serves. Lukes doesn't do it in this article, but one could possibly argue that it would follow from this position that the only morality that is not illusory is some kind (or ideal?) of proletarian ethics, one that does not disguise its interests in false universal claims.

(3) Finally, the idea has been put forward that a defense of ethics and legality would require abandoning Marxism, whilst still being 'Marxist'. This was, for instance, Drucilla Cornell's extremely paradoxical reply to Lukes' essay in *Praxis International*. Her views on what it meant to be a Marxist amounted to the defense of a theory of justice based on abstract principles of right such as those proposed by Jürgen Habermas in his jurisprudential model of communication and formation of discursive will. It obviously exceeds the limits

---

[25]Georg Lukács, 'The Role of Morality in Communist Production', *Political Writings, 1919-1929* (London: N.L.B., 1972). Reproduced in: www.marxists.org/archive/lukacs/works/1919/morality.htm (March 2009). See also Agnes Heller's critique of Lukács: Agnes Heller, 'The Legacy of Marxian Ethics Today', *Praxis International* 4 (1981): pp. 356–364, here pp. 358–9.
[26]Agnes Heller offers a good reconstruction of Marx's and certain Marxists' (Plekhanov, Lenin, Bauer, Kautsky and Lukács, amongst others) views on morality, also with respect with the problem of alienation, which I cannot discuss here. Her own position, after rightfully dismissing Marxism's tendency to metaphysics (what she terms its 'commitment to the absolute'), too quickly lapses into what I here describe as position (3): a defense of the liberal post-Marxism of Jürgen Habermas. Ibid., pp. 360–3.
[27]Steven Lukes, 'Can a Marxist Believe in Human Rights?' *Praxis International* 4 (1981): pp. 334–345. He also discusses Engels' *Anti-Dühring*, Lenin's claim at the 1920 Komsomol Congress that in Marxism there is not a grain of ethics, as well as Trotsky's pamphlet *Their Morals and Ours*.
[28]Ibid., p. 342.

of this article to discuss in detail Habermas' theses, or Cornell's appropriation of them. However, in order to grasp the motivation that is at the basis of their position, it should suffice us to quote Cornell's own words, when she states that 'the move beyond Marx is consistent with the early Marx's underlying critique of right and with his staunch support of the free press and of universal suffrage'.[29] Except the adjective 'Marxist', not much of Marx is left in her (or arguably in Habermas') position.[30] As explicitly stated, the idea is to 'move beyond Marx' as Marxism (and it should be noted that by Marxism Cornell only takes into consideration Lukes' version of Marxism) is incapable of having a proper account of ethics, and concomitantly tends to dangerously negate legality. This mistake 'undoubtedly has its roots in the later Marx's own reliance on scientific rhetoric',[31] so the only thing that is worth rescuing in Marx, she concludes, is the liberal impulse that inspires his early writings. We can also dismiss as 'scientific' the analysis of the economy or of the capitalist mode of production.

I would like to claim that what these three positions about Marxism and ethics share is their incapacity to articulate the subject as simultaneously knotted along the registers of the economic/social, the ethical, and the legal/juridical. It follows from this incapacity that the subject is either viewed as a pure proletarian subjectivity (Lukács and Lukes), or as a purely political (liberal) subject, as we have seen in Cornell. To put it briefly, in the utopian socialist view of Lukács, the proletarian subject is a pure economic subject, inserted in the full development of the forces of production. That is, someone who actually bypasses the problem of the juridical (which is precisely what Cornell sees as being so problematic in Marxism). Similarly, in the reductive Marxist view of Lukes, the juridical and morality are mere forms of false consciousness, that is, illusory representations of the real economic conditions of production. Nevertheless, Lukes doesn't actually derive from this view any alternative model of ethics that could allow us to properly give an account of how to conceptualize a Marxist model of an ethical subject.[32] Finally, Cornell just takes the last step of actually getting rid of Marxism altogether, with the unavoidable problem that she can only thematize the subject as a liberal one, thus completely ignoring the register of the economic (and the problem of capitalism altogether).

---

[29] Drucilla Cornell, 'Should a Marxist Believe in Rights?' *Praxis International* 4.1 (April 1984): pp. 45–56. The adjective 'Marxist' was abandoned after this debate took place, once Habermas decreed the end of Marxism, and the entrance into a new epoch of Habermasian post–Marxist discursive ethics and legality. The journal was henceforward named *Constellations*. The same move was made by Agnes Heller in 'The Legacy of Marxian Ethics Today'.
[30] A similar debate, also in the 1980s and this time around Marxism and justice, took place in the Anglo–Saxon world. It also ended up with similar conclusions. See an overall view of the debate in Norman Geras, 'The Controversy About Marx and Justice', *New Left Review* I/195 (March-April 1985): pp. 47–85. In the more specific field of analytical philosophy, see G. A. Cohen, 'Freedom, Justice and Capitalism', *New Left Review* I/126 (March-April 1981): pp. 3–16. Here Cohen argues, in a similar way to Lukes, that ideology is a form of 'illusion' and 'conceptual confusion'. He then concludes in the most Tui (Brecht's expression) way, that Marxism serves to convince capitalists of the error they live in.
[31] Cornell, 'Should a Marxist Believe in Rights?' p. 46.
[32] Only four years later Steven Lukes wrote a whole book on the issue of Marxism and morality, where he tried to prove that Marxism is by itself not enough to offer a proper account of morality, because it is 'consequentialist', 'long-range and perfectionist', and because it presumes 'to foresee the future, in which its eventual realization is somehow guaranteed, it forswears both the clarification of the long-term consequences by which alternative courses are to be judged'. Steven Lukes, *Marxism and Morality* (Oxford: Oxford University Press, 1985), p. 142 and p. 146. This is similar to what Agnes Heller calls its 'commitment to the absolute', the fact that Marxism is oblivious to real people and their subjective wealth and complexity.

What these three positions also have in common is the idea that Marxism inevitably leads to a reduction of the legal or the ethical to the metalanguage of the economy, i.e. the essentialist idea according to which the economy (the forces and relations of production) determines all modes of existence including of course ethics and subjective responsibility. This is certainly what Lukács is defending when he states that in a perfect socialist society the realization of morality is tantamount to the full development of the economy, or what Lukes is writing about when he affirms that in capitalism the ethical and the juridical are simply illusions or false representations of the actual relations of production. It is also what is lurking behind Cornell's arguments when she abandons Marxism in order to endorse an abstract model of legality in the form of ideal intersubjective or discursive ethical principles. At the end of the day, what they all presuppose is that Marxism can only think of the social in terms of the architectonic metaphor of the base and the superstructure: the idea that there is a real or material base (of real or material conflict between forces and relations of production) upon which a spurious or illusory superstructure (which includes all kinds of ideology: from religion and the juridical, to of course ethics) erects itself.

2. A BRECHTIAN ETHICS

Bertolt Brecht consistently lamented the tendency of Marxist thought to ossify into a formal and formalist framework insensitive to the wealth, and contradictoriness, of ethical experience. In what follows I would like to argue, concentrating on a text of Brecht that I have already mentioned, *Die Geschichten vom Herrn Keuner*,[33] that not only can we dismiss as false an alleged essentialism of Brecht, but also that, contrary to the contemporary rejection of his Marxist thought, the latter in fact allows for the theorization of an ethical model of action that takes into account, in one go, economic and subjective issues, material and cultural problems. My claim will be that, at his best, Brecht neither neglects economic issues, nor dismisses the subjective responsibility and fundamental contradictoriness that lies at the source of ethical actions. By carefully analyzing a few passages from the above mentioned, and wonderful, text, I will try to show that Brecht tries to integrate the political, the juridical, the ethical and/or the subjective *into* an analysis of the economic;[34] in other words, that he tries to effectively do away with the rather tried and overplayed metaphor of the ideological superstructure and the economic base. According to this metaphor, there is, on the one hand, at one level, the economy ruled by its own deterministic laws, and on the other hand, at another distinct level, the rest of life. A great amount of interpretations of Marxism maintain that Marxism effectively does away with the second level by reducing it to the determination of the economy, as if the economy were a metalanguage that could account for everything human–that could end up eliminating, in its dryness and abstraction, the contradictoriness and wealth of subjectivity. These interpretations are not entirely incorrect; as we have already seen, a great deal of Marxism has indeed tended to reduce subjectivity to the determinations of the economy.

---

[33] I follow the recent English translation by Martin Chalmers. Bertolt Brecht, *Stories of Mr. Keuner* (San Francisco: City Lights Books, 2001).

[34] The last episode in the history of the rejection of Brecht's Marxism is a recent article on Herr Keuner, in which no economic motives appear at all, and Keuner is interpreted as a merely political subject of power and resistance. See Samuel McCormick, 'The Political Identity of the Philosopher: Resistance, Relative Power, and the Endurance of Potential', *Philosophy and Rhetoric* 42.1 (Spring 2009): pp. 72–91.

Keeping this in mind, I will argue that in Brecht's model of ethics, the economy is never a metalanguage that underpins and explains political, symbolic or subjective contingency, but rather the space or field of forces where this political, symbolic, ethical or subjective contingency is allowed to irrupt or come to the fore in the first place.

Motives instead of Principles

We will begin by considering a few ethical motives in *Herr Keuner*. The first thing that I would like to argue is that from the different situations depicted in each of the stories one cannot derive universal principles in the sense of generalizations, laws or rules of action valid in any case or circumstance, or for everybody. Rather, these stories put forward ethical motives in which a subject is forced to confront or deal with a concrete situation, and whose response will necessarily have important effects on other people. What they prove is that Brecht is not operating here with a base / superstructure model of representation, i.e. that the depicted actions do not attempt to portray mediations between two supposedly distinct levels: the political and the ethical, on the one hand, and the economic or material, on the other. The reason for this lack of mediations in his mode of representation lies in the simple fact that for Brecht an ethical or political act is always already economic and material. I will also try to show that Brecht's mode of representation tries to thematize *one* single level, that of the capitalist mode of production–but one that, at any moment, can be altered, reshaped and contested by the insertion of subjectivity, or the possibility of an ethical act, or even the political, within it.

The opening of the economy by the subjective ethical act is, I would maintain, the main characteristic of Brecht's dialectical method: in his work, he carefully observes a situation in which an ethical response is required; he also reveals that this ethical response is in itself only relevant, or even made possible, by the consideration of material or economic elements (in his words: needs, satisfactions, hunger–the economic in the broadest sense), and, finally, he shows that these material elements appear to be, without the need for mediations, completely impregnated by ideas, philosophy, ideology, etc. As we shall also see, the intertwinement of ethical or subjective and economic motives will also help us explain the political struggle in which Brecht locates himself. His objective is to combat ideological (he would like to say: philosophical) attitudes that do not take into account the material motives that are necessarily intertwined with them.

I will consider and analyze, then, two kinds of motives that appear in *Herr Keuner* in order to show how Brecht tries to avoid any architectonic framework of base and superstructure. The economic, the political, the legal and the subjective co-imply each other, without gaps or mediations. In order to anticipate the meaning of the anecdotes and clarify the motive that is at stake in each case, I will also provide tentative titles to each of them. The two kinds of motives are:

1) Ethical and subjective motives
2) Ideological or philosophical motives

Ethical motives

a) *The primordiality of the practical.* In the story 'The question of whether there is a God', Brecht writes that somebody asked Herr Keuner whether God existed. Herr Keuner's reply is the following:

I advise you to consider whether, depending on the answer, your behavior would change. If it would not change, then we can drop the question. If it would change, then I can at least be of help to the extent that I can say, you have already decided: you need a God.[35]

Two aspects come to the fore in this parable, both of which point at the insertion of the subject's own position in the question that is being posed. Firstly, Brecht replies that you need to observe your own behavior. This self-observation will give you the answer to the question about God. However, the moment you ask not only about God, but also about why you are asking about God, you come to realize that the first question did not demand a theoretical answer, but rather a question about your own behavior. Secondly, Brecht writes that you have to observe what you already do, that you don't have to look for the answer somewhere else. The primordiality of the practical in Brecht's model is tantamount to the fact that the truth about yourself is something that is already there in you, that you are, so to say, already accomplishing or executing it. In the last instance, therefore, even a question about God's existence is a question about your own practice, about ethics.

b) *The truth is already there: it is a practice, it is being realized*. In 'About truth' Brecht juxtaposes the question of truth with the price one pays when buying fish:

> Deep, the student, came to Mr. Keuner, the thinking man, and said: 'I want to know the truth.' 'Which truth? The truth is well known. Do you want to know the truth about the fish trade? Or about the tax system? If, because they tell you the truth about the fish trade, you no longer pay a high price for their fish, you will never know the truth,' said Mr. Keuner.[36]

Herr Keuner needs to explain his first rather cryptic answer about the truth being well known by stating that the truth is in the very act of buying their fish. There is no need to dig very deep in order to see what is the truth of profit making, or even about production; the truth is realized each time one buys or sells. The truth is related to the subjective element of taking part in the whole (objective) process. It is known precisely because it is a practice. It is already there, being realized each time one buys or sells. One cannot find a final theoretical answer to the truth about the fishing industry, or to the truth about anything. The truth about any situation lies in the subjective and ethical insertion of the question that is being posed about the content of what is being said. Therefore, knowledge is first of all a practical thing, a process that constantly requires studying.

In a similar vein, Brecht writes in 'Socrates' that Herr Keuner doesn't like those philosophers who present things as unknowable—those who, like Socrates, claim to know nothing at all.[37] One has to study. Indeed, as Brecht's friend Walter Benjamin recalls in his texts on epic theater, Brecht had on a window ledge in his room a little donkey that nodded its head. Brecht had put a little notice around its neck that said: 'I, too, must understand it.'[38]

---

[35]Brecht, *Keuner*, p. 14.
[36]Ibid., p. 72.
[37]Ibid., p. 41.
[38]Walter Benjamin, 'Notes from Svendborg, Summer 1934', in *Selected Writings. Vol. 2. 1927–1934* (Cambridge, Mass. and London: The Belknap Press of Harvard University Press, 1999), p. 785.

c) *Procedures and formulas have nothing to say about justice and ethics*. In 'A good answer' Brecht comes up with another interesting example that can help us understand the previous idea:

> In a court a worker was asked whether he wanted to take the lay oath or swear on the Bible. He answered: 'I am unemployed.' 'This was not simply absentmindedness,' said Mr. K. 'By this answer he showed that he found himself in a situation where such questions, indeed perhaps the whole proceedings as such, have become meaningless.'[39]

Brecht is here trying to show how on certain occasions the usual set of questions about which formula to use, even more, the whole procedure, do not make any sense. But isn't the worker's comment something one would never say in front of a jury? Why? Because it belongs to an order that is presupposed, which is always already there, and which requires no further consideration. According to this implicit order, it is known that you have to have the material means that allow you to make a statement in front of a jury. However, this knowledge does not need to be explicitly discussed, it remains, so to say, in the background. One could add: it is a practice that is not even known in the sense of anyone having a full awareness of it. It is something that is being practiced. Like the truth about you or the situation in which you are, it is already there, and is effective. One could phrase this idea in a different way: the economic motive (uttered by the worker) and the statement in front of the jury (about the procedure) are in the same world, but it is as if this world was split itself in two: one side which deals with economics, another which deals with procedures, formulas, symbolic rituals, and so on. Are they in some way connected? Brecht would say that they belong to the same world, that the statement in front of the jury leads without mediations to the question of the material needs, and vice versa, that the statement about economics has also something to do with the order that allows us to presuppose certain silence about it. Brecht's dialectical thinking/acting would consist in grasping both statements simultaneously, as one reality that is split into two.

d) *'Form and content'*. There is another thought of Herr Keuner that allows us to see the necessary connection between the material needs of practical life and, in this case, art:

> Mr. K. looked at a painting that gave certain objects a very unconventional form. He said: 'When they look at the world, some artists are like many philosophers. In the effort to find a form, the content gets lost. I once worked for a gardener. He handed me a pair of shears and told me to trim a laurel tree. The tree stood in a pot and was hired out for celebrations. For that it had to have the form of a sphere. I immediately began to prune the wild shoots, but no matter how hard I tried to achieve the form of a sphere, I did not succeed for a long time. First I lopped off too much on one side, then on the other. When the tree had at last become a sphere, the sphere was very small. Disappointed, the gardener said: "God, that's the sphere, but where's the laurel?"'[40]

In this parable, Brecht is once again emphasizing the interrelation between material and practical motives and artistic or intellectual ones. One cannot lose sight of the content at the basis of the laurel, that is, one cannot erect a so-called autonomy of the form executed by the artist as it could be abstracted from the practice into which it is built. This doesn't

---

[39] Brecht, *Keuner*, p. 33.
[40] Ibid., p. 24.

mean –and at this point, however, we would move a little bit beyond Brecht – that form is to be neglected at the expense of content. That is, that one could speak of a content that is prior or more substantial or real than form. Content only exists in a specific form. What Brecht is defending is the possibility of a consideration of a practice that, in the terms that he employs here, allows for a form that doesn't deny or suppress its constitutive content. But, what content is Brecht talking about here?

e) *Change.* The previous question could be addressed considering the anecdote called 'Meeting again': 'A man who had not seen Mr. K. for a long time greeted him with the words: "You haven't changed a bit." "Oh!" said Mr. K. and turned pale.'[41] In 'Knowledge of human nature' writes Brecht: 'Thinking means making changes.'[42] These two reflections on change point at the priority of the practical as the insertion of the subject into that which is being said/done. They can also underline the idea of self-transformation, in the sense that the subject who inserts himself or herself into what is being said/done is always on the make, always within a certain field of forces and responsible for the effects of his/her actions. Another interesting anecdote about change is 'Mr. Keuner and the flood tide':

> Mr. Keuner was walking through a valley when he suddenly noticed that his feet were walking through water. Then he realized that his valley was in reality an arm of the sea and that high tide was approaching. He immediately stood still in order to look round for a boat. But when no boat came in sight, he abandoned his hope and hoped that the water would stop rising. Only when the water reached his chin did he abandon even this hope and begin to swim. He had realized that he himself was a boat.[43]

According to this parable, instead of waiting for the situation to improve, one transforms oneself into what one thinks the situation requires of oneself. A more straightforward (and certainly utopian today, in the age of global mass media) example of a similar phenomenon is given in 'Mr. Keuner and the newspapers' when somebody called Herr Wirr (Mr. Muddle) complains about newspapers. Herr Keuner says that a complaint serves no purpose; that one has to imagine, instead, how one would like a newspaper to be, and then try to do something about it: 'Mr. Muddle thought highly of man and did not believe newspapers could be made better, whereas Mr. Keuner did not think very highly of man and believed newspapers could be made better. "Everything can be better," said Mr. Keuner, "except man."'[44] Instead of assuming the givenness of the world, one transforms it by actually taking part in it. The matter about which Brecht talks is an action which doesn't neglect nor suppress one's own subjective insertion into what is being said/done. Only in this way does one stop theorizing about man and starts transforming the world and oneself. Similarly, Herr Keuner repeats a thousand times that a complaint that is not productive serves no purpose except that of the sheer reproduction of the given. And it starts to be productive when one decides to change oneself by transforming the conditions in which it is uttered.

f) *Productive complaint.* When you complain, it has to be heard: this statement is repeated by Herr Keuner throughout the entire work. If injustice is done to you, make sure you are

---

[41] Ibid., p. 20.
[42] Ibid., p. 61.
[43] Ibid,, p. 62.
[44] Ibid., p. 65.

heard; otherwise you don't deserve to complain. The parable 'The helpless boy' illustrates this point:

> A boy was crying to himself and a passerby asked what was wrong. 'I had saved two dimes for the movies,' said the boy, 'when a big lad came and grabbed one from me/ and he pointed at a lad who could be seen some distance away. 'Did you not shout for help?' asked the man. 'I did,' said the boy and sobbed a little more loudly. 'And didn't anyone hear you?' the man went on, stroking him fondly. 'No,' sobbed the boy and looked at the man with new hope. Because he was smiling. 'Then give me that one as well,' said the man and took the second dime out of the boy's hand and walked away unconcerned.[45]

Herr Keuner is disturbed by the boy's complaint, yet not so much by the content of the cry itself, but by the fact that it is not loud enough. When a complaint is not effective, when the cry is not loud enough, it is as if it wasn't really uttered. So why utter it in the first place? The acknowledgment of one's subjective position in what is being said/ done demands that the complaint is made productive, that it has effects, that it is useful ('usefulness' is another expression Brecht always liked).

This kind of coldness and lack of sympathy in Brecht has been fiercely criticized. Philosophy has termed this attitude 'consequentialism' in the sense of only taking into account the consequences of one's actions, not the moral motivations that ground them. One fast Brechtian answer to this kind of position would be: but who is fully aware of one's own motivations? Are individual motivations or individual moral grounds good indicators of anything? Brecht would not deny that there are motivations and principles; what he would question, however, is the kind of subject that a purely principled theory of ethics implies. For what this kind of theory implies is a subject that fully identifies with his or her principles, who is capable of rising above the contradictoriness of the social. Brecht's Herr Keurner is not self-identical, he is not fully aware of his desires and principles: in fact, he only knows what takes place, and sometimes only when it is too late, never before the action.[46] This is precisely his ethical stance.

Ideological or philosophical motives

a) *The need to interrupt those who speak, so they don't construct wholes.* Brecht's suspicion of philosophy and intellectuals in general is well known. Its most important manifestation appeared in his last play, *Turandot,* where intellectuals (also called 'Tuis') are considered to be whitewashers, the great creators of ideology. We can already discern in Herr Keuner a few reasons for this suspicion. Brecht writes in 'On systems' that Herr Keuner likes interrupting people.[47] This is because of their tendency to construct deceiving wholes in which all the parts seem to fit perfectly, as if there was no rupture between them and everything functioned harmoniously. According to Brecht, there are different elements that introduce this rupture–which can be disruptive in the order of knowledge – and that one always needs to look for.

---

[45]Ibid., p. 16.
[46]Bertolt Brecht says in *Me-ti*: 'Not to be identical with oneself, to embrace and intensify crises, to turn small changes into great and so forth -one need not only observe such phenomena, one can also act them out.'
[47]Ibid., p. 92.

b) *The subjective positioning (or attitude) is intrinsic to philosophy.* As we have seen, in Brecht's view, the content of what is being said/done, is necessarily connected to the place from where it is being said, its subjective enunciation. Brecht also states that the content of what is said is in immediate relationship with *how* it is said (for instance, the posture, attitude, gestures, voice etc.). A very remarkable story exemplifies this idea:

> A philosophy professor came to see Mr. K. and told him about his wisdom. After a while Mr. K. said to him: 'You sit uncomfortably, you talk uncomfortably, you think uncomfortably.' The philosophy professor became angry and said: 'I didn't want to hear anything about myself but about the substance of what I was talking about.' 'It has no substance,' said Mr. K. 'I see you walking clumsily and, as far as I can see, you're not getting anywhere. You talk obscurely, and you create no light with your talking. Seeing your stance, I'm not interested in what you're getting at.'[48]

This dialogue between the philosopher and Herr Keuner exemplifies Brecht's inversion of the common idea according to which knowledge or wisdom amount to the content of what is being said. For him, the content doesn't matter so much; at least if it is considered independently of how, and by whom, it is being said. Herr Keuner's reply to the professor inverts that common idea by declaring that wisdom is a consequence of attitude, and not the other way round. Attitude is at the root of any act, also of thinking. Herr Keuner tells us elsewhere about the necessary attitude intrinsic to ethics and philosophy:

> A false student came to Mr. Keuner, the thinking man, and told him: 'In America there is a calf with five heads. What do you say to that?' Mr. Keuner said: 'I don't say anything.' The false student was pleased and said: 'The wiser you were, the more you would be able to say about it.'
>
> The stupid man expects much. The thinking man says little.[49]

What does this parable mean? Besides the fact that it is important to separate between important questions and nonsense, it also tells us about Herr Keuner's silence as an accurate response to a fool. There is no content to what Herr Keuner replies, for there was no real content in the fool's question, except the fact that he wanted to mock his master, to put him down. To this intention, a reply would have meant surrender.

c) *What is an attitude? Or, what is the condition of possibility of a certain attitude?* We have seen that Brecht places attitude–or the subjective act – at a higher level with respect to content. The condition of possibility of this attitude is to be aware of one's needs and to act according to one's subjective insertion into what is said/done. The following thought of Herr Keuner is in this respect revealing:

> I often observe, says the thinking man, that I have my father's stance. But I do not do what my father does. Why are my deeds different than his? Because what is necessary is different. But I observe that the stance endures longer than the form of action: it resists what is required.[50]

---

[48]Ibid., p. 1.
[49]Ibid., p. 79.
[50]Ibid., p. 80.

Attitude or stance is similar to character: one can act in different ways depending on the circumstance (it is impossible to generalize about rules of behavior), but one's stance depends on a subjective disposition to act in different ways. This subjective disposition is different to the way one acts, but it can only be known by acting.

d) *What is a need?* We recall at this point the answer the worker gives to the jury when he is asked about the way he would like to formulate his oath. A need irrupts the normal functioning of any kind of order, pointing at other elements that should be considered. But this does mean that need (i.e. material need or interest), as the source of disruption, is not affected by knowledge, theory, or by the ideas we live in: 'The principal reason that interests need to be satisfied is that a large number of ideas cannot be thought because they run counter to the interests of the thinkers.'[51] Ideas are rooted in interests' satisfaction. Every enterprise (philosophy too) is materially grounded-it produces some kind of material satisfaction. ('I can be hungry anywhere,' says Herr Keuner elsewhere).[52] But ideas also have an impact on the possibility of this satisfaction, hence Brecht's combat in the world of ideas. 'If it is impossible to satisfy interests, it is necessary to point to them and to emphasize their dissimilarity, because only in this way can the thinking man think thoughts that are of service to the interests of others.'[53] Ethical ideas are those that expose the fact that some people's needs are not being satisfied.

3. BRECHT'S MARXIST SUBJECT

The idea according to which there are two different spheres (the economy on the one hand, and subjective life on the other) derives from the metaphor of the base and the superstructure, which implies that society has two distinct levels, and the latter is reducible to the former. Contrary to this extremely problematic explanatory scheme, in Brecht's Marxist ethics, the subject is inserted in a complex and contradictory field of forces which is both material and ethical, and which demands action in terms of the economy, but not at the expense of other spheres of life. This is simply because all spheres of life (politics, the juridical, and even the religious, as we have seen) are operative within the same mode of production–capitalism – and, as such, are not totally independent of it, even if they partially function according to their own rules. Contrary to what some of his critics have pointed out, we have seen that neither do dryness and abstraction reign in Brecht's stories, nor do his characters imperiously distance themselves from the complexity of human affairs. In fact, if they try to think beyond themselves, beyond their own personal interests, it is only due to the fact that capitalism is a mode of production that operates beyond the individual, i.e. it has effects on every sphere of the individual's life, and in many instances these are totally beyond his or her individual control. Consequently, the Brechtian's model of going 'beyond the individual' is not tantamount to the abolition of the subject, but rather the opposite, the recognition of his subjective implication in the situation depicted, – a complex and contradictory field of forces.

Let's consider another motive, which could be called *How to revolutionize the law*, in order to begin to put forward a few conclusions. It points at how Brecht's ethical model

---

[51] Ibid., p. 68.
[52] Ibid., p. 9.
[53] Ibid.

of action, to reiterate, demands the subjective implication of the ethical agent in spheres that are usually taken for granted:

> I know a driver who has the traffic regulations at his fingertips, obeys them, and is able to use them to his own benefit ... Another driver I know proceeds differently. Even more than in his own route he is interested in the traffic as a whole and he regards himself as a mere particle of the latter. He does not take advantage of his rights and does not make himself especially conspicuous. In spirit he is driving with the car in front of him and the car behind him, with constant pleasure in the progress of every vehicle and of the pedestrians as well.[54]

In the case of the second driver, the law is not felt as a coercive structure imposed upon the subject, but a mode of action that is not only endorsed, but also recreated by the subject in his implication in it. This is the reason why the second driver tries to consider not just his own individual interests, but also those who share the rules with him. He is acting from the perspective of his own subjective insertion in the common law.

This paper has tried to show that, contrary to the contemporary rejection of Brecht's Marxism, which is based on his supposed tendency to reductionism and abstraction, it is precisely his Marxism that allows him to have an account of ethics and the subject in the first place. One can of course disagree about Keuner's (or Brecht's?) motives of action in each of the depicted situations.[55] One can also dislike the consequences of Keuner's actions. And today – a time in which only the Right (for instance, Sarkozy) or the church appeal to ethical authorities – one could also find a bit outdated, – or even too 'Brechtian'! – Brecht's very authoritative voice and/or his recourse to the figure of the master or educator.[56] But Brecht's Marxism is precisely what allows him to articulate a non-essentialist notion of the subject, that which prevents him from lapsing into economic reductionism. Brecht's model of action shows that in the capitalist mode of production the economy can be opened and disrupted by the ethical act, and that the subject is knotted along different registers, none of which can be reduced to the rest.

The subjective insertion of the subject implies that, in Brecht's model, it doesn't make any sense to speak of an opposition between subject-object, or an opposition between the internal/the mind, on the one hand, and the external world, on the other (as in psychology). These oppositions rely on the idea of an individual that is separated from, or who locates himself above, the social. In the humanist version of Marxism, these oppositions stem from the notion of an economic world that totally alienates the supposedly pure or human essence of the individual. The Brechtian subject has no essence and doesn't rise above the social; it is perpetually non-identical, constantly divided along the registers of the economic, the political and the legal. The Brechtian subject has no non-alienated human essence to appeal to. Principles of action (liberal or so-called proletarian) can be generally formulated as some kind of basic orientation in life, as rules of thumbs for example, but when it comes to ethics and action, they simply don't work any more, because ethics is

---

[54]Ibid., p. 55.

[55]Max Frisch writes about Brecht: 'Brecht, like few people, is so unconceited in regard to himself; Brecht, moreover, like perhaps all people of independent means expects no agreement whatever; on the contrary, he expects opposition'. Max Frisch, 'Recollections of Brecht', *The Tulane Drama Review* 6.1 (September 1961): pp. 33–38, here p. 33.

[56]Günther Anders finds it a bit too authoritative or even authoritarian, similar in this respect to Nietzsche. See Günther Anders, 'Bertolt Brechts Geschichten vom Herrn Keuner', *Merkur* 33 (1979): pp. 882–892, here p. 889.

the realm where there is no guarantee for our actions, and no predetermined path for anything. In fact, as we have seen in the examples that we have discussed, principles or procedures have nothing to do with ethics. Marxist Ethics has to do with what I have called before the primordiality of the practical. This is the realization that, when it really comes to ethics, there is going to be no morally elevated goal to be appealed to, no human essence to be rescued, no procedural mode of behavior to ascertain, and no (bourgeois or proletarian) regulative ideal of action to be followed.

PERMISSIONS ACKNOWLEDGEMENTS

Excerpt from *Brecht in Augsburg. Erinnerungen, Texte, Fotos*. Eine Dokumentation von Werner Frisch und K.W. Obermeier unter Mitarbeit von Gerhard Schneider. © Suhrkamp Verlag Frankfurt am Main 1976. All rights reserved by and controlled through Suhrkamp Verlag Berlin.

Tom Kuhn, 'Ja, damals waren wir Dichter', from Hanns Otto Münsterer, *Bertolt Brecht and the Dynamics of Literary Friendship*, pp. 48–66. Copyright 1996 by the International Brecht Society. All rights reserved.

Philip Glahn, 'Sachlichkeit', in *Bertolt Brecht* by Philip Glahn. Published by Reaktion Books Ltd., 2014. Copyright © Philip Glahn, 2014. Reproduced with permission of the Licensor through PLSclear.

Stephen Parker, 'A Life's Work Curtailed? The Ailing Brecht's Struggle with the SED Leadership over GDR Cultural Policy', from Laura Bradley and Karen Leeder (eds.), *Brecht and the GDR. Politics, Culture, Posterity*. Copyright © 2011 the Editors and Contributors. Reprinted by permission of Boydell & Brewer Inc.

Excerpt from Bertolt Brecht, 1933–1947. *Schriften zum Theater*. Band 3. © Suhrkamp Verlag Frankfurt am Main 1963. All rights reserved by and controlled through Suhrkamp Verlag Berlin.

R. C. Speirs, 'Brecht's Plays of the Weimar Period', in Alan F. Bance, (ed.) *Weimar Germany: Writers and Politics*. 1982. pp. 138–152. Reprinted by permission of the author.

Herbert Ihering, 'Review of Drums in the Night', in Monika Wyss, *Brecht in der Kritik*. 1977, 4–6 (Munich: Kindler, 1977).

Monty Jacobs, 'Review of The Threepenny Opera,' in Monika Wyss, *Brecht in der Kritik*. 1977), pp. 80–2.

Excerpt from Bertolt Brecht, 1918–1933. *Schriften zum Theater*. Band 2. © Suhrkamp Verlag Frankfurt am Main 1963. All rights reserved by and controlled through Suhrkamp Verlag Berlin.

Andrzej Wirth, 'The Lehrstück As Performance', *TDR/The Drama Review*, 43:4 (T164-Winter, 1999), pp. 113–121. © 1999 by New York University and the Massachusetts Institute of Technology. Reprinted by permission of MIT Press Journals.

Durus, 'Review of The Measures Taken', in Monika Wyss, *Brecht in der Kritik*. 1977), pp. 134–6.

Excerpt from Bertolt Brecht, 1918–1933. *Schriften zum Theater*. Band 2. © Suhrkamp Verlag Frankfurt am Main 1963. All rights reserved by and controlled through Suhrkamp Verlag Berlin.

Ehrhard Bahr, 'Brechts Episches Theater als Exiltheater', in Alexander Stephan, (ed.); Hans Wagener, (ed.), *Schreiben im Exil: Zur Ästhetik der deutschen Exilliteratur 1933-1945*. 1985. pp. 109–122. Bonn: Bouvier, 1985). Reprinted by permission of author.

Hans Ott, 'Review of Mother Courage and her Children', in Monika Wyss, *Brecht in der Kritik*. 1977), pp. 210–12.

Berliner Ensemble Adaptations by Bertolt Brecht, edited by David Barnett. © Bertolt-Brecht-Erben / Suhrkamp Verlag 2014. Introduction © Bloomsbury Methuen Drama 2014. Reprinted by permission of Bloomsbury Methuen Drama.

Gerhard Wahnrau, 'Review of Mother Courage and her Children', in Monika Wyss, *Brecht in der Kritik*. 1977, pp. 216–18.

Franz Schonauer, 'Review of Coriolan', in Monika Wyss, *Brecht in der Kritik*, 1977, pp. 396–8.

Judith Wilke, 'The Making of a Document: An Approach to Brecht's Fatzer Fragment', *TDR/The Drama Review*, 43:4 (T164-Winter, 1999), pp. 122–128. © 1999 by New York University and the Massachusetts Institute of Technology. Reprinted by permission of MIT Press Journals.

David Midgely, 'The Poet in Berlin: Brecht's City Poetry of the 1920s', in *Empedocles' Shoe* by Bertholt Brecht (trans. Karen Leeder and Tom Kuhn), 2002, Bloomsbury Methuen Drama.

Tom Kuhn, 'Visit to a Banished Poet: Brecht's Svendborg Poems and the Voices of Exile', in Ronald Speirs (ed.), *Brecht's Poetry of Political Exile*. 2000, pp. 47–65. Copyright © Cambridge University Press 2000, reproduced with permission.

David Constantine, 'Brecht's Sonnets', in *Empedocles' Shoe* by Berholt Brecht (trans. Karen Leeder and Tom Kuhn, 2002, Bloomsbury Methuen Drama.

Karl H. Schoeps, 'Brecht in Buckow: The Buckow Elegies', in *Germanic Review*, vol. 61, no. 4 (1986), pp. 168–76. Reprinted by permission of the publisher (Taylor & Francis Ltd, http://www.tandfonline.com).

Klaus-Detlef Müller, 'Der nichtaristotelische Roman: Brechts Beitrag zum Roma der klassischen Moderne', in Robert Gillett and Godela Weiss-Sussex (eds.), *'Verwisch die Spuren!' Bertolt Brecht's Work and Legacy. A Reassessment*. (2008). Reprinted with permission of the publisher, Brill/Rodopi.

Sonia Arribas, 'The Subject Herr Keuner. Towards a Brechtian Ethics', from *The Brecht Yearbook*, 35 (2010), pp. 2–23. Copyright 2010 by the International Brecht Society. All rights reserved.

Every effort has been made to trace copyright holders and to obtain their permission for the use of copyright material. The publisher apologizes for any errors or omissions in the above list and would be grateful if notified of any corrections that should be incorporated in future reprints or editions of this book.

INDEX

Abusch, Alexander 58
acting 62–3, 77, 86, 91–2, 94, 96, 99, 103, 112–13, 115–18, 126, 148–9
'Actor's Speech About How to Portray a Little Nazi, The' (Brecht) 116
'Actress in Exile, The' (Brecht) 112
Adorno, Theodor 35
Albers, Hans 51
Alder, Vastius 229
alienation 27, 28, 33, 35, 76, 94, 155, 168, 189, 238
Althusser, Louis 238
America 75, 238
'Amt für Literatur, Das' (Brecht) 59
'An die Nachgeborenen' (Brecht) 200
anti-Aristotelian novel 217–32
anti-fascist exiles 170
Antigone of Sophocles, The (Brecht) 113
antimetaphysical art 237
Antony and Cleopatra (Shakespeare) 139
Arbeiter Illustrierten Zeitung 28
Arbeitsjournal (Brecht) 200, 204, 206, 211
Arendt, Hannah 238
Aristotelian novel 221
artistic act 228
Auerbach, Erich 167
Auerochs, Bernd 218
Aufricht, E. R. 80, 87
Aufstieg und Fall der Stadt Mahagonny/ The Rise and Fall of the City of Mahagonny (Brecht) 154
'Augsburger Kriegsbriefe' (Brecht) 70
Augsburger Volkswille 81
Augsburg Sonnets 189–90, 193
Aus einem Lesebuch für Städtebewohner/ From a Reader for Those who Live in Cities (Brecht) 35, 157, 158, 159, 161–4, 189–90, 195
autarkic (self-sufficient) metatheatre 96

Baal (Brecht) 2, 21–2, 69, 70–2, 71 n.4, 125, 191
'Baals Lied' (Baal's Song) 19

Baden-Baden Lesson on Consent, The (Brecht) 92, 162
Badiou, Alain 27
Banholzer, Paula 14, 16, 22 n.23
Banners and *Tidal Wave* (Paquet) 77
Barlach, Ernst 56–7
Barthel, Kurt 207
Barthes, Roland 238
Beaver Coat, The (Hauptmann) 133
Becher, Johannes R. 168
Beggar's Opera, The (Gay) 34, 35, 80, 87, 125
Behaviourism 79
'Bei der Lektüre eines spätgriechischen Dichters' (Brecht) 208
'Beim Lesen des Horaz' (Brecht) 210–11
Benjamin, Walter 32, 33, 110, 111–12, 146 n.2, 160, 161, 218, 230
Benn, Gottfried 77
Bentley, Eric 96
Berlau, Ruth 42, 53, 176
Berlin Alexanderplatz 219 n.9
Berliner Börsen-Courier 33
Berliner Ensemble (BE) 94, 94 n.2, 99–100
  adaptations for 125–35
  Brecht and 125–35
  Shakespearean adaptation 129–30, 133
  Trial of Joan of Arc at Rouen, 1431, The (Seghers) 130–1, 134
Bert Brecht: Erinnerungen aus den Jahren 1917-22 (Münsterer) 12, 15
Bertolt Brecht Archive (BBA) 9–10, 19, 144
Besson, Benno 130
Bezold, Otto 13, 15, 20
Bienek, Horst 56
Bildungsroman 28
Bingen, Julius 9
black Expressionism 72
Bloch, Ernst 116
Bohnen, Michael 27
Bolshevism 81
'Böser Morgen' (Brecht) 209
boxing 27–8
Brady, Philip 159

Brandl, Erich 27
Brandt, Thomas O. 202
Brecht: A Choice of Evils (Esslin) 115
Brecht, Bertolt
    artistic exploration 2–3
    Augsburg circle of 11–13
    Berliner Ensemble and 125–35
    biography 23, 170–4, 179, 228–30
    career as writer 11–13
    city poetry of 1920s 152–64
    collaborations 125
    on cultural bureaucracy 59–60
    in cultural-political controversies 50
    in Danish exile 49
    death 50
    diary 13
    elegies 199–213
    as emblematic figure of twentieth century 27
    epic theatre as exile theatre 108–18
    ethics 235–51
    exile 2, 39–46, 108–18, 167–80, 203–13
    friendship 11–13
    in German Democratic Republic 1, 2, 39, 49–61, 199, 203–13
    and Girnus 55
    Gruppe 25 and 31, 82
    health and activities 50
    imaginative flights 16
    Marxism 24, 235–42
    Marxist ethics 249–51
    medical history 51–2
    and momentous events around 17 June 1953 58–61, 205–13
    and Münsterer, friendship between 14–24
    non-Aristotelian theatre 112
    novel of classical modernity, contribution to 217–32
    obscenity 189
    opera project 33
    Piscator, Erwin and 33
    plays of Weimar period 69–83
    poems 17–18, 199–213
    productions of plays, reviews of 4
    as productive collaborator 2–3
    robbing and owning, constructions of 35
    with Samson-Körner 28
    with SED 50, 52–8
    Shakespeare and 129–30, 133, 139–40
    as socialist 93–4
    sonnets 183–96
    speech 29
    Stasi interest in 54
    stylizations 16
    theatrical theory and practice 108–18
    U. S. immigration 39–46
    urological problems 51–2
    utopian theory 96
    and Weill 34
    in Weimar Republic 2, 31–6
    works 2, 3, 31, 69–83
        'Actor's Speech About How to Portray a Little Nazi, The' 116
        'Actress in Exile, The' 112
        'An die Nachgeborenen' 200
        Antigone of Sophocles, The 113
        'Augsburger Kriegsbriefe' 70
        Aus einem Lesebuch für Städtebewohner (From a Reader for Those who Live in Cities) 157, 158, 159, 161–4, 189–90, 195
        Baal 2, 21–2, 69, 70–2, 71 n.4, 125, 191
        Baden-Baden Lesson on Consent, The 92, 162
        'Bei der Lektüre eines spätgriechischen Dichters' 208
        'Beim Lesen des Horaz' 210–11
        'Böser Morgen' 209
        Büsching 60
        Business Affairs of Mr Julius Caesar, The 227–31, 232
        Caucasian Chalk Circle, The 113, 175
        'Cities, The' 31
        'Constructing a Role: Laughton's Galileo' 114
        Courage Model 1949 4
        'Das Amt für Literatur' 59
        Days of the Commune, The 135
        Decision, The 91, 102–3
        Der Brotladen 82
        'Der Einarmige im Gehölz' 52, 211
        'Der Himmel dieses Sommers' 211, 213
        'Der Narr'/'The fool' 183
        Der Ozeanflug (The Flight over the Ocean) 94
        Die Augsburger Sonette 184
        'Die Gewaltigen'/'The mighty' 183
        'Die Kelle' 209

'Die Lösung' 207, 208
'Die Musen' 208
'Die Schneetruppe'/'Snow unit' 184
'Die Wahrheit einigt' 208
Dreigroschenoper 69, 143, 146, 157
'Eigenarten des Berliner Ensembles' 3–4, 62–3
'Emaus'/'Emmaus' 183
Fatzer fragment 82, 95, 95 nn.3–4, 97–8, 143–8
Fear and Misery of the Third Reich 108, 109, 111–12, 113, 115, 171
'Gedanken über die Dauer des Exils' ('Thoughts on the duration of exile') 170
Gedichte im Exil (Poems in Exile) 171
'Gewohnheiten, noch immer' 211
Good Person of Szechwan, The 111, 113, 129
Good Woman of Setzuan, The 39
'Große Zeit, vertan' 208–9, 212
Harvest, The 9–10
Hauspostille/Domestic Breviary 155, 157, 161, 184, 188–9
Heimat (Homeland) 168
'Heißer Tag' 211
Herr Keuner 243–9
Herrnburger Bericht 56
Horatians and the Curiatians, The 91
imaginative flights 16
Im Dickicht der Städte (In the Jungle of the Cities) 75–6, 154
'In finsteren Zeiten' 24
Katzgraben 57, 58, 200
'Kohlen für Mike'/'Coal for Mike' 187
'Kulturpolitik und Akademie der Künste' 206, 207
'Landscape of Exile, The' 46
'Lebensmittel zum Zweck' 211
Lehrstück 3, 20, 91–2, 93–100, 162
Lesebuch 35
Lieder Gedichte Chöre (Songs, Poems, Choruses) of 1934 171
Life of Eduard II of England, The 76, 77, 78, 125
Life of Galileo 39, 111, 113–14
'Little Piece of Advice About Producing Documents, A' 228

Lucullus 44, 208
Man Equals Man 76–9, 87
Manual of Piety 87, 88
Measures Taken, The See Decision, The (Brecht)
'Meine Achillesverse'/'My Achilles verses' 188
Messingkauf, The (Buying Brass) 109–10, 115–17
Mother Courage and Her Children 4, 39, 53, 119–21, 136–8, 199
Mr Puntila and his Man Matti 39, 113
Neinsager 99–100
'Nicht feststellbare Fehler der Kunstkommission' 59
'Ode to a Lofty Dignitary' 43
'On the Aristotelian Novel' 220–1
Private Life of the Master Race 39
Refugee Dialogues 43, 45
Resistible Rise of Arturo Ui, The 39, 113, 135
Rise and Fall of the City of Mahagonny, The 76, 80–1, 110, 154
Round Heads and Pointed Heads 39, 113, 125
'Rudern, Gespräche' 202
Saint Joan of the Stockyards 82
Señora Carrar's Rifles 108, 111, 112–13, 115
Short Organon for the Theatre 110, 117
Sonette and Englische Sonette 184
'Sonett über schlechtes Leben'/'Sonnet on the subject of living badly' 190
'Sonnet on the legacy' 186–8
Studien (Studies) 185
Svendborg Poems 167–80
Tagebücher 23
'Theses for Proletarian Literature' 107
Threepenny Lawsuit 225
Threepenny Novel 217, 221–5, 228, 232
Threepenny Opera, The 34, 69, 76, 80, 80 n.17, 87–8, 125, 157
Trommeln in der Nacht (Drums in the Night) 1–2, 69, 73–4, 73 n.8, 81, 84–6
Tui-Novel 227, 232

Turandot 60, 207
'Über Mangel an Bösem'/'On the lack of wickedness' 189
'Und als sie wegsah'/'And when she looked away' 184
'Und nun ist Krieg und unser Weg wird schwerer'/'And now it's war; our path is growing steeper' (Brecht) 192
'Uppercut, The' 28
Verfremdungseffekte 94, 238
Versuche (Experiments) 185
'Visit to the Banished Poets, A' 168, 172, 174–8
Vita of the Boxer Samson-Körner, The 28
'Vor acht Jahren' 211
Weizen 82
'Zufluchtsstätte' ('Place of refuge') 170
  writings 17–18
  young 11–24
Brecht, Walter 15, 16, 20
Brecht and Method (Jameson) 239
Breitensträter, Hans 27
Broch, Hermann 219 n.9
Bronnen, Arnolt 72
Brummack, Jürgen 222
'*Buckow Elegies, The*' (Brecht) 199–213, 206 n.34
Bundeswehr 132
Busch, Ernst 56, 137
Büsching (Brecht) 60
Business Affairs of Mr Julius Caesar, The (Brecht) 227–31, 232

capitalism 35, 81, 140, 178, 180, 190–1, 201, 242, 249
capitalist economy 221
Castle, The (Kafka) 219 n.9
Caucasian Chalk Circle, The (Brecht) 113, 175
Century, The (Badiou) 27
'Cities, The' (Brecht) 31
class 237
communism 81
Communist Party of Germany (KPD) 49
'Constructing a Role: Laughton's Galileo' (Brecht) 114
Coriolanus (Shakespeare) 129–30, 139–40, 202
Cornell, Drucilla 241–2

Coronation of Richard III, The (Jahnn) 77, 114
Courage Model 1949 (Brecht) 4
Cremer, Fritz 50

Dadaists, Berlin 28
Days of the Commune, The (Brecht) 135
Decision, The (Brecht) 91, 94, 99, 102–3, 147
Decline of the West (Spengler) 77
Der Brotladen (Piscator) 82
'Der Einarmige im Gehölz' (Brecht) 52, 211
Der Einsame (Johst) 71
'Der Himmel dieses Sommers' (Brecht) 211, 213
Der Hofmeister/The Tutor (Lenz) 53, 127–32
'Der Narr'/'The fool' (Brecht) 183
'Der Orangenkauf'/'Buying oranges' 196
Der Ozeanflug/The Flight over the Ocean (Brecht) 94
'Der Radwechsel' (Brandt) 202, 209–10
dialectical pedagogy 176–7
dialectics 1, 30, 176, 180
  applied 112–13
  non-deterministic 1
  political 155
  of revolution 73
Die Abenteuer des braven Soldaten Schwejk (Hašek) 144
Die Abenteuer des braven Soldaten Schweyk (Piscator) 82
Die Augsburger Sonette (Brecht) 184
'Die Gewaltigen'/'The mighty' (Brecht) 183
'Die Kelle' (Brecht) 209
'Die Lösung' (Brecht) 207, 208
Die Maßnahme (The Measures Taken). See *Decision, The* (Brecht)
'Die Musen' (Brecht) 208
'Die neue Mundart' 212
'Die Schneetruppe'/'Snow unit' (Brecht) 184
Dieterle, William 44
Die Verurteilung des Lukullus 56
'Die Wahrheit einigt' (Brecht) 208
directing 54
dissimulation 159
distanciation 78, 95, 112–13, 132, 134, 203–4
Dittberner, Hugo 200
Döblin, Alfred 29, 31, 219 n.9
Don Juan (Seghers) 131, 134

INDEX

Dreigroschenoper (Brecht) 69, 143, 146, 157
Dreigroschenprozeß 175
'Duino Elegies' (Rilke) 203

Ecce Homo 190
Economic and Philosophical Manuscripts 240
economics 221, 245
'Eigenarten des Berliner Ensembles' (Brecht) 3–4, 62–3
'Ein Mann bringt sich zu Bett'/'A man gets himself to bed' 190
Einverständnis (social agreement) 31
Eisenberg, Emanuel 39
Eisler, Hanns 41, 55, 96, 115, 132, 200
elegies 203–13
Eliot, T. S. 175 n.19
'Emaus'/'Emmaus' (Brecht) 183
emotions/feelings 23, 62, 74, 110, 114, 119–20, 158, 162, 163, 228
empathy 99, 108, 111–14, 116, 117, 219–20, 224, 230
Engel, Erich 88, 136
ensemble 99, 126–7, 133, 135, 137–8
epic theatre 34
   audience in 111
   Benjamin's observations on 110, 112
   Brecht's theoretical works on 109–10
   as exile theatre 108–18
   management 115
   maxims and 114
   special aspect of 112
   theory of 116–18
epos 220
Erpenbeck, Fritz 49, 53
Esslin, Martin 115
ethics
   Brechtian 242–9
   Marxism and 235–42
   motives 243–7
      ideological/philosophical 247–9
   vs. principles 243
Expressionism 71–4

Fabel 127
Faber, Erwin 84, 85–6
Falckenberg, Otto 84, 85
false consciousness 237, 237 n.14
Farquhar, George 131
fascism 116–17, 210–11

Fassbinder, Rainer Werner 238
Fatzer fragment (Brecht) 82, 95, 95 n.3–n.4, 97–8, 143–8
Fear and Misery of the Third Reich (Brecht) 108, 109, 111–12, 113, 115, 171
Feuchtwanger, Lion 41
Fiedler, Theodore 208
Fiesco (Schiller) 77
Flechtheim, Alfred 27
For Soviet Power 103
Frank, Bruno 41
Frisch, Max 238

gardens 201
Gaunerjargon (gangster jargon) 30
Gay, John 34, 35, 80, 87
'Gedanken über die Dauer des Exils'/'Thoughts on the duration of exile' (Brecht) 170
Gedichte im Exil/Poems in Exile (Brecht) 171
George, Stefan 29
German Democratic Republic (GDR) 1, 2, 39, 46, 203–13
   audience 199
   Brecht in 49–61, 199
   cultural policy 132
   exile poetry 167–80
   reconstruction of 199
German Revolution 72–3
Gerron, Kurt 88
Gerz, Raimund 207
Geschichten vom Herr Keuner 239
Geschonneck, Erwin 137
gesture 159
gestus 94, 159, 227, 232, 239
'Gewohnheiten, noch immer' (Brecht) 211
Geyer, Georg 9
Giehse, Therese 133
Girnus, Wilhelm 55, 55 n.14, 59–60
Good Person of Szechwan, The (Brecht) 111, 113, 129
Good Woman of Setzuan, The (Brecht) 39
Gorki, Maxim 178
Goslar, Lotte 115
Götz, Curt 88
Grabbe, Christian Dietrich 71
Grass, Günter 202
'Große Zeit, vertan' (Brecht) 208–9, 212
Grosz, George 27, 35, 79, 190
Gruppe 25 31, 82

Habermas, Jürgen 240
Haltung (posture) 179
Harris, Frank 146, 228
Harvest, The 9–10
Hašek, Jaroslav 144
Hauptmann, Elisabeth 23, 34, 81
Hauptmann, Gerhart 133
Hauspostille/Domestic Breviary (Brecht) 155, 157, 161, 184, 188–9
Hays, H. R. 41, 44
'He, he! The Iron Man!' (Küpper) 29
Heartfield, John 27, 28, 145
Hecht, Werner 35, 54
Heimat/Homeland (Brecht) 168
'Heißer Tag' 211
Heller, Agnes 240 n.26
Herr Keuner (Brecht) 243–9
Herrnburger Bericht (Brecht) 56
Hesse, Hermann 69
Heym, Georg 153
Hildebrand, Alexander 202
History of the Great American Fortunes, The 223
Höch, Hannah 28
Hohenester, Max 16
'Hollywood Elegies' 203–4
Homolka, Oskar 41
Honecker, Erich 56
Horatians and the Curiatians, The (Brecht) 91
Houseman, John 115
house music 96
House Un-American Activities Committee 2
Hüdepohl, Ferdinand 52, 52 n.6–n.7
Hurwicz, Angelika 136, 137

ideology 238
Ihering, Herbert 84–6
Im Dickicht der Städte/In the Jungle of the Cities (Brecht) 75–6, 154
'In finsteren Zeiten' (Brecht) 24
Internationale Literatur 119

Jahnn, Hans Henny 72, 77
Jameson, Fredric 239
Jasager 95, 99–100
Jeriah Jip 78
Jessner, Leopold 77
Johann Faustus (Eisler) 55, 59, 132, 144
Johnson, Alvin S. 41, 43
Johst, Hanns 71, 125, 191
Joyce, James 169

Jung, Franz 83
Jünger, Ernst 77

Kafka, Franz 219 n.9
Kaiser, Steffen 1, 27, 74, 81, 99
Kaiser, Wolf 140
Kammerspiele, Munich 84, 85
Kästner, Erich 74, 154
Katzgraben (Brecht) 57, 58, 200
Ketzerbrevier, Das/Heretic's Breviary (Mehring) 155
Kilger, Heinrich 136
Kisch, Egon Erwin 31
Klingsors letzter Sommer (Hesse) 69, 70
Koch, Georg August 138
'Kohlen für Mike'/'Coal for Mike' (Brecht) 187
Konjunktur (Lania) 82, 144
Korsch, Karl 227, 237 n.14
Kortner, Fritz 27, 41
KPD. *See* Communist Party of Germany
Kroder, Armin 18
Küchenmeister, Claus 60
Kuhl, Kate 88
'Kulturpolitik und Akademie der Künste' (Brecht) 206, 207
Küpper, Hannes 29
Kurella, Alfred 49
Kutscher, Artur 71

Laclau, Ernesto 236
Lady Chatterley's Lover (Lawrence) 194
'Landscape of Exile, The' (Brecht) 46
Lang, Fritz 41
Langhoff, Wolfgang 134
Lania, Leo 144
Lao-tsû 168, 170, 178–9
Laughton, Charles 201
'Lebensmittel zum Zweck' (Brecht) 211
Legacy of This Time (Bloch) 116
Lehrstück (Brecht) 3, 20, 162
  as genre 108
  as performance 93–100
  vs. spectacle 94 n.1
  theory of 91–2
  Verfremdung 94
  Verfremdungseffekte in 94
Lenya, Lotte 34
Lenz, J. M. R. 127
  Der Hofmeister/The Tutor 53, 127–32
  plays 128
  Soldiers, The 127

Lesebuch (Brecht). *See Aus einem Lesebuch für Städtebewohner/From a Reader for Those who Live in Cities* (Brecht)
Lethen, Helmut 158
Lieder Gedichte Chöre (Songs, Poems, Choruses) of 1934 (Brecht) 171
'Lieder zur Klampfe von Bert Brecht und seinen Freunden' 19, 23
Life of Eduard II of England, The (Brecht) 76, 77, 78, 125
Life of Galileo (Brecht) 39, 111, 113–14
Literarische Welt 29
'Little Piece of Advice About Producing Documents, A' (Brecht) 228
'Little Red School House, The' (Eisenberg) 39
Lonely Man, The (Johst) 125
Losey, Joseph 115
Louis Ferdinand, Prince of Prussia (von Unruh) 77
Lucullus (Brecht) 44, 208
Lukács, Georg 49, 109, 228, 232, 236, 240–2
Lukes, Steven 240, 241 n.32
Lyon, James K. 114, 115

Macbeth (Shakespeare) 77
Machine-Wreckers, The (Toller) 77
MacNamara, Reggie 29
Magic Mountain, The (Mann) 219 n.9
Magritz, Kurt 56
Mahlke, Stephan 238, 239
Mahoney, Jim 76, 80–1
Man Equals Man (Brecht) 76–9, 87
Mann, Klaus 29–30
Mann, Thomas 29–30, 219 n.9
Mannheim, Ralph 129
Mann ist Mann/*A Man's a Man* (Brecht). *See Man Equals Man* (Brecht)
Manual of Piety (Brecht) 87, 88
Man Without Qualities, The (Musil) 219 n.9
Marsch, Edgar 208
Marxism 24, 200, 241 n.29–n.32
  Brecht's 24, 200, 235–42
  criticisms of 235
  and ethics 235–42
  and morality 240, 241 n.32
Marxist ethics 249–51
materialism/materialist 119, 235–6, 238
Measure for Measure (Shakespeare) 125

Measures Taken, The (Brecht) 94, 96, 99, 102
Mehring, Walter 154–5, 157, 162
'Meine Achillesverse'/'My Achilles verses' (Brecht) 188
Men in Dark Times (Arendt) 238
Mennemeier, Franz Norbert 202
Merin, Peter 119
Messer, Mackie 80, 223
Messiah (Handel) 81
Messingkauf, The/Buying Brass (Brecht) 109–10, 115–17
Michaëlis, Karin 168
Miller, Henry 194
Mittenzwei, Werner 3
Modest Proposal, A (Swift) 221–2, 231
Monk, Egon 133
montage 28, 94, 145
morality 240
Mother Courage and Her Children (Brecht) 4, 39, 53, 54, 119–21, 136–8, 199
Mr Puntila and his Man Matti (Brecht) 39, 113
Mü, Tui Ka 60
Müller, Heiner 239
Münsterer, Hanns Otto 11–13
  Bert Brecht: Erinnerungen aus den Jahren 1917-22 12, 15
  birth 13
  and Brecht 14–24
  diary 12, 16, 21, 23–4
  family 13
  memoir of Brecht 13
  poems 17–18
  writings 17–18
Musil, Robert 219 n.9

'Naive and Sentimental Poetry' (Schiller) 203
Nationale Volksarmee (National People's Army) 132
naturalism/naturalistic 72, 108
Nazism 60, 116–17, 132, 170–1
Nebelung, Elsbeth 13
necrophilia 34
Neher, Carola 49
Neher, Caspar 13, 15, 16, 70, 88
  diary 13, 13 n.6, 14 n.7, 15, 16, 21 n.20
Neinsager (Brecht) 99–100
neo-fascism 208
Neue Preußische Kreuz-Zeitung 34

'Neue Sachlichkeit'   74, 74 n.9, 83
Neues Deutschland   55
'Nicht feststellbare Fehler der Kunstkommission' (Brecht)   59
Nietzsche, Friedrich   71, 95–6
Noh plays   3

obscenity   189
'Ode to a Lofty Dignitary' (Brecht)   43
On Marx (Althusser)   238
'On the Aristotelian Novel' (Brecht)   220–1
Othello (Shakespeare)   112
Owens, Jesse   27

Paquet, Alfons   77
Paulsen, Harald   88
perspectivism   75
Pfanzelt, Georg   15
Phelan, Anthony   175 n.20
piano   96
Pieck, Wilhelm   55
Piscator, Erwin   29, 33, 39, 41–3, 81
   Die Abenteuer des braven Soldaten Schweyk   82
   Rasputin   82, 144
   technical innovations   82
Plebeians Rehearse the Uprising, The (Grass)   202
Pohl, Martin   58
political *vs.* private poems   172–3
Ponto, Erich   88
Portrait of the Artist as a Young Man of 1916, A (Joyce)   169
Private Life of the Master Race (Brecht)   39
proletarian   100
   art   82
   choirs   103
   literature, theses for   107
   revolutionary   102–3
Protestantism   96

Rasputin (Piscator)   82, 144
rationality   42, 77, 110, 119, 161, 222, 226
Reader (Brecht). See *Aus einem Lesebuch für Städtebewohner/From a Reader for Those who Live in Cities* (Brecht)
realism   62–3, 73, 82, 109, 115, 129–30, 131, 208, 218, 227–8
Recruiting Officer, The (Farquhar)   131
Red Hen (Hauptmann)   133
reductionism   235–6

Refugee Dialogues (Brecht)   43, 45
Reinhardt, Max   154
relativity/relativism   75
'Republican Automatons' (Grosz)   79
Resistible Rise of Arturo Ui, The (Brecht)   39, 113, 135
Reyher, Ferdinand   40
Rischbieter, Henning   99
Rise and Fall of the City of Mahagonny, The (Brecht)   76, 80–1, 110, 154
Rodenberg, Ilse   55–6
'Roman Elegies' (Goethe)   203
romanticism   73
Rose Bernd (Hauptmann)   81
Rote Fahne   34
Round Heads and Pointed Heads (Brecht)   39, 113, 125
'Rudern, Gespräche' (Brecht)   202
Ruhr Valley   32
Rülicke, Käthe   56, 57

Sachlichkeit, Neue   29
Sachlichkeit (objectivity)   27–36
Saint Joan of the Stockyards (Brecht)   82, 203
Samson-Körner, Paul   27, 28
satire   222
Schäfer, Gert   136
Schall, Ekkehard   138, 140
Schaustück   96
Schella, Sigrid   99
Schipfel, Josef   10
Schmeling, Max   27
Schneider, Max   9
Schopenhauer, Arthur   71
Schuhmann, Klaus   200
Schulte, Götz   99
Schutzverband Deutscher Schriftsteller   112
SED. See Socialist Unity Party of Germany
Seghers, Anna   130–1, 134
self-assertion   163
self-overcoming   163
Señora Carrar's Rifles (Brecht)   108, 111, 112–13, 115
Shakespeare, William
   Antony and Cleopatra   139
   Brecht and   129–30, 133, 139–40
   Coriolanus   129–30, 139–40, 202
   Macbeth   77
   Measure for Measure   125
   Othello   112
Shattuc, Jane   238

INDEX

Short Organon for the Theatre (Brecht) 110, 117
Silberman, Marc 237
Simmel, Georg 153
Sinn und Form 53
Sleepwalkers, The (Broch) 219 n.9
socialism 53, 62, 155, 160, 180, 199, 209
socialist realism 109
Socialist Unity Party of Germany (SED) 49, 132–3, 205
  Brecht and 50, 52–8, 205
  on cultural policy 54–5
  economic and social transformation, policies for 53
  Formalism Campaign 54–5
  leadership 52–61
society 35, 78, 139–40
  as changeable 93
  French 130–1
  of friends 24
  German 72–4
  individual and 1–2, 135
  machine of 78
  Roman 130
  Weimar 83
Soldiers, The (Lenz) 127
Sonette and Englische Sonette (Brecht) 184
'Sonett über schlechtes Leben'/'Sonnet on the subject of living badly' (Brecht) 190
sonnets
  Augsburg Sonnets 189–90, 193
  Brecht's 183–96, 183 n.1
  on legacy 186–9
Steffin, Margarete 41–2, 186, 191–6, 218
Stein, Gertrude 94
Steinweg, Reiner 108
Sternberg, Fritz 82, 230
'storm and stress,' movement 127
Strittmatter, Erwin 57, 200
Swift, Jonathan 221–2
Syberberg, Hans-Jürgen 134
symbolism 78–9

Tage-Buch, Das 30
Tagebücher (Brecht) 23
'Tarpeja,' (Kroder) 18
Technikkult (Sachlichkeit) 29
Tenschert, Joachim 129
'Theater am Schiffbauerdamm' 80

Theater der Zeit 53
'Theses for Proletarian Literature' (Brecht) 107
Thiele, Dieter 207
Thompson, Dorothy 41
Threepenny Lawsuit (Brecht) 225
Threepenny Novel (Brecht) 217, 221–5, 228, 232
Threepenny Opera, The (Brecht) 34, 69, 76, 80, 80 n.17, 87–8, 125, 157
Toller, Ernst 77
Tretyakov, Sergei 39
Trial of Joan of Arc at Rouen, 1431, The (Seghers) 130–1, 134
Trommeln in der Nacht/*Drums in the Night* (Brecht) 1–2, 69, 73–4, 73 n.8, 81, 84–6
Tropic of Cancer (Miller) 194
Tropic of Capricorn (Miller) 194
Tucholsky, Kurt 154
Tui-Novel (Brecht) 227, 232
Turandot (Brecht) 60, 207

'Über Mangel an Bösem'/'On the lack of wickedness' (Brecht) 189
Uhu 30
Ulbricht, Walter 54, 205, 208
'Und als sie wegsah'/'And when she looked away' (Brecht) 184
'Und nun ist Krieg und unser Weg wird schwerer'/'And now it's war; our path is growing steeper' (Brecht) 192
'Uppercut, The' (Brecht) 28
urbanization 75
Urfaust (Goethe) 133–4
Utopian socialism 155

van den Steinen, Helmut 208
Vatermord (Bronnen) 30
V-effect 91, 114–15
Verfremdung 94
Verhör des Lukullus, Das 54–5
Versuche (Experiments) 185
Viertel, Berthold 52
Villon, Francois 34, 88
'Visit to the Banished Poets, A' (Brecht) 168, 172, 174–9
Vita of the Boxer Samson-Körner, The (Brecht) 28
Volksbühne 126
'Vom Liebhaber'/'The lover' 190

von Hellens, Lawrence 43
von Schiller, Friedrich 203
von Unruh, Fritz 77
'Vor acht Jahren' (Brecht) 211

Wagner, Frank Dietrich 27, 117
Walcher, Jakob 204
Wandel, Paul 208
Wedekind, Frank 71
Weigel, Helene 45, 59, 60, 112, 117, 125, 136, 137, 188
Weill, Kurt 34, 41
Weimar Republic 2, 31–6
  Brecht in 2, 31–6
  choruses of 96

political drama of 112
political theatre in 81–3
Weiskopf, Franz Carl 171
Weiss, Peter 238
Weizen (Brecht) 82
Wekwerth, Manfred 111, 129
Werfel, Franz 29
Willett, John 132
Wilson, Robert 94
Wisten, Fritz 126

'Zufluchtsstätte'/'Place of refuge' (Brecht) 170
'Zur Musik der *Dreigroschenoper*' (Adorno) 35
Zweig, Arnold 59